Arab Media

ARAB MEDIA

Power and Weakness

edited by Kai Hafez

NEW YORK • LONDON

2008

The Continuum International Publishing Group Inc
80 Maiden Lane, New York, NY 10038

The Continuum International Publishing Group Ltd
The Tower Building, 11 York Road, London SE1 7NX
www.continuumbooks.com

Printed in the United States of America
Library of Congress Cataloging-in-Publication Data

Arab media : power and weakness / edited by Kai Hafez.
p. cm.
Includes bibliographical references and index.
ISBN-13: 978-0-8264-2835-6 (hbk. : alk. paper)
ISBN-10: 0-8264-2835-5 (hbk. : alk. paper)
ISBN-13: 978-0-8264-2836-3 (pbk. : alk. paper)
ISBN-10: 0-8264-2836-3 (pbk. : alk. paper) 1. Press and politics--Arab countries.
2. Press--Arab countries. I. Hafez, Kai, 1964- II. Title.

PN5359.A57 2008
073.927--dc22

2008021982

To my wife Nicola—for all those wonderful years.

Table of Contents

Acknowledgments xi

Introduction

Arab Media: Power and Weakness 1
Kai Hafez

Media Effects

Chapter One Political Opportunity Structures:
Effects of Arab Media 17
Marc Lynch

Chapter Two Lack of Influence? Public Opinion and
Foreign Policy Making in the Arab World 33
Russell E. Lucas

Chapter Three The Effects of Islamist Media on the
Mainstream Press in Egypt 46
Carola Richter

Media Audiences

Chapter Four Arab Media Audience Research:
Developments and Constraints 69
Hussein Amin

Chapter Five From Activity to Interactivity:
The Arab Audience 91
Marwan M. Kraidy

Media Content

Chapter Six Arab World Media Content Studies: A Meta-Analysis of a Changing Research Agenda 105
Muhammad Ayish

Chapter Seven The Political Elites' Dominance over the Visual Space: A Qualitative and Quantitative Content Study of Lebanese Television 125
Katharina Nötzold

Media Ethics

Chapter Eight The Unknown Desire for "Objectivity": Journalism Ethics in Arab (and Western) Journalism 147
Kai Hafez

Chapter Nine Agents of Change? Journalism Ethics in Lebanese and Jordanian Journalism Education 165
Judith Pies

Media Economy

Chapter Ten Gaps in the Market: Insights from Scholarly Work on Arab Media Economics 185
Naomi Sakr

Chapter Eleven Orientalism and the Economics of Arab Broadcasting 199
Tourya Guaaybess

Media Law and Policy

Chapter Twelve Media Policy and Law in Egypt and Jordan: Continuities and Changes 217
Orayb Aref Najjar

Media Cultures

Chapter Thirteen Arab Media and Cultural Studies: Rehearsing New Questions 237
Tarik Sabry

Chapter Fourteen Through the Back Door: Syrian Television Makers between Secularism and Islamization 252
Christa Salamandra

The Authors 263

Index 267

Acknowledgments

The editor is indebted to a number of people without whom this book could not have been realized. Special thanks go to David Duke for his help editing the writing of nonnative English speakers, and to my PhD students and coauthors Judith Pies and Carola Richter as well as to my student David Jalilvand for assisting in the editing process. Continuum's assistant editor Katie Gallof was at all times a reliable and effective partner on the other end of the Atlantic Ocean. Last but not least I would like to thank my authors from various continents and countries and my home university at Erfurt, Germany, for participating in the project.

INTRODUCTION

Arab Media: Power and Weakness

Kai Hafez

In the developed democracies of the West, or in other parts of the world, "media power" is usually highly controversial. The mass media are a welcome expression of the participatory communicative link between governments and peoples that is needed even in representative democracies. Politicians need to know what people think, not only during election times but on a daily basis. However, the mass media are not the expression of the ideal "public sphere." There is a deep gulf between "published opinion" and "public opinion." Individual journalistic, entrepreneurial, and market interests underlying all kinds of mass media production reveal that journalists do not hold a political mandate. Each journalist's opinion is as legitimate as any of the voices emanating from the masses that are never presented in the mass media. In the West, therefore, the idea of "media democracy" is mostly debated with respect to the Internet and new means for the individual to go public. At the same time, the political influence of major journalism has been met with scepticism because the media might pose a risk to established democratic institutions (Meyer 2001).

In the Middle East, and particularly in the Arab world, the reception given to the concept of media power has tended toward the optimistic, focusing on high hopes rather than on fears about the media's influence on the political arena. In most Arab countries, which are still characterized by authoritarian rule and the stagnation of political development, more is expected of the media than in the postmodern Western world. Will the media articulate the voices of society and break the political near-monopoly of the state? Questions like this have been dominating the Arab media discourse in recent years. The advent of more than two hundred new Arab satellite stations and likely developments in other media sectors have helped a new public sphere to emerge. The foundation of the modern Arab nation-state after World War I has been followed, almost a century later, by the introduction of a media space that, however tendentious and restricted it might still be, allows for open debate on deep-seated taboos within Arab societies. Not only does the now-famous pan-Arab TV network Al-Jazeera cover "hot issues," regular programs such as Egyptian TV soaps (sg. *musalsal*) also discuss sensitive topics like rape and the social stigmatization of women in Arab societies. Moreover, they now openly discuss politics.

Many analysts from around the world are fascinated in particular by Arab satellite TV's ability to demonstrate that Arab culture is not as hierarchical and traditional as many people had thought, but it encompasses a variety of viewpoints, ideologies, and lifestyle-related worldviews from Nasserism to Islamism and from liberalism to neoconservatism. Without exaggeration one can view Arab media as a balancing power to the other great mobilizing force of the last decade: political Islam. While Islamists seek to mobilize people through moral rigor, social networks, and political organizations, the media have inspired people's minds through their liveliness, plurality, and dynamics. The old idea that a "triangle of taboos: politics, sex, and religion" expresses Arab culture is outdated in the new media age. While religion is still sensitive, hedonism is an element of many Arab programs, and it has become an acceptable part of life to debate politics.

From here it has been only been a small step for many observers to assume that Arab media are the vanguard of a democratic "revolution" and that they, and especially their icon Al-Jazeera, are "rattling" authoritarian governments (Nawawy/Iskandar 2003; Mernissi 2007). Arab media almost seem like a replacement for political parties (Hafez 2006): expressing what people think, especially about politics, moulding public opinion on urgent questions of modernization, sometimes activating the "Arab street" for political demonstrations and at times even influencing the behavior of Arab regimes (Lynch 2006).

But are Arab media actually that powerful? Can the mass media really be considered the counterparts of a social movement like political Islam? How can system change under these conditions be imagined? There are theoretical arguments as well as empirical evidence for a much more modest or even pessimistic approach to Arab media. Theoretically speaking, there is a deep gulf between the existence of a public sphere and democratic change. Transformation theory accepts that mass media and public opinion are important factors for democratic change, but the media are neither social actors themselves nor can they be dissociated from their own institutional interests (Hafez 2006). In the Arab world, like anywhere else, the mass media, especially of press and TV, struggle for their survival as a commercial complex under authoritarian rule. In historical perspective the mass media have never been at the forefront of political change, irrespective of whether change came as a revolution or as a peaceful reform. Throughout modern history it was intellectuals, dissidents, or political movements of various kinds, but never the mass media, that introduced system change. In the Soviet Union, as elsewhere, it was underground "Samizdat" pamphlets that spread opposing political views, but never the press or TV.

It could well be true, as was suggested, that Arab media were operational in organizing solidarity campaigns before and during the wars against Afghanistan in 2001 and Iraq in 2003. Yet was it really the "new power of public opinion" (Lynch 2006, 156) expressed through Arab media that made even pro-Western leaders like

Saudi Arabia and Kuwait hesitant to openly support the American invasion? Were these regimes really intimidated because the media was expressing the Arab people's resentment against such policy? As a matter of fact, in contrast to the Second Gulf War in 1991, the United States in 2003 was unable to build a significant Arab coalition. However, even in 1991, at a time when neither Arab satellite TV nor the Internet existed, Arab regimes were aware of how fragile Arab public opinion was. Mass protests could be seen in many Arab countries, and Egypt alone imprisoned around 30,000 people. The Arab grassroots were marching even without the support of the new Arab media. The main reason why Arab regimes did not cooperate in 2003 as some of them had in 1991 was that the political case for war—Iraq's supposed possession of "weapons of mass destruction"—was much less convincing than in 1991, when Iraq had clearly violated international law when occupying Kuwait.

Are the continuous protests of the U.S. and British governments against the alleged one-sidedness of Arab satellite TV networks, and against Al-Jazeera in particular, which was accused of being a supporter of terrorism, proof of the power of Arab media? A daring thought: a small TV network from Qatar challenging the last superpower on earth and uniting the Arab world against it. It sounds like an Arab version of "David and Goliath" and certainly arouses wishful thinking among many Arabs eager to compete with the West after decades of colonialism and neo-imperialism. It is certainly true that American decision makers disliked the fact that they had lost the monopoly on war coverage that they had held in 1991, when even Arabs watched CNN. These were the same media-sensitive politicians, however, who believed they could fight the widespread anti-Americanism in the Middle East using manipulative public diplomacy and foreign broadcasting stations such as the U.S. Arabic TV network Al-Hurra, which, as most observers agree, has no influence whatsoever in the region. (Arab audiences are used to mistrusting propaganda coming from their own governments, so why should they accept U.S. propaganda?) In the end, the government of George W. Bush was able and willing to pursue the war against Iraq with or without the consent of Arab media. Similarly, the governments in Great Britain, Spain, and Italy cooperated with the U.S. government, even though about 80 percent of Europeans were against that war.

In domestic Arab politics the short-lived mobilization of the Arab street in wartime had no effect on the character of political power. Quite the contrary, authoritarian governments from Morocco and Egypt to Jordan have been able to sustain their grip on their societies. The last real challenge to their power monopoly stemmed from the so-called bread riots that took place in several Arab countries in the late 1980s when the Arab masses protested against the deterioration of social standards. This led to Arab governments (for example, in Algeria and Jordan) conceding increased participation in the political systems. These riots, however, were spontaneous responses to events at a time when neither the new Arab TV nor the Internet existed. Paradoxically enough, the era of the new Arab media is also an era of relatively stable authoritarian government with only minor increases in the inclusion of the populations in political decision making. If we trust the existing freedom indices like those provided by Freedom House, Arab political systems have made no substantial progress towards democracy in the "Al-Jazeera era."[1]

What the media age might have achieved is a change in the basic character of authoritarian government. Arab regimes have been able to cope with the challenges of globalization, although some have been forced to adapt different media policies. While, for example, in Tunisia, Libya or Syria Soviet-style totalitarian propaganda is still intact within the media sector, countries like Morocco, Algeria, Egypt, or Jordan have managed a change from Nasser-style totalitarianism to more liberalized and modernized forms of authoritarian government. The basic trait of the media policies of these Arab countries is a carrot-and-stick approach that allows for tremendous developments within a new public sphere (Eickelman/Anderson 1999) while retaining certain "red lines" as to what constitutes legitimate or legal reporting. As a result, Arab mass media still avoid controversial reporting about their home governments, uttering more criticism of other countries than of their own. External censorship, journalistic self-censorship, and the whole debate about journalistic freedom and the ethics of objectivity under authoritarian rule, all of which were debated in previous decades, are still high on the agenda (Hafez 2003).

It is high time to reassess the role Arab media play in politics and society, the effects they have *on* and the role they play *for* their audiences. Rather than heralding outdated stimulus-response models of strong media effects, scholars and other analysts will have to not only reflect on the various influences on media content that exist but also on the various variables that interfere with media effects and uses. In many Arab countries public spheres have developed in which the contest over public opinion has begun, with governments "spinning" public relations and political challengers trying to widen the definition of authoritarian censorship. For the media to have a powerful impact on changes to the political system (and perhaps on democratization) it will be extremely important to improve their links to civil societies and the political opposition that, outside the Islamist camp, is mostly poorly developed. Winning the media contest is not enough for the transformation of political systems—new Arab media have to be followed by new political and social movements.

Perhaps the real power of Arab media has to be located in a sphere that lies beyond the realm of realpolitik, of governments, parties, and social movements contesting for power. The new Arab public sphere that has opened up over the past decade might be intertwined with the modernization of political values and attitudes and the whole fabric of Arab political culture. Effects *of* the media and interactions *with* the media on that level of social development often escape academic attention, although they can in fact lead to long-term political and societal changes. While Islamist political organizations like the Muslim Brethren have established their "parallel polities" (a term the former Czech president Vaclav Havel once used for oppositional networks in the Soviet Bloc), Arab media might have started to generate a feeling of political participation in the virtual Arab parliaments of their talk shows that could one day contribute to real political change. It is surely possible that despite the limited effect of Arab mass media on the concrete political decisions of those in power they might have a far-reaching influence on the political agenda of public opinion and on the framing of the political discourse that is related to the political opinions, values, attitudes, and political cultures of Arab populations.

Moreover, as a reaction to the seemingly limited short-term effects of Arab media on politics several observers argue that the real revolution brought about by Arab media is not taking place in the field of political reporting and news making but in popular entertainment.[2] The increased diversity of content produced by the more than two hundred television programs and numerous print media, the Internet and blogs could reinforce the trend toward individualization—a development that could be conducive to democratization. However, widespread slogans like "entertainment is political" need to be substantiated. Entertainment is surely societal and cultural—but is it really political? How does one argue with those critics who suspect that the fast-growing popular culture in the Arab world diverts attention away from political change to a long-term "Chinese" coexistence between a modernized socioeconomic sector and a retarded or even stagnating political sphere?

In general, there seems to be no clear or easy definable link among politics, society, and the media. An assessment of the power and weakness of Arab media depends largely on the perspectives that we choose.

Mapping the Field

The links among politics, society, and the media must be analyzed from various angles. Gadi Wolfsfeld's political contest model paves the way for how future research on Arab media could be structured and in which fields it could be located. In Wolfsfeld's concept, authorities and challengers compete by various means for access to the media, which are an important part of the public sphere (Wolfsfeld 1997). The antagonists' capacity to become present in the media depends mainly on their ability to maximize their individual news value through political and social status factors such as organizational resources, "exceptional behavior" (demonstrations, staged events, or even violence) or by controlling the political environment (mainly influence on political developments; Wolfsfeld 1997, 13–30). Although authorities are mostly privileged in all these respects and receive primary attention from the major mass media, challengers—social movements, for example—seek to compensate for their relative weakness through all kinds of exceptional behavior. The media are not passive gatekeepers but actively define and change news routines, news values, the media agenda, and their frames (Wolfsfeld 1997, 31–55). Media output, therefore, is a result of the authorities' and challengers' thematic and framing impulses and journalistic decisions—decisions that might be more or less restricted, depending on the extent of media freedom within the respective media system.

Wolfsfeld's conceptualization of the relations between the mass media and political actors is, like all theoretical concepts are, limited in scope. Such a model could hardly be applied to the small media that exist on the Internet and elsewhere, since this type of media might inherently privilege one side over the other and not work according to the logic that tries to integrate large masses and have a different role to play in society than small partisan media. Nevertheless, Wolfsfeld's political contest model is a valuable starting point for mapping various theoretical fields that could be of interest to future research on Arab media. Since communication thought and theory is extremely diverse, the following outline can only highlight a few interesting issues and suggest a small number of exemplary references.

Research field I—the link between politics (government) and the media. Naomi Sakr argues that Arab governments have adopted TV-friendly modes of conduct since Arab satellite television came into existence (Sakr 2007). This might indicate that traditional authoritarian censorship and other forms of interventions into Arab media have started to give way to modern forms of political spin-doctoring, public relations, and the creation of media events. What is needed are studies that identify old and new forms of intervention by Arab governments in the media system, from executive intervention as part of media policies to media laws and informal networks between journalists and politicians, so-called beat systems, that define a special exchange relation whereby privileged information is granted to loyal media (Molotch et al. 1987).

Research field II—the link between society (challengers) and the media. Questions in this field are centered on the degree to which challengers from civil society have already managed to gain representation in Arab media and how they managed that. As argued above, for the Arab media to have a strong effect on politicalchange, it might be important to improve links with civil society. Traditional public sphere theory has focused on identifying which actors are present in the media—only elites, or also representatives of a pluralist society? Such representation is needed for the public sphere to fulfill its multiple roles: to provide transparency (of political decisions), validation (through discourse in society), and orientation (of people's political opinions). Of course, special interests of organized publics and issue lobbies do not necessarily represent the *volonté générale*, and numerous groups from Western NGOs such as Greenpeace to Middle Eastern Islamists are trying to instrumentalize the media on the basis of sometimes questionable democratic legitimacy. Nevertheless, since it is unclear how changes in the public sphere translate into political change, it would be appropriate to apply modern social movement theory (Van den Donk et al. 2004) to the Arab media sector.

Research field III—media processes 1. Leon V. Sigal argues that media content is influenced by three internal media dimensions: time, space, and staff (Sigal, 1973). Various communication models deal with the media's gatekeeping of incoming information, the influence of external news providers like news agencies on media content (Boyd-Barret/Thussu 1992), social processes in the newsroom (Rühl 1980), news values and news routines (Harcup/O'Neill 2001), or journalistic ethics as guiding principles of news making (Starkey 2007). Although there are many studies on Arab media content, research on the internal processes of media organizations are rare, or they are, as in the case of a number of books on Al-Jazeera, more descriptive or essayistic than informed by communication theories and methodologies.

The above systematization is just part of the story of the politics/society–media link. It reflects *influences on* the media and content-related processes *in the media*, but it does not reflect on *effects the media have*, or might have, *on politics and society*. Again, Wolfsfeld's political contest model is a good starting point for mapping the field (Wolfsfeld 1997, 56–73). In his view, the media's influence on political outcomes depends on the relative effect of value factors like size, status, and the political power of the media's audiences and of dependency factors like official political control, the need for official information and organizational resources (this time of the media themselves). Politicians as much as societies are not thought to be passive in the face of media influences, but their reaction, the changes they make to political strategies, and their political standing can be considered interactions between media outputs and internal processes within the political and societal spheres. In other contexts, such processes are considered to be the intervening variables of media effects.

Wolfsfeld's approach is incomplete since his model is confined to political communication antagonists in the narrower sense (authorities, parties, organizations) and it does not cover large parts of society that, as we have seen in the debate on political attitudes, political cultures, and public opinion, could be important for political change. Moreover, intervening factors that could limit the media's effect on authorities and challengers are not explicitly mentioned. As in the case of *influences on* media, Wolfsfeld provides a rough sketch for the identification of research fields concerning the *influences of* Arab media on domestic and foreign political decision making and on political and social developments within Arab societies.

Research field IV—media processes 2. Media processes determining the media effects of media products are mainly those related to economy, markets, and technology. For Arab media to be effective it is, for example, necessary for that media to be receivable through satellites or other telecommunication infrastructures that are the prerequisites for media distribution. Media cities established in several Arab countries are but one way to enhance the economic capacities of mass media industries. It is certainly true that the growing interest in audience studies in Arab media research partly stems from commercial value such data can have.

In general there is, quite like in many other fields of media and communication studies, a variety of approaches to media economy but no comprehensive concept (Kiefer 2001).

Research field V—the link between the media and politics. The mass media can influence politics by informing politicians about the political process, defining standards of political acceptance and legitimacy, directing a society's attention to a certain agenda, limiting the freedom of political decision making, or changing the speed of processes (O'Heffernan 1991). Recent studies about the CNN effect, however, have demonstrated that such effects are more likely to occur under particular circumstances—namely, splits in elite political ranks, the availability of media images, and clearly definable political crises (for instance, a humanitarian issue in contrast to a regular complex political conflict; Robinson 2002). The probability of such effects is also minimized in special situations like wars or catastrophes that guarantee a greater autonomy of governments from social control than in other situations. In such situations system theory might help to understand fluctuations in media autonomy (Hafez 2000, 35 ff., 44 ff.). It is certainly a challenge to analyze such complexities with respect to Arab media's effects on politics, rather than engage, as is often the case, in fundamental debates about Arab media's power or weakness.

Research field VI—the link between the media and society. Traditionally there exists a great divide between media effect and audience studies, and it is quite an understatement to say that the application of relevant concepts and theories on Arab media's interactions with Arab societies could be improved. Today's most respected, and certainly the best-developed, theory of media effects is the agenda-setting approach that holds that media do not necessarily determine what people think but rather what they think *about* (Dearing/Rogers 1996). There are a number of other important theories, like that of the "spiral of silence," whose basic assumption is that the mass media are interpreted by many to represent the dominant public opinion, which in turn reduces people's willingness to utter and support views that are not represented or even condemned in the media (Scheufele/Moy 2000). It would be challenging to apply such theories to Arab environments. It is still unclear whether theories like the "spiral of silence" can only be applied to fully developed democratic societies with a high level of media freedom and where the media are trusted by many people to reflect public opinion, which is surely not the case in authoritarian systems where many people mistrust state-controlled media. Have we already reached the point in Arab countries where, due to the growth of new and often more liberal media sectors, the media have a strong effect on people's interpersonal political communication? From here it would be just a small step to analyze the effect of media on group formations, on so-called social movements or virtual communities (Rheingold 1993) that are important for the development of various kinds of social capital (Putnam 1993).

It is equally important to study the behavior of audiences. Audience analysis is not the privilege of media and communication studies, which is at the focus of media anthropology and cultural studies as well. Stuart Hall, for example, has paved the way for a better understanding of audiences' "decoding" of media content (Hall 1981). Communication studies on the basis of the uses-and-gratifications approach (Blumler/Katz 1974) have made clear, among other things, that the "effects" of the much debated import of Western films, for example, must be judged with respect to Arab individual and cultural interpretations that "domesticate" Western film products (Liebes/Katz 1990).

Research on Arab Media: Rapidly Growing, but Still in Its Infancy

For research on Arab mass media the terrorist attacks of September 11, 2001, were a real turning point. Starting with the events in New York and Washington, D.C., the worldwide interest in Arab media started to boom. "Al-Jazeera" became one of the most frequently searched-for terms on the Internet, Western media became interested in Arab journalism, and young academics all over the world discovered Arab media as a field of research and academic teaching. Especially the hype about Al-Jazeera, the leading pan-Arab news network that became famous for taboo-breaking journalism but also notorious for the circulation of terrorist videos made by Osama bin Laden and others, attracted the interest of media and communication research, a well-established discipline in the West and an upcoming field in many Arab countries.

The fast development in research has brought about a number of informative and enlightening books and articles (e.g., Sakr 2001, Zayani 2005, Lynch 2006). At the same time, however, the young discipline has also suffered from a number of teething problems. Since the desire for fast information on Arab media was strong, an essayistic culture developed that often provided the academic market with analyses weakened by grave theoretical and empirical deficits. Editors of special academic journals admit that relevant articles rarely ever met the requirements of refereed journals. It is perhaps symptomatic that even years after 9/11 hardly any content analysis on Al-Jazeera exists that combines quantitative and qualitative state-of-the-art methodology. Channels like Al-Jazeera are much debated, but they are still underresearched.

The main reason for these and many other deficits is that research on Arab media lies at the crossroads of various larger disciplines, especially Middle Eastern studies and media and communication sciences. Because Middle Eastern studies are traditionally inspired by political science, economics, cultural studies, philology, and anthropology, they often lack theoretical and methodological ingredients needed for the study of Arab media. Meanwhile, media and communication studies, which could provide such qualifications, have for years almost totally neglected the non-Western world. Until today the large academic corporations like the International Communication Association (ICA) and to a lesser degree also the International Association of Media and Communication Research (IAMCR) have been mainly recruiting their members from North America, Europe, and Australia. These and other conditions are the reason why academic research on Arab media is growing rapidly but is still in its infancy.

When confronted with such critique, non-Arab scholars very often, and quite correctly, point to the specific hurdles they have to overcome before studying Arab media. First, there is the limited access to the Arabic language, which, of course, poses a major stumbling block to any serious research, especially in the field of media content analysis. Second, many authoritarian Arab regimes restrict access to field research in their countries, a fact that has surely hampered the development of all kinds of inquiries, including public opinion polls. Third, there is a deep-seated suspicion that research on Arab media might require completely different theories that are not part of the predominantly Eurocentric canon of media and communication studies.

Of course, any of these arguments are valid efforts to explain why Western scholarship, in particular, has almost completely ignored Arab and other non-European media systems over the past decades, but none of them is sufficient on its own. Language hurdles can be bypassed through translations, permission to research can be acquired, and problems of theoretical applicability can only be defined if we first adapt the existing theories of communication science to the Arab media (standards of media use and effect such as agenda-setting; framing; uses and gratification; cultivation; or special theories in various specific fields—for example, political communication, interpersonal communication, social communication, international communication, etc.). De-Westernizing media studies means that particularly the strong and large communication studies departments in the Western world need to pay more attention to the non-Western world. It is not a culturalist strategy that should be based on the foregone conclusion that existing theories are inappropriate and completely new approaches are needed (see also Curran/Park 2000, 15).

The Book

This book represents an effort to enhance the interdisciplinary merger of systematic social sciences and humanities in the field of media and communication studies with the field of research on Arab media. In a series of chapters some of the foremost experts from Arab countries, Europe and the United States seek to define their views on the state-of-the-art in various fields. The book is grouped in sections that cover most of the above research fields and a large part of the current canon of media and communication studies around the world: content analysis, effect studies, audience research, media ethics, media economy, media law and policy, and media culture. Alternative categorizations—for example, political or social communication—are valid. Since those fields, however, overlap tremendously with many of the other categories that are used in this book, they were left aside.

Some of the texts in this anthology raise problems without always providing sufficient answers. Many authors bemoan a lack of access to empirical data that are needed to reach satisfactory conclusions. The whole project therefore must be understood as an impulse for a long-term revision of the field of Arab media studies.

For Marc Lynch it seems highly likely that Arab media have strong effects on the public agenda or even on the framing of public discourses in Arab countries. He hesitates, however, to concede likely influences on deep structures of political opinion making or even on political decision making. His chapter is a plea for the better integration of political communication studies and Arab media research.

Traditionally public opinion is considered a rather weak influencing factor in foreign policy, where the dominance over decision making and weakly organized that publics benefits governments. Russell E. Lucas, however, cautiously demonstrates, due to a lack of clear empirical evidence, that even in authoritarian countries like Jordan specific conditions—namely, moderate issue salience and the emergence of a public consensus—public opinion can have an effect on the foreign policy of authoritarian regimes.

On the basis of an in-depth comparative content analysis of the Egyptian mainstream and the Islamist press as well as relevant interviews with journalists, Carola Richter reflects on whether Islamist media function as intermedia agenda setters. Her interest is not, as in the other chapters, whether the media influence politicians or public opinion, but whether they affect other media and the media discourse. Richter concludes that the established press merely reacts to the Islamist topical agenda, which, however, mainly serves as a template for critical response. In that sense, Islamists might be able to promote certain issues within the wider public realm, but they are not necessarily capable of favoring their own ideological worldviews on the subjects discussed. The Islamification of the Egyptian media through Islamist organizations and their media has only partially been accomplished.

In an overview of existing research on Arab audiences Hussein Amin shows that despite the fact that the number of studies is growing, many of them lack theoretical sophistication. Three of the many stumbling blocks for audience researchers are limited access to unbiased data, a lack of trained personnel in the Arab world, and "barriers and constraints from inconvenience to imprisonment."

Like Amin, Marwan M. Kraidy argues that a lot more empirical but theoretically grounded research on Arab audiences is urgently needed. Arab television viewers' "decoding" of media messages remains largely a black box. The rapidly developing field of interactive programming can especially reveal a great deal about the political and economic anxieties of Arab populations in still largely authoritarian environments.

In a study of Arab and other research on Arab media, Muhammad Ayish identifies a series of deficits in the current quality of content analysis. According to the author, the bulk of academic work is quite obsessed with development issues, leaving aside many other relevant topics. From a theoretical perspective most studies are quantitative-descriptive rather than qualitative-explanatory, and they are seldom embedded in elaborate theoretical frameworks.

In addition to Ayish's meta-analysis, Katharina Nötzold presents an exemplary case study of Lebanese TV. Although her chapter confirms that sectarian influences are strong, it also demonstrates the capacity of quantitative work to challenge false assumptions and prejudices. Al-Manar, for example, a TV network close to Islamist Hezbollah, does not cover the highest percentage of religious events.

In his chapter on journalism ethics, Kai Hafez concedes that the field is marginal to contemporary Arab media research, although it is perhaps *the* focal point of all debates on Al-Jazeera and the new Arab media. Focusing on the core concept of Western media ethics, on "objectivity," the author compares Arab and Western values and practices in that field. Hafez concludes that many problems caused by conflicting Arab and Western media perceptions and relations are the result not of differences but of commonalities in Western-style professional concepts that leave too much space for conflict-oriented news values and own-community biases. Professional ethics on both sides hardly reflect on the international dimensions of journalism.

Journalism education and ethical coaching have started to flourish all over the Arab world in recent years as a sign of increased professionalization. Judith Pies demonstrates in her case study on Lebanon and Jordan that the approaches of these institutions to ethical teaching can differ enormously. Ethics can be viewed as a regulating device for the profession, designed to secure the unity of the country or as an instrument of mobilization for change in society.

In her analysis of existing research on Arab media economics, Naomi Sakr bemoans the lack of academic literature in the field. Existing problems such as the loss of profitability resulting from widespread piracy, the bad coordination of TV ratings and advertising or government interventions into film markets are hardly dealt with.

Tourya Guaaybess discusses the Orientalist biases in the Western reception of Arab mass media, which are often suspected of having a hidden (anti-Western) political agenda. From her perspective, the development of Arab media economies, media advertising, and media equipment over the past decade reveals the growing relevance of market factors even in authoritarian state capitalist systems.

Orayb Aref Najjar outlines how the terrorism issue has been exploited by governments in Egypt and Jordan to tighten up media laws and, at the same time, to curb the political opposition. However, media law also developed into a double-edged sword for the regimes. Where courts protected free speech the law turned against autocrats to secure some basic independence for the legal system from the political system.

Tarik Sabry argues that the study of Arab media culture, which has so far been almost completely left to Western anthropologists and social scientists, should be renewed by introducing new, mostly indigenous theories and methodologies. As an example, he discusses the concept of a unified Arab culture that he perceives to be an Arab speciality.

Although the Islamification of popular culture in Syria is far from complete, Christa Salamandra has observed growing pressure on Syrian filmmakers to incorporate Islam-influenced elements into their products. Cultural industries are thereby diluting the divide between Islamist and secularist orientations in society.

Notes

1. See the "Freedom in the World" index on freedomhouse.org.
2. See, for example, the statement by Jon Alterman during the conference "Arab Media, Power and Influence" at Princeton University, http://www.wws.princeton.edu/research/specialreports/Arab Media.pdf.

References

Blumler, J. G./E. Katz (eds.) (1974), *The Uses of Mass Communications: Current Perspectives in Gratification Research.* Beverly Hills/London: Sage.

Boyd-Barrett, O./D. K. Thussu (1992), *Contra-Flow in Global News: International and Regional News Exchange Mechanisms.* London et al.: John Libbey.

Curran, J./M.-J. Park (2000), Beyond Globalization Theory. In J. Curran/M.-J. Park (eds.), *De-Westernizing Media Studies.* London/New York: Routledge.

Dearing, J. W./E. M. Rogers (1996), *Agenda-Setting.* Thousand Oaks et al.: Sage.

Eickelman, D. F./J. W. Anderson (eds.) (1999), *New Media in the Muslim World: The Emerging Public Sphere.* Bloomington/Indianapolis: Indiana University Press.

Hafez, K. (2000), The Middle East and Islam in Western Media: Towards a Comprehensive Theory of Foreign Reporting. In K. Hafez (ed.), *Islam and the West in the Mass Media: Fragmented Images in a Globalizing World.* Cresskill: Hampton Press, 27–66.

______. (2003), *Media Ethics in the Dialogue of Cultures: Journalistic Self-Regulation in Europe, the Arab World, and Muslim Asia.* Hamburg: Deutsches Orient-Institut.

______. (2006), Arab Satellite Broadcasting: Democracy without Political Parties. *Transnational Broadcasting Studies* 1 2, 275–297.

Hall, S. (1991), Encoding/Decoding. In S. Hall/D. Hobson/A. Lowe/P. Willis (eds.), *Culture, Media, Language: Working Papers in Cultural Studies, 1972–79.* London: Hutchinson.

Harcup, T./O'Neill, D. (2001), What is News? Galtung and Ruge Revisited. *Journalism Studies* 2, 261–280.

Kiefer, M. L. (2001), *Medienökonomik.* München/Wien: Oldenbourg.

Liebes, T./E. Katz (1990), *The Export of Meaning: Cross-Cultural Readings of Dallas.* New York/Oxford: Oxford University Press.

Lynch, M. (2006), *Voices of the New Arab Public: Iraq, Al-Jazeera, and Middle East Politics Today.* New York: Columbia University Press.

Mernissi, F. (2007), Der Islam schafft Solidaritat. *Die Tageszeitung,* Berlin, September 19.

Meyer, T. (2001), *Mediokratie: die Kolonisierung der Politik durch die Medien.* Frankfurt a.M.: Suhrkamp.

Molotch, H./D. L. Protess/M.T. Gordon (1987), The Media-Policy Connection: Ecologies of News. In D. L. Paletz (ed.), *Political Communication Research: Approaches, Studies, Assessments.* Norwood: Ablex.

Nawawy, M. al-/A. Iskandar (2003), *Al-Jazeera: The Story of the Network that is Rattling Governments and Redefining Modern Journalism.* Cambridge, MA: Westview Press.

O'Heffernan, P. (1991), *Mass Media and American Foreign Policy: Insider Perspectives on Global Journalism and the Foreign Policy Process.* Norwood: Ablex.

Putnam, R. D. (1993), The Prosperous Community: Social Capital and Public Life. *The American Prospect* 13, 35–42.

Rheingold, H. (1993), *The Virtual Community: Homesteading on the Electronic Frontier.* Reading: Addison-Wesley.

Robinson, P. (2002), *The CNN Effect: The Myth of News, Foreign Policy and Intervention.* London/New York: Routledge.

Rühl, Manfred (1980), *Journalismus und Gesellschaft: Bestandsaufnahme und Theorieentwurf.* Mainz: Hase und Köhler.

Sakr, N. (2001), *Satellite Realms: Transnational Television, Globalization and the Middle East.* London/New York: I. B. Tauris.

______. (2007), Approaches to Exploring Media-Politics Connections in the Arab World. In Naomi Sakr (ed.), *Arab Media and Political Renewal: Community, Legitimacy and Public Life.* London/New York: I. B. Tauris.

Scheufele, D. A./P. Moy (2000), Twenty-Five Years of the Spiral of Silence: A Conceptual Review of Empirical Outlook. *International Journal of Public Opinion Research* 1, 3–28.

Sigal, L.V. (1973), *Reporters and Officials: The Organization and Politics of Newsmaking.* Lexington: Heath.

Starkey, G. (2007), *Balance and Bias in Journalism: Representation, Regulation and Democracy.* New York: Palgrave/Macmillan.

Van de Donk, W./B. D. Loader/P.G. Nixon/D. Rucht (eds.) (2004), *Cyberprotest: New Media, Citizens and Social Movements.* London/New York: Routledge.

Wolfsfeld, G. (1997), *Media and Political Conflict: News from the Middle East.* Cambridge: Cambridge University Press.

Zayani, M. (ed.) (2005), *The Al Jazeera Phenomenon: Critical Perspectives on New Arab Media.* London: Pluto.

Media Effects

CHAPTER ONE

Political Opportunity Structures: Effects of Arab Media

Marc Lynch

The state of research on media effects is one of the most notable embarrassments of modern social science.

(Bartels 1993, 267)

Many broad and definitive judgments about the substantive content of mass media are still made without actual content analyses of these media.

(Graber 2003, 140)

Confusion about the political effects of the Arab mass media abounds. Sweeping claims about the pernicious or revolutionary impact of satellite television are easily found: the Arab media promotes democracy, washing away decades of authoritarian political culture; the Arab media fans the flames of radicalism, subverting liberalism and the forces of moderation. But such claims are routinely made based on superficial and impressionistic evidence, with little serious attention to the theoretical underpinnings or causal mechanisms underlying the contentions (Sakr 2007). These debates about Arab media in fact recapitulate earlier debates about the effects of the media in Western societies (Newton 1999; 2006). Early research saw massive effects "because the mass media permeate almost every corner of society, and have a strong impact on almost everywhere they touch" (Newton 2006, 209). These arguments seemed plausible in increasingly media-saturated Western societies, and were attractive both to conservatives who mourned the assumed decline of traditional society and leftists keen to expose the manipulation of the masses by corporate media. Social scientists seeking to document these alleged massive media effects found little supporting evidence, however (Zaller 1996). The "minimal effects" school that rose in its place argued instead that Arab media is "generally a weak force in politics and government...they can and do exercise some direct and independent influence over some aspects of political life, and can even exercise a strong or crucial one under certain circumstances, but normally their impact is mediated and conditioned by a variety of other and more powerful forces" (Newton 2006, 210).

Most discussion of the Arab media today falls by default into the "massive effects" camp, despite the general dominance of the "minimal effects" school in the academic literature and the relative absence of systematic evidence to support the claims. The "massive effects" school of Arab media studies is given superficial plausibility by the seemingly simultaneous rapid expansion of the mass media and political upheavals in the Arab world over the last decade. And just as "massive effects" were politically convenient in the West, the Arab media today makes a convenient scapegoat for a wide range of actors: Americans found it more convenient to blame the media for fueling anti-Americanism or the struggles in Iraq than to consider the effects of their foreign policy, while Arab governments preferred to blame Al-Jazeera for popular unrest than to look at their own failures. As in the earlier generation of Western media effects research, the absence of serious empirical research and undertheorized causal mechanisms allow a politically convenient and superficially plausible "massive effects" assumption to go largely unchallenged.

This chapter places the arguments over the political effects of the Arab media within these wider debates in order to lay the foundations for a practical research agenda. It highlights current deficiencies in the available empirical evidence on audiences, content, and effect, as well as in the theoretical underpinnings of the claimed relationships. I then consider a set of hypotheses drawn from the wider literature that could conceivably be relevant to the Arab case, concluding that the most promising research avenue lies with media effects theories that emphasize framing and agenda setting. I conclude that there is relatively thin support for regionwide claims about mass media effects on political attitudes or behavior, with it being virtually impossible at this point to separate out media effects from other driving forces (such as actual policies, power struggles, and social movements). There is stronger support for more specific claims about specific cases, with the media shaping political strategies and outcomes in particular instances. Given the data shortcomings and regional variation, the best way to make sense of the political effects of the Arab media is through detailed case studies that distinguish between the universal and the specific, and pay close attention to competing explanations. This suggests the utility of reconceptualizing the media as part of the "political opportunity structure" within which actors operate (McAdam et al. 2001, Tilly/Tarrow 2007), rather than as an independent variable directly causing outcomes. Finally, I offer brief illustrations of two issue areas in which the media is claimed to have a major role, one in attitudes (anti-Americanism) and the other in behavior (democratization).

Current Deficiencies

Jim Shanahan and Erik Nisbet's recent work on the relationship between the Arab media and anti-Americanism exemplifies both the prospects and the problems with current Arab media effects research. Shanahan and Nisbet attempt to statistically evaluate a series of hypothesized relationships between the Arab media and Arab attitudes toward America, concluding that "media infrastructure, in terms of access to television and Internet, was the strongest predictor of which countries had substantial increases in anti-American sentiment" during the period between 2002 and 2005 (Shanahan/Nisbet 2007, 2). Although their statistical analysis is solid, their analysis is hampered by the shortcomings in the available data upon which they rely: occasional large-scale public opinion surveys carried out by Gallup, Pew, and Zogby, supplemented by content analysis provided by the German firm Media Tenor. Such data sources are deeply inadequate to the task of isolating the political impact of the media. This is not the fault of Shanahan and Nisbet, but rather an indication of the state of the field. Indeed, it is difficult to pinpoint particular deficiencies in the existing data about the political effects of the Arab media, because those deficiencies are global. The availability of reliable measures of even the most basic data about independent variables cannot be taken for granted in the case of the Arab media. Three particular areas of concern stand out: information about *audiences* for the mass media; information about the *content* of the media; and measures of the *effects* the media is claimed to be having. Finally, data alone will not solve problems that are fundamentally theoretical. Any persuasive theorization of Arab media effects needs to precisely specify the *causal mechanisms* by which media affects political attitudes, behavior, and outcomes, and must balance the homogenizing impact of regional media with the highly variable domestic political configurations across the Arab world.

Audiences

Even determining the audiences for Arab media is surprisingly challenging. Anecdotal evidence abounds: travelogues of satellite dishes sprouting in squalid urban quarters, or vignettes of men in a café with eyes glued to Al-Jazeera's coverage of the invasion of Iraq. We can speak in general terms about the rapid growth of access to satellite television across the region, but the illicit nature of many of these satellite dishes—as well as the common practice of communal viewing in cafés and other venues—makes precise quantification difficult. Nothing comparable to the American Nielsen ratings exists for the Arab market that would allow for reliable tracking of media consumption patterns over time. Public opinion surveys carried out for other reasons have asked about media preferences and usage, but do not follow conventional television ratings methodologies and are not repeated often enough along the same samples to generate useful trend lines. There are studies carried out on behalf of advertisers or particular stations, but their findings are rarely made public and tend to focus only on certain markets (primarily Saudi Arabia, the largest advertising market). In short, even if there is more information available today than in the past, existing audience market data is of limited utility for academic research except for broad generalizations.

The most systematic, useful information about Arab consumption of mass media has been produced by Shibley Telhami's annual survey of six Arab countries (Egypt, Jordan, Lebanon, Morocco, Saudi Arabia, and the UAE).[1] His surveys demonstrate that Al-Jazeera is the overall dominant market leader, with very significant variations by country. In 2004 Al-Jazeera ranked as the primary station for 62 percent of Jordanians, 54 percent of Moroccans, 44 percent of Lebanese, 44 percent of Saudis, and 46 percent in the UAE; and the secondary station for (on average) about 20 percent more in each country. In the 2005 survey, only 10 percent said they never watched Al-Jazeera, while 65 percent named it as either their first or second preference. Again, there was significant variation by country: Al-Jazeera was least viewed in Lebanon (63 percent) and Saudi Arabia (42 percent), for instance, while dominant in Egypt and Jordan. In the 2006 survey, Al-Jazeera remained on top, with 54 percent naming Al-Jazeera as their top choice for international news. Saudi Arabia was the only market in which Al-Jazeera did not lead, a finding reproduced in other market surveys as well. The Lebanese market matched Al-Jazeera against a number of popular local stations. Still, in its strongest four (out of six) countries, Al-Jazeera enjoyed an *average* advantage of over 45 percentage points (62 percent in Egypt and 64 percent in Jordan). In some (such as Yemen, Jordan, and the Palestinian areas) the weakness of local media turns Al-Jazeera and other regional broadcasters into the primary platform for political news and debate. In others (such as Egypt, Saudi Arabia, and Lebanon) the regional broadcasters play an important but not dominant role in a more crowded domestic media arena.

This data, whatever its flaws, allows for some generalizations about the structure of the Arab media market. Prior to the 1990s, most Arab media was either state-dominated or else published abroad, with the mass electronic media primarily "mobilizational" in character (Rugh 2004). The launch of Al-Jazeera revolutionized the political arena with professional and independent reporting, an Arab nationalist and populist ethos, and diverse and contentious political opinion. By the turn of the century, Al-Jazeera enjoyed something like universal presence among Arab political society. This means that by roughly 1998 Al-Jazeera's programming could be reasonably considered what game theorists call the "common knowledge" of Arab political society: every actor would reasonably expect that every other actor was aware of it. This status made it an enormously potent weapon, and hotly contested battlefield, in the aftermath of 9/11. Within a few years, Al-Jazeera's near monopoly had given way to intense market competition, with the market fragmenting (in some markets more than others). Al-Arabiya launched in 2003 with Saudi funding and quickly emerged as a regionwide challenger to Al-Jazeera. Egyptian stations (Dream and Orbit), smaller persian Gulf competitors (Abu Dhabi TV and Dubai TV), other Saudi stations (MBC, ART), and even Iranian and Western Arabic-language broadcasters played a role in specific contexts. Lebanese broadcasters such as al-Manar, New TV, Future TV, LBC—often tied to particular political parties—took on an explicitly political role in the heated events after the 2005 assassination of Rafik Hariri. The Arab media market has therefore gone through distinct phases rather than remaining constant in its structure or political dynamics.

Content

The literature on Arab media effects also lacks basic information about its content (see Ayish and Nötzold in this volume). Serious content analysis of the Arab media remains very thin, leaving analyses to simply impute content to stations based on assumption or anecdotal evidence. Recent comparative work has attempted to include Arab media sources, but these studies remain very limited in their penetration or interpretive grasp of Arab media discourse (Aday et al. 2005; Falah et al. 2006). Even work that cites examples of Arab media content tends to select them on an unscientific and potentially unrepresentative basis, producing argument by anecdote rather than by systematic, representative content analysis (Fandy 2000, Ajami 2001). Virtually nothing in Arab media studies approaches the sort of empirically sophisticated content analysis formed on the Chinese media by Iain Johnston and Daniele Stockman (2006), to say nothing of the norms of empirical analysis of English-language media. This is a problem with statistical analyses that use "Al-Jazeera viewing" as a proxy for exposure to anti-American content (Gentzkow/Shapiro 2004; Nisbet et al. 2004); to the extent that Al-Jazeera's content is more diverse and contentious, such inferences would not hold (Nawawy/Iskander 2002; Lynch 2005b; Miles 2005.)

To show why the limited availability of content analysis matters, consider that one of the strongest findings in the literature has to do with the effects of "exposure to dissimilar views via the media" (Mutz/Martin 2001, 99). As Bartels (1993) puts it, "Consistent, distinctive media messages favoring one side or the other in a political controversy are...likely to produce sizable opinion changes over time. Thus, studies of when and why such consistent, distinctive media messages get produced should be among the highest priorities for research on the political impact of the mass media." Does the Arab media reinforce balkanized views or does it provide a diversity of views? Does the rise of Al-Arabiya and the fragmentation of the Arab media market offer Arab viewers a wider array of competing messages? Ajami and Fandy's presentation would suggest not, that the new Arab media is full of very similar, mutually reinforcing content. Others argue that not only does Al-Jazeera itself feature highly diverse content and multiple points of view, but that the rise of a fragmented market (which includes stations such as Al-Arabiya that have self-consciously set out to offer a political alternative to Al-Jazeera) means that a wide variety of political perspectives are now available to channel-surfing Arab viewers. Rigorous content analysis—whether statistical or more interpretive discourse analysis—would at least begin to fill in the empirical void.

Causal Effects

Finally, measures of the dependent variables of interest to political scientists are improving but remain limited and rudimentary. Part of the problem is conceptual: defining the political attitudes or behaviors of interest, and their relationship to political outcomes. Another part is empirical: the availability of reliable measures of those variables. The latter problem is beginning to change, to some extent. Public opinion survey research in the Middle East has taken off since 9/11, with a growing body of research of widely varying quality on Arab political attitudes (Tessler 2003; Lynch 2006; Moaddel 2006). As early as the 1990s, several governments and agencies were beginning to survey national public opinion in the region. After 9/11, international research agencies such as the Pew Foundation, Zogby International, and the Gallup Organization began carrying out major cross-national survey research on a wide range of questions of concern to American foreign policy. An upgraded Arab component of the World Values Survey and a number of National Science Foundation reports supported single country and multi-country studies. As a result, we now have a far more rigorous and useful set of data on Arab and Muslim public opinion than ever before, and it is increasingly being exploited by statistically oriented political scientists.

Political attitudes as measured by survey research are only one component of the "political effects" of concern to political scientists, however. Consider two of the most widely studied issue areas in Arab media studies: anti-Americanism and democratization. Anti-Americanism is an *attitude*, to be measured in opinion surveys and public discourse, whose manifestation does not necessarily lead to any particular political effects (which are mediated through all the various political institutions and processes through which public opinion might or might not matter politically). It is worth distinguishing between relatively transient opinions, which might change easily in response to changed circumstance, and more entrenched interpretive schemas that constitute relatively stable worldviews (Katzenstein/Keohane 2007). Democratization is a political process, whose manifestation can be seen in political behavior—elections, protests, parliamentary maneuvering—that is not reducible to attitudes. There have been a number of fairly free, contested elections in the Middle East in recent years (Bahrain, Egypt, Iraq, Kuwait, Lebanon, Palestine, etc.), and these offer a chance to tentatively begin the kind of voting behavior questions that dominate much of the "political effects of the media" literature (Sheafer/Weimann 2005). There has also been a parallel explosion of contentious political behavior that would lend itself to constructing data sets about protests, strikes, and other mobilizational activity. Distinguishing between attitudes and behavior is necessary for developing useful theories of the political effects of the Arab media.

It is important to note, however, that the problems are not simply data related. There are also serious methodological, conceptual, and theoretical issues that have hardly begun to be resolved. The media effects literature has long struggled with disentangling the various possible explanatory factors driving political opinions and behavior. The sophisticated statistical analysis that goes into these efforts would simply be impossible in the data-poor Arab context. Any serious analysis of media effects, however, must at least attempt to go beyond correlation and specify causal mechanisms. How does the Arab media have the claimed effects? The mechanisms could be psychological (priming, agenda setting, motivated bias) or political (strategies, power resources, opportunity structures). The next section begins to flesh out some of these possible causal mechanisms, which should be elaborated even if solving the data problems remain a long-term agenda.

Hypotheses about the Arab Media

Research on the political effects of the Arab media should integrate theories of *agenda setting*, or how the media decides which issues become major themes in public opinion; *framing*, or how they are linked together into political narratives (Scheufele 1999; Takeshita 2005); and *political opportunity structures*, or how the media changes the prospects for these attitudes to be translated into political action (Tilly/Tarrow 2006). *Agenda setting* works by priming viewers, highlighting certain issues and identifying them as important while neglecting others. Whether as passive recipients or as active learners, viewers infer from the media which issues matter. These are not solely media constructs, of course: the progression from the second Palestinian Intifada, through 9/11, the 2002 Israeli reoccupation of the West Bank, the invasion of and subsequent violence in Iraq, and the 2006 Israel-Lebanon war has meant that a steady stream of violent, bloody images—punctuated by moments of political enthusiasm, such as the Lebanese and Egyptian protests of 2005—has dominated the regional agenda. *Framing* refers to the normative evaluation of the issues built into the coverage, and the narrative into which the issues fit, which together construct the meanings that inform viewers about how they should be understood (Scheufele 1999). Framing and agenda setting can be integrated effectively into an understanding of the media's effects rooted in theories of contentious politics. Rather than a stand-alone variable, the media should be understood as a vital part of what Charles Tilly and Sidney Tarrow (2006) call the "political opportunity structure."

The key framing and agenda-setting contributions of the new Arab media, especially satellite television, have been to unify the Arab political agenda and to shatter the ability of states to control information or the range of permissible opinion. Whether for ideological reasons (residual Arab nationalism or Islamist pan-nationalism) or for market reasons (regionwide broadcasters need to emphasize issues of wide appeal), the main satellite television stations have structured a news agenda that emphasizes an overarching Arab identity (Telhami 2007). The transnational Arab media, it is often argued, promotes Arab identity at expense of national identity (Alterman 1998). The public sphere has a powerfully constitutive effect on political identity, so that the common news agenda and common political debates of Al-Jazeera and its regional competitors engage average citizens in the wider Arab identity.

Palestine and Iraq are the most obvious examples of this regionwide Arab frame. But issues of reform and democratization have similarly been cast as part of a wider Arab story. Al-Jazeera's framing of the political agenda establishes a common, core Arab narrative that in the past had existed only in a more abstract sense (Lynch 2005b). It places events across the Arab world within a single narrative, drawing connections by implication (in the news) and explicitly (in talk show discussions).

The common regionwide agenda has not led to the predicted detachment from local politics but instead has reframed local politics around wider regional themes. Elections in Egypt or explosions in Morocco become part of an overarching Arab narrative as well as political episodes of local import. When Egyptians protested in one part of Cairo, in the past other Egyptians would have heard about it only via word of mouth, since Egyptian television would not have covered it. Now, virtually any protest, election, or political event is immediately covered by Al-Jazeera and its many competitors, rendering them visible and giving them meaning not only to other Egyptians but to all other Arabs. This points to one of the truly important political effects of the Arab media: its redefinition of the field of contention and its recasting of the political opportunities available to a wide range of political actors (McAdam et al. 2001). The contributions of the Arab media to both democratization and anti-Americanism, as discussed above, may be linked to this framing and agenda-setting mechanism: the rise in anti-Americanism in the region might be driven by a common narrative linking America as the common denominator for each of these otherwise distinct issues, while the rise in contentious democratic politics may similarly be supported by the same overarching Arab media–promoted narrative.

The transnational quality of the Arab media, with its very self-conscious invocation of a common political identity and its attempt to maintain a coherent political dialogue across national borders, is one of its most distinctive qualities. Compared to even the European media, the Arab media has succeeded in establishing these genuinely transnational qualities in unique ways. Viewed at that level, it makes sense to look for regionwide political effects—for instance, heightened identification with transnational identities (Arab, Islamic), or the greater emotional response to events triggered by the power of broadcast images. At the same time, the concrete political effects of the Arab media are always mediated through local political and social structures. The transnational media will matter differently in a media-saturated, politically dense arena such as Egypt and a media-starved, relatively uninstitutionalized country such as Yemen.

Finally, the changing structure of the Arab media market discussed above offers the opportunity to test some of the hypotheses that follow from agenda-setting and framing models. For instance, as it has risen to prominence since 2003, the Saudi-backed Al-Arabiya has pointedly attempted to reframe and reprioritize the Arab agenda against the narrative offered by Al-Jazeera. It has self-consciously offered a more "moderate" alternative, promoting critics of radical Islamism and favoring the views of status quo Arab regimes (such as Saudi Arabia) over popular Islamist movements. This means that significant numbers of Arab media viewers in 2005 or 2006 were exposed to a different agenda and normative framing than they would have been exposed to in 2002 or 2003, offering a perfect opportunity for testing these hypotheses.

Attitudes: Radicalism and Anti-Americanism

The impact of the Arab media on anti-Americanism has been one of the most systematically studied issue domains (Chiozza 2007). Several correlational studies have been published based on the 2002 Gallup Organization survey of nine Muslim countries. Nisbet et al. (2004), found that "attention to TV news coverage contributes significantly to anti-American perceptions." They did not argue that Arab media caused anti-Americanism, but rather that it *amplified* preexisting attitudes. But the study did little to determine whether the Arab media caused those attitudes, or whether people with such attitudes simply preferred to watch Al-Jazeera. Since the finding was correlated with TV news viewing rather than with any content analysis of specific stations, it also seems plausible that those coded as higher consumers of the media were simply more politically aware. Gentzkow and Shapiro (2004), looking at the same data, found little impact of media exposure, but that those for whom Al-Jazeera was the first choice were less likely to consider the 9/11 attacks unjustifiable and more likely to be hostile to the United States. But once again, they can do little to separate out causality. Finally, Chiozza's (2007) cross-regional study of anti-Americanism found that watching an international channel for news (i.e., CNN or BBC rather than Al-Jazeera) was significantly associated with more favorable views of the United States but could not determine whether this represented cause or effect (i.e., those more inclined to like America watched Western stations).

There are obvious problems with blaming the Arab media for anti-Americanism, such as the parallel rise of anti-Americanism across the world, in places that do not watch Al-Jazeera (Lynch 2007). Beyond such critiques, it is necessary to separate out "bias" arguments from "amplification" arguments: "bias" would mean that the Arab media is creating anti-American anger based on misleading or false presentations of American policies; "amplification" would mean that anti-Americanism is driven by the Arab media's relatively accurate presentation of American policies. The Arab media's airing of the Abu Ghraib scandal or the detentions at Guantanamo Bay angered Arab audiences, but each was rooted in very real American actions. Determining what is "fair" and what is "biased" brings the researcher deep into the heart of political controversy, unfortunately, with little solid ground upon which to stand. But the two different mechanisms would lead to very different prescriptions: "bias" would point to changing the Arab media, while "amplification" would point to changing American policies.

Perhaps the most extreme charge against the Arab media is that it incites violence—particularly in Iraq, where American and Iraqi officials routinely blame Al-Jazeera and other Arab media for the horrific violence. In the past, Palestinian suffering was something abstract and distant, but today Arabs are bombarded daily with graphic images of bloodied Iraqis and Palestinians. This direct, immediate visual access to political developments abroad has arguably made politics more real and reactions more intense. The graphic images of bloodshed from Palestine and Iraq, televised day after day into living rooms all over the Arab world, may well drive viewers to anger and political mobilization or to disgusted apathy and political withdrawal. As with other media effects, research on the social effects of televised violence are at best inconclusive: "people are affected by media in highly individualized ways ... the social factors underlying aggression and crime are influenced by far more than violent media" (Trend 2007, 2). In the Arab context, some viewers of televised carnage in Iraq may be inspired to set off to fight a violent jihad—but most will not, and explaining why some are radicalized and others are not requires more than looking at their common media-viewing habits. To this point, there has been no empirical research to support either case.

If direct effects of televised violence are difficult to ascertain, there is more evidence of the media as a key part of the political opportunity structure, shaping the political strategies and opportunities of insurgents and other violent actors. Alterman (2004) has described the kidnappings and beheadings in Iraq as "made for television events," designed for an impact on the mass public rather than directly on the local scene (although it is worth noting that no Arab satellite television station of which I am aware, including Al-Jazeera, ever aired a beheading video). Al-Jazeera's coverage of the battle for the city of Fallujah in April 2004 demonstrably hampered American military efforts there. The rise of sectarian Iraqi media, with Shia, Sunni, and Kurdish stations each playing to communal prejudices, may have more responsibility than the pan-Arab stations—certainly in other contexts the rise of sectarian media has been seen as a key explanatory variable for the outbreak of violent ethnic conflict. Al-Qaida has exploited the violence in Iraq in its propaganda, primarily disseminated on the Web but often seeping into televised media coverage. But once again we run into the need to consider competing explanations. The distinctive characteristics of the Arab media may have shaped the political strategies of the Iraqi insurgency, but it seems implausible to leap from this to blaming the Arab media for the existence of the insurgency, as American and Iraqi officials were too often wont to do.

Set against claims about the radicalizing effects of the Arab media should be the prevailing conventional wisdom at the global level—that transnational media tends to be depoliticizing (Bennett 2004). Indeed, Monroe Price argues that globalization of the media is "virtually synonymous with a tendency toward depoliticization" (1996, 17). As Lance Bennett summarizes this critical consensus, a market-oriented transnational media tends to "increase generic programming in both entertainment and public affairs," creating "a reconstructed political media space that excludes much of local politics, citizen activism, public policy analysis, and deliberation." The "emphasis on low-cost, attention-getting sensationalism" tends to promote "discouraging antisocial and antipolitical images," creating a passive citizenry focused on consumption rather than on politics (Bennett 2004, 126–127). Against this consensus, some argue that Arab media is not truly "globalizing," but regionalizing (Kraidy 2002). The distinctively political focus of Al-Jazeera and its competitors, and their elaboration of a pan-Arab political frame, likely cuts against the depoliticization found in other settings.

Finally, one variant of the radicalization thesis is what might be called the "frustration thesis": that the new Arab media generated great expectations for political change, the failure of which has soured newly empowered citizens on politics and given birth to an ugly new populism. This thesis has the virtue of offering a specific mechanism for attitude change—raised and then dashed expectations—as well as the suggestion of a clear sequence that could be measured through iterated survey data.

Behavior: Democratization

Arguments about the impact of Arab television on democratization concern institutions and behaviors rather than attitudes. Here I argue that an approach based on political opportunity structures makes more sense than does a search for unique media effects. "Political opportunity structure" is a fairly elastic concept that generally refers to how the institutional and political environment shapes the incentives and opportunities of political actors: "Changes in political opportunity structure shape the ease or difficulty of mobilization, the costs and benefits of collective claim making, the feasibility of various programs, and the consequences of different performances in the available repertoire" (Tilly/Tarrow 2006, 75). While Tilly and Tarrow do not include the media in their most recent elaboration of the concept, the media appears in many of their *examples* as something providing new opportunities to previously ignored actors. The new Arab media described above clearly makes an impact at these levels, making mobilization easier and giving it greater potential impact, thus lowering the costs and increasing the potential benefits of contentious politics (Hafez 2005).

Above I outlined a succession of shifts in the structure of the Arab media realm. Each of these phases offers a distinctive political opportunity structure. In the first, pre–Al-Jazeera phase, regimes were largely able to control the flow of information and opinion; even if elites could access Western media or the London-based Arab press, these had only limited wider political impact. Control over the media represented a key part of the authoritarian structure of politics, denying regime opponents the ability to be seen or heard by most of the citizenry. Opportunities for political activism were thus sharply limited, since activists had few means by which to gain access to the public realm. The second phase, the "Al-Jazeera era" spanning 1998 to 2003, decisively overturned this situation, offering significant opportunities for political action and conveying real power on sometimes quite small political movements. Al-Jazeera cameras conveyed power and protection, at least for a while, as the regime initially shied away from overt repression when the cameras were rolling. Small rallies that in the past would have been easily ignored by the state media now became important political events. As much as this created new opportunities, however, it also created vulnerabilities for these political activists. By initially exaggerating their importance, the media coverage unrealistically raised expectations that were inevitably frustrated—while also triggering the fears of the regimes and likely fueling an inevitable repressive crackdown.

In the third phase, the period of intense competition dating from roughly 2003, the greater number of competing media outlets provided more opportunities for coverage, but the fragmentation of the media market had some countervailing effects in other areas. The political significance of this fragmenting, hypercompetitive media market remains almost completely unexplored. One argument might be that media fragmentation limits the ability of any actor or movement to dominate the agenda due simply to the dizzying diversity of available outlets and agendas: where bin Laden could monopolize the public realm after 9/11, no movement or actor is likely to regain such ability. At some points—such as Nasrallah's prominence during the Israel-Lebanon war—the agenda regained coherence, but much of the time the media fragmentation has meant that viewers are more exposed to mixed messages and competing frames than in the past. Another possible difference lies in the incentives created by market competition. The intense need to attract audiences might drive competing satellite television stations toward a more sensationalist approach (coverage of Iraqi bloodshed, for example), or toward heavy coverage of populist issues (like the Danish cartoons crisis, for instance).

Enthusiasts for the new media argue that Al-Jazeera and the new Arab media are contributing to building democracy in the Arab world by undermining state power and encouraging new forms of political activism. But in the Arab case, the media cannot yet provide such foundations. As Lynch (2005a) puts it, "satellite television alone will not suffice to overcome entrenched authoritarian regimes. [They] can not stand in for the hard work of politics: party organization, mobilization, bargaining, and negotiation." The attention of the transnational media is fickle and unsustained, and tends to force domestic processes toward grand regional narratives into which they might not comfortably fit.

Other mechanisms linking the media and democratic outcomes are worth exploring. Lynch (2005b; 2005b), for instance, argues that the new Arab media has created the foundations for a new public sphere (Eickelman/Anderson 1999). Increased access to information and opinion "opened up the realm of possibility across the Arab world, inspiring political activists and shifting the real balance of power on the ground" (Lynch 2005a). These new forms of engagement would represent a secular change independent of specific political events or outcomes. For instance, Lynch (2005b) proposes that "talk shows on Al-Jazeera and other Arab television stations have contributed enormously to building the underpinnings of a more pluralist political culture, one which welcomes and thrives on open and contentious political debate." Hisham Sharabi (2003) similarly argues that the new media have raised the general political consciousness of Arabs, increased their ability to take political stands, and fueled collective action.

Against these claims that Arab television programs have increased political consciousness and engagement, critics see a depoliticizing dimension that would make this mechanism work in precisely the opposite direction. Rami Khoury (2001) has argued that "Arab satellite stations... may be having precisely the opposite impact—they may be entrenching autocratic, top-heavy Arab political regimes, rather than loosening them and promoting democracy and accountability." Khaled Al-Hroub complains that in the 1980s "the people were not captive to their television screens, which have robbed them of their ability to act" (2006, 103). Critics of Al-Jazeera charge that it sets up falsely polarizing debates and emphasizes sensational, violent news for the sake of ratings (Fandy 2000; Zayani/Ayish 2006). Some of this skepticism builds upon common criticisms of the media's claimed effects in Western democracies: spreading cynicism and alienation, undermining faith in democracy, spreading ignorance and incomprehension, and debasing public discourse (Newton 2006, 212–214). Here I do not endorse one view or the other, but only wish to point out that such an argument over the impact of talk shows on political engagement offers competing causal claims and hypotheses that could be tested more rigorously than can broad sweeping claims about "democracy."

The strongest argument for significant political effects of the Arab media is frustratingly circular: the opening of political discourse has, indeed, *dramatically* opened political discourse. The shattering of taboos in the Arab media is itself politically significant, but it is not at all clear how it translates into other, more "real" political outcomes. How can it not matter that people have become accustomed to contentious public discourse, public political dissent and protest? Although the extent of the transformation varies by country, and some governments have tried harder than others to maintain control, most Arab countries have seen their politics transformed in some way by the new media realm (Popkin 2006).

The impact of the media on democratization can best be described as shaping the political opportunity structure, transforming the strategies and repertoires of political activists. Under the glare of satellite television cameras, regime forces may be more reluctant to apply brutal repressive force. Satellite TV outlets can magnify the political power of relatively small groups by choosing to cover their rallies and demonstrations. And creative political actors can work the media (or even work with it) to take advantage of the new opportunities. But the attention of transnational media is episodic at best and tends to focus on some countries more than others. The proliferation of outlets would make it conceivable that these problems might be overcome: Al-Jazeera might cover Saudi politics even when they are ignored by Al-Arabiya, while Al-Arabiya covers Qatari politics that are neglected by Al-Jazeera. But even there, market competition might well lead multiple stations to concentrate upon the same small constellation of headline stories.

Conclusion

The Arab media clearly matters politically, even if measuring those effects remains an infant science. Satellite television has reshaped the structure of political opportunities for activists and governments alike, empowering new forms of collective action (both peaceful and violent) and restricting some forms of repression. Al-Jazeera and its imitators have played a significant role in setting the Arab political agenda and framing events within a common narrative. At the same time, there is little evidence to support the assumption that the Arab media has "massive effects" on Arab political opinions, behavior, or outcomes. Its impact varies by case and tends to interact in complex ways with a wide range of other political forces. Serious empirical research into audiences, content, and precise causal effects may ultimately vindicate the "massive effects" view, but more likely such evidence would cast it into doubt as it has in Western societies.

Notes

1. These surveys are available for download at http://www.bsos.umd.edu/SADAT/ and are interpreted in Telhami (forthcoming).

References

Aday, S./S. Livingston/M. Hebert (2005), Embedding the Truth: A Cross-Cultural Analysis of Objectivity and Television Coverage of the Iraq War. *Harvard International Journal of Press/Politics* 1, 3–21.

Ajami, F. (2001), What the Muslim World Is Watching. *The New York Times Magazine*, November 18, 48–53, 76–78.

Al-Hroub, K. (2006), Satellite Media and Social Change in the Arab World. In *Arab Media in the Information Age*. Abu Dhabi: Emirates Center for Strategic Studies and Research, 89–120.

Alterman, J. B. (1998), *New Media, New Politics? From Satellite Television to the Internet in the Arab World*. Washington DC: Washington Institute for Near East Policy.

———. (2004), Made for Television Events. *Transnational Broadcasting Studies* 13, http://www.tbsjournal.com/Archives/Fall04/alterman.html.

Bartels, L. (1993), Messages Received: The Political Impact of Media Exposure. *The American Political Science Review* 2, 267–285.

Bennett, W. L. (2004), Global Media and Politics: Transnational Communication Regimes and Civic Cultures. *Annual Review of Political Science*, 125–148.

Chiozza, G. (2007), Disaggregating Anti-Americanisms. In P. Katzenstein/R. Keohane (eds.), *Anti-Americanisms in World Politics*. Ithaca: Cornell University Press, 93–128.

Eickelman, D. F./J. W. Anderson (1999), *New Media in the Muslim World*. Bloomington: Indiana University Press.

Falah, G.-W./C. Flint/V. Mamadouh (2006), Just War and Extraterritoriality: The Popular Geopolitics of the United States' War on Iraq as Reflected in Newspapers of the Arab World. *Annals of the Association of American Geographers* 1, 142–164.

Fandy, M. (2000), Information Technology, Trust, and Social Change in the Arab World. *Middle East Journal* 3, 378–394.

Gentzkow, M. A./J. M. Shapiro (2004), Media, Education and Anti-Americanism in the Muslim World. *Journal of Economic Perspectives* 3, 117–133.

Graber, D. (2003), The Media and Democracy: Beyond Myths and Stereotypes. *Annual Review of Political Science*, 139–160.

Hafez, K. (2005), Arab Satellite Broadcasting: Democracy without Political Parties? *Transnational Broadcasting Studies* 15, http://www.tbsjournal.com/Archives/Fall05/Hafez.html.

Johnston, A. I./D. Stockman (2007), Chinese Attitudes toward the United States and Americans. In P. Katzenstein/R. Keohane (eds.), *Anti-Americanisms in World Politics.* Ithaca: Cornell University Press, 157–195.

Katzenstein, P./R. Keohane (eds.) (2007), *Anti-Americanisms in World Politics.* Ithaca: Cornell University Press.

Khoury, R. (2001), Arab Satellite TV—Promoting Democracy or Autocracy? *Jordan Times*, May 9.

Kraidy, M. (2002), Arab Satellite Television between Regionalization and Globalization. *Global Media Journal* 1, http://lass.calumet.purdue.edu/cca/gmj/fa02/gmj-fa02-kraidy.htm.

Lynch, M. (2005a), Reality Is Not Enough: Assessing the Democratizing Potential of Satellite TV. *Transnational Broadcasting Studies* 15, http://www.tbsjournal.com/Archives/Fall05/Lynch.html.

_______. (2005b), *Voices of the New Arab Public: Iraq, Al-Jazeera, and Middle East Politics Today.* New York: Columbia University Press.

_______. (2006), Public Diplomacy and Public Opinion Survey Research. In J. S. Fouts (ed.), *Public Diplomacy: Practitioners, Policy Makers, and Public Opinion.* Los Angeles: USC Center for Public Diplomacy.

_______. (2007), Anti-Americanisms in the Arab World. In P. Katzenstein/R. Keohane (eds.), *Anti-Americanisms in World Politics.* Ithaca: Cornell University Press, 196–226.

McAdam, D./S. Tarrow/C. Tilly (2001), *Dynamics of Contention.* New York: Cambridge University Press.

Miles, H. (2005), *Al-Jazeera: The Inside Story of the Arab News Channel that Is Challenging the West.* New York: Grove Press.

Moaddel, M. (2006), The Saudi Public Speaks: Religion, Gender, and Politics. *International Journal of Middle East Studies* 1, 79–108.

Mutz, D./P. Martin (2001), Facilitating Communication across Lines of Political Difference: The Role of Mass Media. *American Political Science Review* 1, 97–114.

Nawawy, M. al-/A. Iskander (2002), *Al-Jazeera: How the Free Arab News Network Scooped the World and Changed the Middle East.* Boulder: Westview Press.

Newton, K. (1999), Mass Media Effects: Mobilization or Media Malaise? *British Journal of Political Science* 4, 577–599.

Newton, K. (2006), May the Weak Force Be with You: The Power of the Mass Media in Modern Politics. *European Journal of Political Research* 2, 209–234.

Nisbet, E. C./M. C. Nisbet/D. A. Scheufele/J. E. Shanahan (2004), Public Diplomacy, Television News, and Public Opinion. *Harvard International Journal of Press/Politics* 2, 11–37.

Popkin, S. (2006), Changing Media, Changing Politics. *Perspectives on Politics* 2, 327–341.
Price, M. E. (1996), *Television, the Public Sphere, and National Identity.* Oxford: Oxford University Press.
Rugh, W. (2004), *Arab Mass Media: Newspapers, Radio, and Television in Arab Politics.* New York: Praeger.
Sakr, N. (ed.) (2007), *Arab Media and Political Renewal: Community, Legitimacy, and Public Life.* New York: I. B. Tauris.
Scheufele, D. A. (1999), Framing as a Theory of Media Effects. *Journal of Communication* 1, 103–122.
Shanahan, J./E. Nisbet (2007), *The Communication of Anti-Americanism: Media Influence and Anti-American Sentiment,* Report Presented to United States Institute for Peace.
Sharabi, H. (2003), The Political Impact of Arab Satellite Television on the Post–Iraq War Arab World. *Transnational Broadcasting Studies* 11, http://www.tbsjournal.com/Archives/Fall03/Hisham_Sharabi.html.
Sheafer, T./G. Weimann (2005), Agenda Building, Agenda Setting, Priming, Individual Voting Intentions, and the Aggregate Results: An Analysis of Four Israeli Elections. *Journal of Communication* 2, 347–365.
Takeshita, T. (2005), Current Critical Problems in Agenda-Setting Research. *International Journal of Public Opinion Research* 3, 275–296.
Telhami, S. (2007), *Reflections of Hearts and Minds.* Washington DC: Brookings Institution Press.
Tessler, M. (2003), Arab and Muslim Political Attitudes: Stereotypes and Evidence from Survey Research. *International Studies Perspectives* 2, 175–181.
Tilly, C./S. Tarrow (2006), *Contentious Politics.* Boulder: Paradigm.
Trend, D. (2007), *The Myth of Media Violence: A Critical Introduction.* Malden: Blackwell.
Zaller, J. (1996), The Myth of Massive Media Impact Revived: New Support for a Discredited Idea. In D. C. Mutz./P. M. Sniderman/R. A. Brody (eds.), *Political Persuasion and Attitude Change.* Ann Arbor: University of Michigan Press, 17–78.
Zayani, M./M. Ayish (2006), Arab Satellite Television and Crisis Reporting: Covering the Fall of Baghdad. *International Communication Gazette* 5–6, 473–497.

CHAPTER TWO

Lack of Influence? Public Opinion and Foreign Policy Making in the Arab World

Russell E. Lucas

Does public opinion influence foreign policy decision making in the Arab world? One would be tempted to say that it does not, given the popular view of malevolent Arab dictators whipping up a xenophobic Arab street to spew venomous anti-Americanism. After all, what is the use of having coercive control over a public if its wishes are to be listened to and honored? In contrast, in mature Western democracies, voters punish elected leaders for pursuing unpopular wars. On the other hand, scholars still debate the impact of public opinion in democracies on foreign policy decisions. However, authoritarian elites that fall out of touch with their population run the risk of being overthrown. Thus, more rigorous theoretical and empirical approaches are needed to answer this question.

The question on the impact of public opinion on foreign policy decisions links the subfields of political science of international relations, American politics, and comparative political studies of the Arab world, which do not always enter into dialogue with each other. However, useful approaches from each of these subfields can be borrowed to enrich the study of public opinion and foreign policy. This chapter first locates research traditions that focus on the domestic causes of foreign policy decisions. Then, it uses studies of public opinion and foreign policy to present a linkage model modified to accommodate nondemocratic political regimes and non-Western cultural environments. Brief case studies from the Hashemite Kingdom of Jordan in the 1950s and 1990s suggest the utility of this contextualized model for analyzing Arab cases.

Public Opinion and Foreign Policy in the Study of International Relations

The study of foreign policy in Western social science has traditionally been the province of international relations scholars. Proponents of the realist paradigm emphasize the realpolitik between states, and this approach has dominated studies of world politics. Classical realist authors emphasize the role of power in determining relations between states. Foreign policy, therefore, is a product of the distribution of military, political, and economic resources (Morgenthau 1954). Neorealist scholars argue that international politics, not foreign policy choices, are the proper locus of study. They negate the importance of domestic public opinion both empirically and normatively (Waltz 1979). Therefore, in the dominant tradition of international relations, public opinion is at best a weak intervening variable in the conduct of foreign policy.

However, other approaches have increasingly challenged the dominance of realism. The constructivist response to realism argues that states' identities are as important as interests. Debates about identity and relations between states in international and regional societies provide better explanations of state behavior than material factors (Wendt 1999; Finnemore/Sikkink 2001). These debates take place in the public sphere—the realm of interpersonal discourse with the goal of changing attitudes about interests and identities. The public sphere can exist domestically or transnationally when linguistic and imagined social communities cross state boundaries—a phenomenon that applies to the Arab world. Discourse and debate persuade actors to change their perception of identity, which explains changes in state behavior (Barnett 1998; Lynch 1999). Constructivist approaches to the public sphere offer a compelling critique to the reductionism of realism since elements of domestic politics reemerge in the analysis.

Yet, an exclusive focus on the public sphere leaves a number of issues unresolved. First, the constructivist approach often neglects to explain how identity change in the public sphere translates into behavioral change. What are the belts of transmission from the public sphere to political mobilization? A second issue points to a failing of both realism and constructivism in that they both tend to ignore the institutional environment of domestic politics.

The other major challenger to realism is the liberal paradigm in international relations. Although a number of authors could be placed in this tradition that would object to the term "liberal" (e.g., Halliday 2005), most authors tend toward the conviction that foreign policies are a function of state-society relations (Foyle 1999; Western 2005). Foreign policies are chosen based on the "pulling and hauling" of the political process (Hilsman et al. 1993). Authors often invoke the metaphor of (or even formally model) a two-level game to explain the behavior of foreign policy elites caught between their foreign interlocutors and domestic actors (Putnam 1988). In the Middle East, studies have shown that Arab rulers will sacrifice foreign policy consistency to ensure regime survival (Seale 1987; Hinnebusch/Ehteshami 2002). Therefore, although external forces remain important in the liberal approach, the key determinants of foreign policy choices are usually domestic in nature.

The field of comparative politics (or in the United States, the separate field of American politics) has more frequently addressed the explanatory causes of domestic politics. The "new institutionalist" approach in comparative politics argues that differing structures of domestic authority explain varying outcomes in policy choice and implementation. Thus, this chapter synthesizes the conclusions drawn from research done on the public opinion–foreign policy linkage in these various traditions on advanced democracies with modifications for modeling the linkage in the cultural and institutional environments in the Arab world.

Public Opinion and Foreign Policy in Democracies

Scholars tend to fall into three camps in evaluating the importance of public opinion in determining elite foreign policy decisions in democracies—especially in American politics (Manza et al. 2002). The first argues that the aggregate public mood influences elite decisions resulting in policy changes need to be reelected to their positions. Thus, as the public mood changes, elites, "like antelope in the open field," adapt "their behavior to please their constituency" (Stimson et al. 1995, 559, 545). Authors of this persuasion base their conclusions on the correlation between aggregate analyses of time-series data and associated policy changes (Erikson et al. 2002; Stimson 2004). A second tradition rejects that claim and instead offers an argument that public nonattitudes allow elites to manipulate public opinion in support of their chosen policies (Page/Shapiro 1992; Domhoff 2002). The third highlights institutional and historical conjunctures in delineating the linkage between public opinion and policy (Herbst 1998, Lee 2002a). It rejects the possibility of a uniform unidirectional relationship between the two. Rather, this third approach stresses the contextual features of specific times and places to draw more middle-range theories on "if," "how," and "why" public opinion influences elite decisions. This approach also links with the "new institutionalism" in comparative politics, which argues that differing structures of domestic authority can explain varying outcomes in policy choice and implementation (March/Olsen 1989, Steinmo et al. 1992). Given the adaptation of the models from the American context, this chapter will tend to borrow more from the third approach.

In adapting models in their third vein of research from Western democracies to Arab cases two significant issues require attention: the authoritarian nature of politics in the Arab world, and cultural differences between Americans and Europeans on one hand and Arabs and Muslims on the other. By seeing regime structures in terms of patterns and networks of representation, the basic institutional differences between democratic and authoritarian regimes can be incorporated into a model of public opinion and foreign policy. The patterns of linkage may be altered from democratic to authoritarian contexts, but authoritarian regimes do not inherently sever links to society in their entirely (Linz 2000). Likewise, cultural differences can be incorporated into the model by identifying competing normative preferences as explanatory variables (Wiktorowicz 2004). This approach supersedes a reified thinking about cultural differences where a monolithic Arab-Islamic culture contrasts to the pluralistic West.

A Model of Public Opinion and Foreign Policy

A number of works address possible linkages between public opinion and foreign policy in the United States and other Western democracies (Risse-Kappen 1991; Shiraev/Sobel 2003; Holsti 2004) and in the Middle East (Lynch 1999; Telhami/Barnett 2002; Halliday 2005). A reading of these works, combined with the model of Powlick and Katz (1998), identifies five crucial components in the translation of public opinion into foreign policy decisions in the Arab world: the public sphere, mass individual attitudes, organized political mobilization, institutional structures, and individual foreign policy decision-making elites. As debates in the public sphere produce consensus on issues among individuals, attitudes change, producing opportunities for political mobilization, which if realized can influence policy decision makers to adopt or change foreign policies. However, does this possible chain of events often result in public opinion's influence on foreign policy decisions?

Public opinion as processed through these stages can result in a continuum of outcomes in influencing elite foreign policy decisions. At one end, public opinion may have absolutely no influence on the decisions of foreign policy makers—a result possible in democratic as well as authoritarian regimes. On the other, the public mood may constitute the basis for such decisions—also regardless of regime type. Or in between, public opinion may constrain foreign policy elites. In other words, the dependent variable lies somewhere along this continuum (Sobel 2001, 5).

Five major variables based on these components explain the degree to which public opinion influences foreign policy. The first variable, the salience of the international issue, is external to the domestic system presented in the model. However, the nature of the issue that necessitates a decision by foreign policy elites often determines the role that public opinion will play in the elites' calculations. Both rapid, highly salient foreign policy issues (e.g., invasion) or slow-moving, low-salience issues (e.g., international trade negotiations) may render negligible the importance of public opinion (Foyle 1999, Jacobs/Shapiro 2002). Moreover, the longer the issue remains salient the greater the attentiveness of public opinion becomes due to prolonged debates about the topic (Burstein 2002).

The second variable, the existence of divisions among elites, contributes to this debate. Common divisions in both democracies and authoritarian regimes include partisan and ideological splits between major political actors in which divergent foreign policy preferences may emerge (Przeworski 1991; Katz 1998; Foyle 1999). Such divisions may be necessary for a greater likelihood of the influence of public opinion on foreign policy decisions, but they themselves are not a sufficient cause.

The third variable, a consensus in the public sphere of discourse, especially one in opposition to preferences of foreign policy elites, leads to the activation of public opinion. Only if there is a "real debate" in the public sphere does public opinion move from being either acquiescent or supportive of elites (Lynch 1999). If opposition groups can provoke such a debate over foreign policy in terms that resonate with interpretative frames of large sections of the public, then opposition forces can shift public attention (Powlick/Katz 1998, 35–39). A consensus in the public sphere in opposition to foreign policy decisions (or preferences) provides a necessary but not sufficient cause of bringing public opinion into foreign policy decisions.

As long as the public attitudes remain in the discursive realm, foreign policy elites can choose to ignore the public and continue to promote unpopular policies. Governing elites, however, fear the mobilization (actual or potential) of the public by opposition groups in the political arena, be it in the streets, or in legislative chambers—the fourth variable. These organizational activities promote a feedback into the public sphere, where debate about the issue is joined with discussion about the mobilization against it. Opposition mobilization in the political arena again may be necessary for public opinion to influence foreign policy decisions, but it may not be sufficient in and of itself—elites may ignore it (but at their possible peril).

Mobilization in the political arena can take many different manifestations. In all of its forms, however, it takes place in an environment regulated (or emancipated) by the state. Thus, institutional rules, both formal and informal, come to bear in shaping how political entrepreneurs bring other individuals to act on their shared opinions—the fifth variable (Risse-Kappen 1991; Powlick/Katz 1998; Shiraev/Sobel 2003). Although in democratic regimes institutional limits to discourse and mobilization may vary, the restrictions are generally much more lightly regulated than the limits authoritarian regimes can place. Such authoritarian intrusions also vary. They often act as grappling hooks by restricting debate in the public sphere (through censorship; Lucas 2003b) or by limiting the channels of mobilization in the political arena (from the altering of electoral rules to privilege particular parties, to a comprehensive coercive clampdown; Lucas 2003a, 2005). Although foreign policy elites could hope that institutional influences would be sufficient to marginalize opposition in the political arena or the public sphere, such manipulations may not be sufficient in limiting the influence of public opinion on foreign policy decisions. Despite its frequent neglect, however, the institutional environment is a feature necessary to be explored.

Thus, one can hypothesize a constellation of these five variables that can constrain or even result in public opinion becoming constitutive of elite foreign policy decisions. Governing elites are more likely to be constrained in situations where they face an issue of moderate salience, divisions exist among important political groups on how to react, opposition groups build a consensus within the public sphere about the issue (which consensus is translated into a mobilization of public opinion into the political arena), and institutional structures allow for mobilization and cannot be manipulated enough to limit opposition mobilization. Theoretically this chain of events could prove constitutive of foreign policy decisions as well; however, based on studies of democratic contexts, one should expect that such occurrences would be less frequent.

Thus, one should not assume that politicians respond reflexively to the public mood, or vice versa. Rather, a range of contextual intervening factors (salience, elite divisions, opposition mobilization, and institutional opportunities) influence the likelihood that a consensus in the public sphere results in specific foreign policy choices.

Application: Jordanian Foreign Policy

An exhaustive test of this hypothesis lies beyond the scope of this chapter. Rather, four brief case studies from the historical experience of the Hashemite Kingdom of Jordan can display the utility of this model and suggest avenues for further research and the methods and resources required for its pursuit. The four cases vary in the value of the dependent variable. One case shows the lack of influence by public opinion (the decision to sign a peace treaty with Israel in 1994), two cases demonstrate constraints public opinion imposed on King Hussein (the decision of King Hussein to not join Britain's Baghdad Pact in 1955, and the decision to cool the normalization of relations with Israel in 1997–98), and one case (albeit arguably) highlights the constitutive role public opinion can play in the king's decision making (the king's decision to dismiss General John Baghot Glubb as commander of the Jordanian Arab Legion in 1956). The four episodes share a number of similar conditions among the independent variables. The comparative control is not complete, and therefore one should understand this section more as a demonstration of the model than as a test hypotheses generated by it.

In 1955 Britain convinced Turkey and Iraq to join the anticommunist mutual-defense treaty known as the Baghdad Pact. The young King Hussein supported the idea of Jordan joining the pact in order to renegotiate the Anglo-Jordanian treaty in the same manner that Iraq's monarchy had. The king, however, could not act alone in making foreign policy decisions because at the time the prime minister held responsibility for negotiating treaty arrangements. Public opinion in Jordan, especially among the Palestinian population, strongly opposed Jordan's joining the pact. Most Jordanians at the time viewed the chief threat to the kingdom's security coming from Israel, not international communism (Aruri 1972, 120–128). The growing Arab nationalist movements in Jordan built on this disjuncture between the government and the people. Support from the transnational public sphere in the form of Nasserist Egyptian radio broadcasts helped forge this consensus (Anderson 2005, 157–167). Thus, in less than a year, the issue would cause the fall of four different cabinets. When the issue came to its head in December 1955, riots and demonstrations broke out that were "the worst the kingdom had ever witnessed" (Satloff 1994, 121). The mobilization of public opinion by opposition forces constrained King Hussein from joining the Baghdad Pact.

Public opinion prevented the king from choosing his preferred policy by following many of the paths laid out above. The Baghdad Pact provided only a moderately salient issue; while serious, it was not existential in nature. Moreover, the issue simmered for a number of months before climaxing in December 1955. The episode displayed significant divisions among Jordan's political elite, between the Arab nationalist and leftist opposition and the range of more conservative supporters of the monarchy. The regime's coalition, however, also divided over the issue of the pact. Some monarchist politicians like Hazza'al-Majali strongly supported Jordan joining Iraq and Turkey. Others, however, like regime stalwart Tawfiq Abd al-Huda preferred Jordan seek neutrality in the emerging Arab cold war (Satloff 1994, 120–125). After a period of debate, a consensus emerged in the public sphere in opposition to the pact—further spurred by foreign radio propaganda. The opposition easily framed the treaty as a further concession of Arab sovereignty to Britain and redirection away from confronting Israel. The opposition mobilized public support through the street protests because the rigged 1954 parliamentary elections prevented the opposition from pressing its agenda through formal institutions. The demonstrations of December 1955 lasted for five days. They most likely would have continued had Prime Minister Majali not resigned. The institutional relationship between King Hussein and the cabinet in relation to foreign policy most likely provided a key ingredient for allowing public opinion to enter the king's foreign policy decision-making process. The new king had not fully wrested executive authority over foreign policy from a series of strong prime ministers since the death of King Abdallah in 1951. Because the cabinet tended to represent the diversity of Jordan's political arena, a parade of ministers resigned from the four different cabinets over the issue of the Baghdad Pact. The insecurity of the cabinet coupled with a lack of the king's firm control over foreign policy hampered negotiations with the British and with domestic opposition forces. Finally, the regime chose not to resort to coercion to override the opposition. Al-Majali "preferred resignation to the shooting of a single soul," most likely because "it was physically impossible to imprison all opponents of the regime" (Aruri 1972, 125, 127). Thus, despite King Hussein's desire to join the Baghdad Pact, he instead chose to remain outside of the treaty. Public opinion had seemingly constrained the king's foreign policy decision in this episode.

Less than six months later, King Hussein decided to fire John Baghot Glubb "Pasha," the British general in charge of Jordan's army. Both domestic and foreign nationalist opposition forces had demanded the Arabization of the Jordanian army. On March 1, 1956, a concern for pubic opinion apparently constituted part of the king's decision. Glubb Pasha had been a pillar of the Jordanian state since the 1920s when he helped found the Arab Legion under Amir Abdallah. However, by the mid-1950s he personified Jordan's continuing dependency on Great Britain. His removal provided the opposition with a major platform position (Satloff 1994, 138; Anderson 2005, 137). King Hussein's relationship with the general nearly three times his age also had grown "frosty" as the king asserted his own decision-making prerogatives (Satloff 1994, 134). The king thought that Arabizing the army would create a constituency loyal to him. Moreover, after public outcry blocked Britain's Baghdad Pact initiative in Jordan, the opposition pushed for Glubb's dismissal, along with the election of a more representative parliament (Anderson 2005, 167–168). The king presented his abrupt decision in terms of military planning, national interest and self-determination (Hussein 1962, 130–138). However, other authors, starting with Glubb himself (1957, 426), cite Hussein's desire to curry favor with the domestic and foreign opposition in motivating the decision (Aruri 1972, 128–131; Satloff 1994, 138; Massad 2001, 184–189; Anderson 2005, 167–168). In the wake of Glubb's dismissal, King Hussein's popularity soared as a nationalist hero. Though they were damaged, Jordan would later repair relations with Britain (Shwadran 1959, 332–334).

This episode shares a number of similar features as with the Baghdad Pact case in terms of the model presented here. One is the moderate salience of Glubb's continued employment: King Hussein could have waited until the end of March, when Glubb's contract expired, to dismiss the general. The divisions between government and opposition continued to exist from the previous months, as did the divisions within the regime coalition. The consensus in the public sphere supported dismissing Glubb, and the opposition used it to mobilize protests. Finally, the institutional environment remained the same. The difference between these two episodes lies in the fact that the king decided to cater to the public mood as compared to trying to repress it. By cutting such a substantial tie to Britain, King Hussein expanded his control over the Jordanian army while garnering domestic and foreign accolades. The Baghdad Pact episode had brought the king confrontation, delegitimation, and embarrassment; the dismissal of Glubb brought him celebration, legitimation, and empowerment. King Hussein's dramatic decision also marked a turn where the king would take the lead in foreign policy—a trend that would solidify over the coming decades.

In 1994 Jordan signed a peace treaty with Israel as part of the American-led push for peace in the Middle East. Although talks had begun in 1991, Jordanian and Israeli negotiations did not become serious until 1993 after the signing of the Palestinian-Israeli Oslo accords. In the wake of Oslo, Jordan would no longer stand outside the Arab consensus in pursuing a separate peace with Israel. Moreover, promises of American aid gave King Hussein an incentive to join in order to end Jordan's post–Gulf War isolation. In July 1994 Jordanian and Israeli negotiators signed the Washington Declaration ending the state of war between the two countries and outlining the peace agreement. Details were negotiated over the next few months, and in October 1994 the treaty was signed to international fanfare in Wadi Araba (Lukacs 1997; Scham/Lucas 2001; Lucas 2004). Opposition groups mobilized conferences and street protests against the treaty. However, the opposition could not delay, let alone block, the treaty's ratification in parliament due to the manipulation of the election law a year earlier, which had stacked the parliament with conservative regime supporters (Lucas 2005, 71–81).

Survey indicators of public opinion toward the treaty were mixed; the public was generally apathetic or taking a "wait and see" attitude (Lucas 2004, 95–96). The Jordanian negotiators gave the appearance of allowing public input into their strategies (Majali et al. 2006, 71–84). However, King Hussein made it clear that the peace treaty was his (rather than the prime minister's): "Thus any opposition to the treaty would be interpreted by the regime as opposition to the monarchy itself—with the resultant consequences" (Lucas 2004, 94–95). In other words, the regime tolerated debate in the public sphere and mobilization in the political arena, but it seemingly felt free to ignore public concerns when negotiating with the Israelis.

Why in this case did the regime successfully ignore public opinion despite opposition objections? Conclusive support for the hypothesis is still lacking without direct evidence from key decision makers (e.g., the king). However, the salience of the issue seems to trump other explanations. For the monarchy, the road to a rapprochement with Washington seemingly ran through Tel Aviv (Majali et al. 2006). Regaining Jordan's traditional good standing with the United States, as well as a return of American financial assistance lost after Jordan's "neutrality" in the Gulf War, while not fully existential, provided an enormous incentive to Jordan (Lucas 2004). Moreover, as the Arab consensus had been broken by the Palestinians, King Hussein felt free to ignore criticism from rejectionist parties like Syria (Milton-Edwards/Hinchliffe 2001, 109). These arguments, coupled with institutional manipulations and a fair dose of coercion of street protests, limited the ability of the opposition to mobilize the public against the treaty. Moreover, the breakneck speed of the negotiations prevented a long, drawn-out public debate over peace.

In contrast, the debate over King Hussein's desire for deepening normalization of relations with Israel dragged until his incapacitation in 1998. As early as the ratification of the peace treaty in November 1994, opposition forces vowed to resist normalization with Israel (Scham/Lucas 2001, 60). King Hussein clearly wished for peace with Israel to not merely end the state of war between Israel and Jordan but to be a building block of a "New Middle East" based on free trade that would develop Jordan's economy and cement its role as Israel's key Arab interlocutor (Lynch 1999). However, the stalling of the Palestinian-Israeli track of the peace process made the king's arguments for a transformed relationship with Israel increasingly difficult over time. By 1997 public opinion began to swing toward the opposition consensus challenging normalization. In addition, the regime coalition began to fray as a number of established conservative stalwarts joined in opposing the treaty (Lucas 2004). The opposition most notably displayed its success in organized mobilization with the boycott of the Israeli trade fair in January 1997 (Clark 2006). In response to the growing strength of the antinormalization forces, the regime engaged in both institutional and coercive maneuvers to curtail the opposition from mobilizing and even fostering public-phere debate about normalization (Lucas 2003a). However, the regime also began to back Jordan away from its desired deeper political, economic, and social links with Israel (Scham/Lucas 2001; Lucas 2004). The regime, however, ignored opposition demands for the canceling of the peace treaty even at the nadir of the Palestinian Al-Aqsa Intifada.

Despite the institutional prerogatives that gave the king a much freer hand in pursuing policies in the 1990s than in the 1950s, a mobilized opposition building on a public consensus could seemingly constrain the regime's foreign policy. Again, decision-making elites backed down on an important, but not existential, policy. A consensus in the public sphere with the antinormalization forces led to an opposition mobilization in the political arena. Despite the regime's electoral manipulations and censorship of the press in 1997–1998, the regime decided to cool normalization. It appears that only massive coercion could have completely silenced the opposition. However, direct access to decision-making elites' explanations for their choices beyond memoirs would be needed in order to more conclusively support this proposition and to rule out competing explanations.

Conclusion

These cases illustrate a hypothesized path in which a foreign policy issue of moderate salience leads to an opposition consensus in the public sphere and a mobilization in the political arena that could explain the constraint of foreign policy elites. In both the cases of the Baghdad Pact and of normalization with Israel, the regime abandoned plans of deeper foreign linkages seemingly in response to domestic discontent. In the case of the firing of Glubb Pasha, it is likely the regime sought to build on opposition demands in its foreign policy, making public opinion a constitutive element in the foreign policy decision. On an issue of higher salience—the peace treaty—however, governing elites most likely felt compelled to ignore the public for more existential methods of regime survival. These four cases cannot fully test these relationships between public opinion and foreign policy decisions. Rather, they are illustrative of the types of research questions emerging through the model.

These brief illustrations generally relied upon secondary historical sources. However, a rounded evaluation of the model and its hypotheses should rely on a variety of sources. As public opinion surveys in the Arab world become more regular and frequent, further correlation analyses also will help analyze the linkages discussed above (à la Erikson or Stimson). However, a key component of the hypothesis is the calculations of decision-making elites, more direct access to their state of mind is required than can be presented in this chapter. Such data usually is obtained through personal interviews of these elites (i.e., King Hussein, Prince Hassan, their various prime ministers, and foreign ministers, and opposition figures) as well as an investigation of their memoirs and writings—a research method used by a number of the authors cited above (Anderson, Lucas, Lynch, Massad, and Staloff, to cite a few). Moreover, authors like Herbst (1998) and Lee (2002b) who study the well-polled American public argue that public opinion can be—and perhaps should be—measured using methods other than surveys. How different actors in the model presented above define and come to know what public opinion "is" provides another avenue for future research that would compliment the analysis of this model and its hypothesis.

Moreover, the sequence of linkages hypothesized here by no means exhausts the available combinations of the independent variables. Other paths or combinations of linkages in the model may provide useful and interesting explanations that can deepen the understanding of how public opinion influences foreign policy decisions not only in the Arab world but also in a global perspective.

References

Anderson, B. S. (2005), *Nationalist Voices in Jordan: The Street and the State.* Austin: University of Texas Press.

Aruri, N. H. (1972), *Jordan: A Study in Political Development (1921–1965).* The Hague: Nijhoff.

Barnett, M. N. (1998), *Dialogues in Arab Politics: Negotiations in Regional Order.* New York: Columbia University Press.

Burstein, P. (2002), Public Opinion and Congressional Action on Labor Market Opportunities, 1942–2000. In J. Manza/F. L. Cook/B. I. Page (eds.), *Navigating Public Opinion: Polls, Policy, and the Future of American Democracy.* New York: Oxford University Press, 86–105.

Clark, J. A. (2006), The Conditions of Islamist Moderation: Unpacking Cross-Ideological Cooperation in Jordan. *International Journal of Middle East Studies* 4, 539–560.

Domhoff, G. W. (2002), The Power Elite, Public Policy, and Public Opinion. In J. Manza/F. L. Cook/B. I. Page (eds.), *Navigating Public Opinion: Polls, Policy, and the Future of American Democracy.* New York: Oxford University Press, 124–137.

Erikson, R. S./M. B. Mackuen/J. A. Stimson (2002), *The Macro Polity.* New York: Cambridge University Press.

Finnemore, M./K. Sikkink (2001), Taking Stock: The Constructivist Research Program in International Relations and Comparative Politics. *Annual Review of Political Science,* 391–416.

Foyle, D. C. (1999), Counting the Public. In *Presidents, Public Opinion, and Foreign Policy.* New York: Columbia University Press.

Glubb, J. B. (1957), *A Soldier with the Arabs.* New York: Harper.

Halliday, F. (2005), *The Middle East in International Relations: Power, Politics and Ideology.* New York: Cambridge University Press.

Herbst, S. (1998), *Reading Public Opinion: How Political Actors View the Democratic Process.* Chicago: University of Chicago Press.

Hilsman, R./L. Gaughran/P. A. Weitsman (1993), *The Politics of Policy Making in Defense and Foreign Affairs: Conceptual Models and Bureaucratic Politics* (3rd edition). Englewood Cliffs: Prentice Hall.

Hinnebusch, R. A./A. Ehteshami (2002), *The Foreign Policies of Middle East States.* Boulder: Lynne Rienner.

Holsti, O. R. (2004), *Public Opinion and American Foreign Policy* (revised edition). Ann Arbor: University of Michigan Press.

Hussein (1962), *Uneasy Lies the Head: The Autobiography of His Majesty King Hussein I of the Hashemite Kingdom of Jordan.* New York: B. Geis.

Jacobs, L. R./R.Y. Shapiro (2002), Politics and Policymaking in the Real World: Crafted Talk and the Loss of Democratic Responsiveness. In J. Manza/F. L. Cook/B. I. Page (eds.), *Navigating Public Opinion: Polls, Policy, and the Future of American Democracy.* New York: Oxford University Press, 54–75.

Lee, T. (2002a), *Mobilizing Public Opinion: Black Insurgency and Racial Attitudes in the Civil Rights Era.* Chicago: University of Chicago Press.

______. (2002b), The Sovereign Status of Survey Data. In J. Manza/F. L. Cook/B. I. Page (eds.), *Navigating Public Opinion: Polls, Policy, and the Future of American Democracy.* New York: Oxford University Press, 290–312.

Linz, J. J. (2000), *Totalitarian and Authoritarian Regimes.* Boulder: Lynne Rienner.

Lucas, R. E. (2003a), Deliberalization in Jordan. *Journal of Democracy* 1, 137–144.

______. (2003b), Press Laws as a Survival Strategy in Jordan, 1989–99. *Middle Eastern Studies* 4, 81–98.

______. (2004), The Death of Normalization in Jordan with Israel. *Middle East Journal* 1, 93–111.

______. (2005), *Institutions and the Politics of Survival in Jordan: Domestic Responses to External Challenges,* 1988–2001. Albany: State University of New York Press.

Lukacs, Y. (1997), *Israel, Jordan, and the Peace Process.* Syracuse: Syracuse University Press.

Lynch, M. (1999), *State Interests and Public Spheres: The International Politics of Jordan's Identity.* New York: Columbia University Press.

Majali, A. A.-S./J. A. Anani/M. J. Haddadin (2006), *Peacemaking: The Inside Story of the 1994 Jordanian-Israeli Treaty.* Norman: University of Oklahoma Press.

Manza, J./F. L. Cook/B. I. Page (eds.) (2002), *Navigating Public Opinion: Polls, Policy, and the Future of American Democracy.* New York: Oxford University Press.

March, J. G./J. P. Olsen (1989), *Rediscovering Institutions: The Organizational Basis of Politics.* New York: Free Press.

Massad, J. A. (2001), *Colonial Effects: The Making of National Identity in Jordan.* New York: Columbia University Press.

Milton-Edwards, B./P. Hinchcliffe (2001), *Jordan: A Hashemite Legacy.* New York: Routledge.

Morgenthau, H. J. (1954), *Politics among Nations: The Struggle for Power and Peace* (2nd revised and enlarged edition). New York: Alfred A Knopf.

Page, B. I./R. Y. Shapiro (1992), *The Rational Public: Fifty Years of Trends in Americans' Policy Preferences.* Chicago: University of Chicago Press.

Powlick, P. J./A. Z. Katz (1998), Defining the American Public Opinion/Foreign Policy Nexus. *Mershon International Studies Review* 1, 29–61.

Przeworski, A. (1991), *Democracy and the Market: Political and Economic Reforms in Eastern Europe and Latin America.* New York: Cambridge University Press.

Putnam, R. D. (1988), Diplomacy and Domestic Politics: The Logic of Two-Level Games. *International Organization* 3, 427–460.

Risse-Kappen, T. (1991), Public Opinion, Domestic Structure, and Foreign Policy in Liberal Democracies. *World Politics* 4, 479–512.

Satloff, R. B. (1994), *From Abdullah to Hussein: Jordan in Transition.* New York: Oxford University Press.

Scham, P. L./R. E. Lucas (2001), "Normalization" and "Anti-Normalization" in Jordan: The Public Debate. *Middle East Review of International Affairs* 3, 54–70.

Seale, P. (1987), *The Struggle for Syria: A Study of Post-War Arab Politics, 1945–1958.* New Haven: Yale University Press.

Shiraev, E./R. Sobel (2003), *International Public Opinion and the Bosnia Crisis.* Lanham: Lexington Books.

Shwadran, B. (1959), *Jordan, a State of Tension.* New York: Council for Middle Eastern Affairs Press.

Sobel, R. (2001), *The Impact of Public Opinion on U.S. Foreign Policy since Vietnam: Constraining the Colossus.* New York: Oxford University Press.

Steinmo, S./K. Thelen/F. Longstreth (eds.) (1992), *Structuring Politics: Historical Institutionalism in Comparative Analysis.* New York: Cambridge University Press.

Stimson, J. A. (2004), *Tides of Consent: How Public Opinion Shapes American Politics.* New York: Cambridge University Press.

Stimson, J. A./M. B. Mackuen/R. S. Erikson (1995), Dynamic Representation. *American Political Science Review* 3, 543–565.

Telhami, S./M. N. Barnett (2002), *Identity and Foreign Policy in the Middle East*, Ithaca: Cornell University Press.

Waltz, K. N. (1979), *Theory of International Politics.* Boston: McGraw-Hill.

Wendt, A. (1999), *Social Theory of International Politics.* New York: Cambridge University Press.

Western, J. W. (2005), *Selling Intervention and War: The Presidency, the Media, and the American Public.* Baltimore: Johns Hopkins University Press.

Wiktorowicz, Q. (2004), *Islamic Activism: A Social Movement Theory Approach.* Bloomington: Indiana University Press.

CHAPTER THREE

The Effects of Islamist Media on the Mainstream Press in Egypt

Carola Richter

Since the 1980s the Arab world has faced a revitalization of Islamist movements.[1] The Islamists' success is based on their reliable objection to the politics of the ruling Arab regimes. Whether those regimes are labeled democracies, republics, or monarchies, most of the Arab postcolonial regimes have instituted an authoritarian, nonparticipative style of ruling aimed at asserting the incumbents' interests. Islamists, however, have been able to mobilize social and political protest on the margins of the system by "presenting activism as a religious obligation" (Wickham 2002, 120).

This chapter examines the Islamists' contribution to the process of political transformation, focusing on the role of the media within their political strategies. The analysis will be exemplified by the Muslim Brotherhood's media in Egypt. After introducing the subject with a short overview of the theoretical approaches to the relationship between protest groups and the media, the article describes the Muslim Brotherhood's media strategy in contemporary Egypt. The empirical section that follows features a content analysis of the official Muslim Brotherhood's website (www.ikhwanonline.com) and compares it to the content of three major Egyptian newspapers.

Both the mainstream Egyptian media and the media of political protest groups are elements of a public sphere that functions as an intermediary between the political regime and society. However, the authoritarian character of the Egyptian media system aims to exclude nonconformist actors from the public sphere. At the same time, the rapid development of information technology, as well as internal and external pressure on the regime to liberalize the politics and the economy, has opened up opportunities for political challengers. Therefore, a more inclusive approach toward protest groups and their views can be expected. This analysis tries to reveal whether such an inclusion actually happens in Egypt, and if so, how this inclusion is characterized.

The media are suitable for examining such a process, as they traditionally reflect the Egyptian regime's strategy for responding to challengers. The effect that the Muslim Brotherhood's marginal media has on the mainstream press would suggest an intermedia influence that, for the first time, allows potent domestic challengers to influence public discourse. It is assumed that access to the mainstream media might lead to greater influence on the political sphere as well, therewith representing an incentive for political change.

Political Transformation and the Media

The mainstream approach to the media's role in democratization processes generally focuses on mass media content, journalistic ethics, or the media system's legal framework. Within this context, the media's functions are assessed by applying Western democracy's expectations about the outcomes of such a process (Rozumilovicz 2002).

However, the early phases of political transformation need a different approach: In authoritarian systems mass media are not conceded an autonomous and independent space to operate. Instead, they are closely watched by the ruling elites, who generally expect the media to support their politics. Openings for nonconformist actors to reach the public turn up on the margins of the controlled mass media spaces—these are small media like leaflets, books, cassettes, or CDs as well as the Internet and interpersonal communication. Nevertheless, neither small nor mass media themselves create change. Their potential depends on the ability of political or social actors to use the media within their protest strategies. Therefore, references to theoretical approaches that focus on social and political actors are useful. Tarrow is one advocate of the school of social movement theory and argues that transformation can be fostered by "collective action (that) becomes contentious when it is used by people who lack regular access to institutions, who act in the name of new or unaccepted claims, and who behave in ways that fundamentally challenge others or authorities" (1998, 3).

Schubert, et al. transfer this concept into an authoritarian political context, arguing that the struggles for change within a political system are fought out between strategic and contentious groups. Strategic groups represent the ruling elites that compete for a share of power without contesting the rules of the system itself. Contentious groups, on the other hand, are potent actors who challenge the status quo if they are able to act autonomously in certain social or political sectors, can withstand co-optation by the regime, appear as a credible alternative to the people or a large part of the people, and openly delegitimize the regime (1994, 68ff.). Wolfsfeld uses a similar approach to describe the struggle over media access as a struggle of challengers versus incumbents, arguing that "one cannot, and should not, distinguish between the contest over the news media and the more general contest over political control" (1997, 13). Sreberny-Mohammadi and Mohammadi (1994) and Downing (1996) prove that this approach is right by describing in case studies for Iran 1979 and the Eastern Bloc in the 1980s how small media were used by oppositional actors to disseminate a parallel agenda, or—in Gramsci's sense—counterhegemonic discourses that contributed to the breakdown of both regimes.

Therefore, authoritarian systems struggle hard to retain control of public discourse. By dominating the public sphere and excluding other actors, the regime secures its position so as to legitimize its political program and actions. Among the common restrictions placed on political antagonists are the following: the marginalization of oppositional media by means of obligatory licensing, the co-optation or imprisonment of journalists, or the banning of media outlets. However, internal pressure from business lobby groups in most of the Arab and Islamic world have resulted in a guided deregulation of the media sector, opening up spaces for nonregime actors, especially on the Internet. Access to the public sphere offers antagonists opportunities to force the regime to make political processes more transparent and to demand their views to be considered in decision making. Dieter Rucht, one of the authors who link actor-centred models with theories of the public sphere, claims that not the direct confrontation between the regime and its challenger effects the regime's politics but "the resonance that has been provoked by the reflection of the confrontation in the media" (1994, 347). Within this context, the media of capable contentious groups can be a powerful tool for opening up the political arena in authoritarian settings, thus setting the preconditions for a transformation process.

Egypt, Democratization, and the Islamists

Egypt is commonly classified as a transitional country (see Albrecht/Schlumberger 2004 for a detailed criticism of this approach). In fact, the country still seems to be stuck at the very beginning of a democratic transition. Admittedly, other factors suggest that Egypt is making steady progress toward becoming a democracy: Sadat's reintroduction of the multiparty system in 1976, Mubarak's implementation of structural adjustment measures in 1991 and the existence of more than 21,000 registered NGOs.[2]

However, Kienle (2004, 72) exposes the putative democratization of Egypt as a delusion: "*What (...) appeared to be a process of political liberalization and democratization was indeed a far more complex attempt to moderately enhance liberties in ways that could not harm the regime.*" Parties were meant to support and legitimize the regime's politics rather than to act as real opposition, economic deregulation turned out to be merely a redistribution of state-owned enterprises into the hands of bigwigs close to the regime, and NGOs remained elitist associations that had no sustainable effect on political decisions (Bianchi 1989).

Both moderate and militant Islamists, however, tended to withstand co-optation. Therefore, to secure its own persistence, the Egyptian regime chose exclusionary strategies to contain Islamist influence (Albrecht/Wegner 2006). In contrast to the militant repression suffered by violent Islamist movements like

Al-Jihad or the Gamaat Islamiya, moderate Islamists like the Muslim Brotherhood meandered between forced exclusion and limited acceptance.[3] This "carrot and stick" policy gave the Brotherhood the possibility to occupy nonpolitical niches on the periphery of the system, enabling it to establish itself as a credible social actor, for example, in the social service sector (Clark 1995; Rieger 1996; Wickham 2002).

However, marginalization of the Brotherhood's influence to niches proved a successful strategy only as long as its possibilities for mass mobilization could be stemmed through restriction of its access to mass media. The spread and success of pan-Arab media, as well as new information technologies starting in the 1990s, offered marginalized groups a new gateway to international and national publics. It will be shown that these new media options also had an impact on the Muslim Brotherhood's political strategy.

The Evolution of the Brotherhood's Media Strategy

The early years from 1928 until 1954—when Egypt was still a monarchy under British mandate—witnessed three waves of political and media activity by the movement, each followed by a temporary ban on its political activities and its media after violent turmoil shook Egypt (At-Tahir 2002, 195–218). Nevertheless, the Brotherhood managed to publish no fewer than twelve different newspapers and magazines, of which *Al-Dawa* and *Al-Ikhwan Al-Muslimun* were the most renowned. These newspapers functioned as forums for intellectual discussions targeting the educated Muslim elite.

When Nasser took over power in 1954, he banned the movement and its public outlets completely, restricting the Brotherhood's communication to clandestine internal contacts. The Muslim Brotherhood regained limited legality only in the 1970s after Sadat strategically positioned the movement as the antipode to the feared strong leftist groups. New Brotherhood cells constituted themselves at Egyptian universities, forming the so-called middle generation that would—in contrast to the old guards of the movement—in the 1990s start to adjust the Brotherhood's ideology to the requirements of being a political party. Traditional interpersonal communication in combination with the provision of social services helped to mobilize support for an agenda of political change (Wickham 2002).

On the other hand, *Al-Dawa* magazine was permitted to relaunch in 1976, confirming it as the semiofficial organ of the Brotherhood. The magazine was edited by the older generation, who avoided outright criticism of Sadat's domestic politics (Kepel 2003, 104). However, following Sadat's assassination in 1981 the newspaper disappeared forever.

Subsequently, the idea of becoming a legitimate actor in the political arena established itself within the movement. Starting in 1984 the politically illegal Muslim Brotherhood built alliances with different legal opposition parties in order to enter the parliament via the national elections. The same piggybacking strategy was used to publish newspapers, for only legal political or social institutions like parties could apply for newspaper licenses. Typically, the movement used the newspapers of their allies to address the public with an Islamist agenda. Temporarily, the neoliberal *Al-Wafd*, the socialist *Al-Shaab,* and the leftist *Al-Ahrar* served as mouthpieces of the Brotherhood. In the 1990s, the leader of the Liberal Party conceded one of the party's licenses to the Brotherhood, enabling it to unofficially publish its own newspaper. The results of this strategy—*Al-Nur* and its successor *Afaq Arabia*—were actually reservoirs for Islamist journalists who were not employed in the national media rather than sought-after investigative newspapers. However, after the massive success of the Brotherhood in the 2005 parliamentary elections, the regime found *Afaq Arabia* potentially dangerous and canceled its license in March 2006, leaving the Brotherhood again without a print organ (Howeidy 2006).

Wickham writes of a "classic cycle of mobilization and counter-mobilization" between the antagonists and the regime (2002, 208). She explains the success of the regime's countermobilization in the 1990s with the Islamists' failure to raise support beyond their traditional supporters. Additionally, the secular elite could not be reached with the Movements' particular discourses (2002, 209).

New Islamist Strategies: Changing Media, Changing Politics

When the new General Guide, Mohammad Mahdi Akif, took over as head of the Muslim Brotherhood in 2004, the aim of being publicly accepted and legally recognized as a political party required turning away from the rather subversive strategies of piggybacking (El-Ghobashy 2005, 389f.). Instead, the traditional clientele was to be kept while the masses were to be approached. As a result, the Brotherhood made consistent use of the new media to reappear as an autonomous and potent political actor embracing the entire Egyptian public.

First, the Brotherhood's small-scale presence on the World Wide Web was developed into a communication platform with different wings. The website www.ikhwanonline.com serves as the focal point of the Internet network targeting the Egyptian and Arab publics, while the English-language website www.ikhwanweb.com targets an international audience. Both sites serve as a mixture of news portal, forum for journalistic analyses, and public relations tool that resembles more or less that of a party newspaper in Egypt. In March 2007, the website www.barlman.com was launched to disseminate news and background information to the public about the parliamentarian work of the Brotherhood's bloc.[4] In addition, at least sixteen regional branches of the Muslim Brotherhood in the twenty-six Egyptian governorates, as well as four branches in Greater Cairo, run their own websites.[5] These serve as a decentralized network covering local events so as to spread information among the interested public and members of the branches. Their importance as local information tools became obvious during the presidential and parliamentary elections in 2005 when they posted up-to-date documentation of local electoral fraud.

Besides the development of its own communication outlets, the Brotherhood embraced pan-Arab media. The London-based opinion-leading newspapers *Al-Hayat* and *Asharq Al-Awsat*, as well as the Qatarian Al-Jazeera news channel, all classify news according to their own news factors without reference to ideological biases. Therefore, the Muslim Brotherhood's political struggle against the Egyptian regime is a sought-after topic and has been featured regularly. Furthermore, in a phase of liberalization since 2000, it has been permitted to establish private newspapers in Egypt. This has given the Muslim Brotherhood the opportunity to be featured in the media more often. The guidance bureau of the Brotherhood reacted to this demand with a forward-thinking strategy by providing media training to its high-ranking members and parliamentarians, by sending regular newsletters to leading journalists and by naming competent contact persons.[6] This was all done despite the fact that the Brotherhood has had to operate in a more or less semiclandestine manner: its headquarters and the media center are located in unregistered flats and its members constantly face the threat of being imprisoned.

The self-centered, introversive communication strategy of the Muslim Brotherhood until the 1990s gave way to a committed extroversive media use. This new proactive strategy contradicts the marginalization attempts of the Egyptian regime.

Case Study: Approach and Methodology

The prerequisites for levering the authoritarian political climate are set. Whether the Muslim Brotherhood's own media has an impact on the process of transformation will be examined by means of a case study of their central media organ, ikhwanonline.com. The obvious difficulty of evaluating the potential of media content to foster the democratization process again needs some clarification. As outlined above, the contest over political struggle is also reproduced in the contest over media access and content. In this text it has been argued that only capable political actors are likely to establish sustainable counterdiscourses that trickle into public discourse and thereby challenge the regime's agenda. The first step on this road is the pluralization of the mass media's political agenda.

The analysis needs to be tackled through three successive questions:

- What distinguishes ikhwanonline.com's content from other media in Egypt? Does it have a relevant different agenda—so to say, a counteragenda?
- How does the website's framing of topics differ from that of the other media?
- Does the website influence the political agenda of the mainstream media?

The questions will be answered by applying comparative content analysis supplemented by a framing analysis and interviews with editors in chief of Egyptian newspapers to gain better understanding of the processes of agenda building and gatekeeping. All the featured articles appeared within one week from February 13–19 in 2007 and were downloaded from ikhwanonline.com and classified according to their topic. The same was done for three major Egyptian daily newspapers of differing political approaches: the privately owned *Al-Masry Al-Yawm*, established in 2004, which quickly won fame as an objective and critical newspaper and sells 50,000 to 70,000 copies per day; the Liberal Party paper *Al-Wafd*, set up in 1984, which is one of the few remaining papers of the once-powerful party press and serves the interest of the secular-oriented Wafd Party, selling 25,000 to 40,000 daily copies; and the widely known semigovernmental and conservative *Al-Ahram*, which sells 250,000 to 400,000 copies, per day.[7]

To answer the first question, the different topics within the respective medium were identified and counted using the statistical analysis program SPSS.[8] Thus, the internal agenda of each medium could be described. To identify distinctions regarding the mainstream media in Egypt, ikhwanonline.com's agenda was compared with that of the other media.[9]

To answer the second question, three major topics that occurred during the period of analysis were chosen for framing analysis. For each relevant article featuring one of the topics the central frame was identified.[10] Frames are "conceptual tools which media and individuals rely on to convey, interpret and evaluate information" (Semetko/Valkenburg 2000, 94). For Entmann, framing results from the work of journalists who are embedded in a certain context and "select some aspects of a perceived reality and make them more salient in a communicating text, in such a way as to promote a particular problem definition, causal interpretation, moral evaluation, and/or treatment recommendation" (1993, 52). Through intermedia comparison of the identified frames, framing policy that was at variance to that of ikhwanonline.com could be examined.

Regarding the third question, statistical content analysis could not reveal whether the topics set by one medium were adopted by another one or whether other variables intervened in the agenda-building process of each medium. The reasons are numerous: the website ikhwanonline.com can—due to the easier production process—be one day ahead of the newspapers; news agencies often determine the overall media agenda and most of the topics that occur are generally virulent. Nevertheless, to get an impression of potential intermedia agenda-setting impact, the chief editors of five Egyptian newspapers—including those that were analyzed—were interviewed on their respective dealings with ikhwanonline.com and the Muslim Brotherhood's agenda.[11]

Findings

Ikhwanonline.com: Serving the Counteragenda?

For the period of analysis, 2,643 articles that dealt with 238 different topics were coded. These topics included mainly issues of domestic, foreign, and international politics, as well as a wide range of societal, economic, and religious issues. The topics were coded inductively according to their appearance. Some of the topics occurred regularly containing the same spin, while others approached very different aspects of a topic. Different codes were therefore attributed if approaches varied widely—for example, for the "Palestinian-Israeli conflict," for which (1) the struggle over the government of national unity, (2) the role of the West in the conflict and (3) the conflict over Israeli archaeological digging on the foundations of the Al-Aqsa Mosque were coded separately. On the other hand, topics that had a similar approach but varied in some details were counted as one topic. For example, the topic "blood donation" is found in several reports about people donating blood in Giza, Alexandria, and so on. Similarly, if a bridge was built in one of the provinces or a highway in another province, both items were counted under the label "infrastructural improvements."

Of the 2,643 articles, 1,214 (almost 46 percent) belonged to *Al-Ahram*, highlighting the broadness and holistic approach of this medium, 528 belonged to *Al-Masry Al-Yawm*, 764 to *Al-Wafd*, and ikhwanonline.com's articles add up to 137 articles (see table 1).

Table 1: Distribution of Articles and Topics Dealt with According to Media

	Number of Articles	Percent of all Articles	Number of Topics	Percent of all Topics
Ikhwanonline.com	137	5.2	53	22.3
Al-Ahram	1214	45.9	203	85.3
Al-Masry Al-Yawm	528	20.0	162	68.1
Al-Wafd	764	28.9	165	69.3
Total	**2643**	**100**	**238**	-*

*sum of percentages exceeds 100 due to multiple coding of occurring topics in the different media

Ikhwanonline.com reports on only about 22.3 percent of all topics (see table 1). This indicates a strong focus on a very limited number of issues. On the other hand, *Al-Wafd*, which also belongs to a political movement, picks up 69.3 percent of all topics featured and thus resembles the private daily *Al-Masry Al-Yawm* with its 68.1 percent share of all topics dealt with. *Al-Ahram*, however, covers 203 topics, 85.3 percent of all topics published.

Figure 1: Thematic Intersections between Four Media

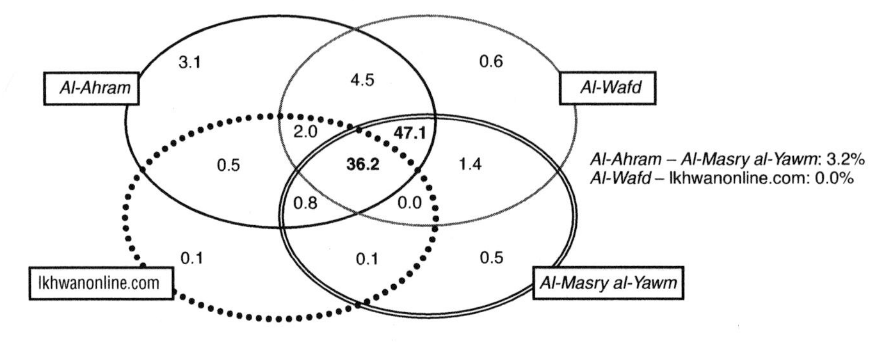

in percent, n = 2643

To ascertain thematic intersections among the different media, all articles were aggregated in a new data record, the unit of analysis now being the topic and not the article. For each topic, the number of articles appearing in each media was counted. The number of articles covering each topic served as a measuring factor. Thus, not only the sheer number of thematic intersections could be counted but also the importance attributed to each topic. Then, all possible intersections were computed. The results can be summarized as seen in figure 1.

The results reveal that 36.2 percent of all articles deal with topics that all four media picked up. A further 47.1 percent of all thematically similar articles are picked up by the three newspapers, but not by ikhwanonline.com. The remaining intersections among every two or every three media as well as the share of exclusive reporting are nearly negligible. The relatively high mutual share of topics between *Al-Ahram* and *Al-Wafd* can be traced to similar treatment of the subject of religion, while the relatively high share of exclusive reporting by *Al-Ahram* results from its focus on non-Arab international politics and societal issues that are not dealt with in other media.

Besides the extremely low thematic fragmentation—one can speak of nearly homogeneous reporting—by the Egyptian media, the Brotherhood's media organ ikhwanonline.com does not, surprisingly, stand out at all when it comes to setting an exclusive agenda. Only one exclusive topic enters on its credit side: a report about the banning of a demonstration. Thus, it does not seem suitable to speak of a Muslim Brotherhood counteragenda, at least not in the sense that ikhwanonline.com sets exclusively new topics that might broaden the mainstream media's focus.

However, three intervening remarks are to be made to this precipitous conclusion. First, the development of the media sector in Egypt and the Arab world has already put topics on the agenda of the mainstream media that might have been neglected before. For example, corruption as a nonnegligible negative outgrowth

Figure 2: Major Topics' Share on Ikhwanonline.com Compared to Their Share in Other Media

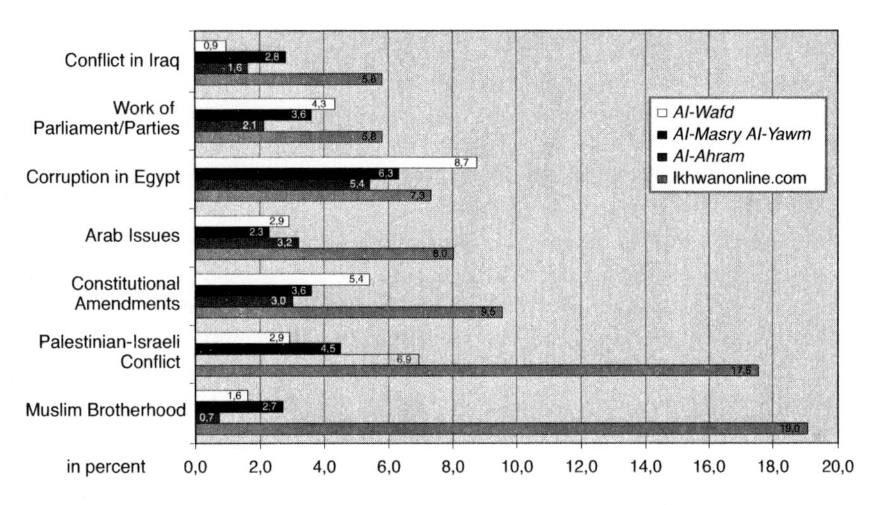

of the political and economic system has become a typical popular topic used to attract the public, especially in the party-owned and privately owned newspapers. Under these new circumstances it does not seem necessary for the Muslim Brotherhood to kick at an open door, as the foundations for critical reporting have been already laid. It is more likely that the intense focus of ikhwanonline.com on virulent topics might lead other media to devote more of their reporting to issues covered on the website. Obviously, ikhwanonline.com omits all "unnecessary" mass media ballast on behalf of intensified reporting about controversial domestic issues. The discussion about the constitutional amendments as well as issues of parliamentarian work are covered more often than in the other newspapers, whereas topics relating to ecology, education, cultural, or health issues are almost neglected on ikhwanonline.com (see figure 2).

Ikhwanonline.com's reporting signals to the political system and the other media the importance that the Brotherhood attributes to certain topics. Since the Brotherhood's agenda as a major antagonist of the regime is newsworthy to the private media and causes the regime and the political parties to react, it can be assumed that the other two media will not ignore the important topics on ikhwanonline.com but feature them as well.

Second, ikhwanonline.com features an agenda that clearly serves the aim of triggering broad mobilization. Ikhwanonline.com's articles that target domestic politics are embedded in a broad spectrum of topics on the Arab-Muslim struggle. It reports more often than average on the conflicts in Iraq, Somalia, Sudan, Yemen and Jordan, and its coverage of Palestinian issues is strong. Of its overall reporting, 17.5 percent is on the Palestinian-Israeli conflict (see figure 2). *Al-Ahram* follows with a mere 6.9 percent, and the others report even less. This finding does not come as a surprise, for the general reference of the Muslim Brotherhood to Arab-Muslim issues serves as a major foundation of its ideology (see also Sadiki 1998 and Abdelnasser 2000). Furthermore, conflictual issues within the Arab world are predestined for allegorizing the struggle between the West and the Arab-Muslim world as well as struggles between a Western-bound authoritarian government and domestic (Islamist) opposition. On the other hand, topics covering Egyptian foreign policy that would put government protagonists into the limelight are mainly excluded from ikhwanonline.com's agenda. Reporting on politics in non-Muslim countries occurs rarely, and if so, the connection to Arab or Muslim issues is obvious. Referring to these topics serves to stir up emotions among the Brotherhood's clientele and Muslim Arabs in general and to build a collective identity among them. Strong collective identity combined with particular mobilization capabilities, argues Wickham, leads to increased political engagement (2002, 151).

Thirdly, ikhwanonline.com serves as a tool with which the Brotherhood can launch information about its program, political actions, and personalities, the website functioning as the drop-in center for media inquiries. The Brotherhood itself is ikhwanonline.com's most prominent topic, totaling 19 percent of all reported news. This self-centeredness results from the Brotherhood's position as a semi-illegal organization that does not have other media channels at its disposal. The website, therefore, is the only point of reference for reliable information about what is happening to the Brotherhood. Reports about the imprisonment of Brotherhood members and the group's strategies for achieving legitimacy made up 2.7 percent of the reporting by the other newspapers (see figure 2). This shows that the putative self-centeredness rather reflects public interest.

In returning to the initial question, it is possible to regard ikhwanonline.com as being the tool of a counteragenda. However, this counteragenda does not rely on exclusiveness, as might be expected. Rather, the agenda distinguishes itself from that of the other media in the intensity of reporting on virulent domestic issues that spill over into the mass media because of the importance attributed to them by such an important political actor as the Muslim Brotherhood.

Ikhwanonline.com: Framing the Difference?

After analyzing the overall media agenda with a special focus on ikhwanonline.com's characteristics, one controversial, virulent topic has been chosen for the analysis of whether ikhwanonline.com also distinguishes from other media in its approach to the topics. Furthermore, the intention was also to examine whether ikhwanonline.com's framing affects the mainstream media's dealing with the topic.

The discussion about the constitutional amendments in Egypt was chosen for framing analysis. In 2005 President Mubarak initiated the process to amend thirty-four articles of the Egyptian constitution. In the period of analysis, the intense political discussion about the amendments was about to reach its peak. The discussion involved the content of the proposed changes that were meant to foster Egypt's democratization. At the same time, these changes were heavily criticized for the possible restrictions they would impose on civil liberties. The focus was also on the role of religion in politics that is ambivalently dealt with in different constitutional articles. On the other hand, the amendment process itself was the subject of discussion. The articles to be amended were chosen and revised by a committee dominated by the ruling National Democratic Party, which occupies over two-thirds of the seats in parliament. Therefore, it was clear from the beginning that the amendments would be adopted by the parliament as proposed. The following referendum on March 26, 2007, officially saw a turnout of 27.1 percent of eligible voters, of which the majority voted in favor of the amendments, while the opposition—which had finally called for a boycott of the referendum—spoke of a mere 5 percent turnout.

The framing of this debate meandered between negatively stressing the meaninglessness of the amendments for the people and a very positive approach emphasizing that the amended constitutions would push forward reform on all societal levels (see table 2). In addition to these two borderline frames, six other more constructive frames could be identified—two of them rather negative, four of them pragmatic. The two other negative frames—the "endangering" and "fabrication" frames—imply the regime had bad intentions. The former suggests that the regime is trying to pave its way to creating a police state; the latter assumes that the amendments are only cosmetic and signal to the international community a putative willingness to democratize.

Table 2: Media Framing of the Debate about the Constitutional Amendments (CA)

FRAME	**Ikhwan-online.com**	*Al-Ahram*	*Al-Masry Al-Yawm*	*Al-Wafd*	TOTAL
negative					
CA are irrelevant for the people	15.4%	0.0%	10.5%	4.9%	**5.5%**
CA endanger civil liberties	15.4%	2.8%	15.9%	14.6%	**11.0%**
CA are only a cosmetic fabrication	7.7%	0.0%	26.3%	7.3%	**8.3%**
Pragmatic					
CA should, but do not stimulate more democracy	30.8%	8.3%	26.3%	26.8%	**21.1%**

FRAME	Ikhwan-online.com	*Al-Ahram*	*Al-Masry Al-Yawm*	*Al-Wafd*	TOTAL
CA should take care of religion in politics	7.7%	8.3%	0.0%	2.4%	**4.6%**
CA should strengthen national unity	0.0%	16.7%	10.5%	7.3%	**10.1%**
CA should be a product of public participation	23.1%	33.3%	10.5%	31.7%	**27.5%**
Positive					
CA will improve many sectors of society	0.0%	30.6%	0.0%	4.9%	**11.9%**
	n = 13	n = 36	n = 19	n = 41	**n = 109**

Ikhwanonline.com (38.5 percent) frames more than one-third of its reporting negatively, emphasizing the perfidious politics of the regime. This share is only topped by the privately owned *Al-Masry Al-Yawm* (52.7 percent), which is very skeptical about the regime's intentions, while the regime-loyal *Al-Ahram* devotes only 2.8 percent to negative reporting.

However, the largest share of ikhwanonline.com's reporting (30.8 percent) and a major share of *Al-Wafd*'s (26.8 percent) and *Al-Masry Al-Yawm*'s (26.3 percent) reporting consists of the "more democracy frame." This frame is applied to approaches that inform relatively neutrally about possible variations to the amendments, thus making it clear how they could generate democratic political competition and broad participation. Within this frame, different positions are described and discussed in a rather objective manner. It is interesting that the Muslim Brotherhood in particular follows this constructive approach. Furthermore, *Al-Masry Al-Yawm* refers directly to the Brotherhood's positions toward the amendments in its articles, loading this frame. This finding reveals the spill-over of some of the Brotherhood's political positions into the mainstream media.

The "public participation frame" is strongly applied by the two political organs ikhwanonline.com (23.1 percent) and *Al-Wafd* (31.7 percent) but even more by *Al-Ahram* (33.3 percent). All three media try to mobilize their respective followers and sympathizers with announcements concerning meetings to discuss the amendments and their implications. *Al-Masry Al-Yawm*, however, loads this frame with only a few articles (10.5 percent) that look from a distance at the lack of participation and comment skeptically instead of trying to mobilize people.

The two remaining frames are antagonistic approaches to the controversial role of religion in the Egyptian state. Only two out of thirty-four articles to be amended deal with the role of religion, but they are featured most prominently in the newspapers. The discussion focuses on the struggle to define the Egyptian nationhood in either religious or secular terms. At the same time, it resembles the struggle about the Muslim Brotherhood's integration of religious attitudes into politics. The newspapers brought up the "national unity frame," which tries to push aside religious values as foundations of the state and promotes the concept of national unity as the underlying premise defining citizenship. On the other hand, the "religion frame" refers to the positive influences of religious values on the state—for example, shared moral foundations and an inherited collective identity. Although, as expected, the first is neglected completely by ikhwanonline.com, the second also is paradoxically not a strong item in its coverage (7.7 percent). However, ikhwanonline.com devotes an additional 2.9 percent of its coverage to the relation between the state and religion without direct reference to the constitution. But even *Al-Ahram* and *Al-Wafd*, which brought up the "national unity frame" as a direct countermeasure to the Muslim Brotherhood's religious attitude, do not shy away from presenting the relation between religion and state somehow sympathetically (8.3 percent and 2.4 percent, respectively). *Al-Ahram* especially seems to follow the guidelines of the government, which is trying to incorporate Islam into its ruling strategies in order to attract the Brotherhood's clientele.

Dealing with the topic of the constitutional amendments, ikhwanonline.com and *Al-Wafd* feature the role of the sedulous educator, in contrast to *Al-Ahram*, which distorts the debate and palliates the negative sides, while *Al-Masry Al-Yawm* also offers a constructive informative approach but merely induces fatalism instead of participation with its skeptical attitude. Regarding the effects that Islamists have on the mainstream press, it can be said that the Brotherhood's positions are directly featured by the party-owned and privately owned press. On the other hand, the semigovernmental press includes the Muslim Brotherhood's position indirectly by prominently covering those aspects of the topic that are mostly discussed in connection with the Brotherhood, like the debate about religion interfering with politics.

Ikhwanonline.com: An Intermedia Agenda Setter?

In developing countries like Egypt, the pull-medium Internet cannot be attributed to broad public outreach. Mainstream media like television and newspapers are far more important agents in the forming of public opinion. However, online media target an educated elite as well as opinion leaders and gatekeepers of the mainstream media. Therefore, proven intermedia agenda setting initiated by an Islamist website would signal that the Muslim Brotherhood is able to influence the public political agenda through its media.

To clarify the effects of ikhwanonline.com on the mainstream media described in previous sections, five editors in chief of Egyptian newspapers, representing private (*Al-Masry Al-Yawm*, *Al-Dustur*), party (*Al-Wafd*, *Al-Ahrar*) and semigovernmental media (*Ruz Al-Yussif*) were interviewed on their dealings with the Brotherhood and its media.[11]

Not surprisingly, the newspapers' affiliation defines also the broad categories that group the different medias' approaches to the Brotherhood and its media. For a long time, the strategy of the semigovernmental press was to hush the existence of a moderate Islamist opposition in Egypt. They either chose to neglect its existence by not reporting about it or they chose the strategy of countermobilization, presenting the Muslim Brotherhood as a dangerous and illegal, even terrorist, association. Despite the disclosing role of pan-Arab news media, the strategies described here prevail in the semigovernmental media. While the more populist state-owned media like *Al-Akhbar* and *Al-Gumhuriya* merely exclude the Brotherhood from their reporting, *Ruz Al-Yussif*, which has a secular-liberal tradition going back to the 1920s, targets intellectuals and was co-opted by the government in the 1990s to serve as the government's instrument for counteracting Islamist discourse. Abdallah Kamal, chief editor of *Ruz Al-Yussif*, states that he regularly picks up on topics set by the Muslim Brotherhood in order to investigate their statements and counteract their argumentation.[12] *Ruz Al-Yussif* would not speak with the Islamists directly, says Kamal, but receives their e-mail newsletters and checks out their website. However, the Brotherhood's topics and argumentation serve only as a template to critical response. Several journalists and experts label this kind of criticism as defamation. Paradoxically, *Ruz Al-Yussif*, by reflecting negatively on the Muslim Brothers' discourses, injects them into the public agenda.

Al-Ahram meanders between neglecting and counteracting. In the period of analysis, eight articles appeared dealing directly with the Brotherhood, although only three of them exceeded the length of short news and all of them presented the Brotherhood as failing. However, as was shown through framing analysis, *Al-Ahram* indirectly picks up on relevant Islamist topics like the relationship between religion and politics and discusses these issues according to its guidelines without directly referring to the Brotherhood.

It remains difficult to determine whether or not ikhwanonline.com plays a central role for gathering the information that is to be counteracted. The chief editors of the party papers Al-*Wafd* and *Al-Ahrar*—Anwar Al-Hawry and Issam Kamil, respectively—both state that during their journalistic careers they have made their minds up about the Brotherhood's goals and strategies.[13] Therefore, the Islamists' website content is regarded more as populist propaganda than as useful information. Instead, news and rumors are verified through contacts to acquaintances among the Brotherhood itself. Nevertheless, the Brotherhood's topics and argumentation are discussed with reference to the agenda of the party a newspaper is affiliated with. *Al-Ahrar*'s Kamil says that, in particular, conflictive topics like civil rights and liberties, freedom of religion, and definitions of citizenship provoke the newspapers' stance against the Brotherhood. Al-Hawary of *Al-Wafd* similarly aims to criticize the Brotherhood's political concepts, taking the party program as a basis for constructive criticism. His aim is to explode the Brotherhood's myths, presenting them as a political force with all its programmatic defects. However, the party papers do not hesitate to present the Brotherhood, embracing its positions if these support their own arguments or if the regime's unlawful way of dealing with the Brotherhood symbolizes its lack of legitimacy.

The newly established private press reports regularly on the Muslim Brotherhood, sharing one characteristic: it refers to the newsworthiness of the Muslim Brotherhood to explain its coverage. Muhammad Samir, one of *Al-Masry Al-Yawm*'s chief editors, and Ibrahim Issa, chief editor of *Al-Dustur*, welcome the Brotherhood's website ikhwanonline.com, their e-mail newsletters, and their press conferences as the public relations outlets of a political actor.[14] Both emphasize that their use of the Brotherhood's communication tools does not mean that they share its views. Instead, the information the tools provide is supposed to be the basis of a critical debate of the Muslim Brotherhood's arguments. Both newspapers interview high-ranking members of the Brotherhood and present its positions on virulent issues, as both did on the debate about the constitutional amendments.

However, there are also fundamental differences among the private papers. *Al-Dustur*, for example, does not see itself as a neutral paper. According to Issa, the paper takes a stand against the restrictive regime and features those oppositional actors that demand political liberalization, irrespective of their ideological affiliation. Regime bashing by some is counteracted by "Brotherhood bashing" by some other private newspapers.

At the center of this dichotomous media environment *Al-Masry Al-Yawm* tries to hold its position as the flagship of neutrality. While increasing sales figures are an obvious indication of readers' appreciation of its balanced coverage, the newspaper faces constant assaults from different political wings. "When we interviewed Mubarak we were accused of being a governmental mouthpiece, when we covered the Brotherhood's positions during the parliamentarian elections we were accused of being their mouthpiece," says Muhammad Samir. After featuring a governmental report about the Brotherhood's possible involvement in money laundering in March 2007, the Brotherhood answered with an open letter accusing *Al-Masry Al-Yawm* of waging a campaign against it.

The Muslim Brotherhood itself has become part of the political agenda in Egypt. It is also able to launch its programmatic positions in the news media—especially the privately owned media. However, mainstream media in Egypt mostly pick up on the Brotherhood's topics in order to use them for critical evaluation. The Brothers reacted to this phenomenon professionally, providing media training for their parliamentarians, and starting political PR. But then again, they themselves still understand the media system as a dichotomy—either against them or with them. Avoiding dichotomization and focusing on news factors by communicating their program, positions, and actions, the Brotherhood would at least stimulate the private newspapers to include their agenda.

Conclusion

Do the Muslim Brotherhood's media have an effect on the Egyptian mainstream press? The findings of this empirical study answer this initial question positively. Ikhwanonline.com focuses on specific political and social issues aiming to mobilize collective action. It can be argued that the importance the Muslim Brotherhood's media attribute to virulent domestic topics is reflected in the agenda of the mainstream press. Both the framing analysis and the interviews with chief editors confirm this interpretation. The private press features the Muslim Brotherhood's topics and positions directly, aiming to attract the broader Egyptian public. On the other hand, the semigovernmental and party presses also react to the political positions of the Muslim Brotherhood, albeit indirectly. They create frames that are meant to counteract the program and ideology of this Islamist movement. It is too early to speak of a full inclusion of the Muslim Brotherhood in the Egyptian public sphere. The semilegal status of the Brotherhood undermines its acceptance as a legitimate political actor. This status quo is also reflected in its ambivalent coverage in the mainstream press. But by effectively using the current technical and political opportunities, the Muslim Brotherhood has succeeded in transferring its contents and views from its marginalized media into the mainstream press, thus creating a new public space for political challengers. Their issues are present in the media even though the organization is still marginalized as an actor. Even this small-scale access to the public sphere can create a public "resonance," in Rucht's sense, that might be able to induce future political change.

However, the more accurate measuring of media effects requires a holistic approach. This study was limited to content analysis of a narrow period of time supplemented by interviews. Long-term content analyses could reveal changes of the mainstream media's agendas with respect to what occurs on Islamist media channels. Interviews with journalists of the different media could identify obstacles blocking the access of political antagonists like the Muslim Brotherhood and their discourses to the mainstream media and clarify how antagonistic media can target the gatekeepers of the mainstream media. Finally, the dimension of media effects on the users should be emphasized. By comparing the agenda of users of ikhwanonline.com with the agenda of users of other media, possible agenda-setting effects of ikhwanonline.com could be identified.

Notes

1. Examples are the Muslim Brotherhood in Egypt, Hezbollah in Lebanon, the FIS in Algeria, and Hamas in the Palestinian Territories, as well as different Islamist parties in Sudan, Morocco, Tunisia, and Jordan. The term "Islamist" is commonly used as a collective name for a diversity of movements that aim to (re-)introduce Islamic values into the political, economic, and social systems. This article uses the term "Islamist" in reference to moderate Islamist groups

that choose nonmilitant means to put their aims across—as, for example, movements in Morocco, Tunisia, Jordan, or Egypt.

2. *Year Book 2006*, Political System, Egypt State Information Service, 2006, http://www.sis.gov.eg/En/Pub/yearbook/yearbook2006/110104000000000003.htm.
3. Hudson (1995) developed a classification of Arab regimes' reactions toward the Islamists and distinguishes five categories: (1) forced exclusion, (2) marginalization, (3) preemption, (4) limited accommodation, and (5) full inclusion.
4. The site is redirected to the proxy www.nowabikhwan.com.
5. Dates are as of March 2007; see, for example, East Cairo, http://www.ikhwan-sharq.com/ or Assiut, http://www.assiutonline.com/.
6. Interview with Mohammad Habib, Deputy General Guide, March 8, 2007.
7. To get reliable figures of newspaper distribution is very difficult because they are constantly overestimated by the newspapers themselves while trying to persuade researchers to believe in their major importance. The figures given here are reliable estimates according to statements of Salah Al-Asyuti, manager of *Al-Ahram's* distribution house and Ibrahim Issa, editor in chief of the private newspaper *Al-Dustur* (personal interviews February 22, 2007 and March 1, 2007).
8. All items featuring sports news, star news, and stories on crime and accidents were coded but finally omitted from the analysis so as not to warp the sample although they represented on average 40.6 percent (*Al-Masry Al-Yawm*), 23.2 percent (*Al-Ahram*), and 27.3 percent (*Al-Wafd*) of the newspapers' content, respectively, but do not appear at all in the analyzed medium ikhwanonline.com.
9. For detailed discussion of the methodological procedure of comparing news agendas see Rössler 2001.
10. For detailed discussion of the methodological procedure of framing newspaper topics see Gamson 1992.
11. This excludes Usama Saraya of *Al-Ahram* newspaper, who was not available for an interview.
12. Interview with Abdallah Kamal, March 7, 2007.
13. Interview with Anwar Al-Hawary, March 3, 2007; interview with Issam Kamil, February 21, 2007.
14. Interview with Muhammad Samir, February 17, 2007; interview with Ibrahim Issa, March 1, 2007.

References

Abdelnasser, W. M. (2000), Islam and the West: Perspectives from the Egyptian Press, With Particular Emphasis on Islamist Papers. In K. Hafez (ed.), *Islam and the West in the Mass Media: Fragmented Images in a Globalizing World*. Cresskill: Hampton press, 141–156.

Albrecht, H./O. Schlumberger (2004), "Waiting for Godot": Regime Change without Democratization in the Middle East. *International Political Science Review* 4, 371–392.

Albrecht, H./E. Wegner (2006), Autocrats and Islamists: Contenders and Containment in Egypt and Morocco. *Journal of North African Studies* 2, 123–141.

Bianchi, R. (1989), *Unruly Corporatism: Associational Life in Twentieth-Century Egypt.* New York: Oxford University Press.

Clark, J. A. (1995), Democratization and Social Islam: A Case Study of the Islamic Health Clinics in Cairo. In R. Brynen/B. Korany/P. Noble (eds.), *Political Liberalization and Democratization in the Arab World,* vol.1: *Theoretical Perspectives.* Boulder: Lynne Rienner, 167–186.

Downing, J. D. H. (1996), *Internationalizing Media Theory: Transition, Power, Culture. Reflections on Russia, Poland and Hungary 1980–1995.* London: Sage.

Entmann, R. (1993), Framing: Toward Clarification of a Fractured Paradigm. *Journal of Communication* 4, 51–58.

Gamson, W. A. (1992), *Talking Politics.* Cambridge: Cambridge University Press.

Ghobashy, M. el-(2005), The Metamorphosis of the Egyptian Muslim Brothers. *International Journal of Middle East Studies* 3, 373–395.

Howeidy, A. (2006), Democracy's Backlash. *Al-Ahram Weekly,* March 9–15, http://weekly.ahram.org.eg/2006/785/eg3.htm.

Hudson, M. C. (1995), Arab Regimes and Democratization: Responses to the Challenge of Political Islam. In L. Guazzone (ed.), *The Islamist Dilemma: The Political Role of Islamist Movements in the Contemporary Arab World.* Berkshire: Ithaca Press, 217–244.

Kepel, G. (2003), *Muslim Extremism in Egypt: The Prophet and Pharao.* Berkeley: University of California Press.

Kienle, E. (2004), Transformation without Democratization? Egypt's Political Future. *Internationale Politik und Gesellschaft* 4, 70–86.

Rieger, B. (1996), *Überleben ohne Staat. Soziale Sicherung und die islamischen Parallelstrukturen in Ägypten.* Baden-Baden: Nomos.

Rössler, P. (2001), Visuelle Codierung und Vielfalts-Analysen auf Mikroebene. Kategorisierungs-und Auswertungsstrategien für die ikonographische Untersuchung journalistischer Berichterstattung. In W. Wirth/E. Lauf (eds.), *Inhaltsanalyse. Perspektiven, Probleme, Potentiale.* Cologne: Halem, 140–156.

Rozumilowicz, B. (2002), Democratic Change: A Theoretical Perspective. In M. E. Price/B. Rozumilowicz/S. G. Verhulst (ed.), *Media Reform: Democratizing the Media, Democratizing the State.* London: Routledge, 9–26.

Rucht, D. (1994), Offentlichkeit als Mobilisierungs factor für soziale Bewegungen. In F. Neidhardt (ed.), *Öffentlichkeit, öffentliche Meinung, soziale Bewegungen.* Opladen: Westdeutscher Verlag, 337–358.

Sadiki, L. (1998), Occidentalism: The "West" and "Democracy" as Islamist Constructs. *Orient* 1, 103–120.

Schubert, G./R. Tetzlaff/W. Vennewald (eds.) (1994), *Demokratisierung und politischer Wandel. Theorie und Anwendung des Konzeptes der strategischen und konfliktfähigen Gruppen (SKOG).* Münster: Lit.

Semetko, H. A./P. M. Valkenburg (2000), Framing European Politics: A Content Analysis of Press and Television News. *Journal of Communication* 2, 93–109.

Sreberny-Mohammadi, A./A. Mohammadi (1994), *Small Media, Big Revolution: Communication, Culture and the Iranian Revolution.* Minneapolis: University of Minnesota Press.

Tahir, K. K. at-(2002), The Essays of Sheikh Muhammad al-Ghazali [in Arabic]. Unpublished master's thesis, Al-Azhar-University.

Tarrow, S. (1998), *Power in Movement: Social Movements and Contentious Politics* (second edition). Cambridge: Cambridge University Press.

Wickham, C. R. (2002), *Mobilizing Islam: Religion, Activism, and Political Change in Egypt.* New York: Columbia University Press.

Wolfsfeld, G. (1997), *Media and Political Conflict: News from the Middle East.* Cambridge: Cambridge University Press.

Media Audiences

CHAPTER FOUR

Arab Media Audience Research: Developments and Constraints

Hussein Amin

The television industry in the Arab world has witnessed enormous growth and development in the past ten years. With more than 190 million inhabitants and over 36 million households, the Arab world's strong population growth combined with continued economic development make it a highly attractive market for broadcasters. Arab countries have more than 150 free-to-air television channels available to most homes. Multichannel free-to-air television reaches 35 percent of households in Egypt and up to 90 percent in Saudi Arabia and the Gulf. At the same time, the Arab world's pay-TV industry is also rapidly expanding, with subscriber growth averaging 40 percent per year over the past several years. Pay-TV penetration is still low, however, varying from 5 percent in Egypt to 29 percent in the UAE.[1]

Demand for and consumption of television broadcasting is significantly stronger in the Arab world than in most other developing countries. Close family ties combined with often harsh weather conditions, low literacy rates, and a culture of oral communication have made television the centerpiece of family life in many Arab countries. Demand for audiovisual content is not, however, homogeneous across countries. Although all the countries in the region share a common language and the majority a common religion, there are differences in culture, television consumption, and viewing preferences across demographic segments and countries. In addition, television preferences are rapidly changing and fragmenting, particularly among age and socioeconomic groups, and competition for viewers' attention is very strong and growing.

Although local programming, such as Arabic series and local news, remains popular, demand is increasing for foreign programming, particularly among affluent segments. Some of the most popular programs in recent years have combined formats, providing local content in a Western programming style. Examples are *Who Wants to Be a Millionaire*, *Star Academy*, *Pop Idol*, cooking shows, talk shows, and news channels such as Al-Jazeera, Abu Dhabi TV, and Al-Arabiya.

Many of these news channels are now leveraging their popularity by adopting an extensive array of thematic channels, with MBC2 (Western movies), MBC3 (children's programming), MBC4 (series/fiction), Al-Jazeera Sports, an Al-Jazeera English news channel, an Al-Jazeera children's channel, and others. Understanding the need to appeal to the cultural and religious sensitivities of its audience, Western movies broadcast on MBC2 are censored to remove scenes of a sexual or extremely violent nature that might offend cultural or religious sensitivities. MBC2 has successfully implemented a strategy of broadcasting popular movies that can be viewed by Arab families, achieving strong ratings of nearly 10 percent in less than two years.[2] In 2004 Al-Jazeera was named one of the top five brands both globally and in Europe and Africa, coming in ahead of the BBC and just behind Nokia.[3] Its combination of Western-style news format, provocative broadcasts, and reporting in Arabic that is, unlike local news broadcasts, uncensored, has earned it a reputation for quality and immense popularity among Arab audiences of all socioeconomic levels.

Audience Research in the Arab World

Audience research in the Arab countries of the Middle East is still in its infancy, impeded by historically authoritarian governments whose strict control and distrust of the mobilizing effects of mass media have hampered the development of indigenous approaches to communications research in general and audience research in particular. Arab communications research has been blocked by inadequate funding and insufficient resources in universities employing overworked, undertrained, and underpaid faculty staff. Professional audience research has likewise been hampered by the lack of well-trained researchers with experience in communications research techniques that meet international standards. But more fundamentally, the politically repressive atmosphere that has for so many years prevailed in Arab national universities has pushed research into narrow channels. Faculty and students have refrained from going down the difficult path of opinion surveys and polling research and have instead been encouraged to conduct media research that promotes politically established goals of national development and national unity. They have, in fact, been recruited into a national enterprise for the production of propaganda. In addition to the myriad permissions that a public survey must receive, there is a broadly interpreted law that prohibits the publication or distribution of material damaging to the reputation of the country. With penalties ranging from fines to imprisonment, researchers are not always willing to embark on potentially revealing research. In spite of these barriers, many communications researchers in the Arab world have produced outstanding work, particularly in areas relating to the development of media and its impacts on society, yet in general they make little contribution to the broader and deeper understanding of Arab audiences (Amin/Napoli 1997).

Arabs mainly first encountered mass communications scholarship during the postindependence era, when mass media infrastructures were being established as part of national development projects. Communication theory was viewed as a luxury Arab societies could not afford at a time when they were preoccupied with nation-building concerns. Arab elites representing a wide range of political and ideological orientations had high expectations regarding the role of mass media organizations in bringing about social and economic transformation. Communication training programs, sponsored largely by international NGOs, placed heavy focus on the preparation of media practitioners capable of running print and broadcast operations within existing social and political settings (Ayish 2002b).

The political and communications environments in the Arab world have changed drastically in the past decades, and especially in the past few years. Most countries are trying to shake off their legacy of socialism while dealing with their own fundamentalist movements. There are many forces altering the political and economic landscape, including a growing movement toward an open national media system; the proliferation of satellite and cable systems bringing in a host of new channels; signs of slow democratization of the political system; a growing independent private sector; privatization of some state-owned enterprises, including some aspects of the media; a boom in the publication of new magazines, both in Arabic and English; the extension of Internet access; and a surge of growth in the fields of public relations and advertising (Labib 1994). The rush toward globalization, economic and political reform, the freedom and openness of the Internet, and liberalization of the press and broadcasting systems are creating enormous opportunities as well as discontinuities and tensions, as societies struggle to "catch up" and economies strive to create jobs for rapidly growing populations. Things are changing, and media studies, especially regarding Arab audiences, are strongly responding to shifts in the economic and political atmosphere. Communications issues are different to those in the West, particularly since the common element is no longer the notion of Western media imperialism. The rapidity of technological and political change in the region also calls for a renewed commitment to, and reorientation of, communications research. A much more complicated picture has emerged that requires more seriousness and introspection among mass communication researchers than has been previously evident (Al-Sharif 1999).

The mid-1990s witnessed a marked change with the advent of the communications revolution. An interest in surveying the flow and impact of TV programming, especially satellite penetration and viewer habits, emerged. Studies on the content and structure of international communication have continued to occupy a notable place in the research profile since the introduction of the communications satellite and the Internet. Research has focused on national identities, international news agencies, and television news. Studies of communication about the Palestinian-Israeli conflict were at a peak during the 1990s but their popularity has started to decline in the new millennium (Boyd/Amin 1995).

Studies that deal with the uses of the medium by government and by people are ever-present, although studies on uses by the people are more available than those about uses by the government. In the 1990s, studies that dealt with the impact of the medium started to gain popularity for those in the field of advertising and public relations (Amin 1999).

The history of research on Arab audiences has been a complex dance among levels of restriction. Arab governments generally have viewed the strength and the intensity of the message over Arab audiences and their perspectives with trepidation and have enforced restrictions on audience research to avoid publication of negative sentiments. Arab governments have historically used the media for public mobilization and propaganda, viewing the media's influence as the "hypodermic" model, which states that all people will react to the same media messages in the same way once they are exposed to them (Amin 1996). This viewpoint has been reinforced by conservative voices in Arab societies, which claim the media is the main reason behind the breakdown of the "traditional values." At the same time, liberal voices accuse the media of being complicit with the government, causing audiences to remain politically passive and quiet and distracting them with consumerist values (Amin 1999).

Conducting audience research in the region has never been easy. Government restrictions make the procedures for obtaining official permission to conduct research—particularly primary research like opinion polls and surveys for audience studies—problematic, if not impossible. Secondary data collection is also difficult, as there is often little reliable and current data available. The lack of sufficient data on audience demographics, opinions, viewing habits, uses and gratifications, and preferences has hindered the ability of communications researchers to conduct in-depth research. With little reliable data on demographics, viewing habits, and preferences, advertisers are forced to rely on guesses and instinct. Market research spending in the Middle East has increased by nearly 40 percent, yet only a negligible fraction of that is devoted to media research. In addition, newspapers and magazines are sometimes reluctant to begin gathering empirical data on circulation and readership demographics if it will contradict figures previously provided to advertisers.[4]

With the increasing liberalization of the media in the Middle East, however, the situation is poised to change for the better. ACNielsen, Arbitron, and others have recently expressed interest in expanding their presence in the region, and negotiations are underway to allow set-top rating boxes and other audience research mechanisms. In addition, there is a growing push in the region from the large media buying agencies and advertisers to promote the development of circulation auditing in the print media industry and for the introduction of television ratings research.

There are several companies in the Middle East conducting professional media research for marketing and advertising purposes. The three most widely cited are IPSOS, TNS, and the Pan Arab Research Center (PARC), which has a partnership with Gallup International and the Arab Advisors Group. They face, however, the same restrictions as academic researchers. There is little independent research. Television ratings are determined not by independent ratings services but by individual broadcasters hiring research agencies to conduct proprietary research. In most cases ratings are determined through quarterly telephone surveys of viewers. In the absence of a common, reliable, and independent ratings system, advertisers lack critical tools with which to make effective buying decisions and communications researchers lack data with which to analyze viewing habits and preferences.

In 2005 the TV network Showtime commissioned the consulting company Booz Allen Hamilton to conduct a study of television in the Middle East. The study collected information from UN reports, government statistics, and industry analyses, as well as market research and television ratings research from Saudi Arabia, Kuwait, and the UAE. The study found that the region's high television consumption is concentrated around an extended prime time, from 6:00 P.M. till midnight, and during the month of Ramadan, when families traditionally gather around the television after the sunset meal to watch popular Arabic series, game shows, and talk shows.[5]

The study reported that the television preferences of affluent young audiences, Showtime's target market, are characterized by "a rising affinity for progressive programming and underscore the Middle Eastern viewers' growing preference for Western-style content." Television serials received the largest share of ratings points, followed by varieties, movies, news, cultural programs, and sports. Music television has been an instant hit in the Arab world, with more than thirty channels offering music programming, most of it progressive and many offering streaming SMS2T, interactive services, and mobile phone downloads. Religious programming received only 1 percent of the ratings points. In Saudi Arabia, the terrestrial television channels still had strong appeal to older and more traditional audiences. In the UAE, television preferences were more fragmented due to the large expatriate population. Egypt has a more homogeneous, lower-income population, with lower satellite penetration and an extensive government-owned terrestrial television system that has a monopoly on Arabic series and variety programs produced by its studios. Egyptians prefer locally produced family entertainment in Arabic offered on terrestrial channels. The study found, however, that Egyptian television viewers were more liberal than their Persian Gulf counterparts and suggested that cost rather than preference for local material was hindering the spread of pay TV and free-to-air TV in Egypt.[6]

An Overview of Research

The past decade has witnessed increasing communications research in the Arab world, shaped more or less by the same agenda and restrictions found in earlier decades. There have been fewer works on history, propaganda, development communication, and news flow, and more professionally oriented and technologically centered books. A review of communication works generated in the Arab world during the past decade shows that many of these works have largely been an extension of preceding traditions dominant in Arab communication scholarship since the 1950s in that there has been little primary research and most have drawn heavily on translated materials. These materials were not originally designed to be used in a foreign cultural context and often fail to account for the socioeconomic and cultural features of Arab societies (Ayish 1998).

Amin and Napoli (2000) agree that Western models of research dominate, with most of the available texts on mass media in the Arab world focusing on Western—primarily American—examples. Arab scholars inherited a body of scholarship that had evolved in the West around institutions, technologies, and economic and political systems not only foreign but completely opposite to the experience in the Middle East.

Gher and Amin (2000) provide a comprehensive account of the development of media technologies up to the mid-1990s. The authors review the potential social and economic effects of new media technologies on society. The concerns expressed by Arabs must be seen as genuine. Many feel that the constant flow of Western pop culture acts as a threat to both their civilization and to their families' and their children's values. Although such threats have been there for more than a hundred years, the explosive growth and popularity of Western products such as video games, music CDs, computer software, videos and DVDs, films, and television programs have led to an increase in defensive attitudes toward Western culture. Islamic societies and Middle Eastern cultures are quite self-protective of their culture, values, traditions, and religious proprieties. The Arab and Islamic regions are tied together regarding these points, and they are keen to preserve this culture through the use of the Arab language and the kind of media that prevail throughout the Middle East. This view of Arab civilization has been reinforced by the Arab civilization's own enforcement of censorship rules. Within Arab culture this reinforced kind of censorship is regarded as a type of civic responsibility (Gher/Amin 2000).

Gher and Amin (2000) go on to report that Arab audiences have other concerns as well. Some countries are fearful of the possible political and religious backlash to this inflow of alien values. An anti-Western, Islamic fundamentalist reaction to the suddenly easy availability of pop-culture products has been taking place for some time, and the predominant fear of certain governments within the region is the destabilization of both their own government and those of neighboring countries. Islamic groups such as the Muslim Brotherhood disapprove of their members using the media—specifically television, which is felt to have a corrupting, immoral influence on Muslims. Public fear of these negative influences is documented in every Arab state. In addition, Arab media systems are historically authoritarian, and most are sensitive to what they perceive as undesired reporting by international radio and television networks. The lack of tolerance within certain Arab administrations to what they regard as negative reporting has caused drastic responses, ranging from fines and imprisonment for journalists and editors, bans and prohibitions of satellite dishes in Saudi Arabia, and delays to the development of telecommunications infrastructures that are considered the main tools that link the Middle Eastern countries globally.

Although a voluminous amount of Arab communication research has been generated in the Arab world in the past two decades, the majority of these works has been descriptive, historical, or empirically oriented, seeking to test a range of generally American communication theories and hypotheses in Arab settings. On the other hand, a small portion of Arab communication research has emphasized relationships between communications on the one hand and culture, politics, and social processes on the other hand. As Abdel Rahman (1998) notes: "Academic dependency in research is clear in the shortage in media studies on Arab communications. Writings lack originality and relevance to Arab communication concerns such as the history of Arab media, media laws, patterns of media ownership, the role of Arab media in the Arab-Israeli conflict, the relationship between media and political establishment, media role in national development, problems of circulation and printing, and the role of advertising in modern Arab life."

Abdel Rahman (1998) likewise notes a virtual absence of critical communication research in the Arab world, which she attributes to political and professional reasons. On the other hand, Amin (1998) explains that the absence of a solid communication research tradition in the Arab world is the result of several factors: a lack of communication journals in the Middle East; a reward structure in most government institutions that does not favor research productivity; and government sensitivity about research techniques like content analysis, audience preferences, and general utilization of the media.

A study by Amin and Fikri (2002) examined the degree of influence that Western products such as video games, music CDs, computer software, films, and television programs have on Arab families, restating many of the concerns held by families and governments throughout the world. By tackling the impact of violent media programs on audience, the authors say that the policy challenge is twofold: first, there should action plans designed to increase awareness of media violence and the public's sense of responsibility; and second, there should be regulations for the different mechanisms that could initiate and generate improper and undesirable behavior in susceptible individuals. In other words, they argue that this is best achieved by striking a balance between censorship of violence and regulations that explicitly limit the extent to which governments can control what people see and do. They explain that the new technology brings the ability to control content to the individual viewer. The authors recommend that governments work to enhance people's awareness of the importance of choosing what is viewed in the home through public health campaigns and educational campaigns that inform and educate children and adults about the different and required skills necessary for a proper usage of entertainment and information media. The authors also emphasize the importance of lessening the amount of war, crime, and violence broadcast, and that there should be a good number of love, peace, and harmony messages spread within society. Media should be aware and responsible to the public and try to protect individuals who could easily react negatively to violent messages (Amin/Fikri 2002).

Hafiz (1993) reports that audience perceptions of media credibility provide evidence that audiences have little belief in the accuracy of news reports. The credibility of the national Arab media among the elite is receding in comparison to Arab satellite news channels, which are perceived as being more comprehensive, balanced, and true in their information. Hafiz agrees that there is an increasing need for conducting research on Arab media ethics.

Hamada (1996) has designed a case study drawing on the agenda-setting hypothesis to investigate the role of the Egyptian party press in determining the public agenda with respect to the issues of corruption, economic problems, interparty conflicts, and international events. The findings of the study seem to indicate that the party-controlled press made a substantial contribution to the initiation of public discussions on issues previously absent from public agendas.

The uses-and-gratifications theory underlines the role of the audience initiative and activity, with communication behavior considered to be largely goal oriented and purposive. Audience members typically select media or messages from a variety of communication sources that go along with their expectations and desires. These expectations and desires arise from and are bounded by personal traits, social contexts, and interactions. The selection of media and messages affects the outcomes of media use. Studies involving research on audience uses and gratifications have been conducted primarily by Arab students in graduate programs across North America. As a caveat, the majority of the studies have focused solely on Kuwaiti and Saudi audiences. These studies have tended to use the basic assumptions of uses-and-gratifications theory to provide a framework for understanding the correlation between the media and audiences. The inquiries address in broad terms why people in the Arab world generally use a particular medium. Moreover, a portion of the studies factor in particular demographic or personality traits as potential predictors for the motives people are likely to find fulfilled by a particular medium. Most of these studies have shown that audiences in the Arab region watch television for motives very similar to audiences in other countries, such as informational, personal identity, entertainment, integration, and social interaction needs (Amin 1998).

Additionally, there have been a number of studies that have attempted to identify gratifications required from viewing satellite television programming. In a study of the usage made by Egyptian audiences in Cairo of international channels broadcast via direct broadcast satellite, the findings indicate that audiences are deliberately selective and highly involved in the media content that they are watching. The study also finds that most viewers prefer to watch Arab Radio and Television (ART), the Egyptian Space Channel (ESC), the Middle East Broadcast Center (MBC), Dubai TV, and the Lebanese Broadcasting Corporation (LBC), in that order. The study has also found audiences prefer Cable News Network (CNN) programming when looking for news. Moreover, the research finds that one of the main reasons survey respondents buy satellite receivers is because they find the programming on Egyptian television unsatisfactory. More recently, another media researcher, Noha Al-Abd, focused on the uses and gratifications of Egyptian children watching Arab satellite television stations. The purpose of the study was to examine how exposure and activity are related to gratifications in the new transnational media environment (Al-Abd 2005).

A study conducted by Sayyid (1999) focused on Egyptian television newscasts and its role on increasing the political awareness among youth. First, the researcher used content analysis on the 9 P.M. TV newscast for three consecutive months. Second, survey research was also conducted on two different samples: students of a target age of eighteen to twenty-five who study at the four major governmental universities, and employees who work in three ministries (the Ministry of Information; the Ministry of Education, and the Ministry of Planning and International Cooperation). Results show that there is a positive relation between the amount of television watched in general and the number of newscasts watched. A positive correlation was also found between watching television newscasts on Channel One (9 P.M. newscast) and the increase of political awareness among youth. Third, the study finds no relationship between the social and economic level and the viewer's awareness of political life. Thus, the study shows that the newscasts play a vital role in informing and affecting people.

Another study was also conducted by Yussif (1996) to measure the role of television newscasts in promoting the concept of political participation among adolescents living in the capital city. The study aimed to know if political participation was the result of direct exposure to the content of the newscasts or whether there were other intervening variables. The sample was composed of 420 individuals living in Cairo, ranging from sixteen to forty years old. The results showed that 64 percent of the sample depended on television to get news, and 23.6 percent depended heavily and 12.4 percent did not depend on TV. Results also showed 29.5 percent were very concerned about politics, and 60.5 percent were slightly concerned, while 10 percent were not concerned at all. The study also found quite low ratings for people who participate in voting during elections, as only 25 percent of the sample actually voted. Thus, the study shows that although there is a positive correlation between how often people watch newscasts and their concern about politics, this awareness does not increase their actual political participation (Yussif 1996).

Another study was conducted to evaluate the public opinion regarding the content of the newscasts and the news programs presented on Egyptian television.[7] This study aimed to analyze the agenda of the newscasts and the role of the reports in covering the news comprehensively. The study used a sample of 1,400 people from different constituencies all over the city, ranging in age from fifteen to sixty-five, in addition to 91 people from the upper class. The results showed that 79.5 percent of the sample watch the newscasts regularly, and 19.9 percent watch them irregularly. Moreover, the study found that Channel One was regarded as the most important channel for news, being watched by 99.5 percent of all viewers. As for the news genres covered, the results showed that the local news came first, followed by the issue of peace in the Middle East, the issue of Arab unity, and, finally, the European news. The study sample ranked the newscasts highly for the success of the correspondents in reflecting a real picture of what was happening nationally and internationally.

Amr (1981) aimed to study the impact of the content of religious programs on changing the family values of people living in both urban areas and the countryside. The research conducted a survey on a sample of 396 people from three different constituencies with different social backgrounds. The study found that religious programs do not have an impact on changing some of the viewers' values. The programs were only able to promote certain social values, such as importance of education, cooperation and work.

In another study, Ali (1984) aimed toward evaluating the content of the soap operas presented on Egyptian television. The researcher wanted to study the role TV soap operas played in solving some of Egypt's social problems, and used content analysis on a sample of twelve Egyptian soap operas presented on Channel One for three consecutive months in 1982. Results showed that there is a positive relationship between watching soap operas and social change. This is due to the fact that soap operas attract a large proportion of the audience and they indirectly affect it through the drama presented. The study also found that social problems counted for 64.1 percent of the total amount of the problems tackled.

Marghalani, Palmgreen, and Boyd (1998) have observed, with regard to Saudi uses-and-gratifications research, that most of the studies used a potentially non-representative sample composed of high school students, college students, or university professors. This probable bias is equally applicable to most other studies conducted in the region. As an example, nearly 50 percent of studies conducted for theses and dissertations used samples of students. Additionally, Marghalani et al. point out that most studies from the region they reviewed included gratification aspects taken from studies in other countries, particularly the United States, and that none of them focused on the gratifications included in traditional television studies. Marghalani et al. have also found that none of the studies used qualitative methods to indicate motives that are specific to Saudi culture.

With few exceptions, these observations can be applied when examining the literature available in the area. Abdel Rahman's study (1998), which included motives such as viewing censored material, a culturally bound motive, is one such exception. In addition, when Shahin (1996) examined Egyptian viewers' uses and gratifications in viewing Arab satellite stations, she designed her study using qualitative methods and well-defined categories that fit the Egyptian culture and media environment. For example, she studied characteristics such as whether television programs presented an Arab perspective or whether they focused on Egyptian events, giving her study a unique viewpoint.

Shahin's study found that more than 40 percent of the respondents had used satellite receivers for longer than three years. An additional 21 percent had bought receivers within the previous year. Shahin also found that viewing of Arab satellite stations was frequent for more than 99 percent of the respondents. MBC ranked first among viewer preferences, followed by Al-Jazeera and LBC. Furthermore, 51 percent preferred watching Arab stations because of their high quality programming, while 44 percent preferred Arab stations for the perceived objectivity of their news programs. The study also found that 65 percent of the respondents watched satellite television to fulfill the need for information through news content, while 62 percent watched to fulfill their need for entertainment. 92 percent of the respondents tuned to Arab stations as the primary source of news. The study found that the number of viewers of Egyptian terrestrial television dropped by 46 percent, and satisfaction with terrestrial programming dropped by 26 percent. Shahin relates that those who do continue to watch terrestrial programming do so to view favorite shows and local news (Shahin 1996). This last point reinforces the Booz Allen Hamilton survey results, which showed that audiences prefer the perceived higher quality of satellite programming and watch terrestrial channels to view popular local programs and local news.

The implementation of uses and gratifications theory to study media use in the region is not yet mature. Despite the shortcomings, it appears that there is a basic understanding of why and how Arab audiences watch television programming, whether broadcast terrestrially or via satellite. These studies need to be continually updated in order to provide accurate insight and information, as viewing habits and broadcast offerings are changing rapidly in the new media environment.

Several studies were conducted to monitor and assess what an Arab audience thought of the first Arab news satellite channel, Al-Jazeera. The studies found that people are mainly attracted to shows involving heated debates about controversial political issues. It is important to mention that most of the studies conducted focused on the demographics of the audience and on programs that had the greatest appeal, and therefore there was a lack of research regarding audience feedback and what they would like to watch.

Auter, et al. (2004) conducted some rare ratings research on Arab audiences. Their study attempted to answer two research questions: Who is watching Al-Jazeera, and how much time do they spend watching it? The Al-Jazeera audience was described by age, gender, marital status, education, and household income, as well as by the psychographic variable of "religion/life philosophy." The researchers conducted an online survey to gather responses from Al-Jazeera TV viewers from around the world. For a two-week period (August 20, 2002 to September 4, 2002), a survey in the Arabic language was linked to Al-Jazeera TV's website. People who could read Arabic and were willing to participate were able to access the survey by clicking on a link on Al-Jazeera's home page. Usable responses were gathered from more than 5,000 respondents from 137 countries around the world. The bias in the sample is that the respondents were self-selected, literate in Arabic, and able to go online, which clearly is not representative of the majority of Al-Jazeera's audience. However, the survey provided some interesting results, finding that most survey respondents watched Al-Jazeera for many hours at a time, in some cases for nearly half of their waking hours. The most sustained viewing was done by the middle-aged. Those among the respondents with the least education viewed the channel the most, and lower-income viewers watched more than did the more affluent viewers. The number of hours the channel was watched was the same for both Muslims and Christians, yet Jews and those who hold other faiths watched much less. In addition, the percentage of liberal viewers watching Al-Jazeera was higher than that of conservative viewers. These results offer a glimpse of the strength of the network's appeal and the diversity of its global audience.

Kabha (2004) cites ratings research to note that satellite stations helped to coalesce Arab opinion throughout the Arab world during the second half of the 1990s. The most widely watched shows were programs that dealt with the Israeli-Palestinian conflict, such as *The Opposite Direction*, moderated by Faisal Al-Kassim; *More Than One View*, hosted by Sami Haddad; *Without Borders*, moderated by Ahmad Mansur (all broadcast by the Al-Jazeera Channel), or Imad Al-Din Adib's talk show on Orbit.

Abdel Rahman (1998) writes about the changing demands of audiences who want to watch more kinds of information, entertainment, and news programs. The author states that there should be a variety of television programming and these varieties of programming must satisfy both the viewers' expectations and the advertisers' needs in order to strike a balance and attract the desired percentage of audience to the channel. With heavy competition among stations, there is a demand for more creative programs and higher-quality graphics and production standards. The author remarks that one of the obvious differences between Arab and Western channels is the high level of sophisticated graphics and advanced technology used in the Western channels.

The sudden onset of satellite broadcasting in the region has prompted the emergence of many issues, such as regulation, public access, ownership and the social and cultural impacts this new industry might have. Sakr (2001) has sketched and mapped out the industry from the first Arabsat satellite, which was launched in 1985, to the present. She notes that most researchers started to study the phenomena of satellite development in the region after the CNN coverage of the first Gulf War; the late-1980s reorganization of French media and France Telecom's satellite transmissions to francophone North Africa were also critical steps. Although Arabsat was launched in 1985, when it broadcast vividly the annual pilgrimage to Mecca to countries across the region, Sakr notes that satellite broadcasting was not heavily consumed until the 1990s. From this point, Sakr monitored the different stages of development of today's key satellite players, like ART, MBC, Al-Jazeera, LBC, and Future TV.

New, rapid developments in technologies have started to challenge the governmental sources of information, as the Arab audience is being exposed to a variety of channels that provide it with an ample amount of information. This variation in sources enables the Arab audience to get a wider perspective and exposes it to different contexts framing current events. Yet, the audience needs a satellite television channel that serves it by enriching Arab culture and promoting the concept of social capital among the Arab nations, as well as acting as a frame of reference for all the Arab countries. Although some Arab countries have taken the initiative, there is still a need for a positive medium that bonds the Arab world together.

Alterman (1999) has similarly examined the changes that started to take place after the introduction of the new broadcasting technologies in the region. One major effect, he notes, is the declining role of the government and state information ministries and the increasing flow of information outside of the traditional state mechanisms. He notes that government control is becoming more informal and that there is an increase in the amount of information the general public has access to, primarily due to an increase in the number and diversity of information outlets. He agrees with other researchers that this diversity and the growing number of players on the international media scene have led to increased competition for viewers and that as a result broadcasters have developed competitive strategies designed to obtain the maximum share of the audience.

Alterman (2002) postulates that the growth rate of the satellite television audience is slowing down. The shift to digital broadcasting increases costs and the number of channels makes the market more difficult and competitive for a single outlet to attract a big share of the audience, making television a loss-making proposition for almost all players. The result is that the only networks that will remain in the field are those that are subsidized or wholly owned by governments. Equally significant, he notes that the rise of Arab media does not appear to have reduced conflict in the region, although he cites polls by Zogby International that indicate that regular viewers of Al-Jazeera are more positively willing to have peace with Israel, in spite of the frequent use of aggressive talk by show guests and the strong editorializing that creeps into regular news coverage. The author suggests the reason for this might be that exposure to Al-Jazeera's coverage provides the audience with specific details that enable the viewers to be aware of the gray areas in the current Arab-Israeli conflict. He concludes that one of the primary impacts of the success of Arab satellite television is the creation of the regional solidarity concept, or "Arabism from the ground up" (Alterman 2002).

Ayish (2002a) discusses the less-than-impressive contribution of television in the Arab world to cultural enrichment. He concludes that the role of television as a tool for unifying the culture of the Arab world is derived mainly from the forty-year-old modernization paradigm that is considered a powerful media contribution to national social and cultural development. From this perspective, the development of local culture is currently the main force for social change among the Arab countries and societies. According to the integrationists, drawing on a common Arab cultural and religious heritage, television should be able to create a united frame of reference for all the people throughout the Arab world. Ayish describes examples of programming that is designed to integrate Arab countries. For example, the Tunis-based Arab States Broadcasting Union (ASBU) has broadcast a series of programs to increase the awareness of the Arabs about their common culture, values, and traditions. The Arab League Educational, Scientific, and Cultural Organization (ALESCO) also uses television as a medium to promote the principles of Arab-Islamic culture by highlighting unique and common cultural features. The author notes that an unexpected outcome of transnational media is the introduction of Arabic speakers to Arabic dialects that are not familiar to them (Ayish 2002a). In his book *Arab Satellite Television and Politics in the Middle East*, Zayani (2004) agrees, noting that transnational broadcasters such as Abu Dhabi TV, Al-Arabiya and Al-Jazeera have a role to play in creating pan-Arab public opinion, which he calls "The Arab Street." This will contribute to reinforcing the region's political strength.

Amin (2004) describes the development of Nilesat, Egypt's first satellite broadcast network, and its positioning with the Arab audiences. Nilesat is unique among Arab satellites in that it provides a larger variety of digital broadcasting services, including unencrypted channels, encrypted channels, and high-speed data transmission services. The unencrypted channels include quality digital television and radio programs that enable all viewers to equip themselves with a satellite dish and receiver as well as subscription-based services and pay TV. Since its beginning, Nilesat has been a unique media outlet in that although it is owned, controlled, and operated by the Egyptian government it was introduced as a publicly traded corporation in which the Egyptian Radio and Television Union (ERTU), the governmental body responsible for all radio and television broadcasting in the country, is the major shareholder. Amin notes that Arab viewers prefer to be exposed to a number of different channels so as to be able to access different kinds of news and information as well as entertainment. They also prefer to have programs in Arabic rather than in English and other languages. The study reveals that another important reason for the popularity of the Nilesat service is a decrease in the cost of equipment and installation of the Nilesat dish and decoders, which has resulted in greater audience share (Amin 2004).

Technologies have also helped the emergence of the reality shows (a new concept to the Arab world) through which certain ideas such as democracy are indirectly promoted. Lynch (2005) studies the most successful Arab reality TV shows, such as *Super Star*, *Star Academy*, and *Al-Wadi*, and discusses the theory that these shows introduce audiences to democratic concepts. The shows use audience participation and voting through phone calls or mobile text messages to determine the winners of competitions. These methods have proven highly popular in an Arab world characterized by suppressive, nondemocratic governments. The response of the audience has been highly unexpected, with millions of voters participating to support contestants. Thousands of contestants submitted applications to compete, and political figures have shown their backing, calling to support their national contestant. The author notes that although Arab reality TV is considered to be healthy for the political and cultural environment, expectations that these programs help in developing and nurturing democracy within the new generation of Arabs by encouraging the concept of voting are grossly exaggerated (Lynch 2005).

Alterman (1998) suggests that one of the most important outcomes of the new technology—print, satellite, and Internet—is that it facilitates the transmission of information independent of distance. He explains that, in the past, differences could be maintained because geography aided governmental efforts to control information, but now this is no longer possible. Today, information transcends barriers to create something much more closely resembling a single market. He foresees that this ease of information flow will have dramatic consequences for the region's economic and perhaps political unity. Alterman (1999) cites studies showing that the new transnational satellite media has led to the introduction of different Arab dialects and broken down some of the barriers that used to stand against understanding others.

Etefa (2004) has studied the impact of satellite television on identity among Arab immigrants. She states that more people than ever before are moving, crossing cultural and geographic boundaries. The results of this study support the idea of satellite television as a significant element in the formation of ethnoscapes and the development of immigrant identities, with the result that as groups move they stay linked to one another through media such as satellite television and the Internet. Transnational media is changing communication in the Arab world by creating links between Arabs in all parts of the globe.

Music satellite channels have emerged at a fast pace in the Arab region, attracting a large audience base, mainly among the teenagers. Most of the studies conducted among adolescents found that almost 100 percent of university students are frequent viewers of those music channels. Yet, no studies were conducted as to what they dislike about those channels or what they aim to watch.

In Mohammad's study conducted in Egypt in 2004, the researcher tried by comparing three Egyptian universities (Al-Minya, Cairo, and October 6) to confirm Egyptian university students' usage of satellite music channels and what gratifications they get. His results prove that the rates of viewing of these channels were high, ranging from 100 percent for October 6 University, followed by Cairo University with 90 percent, and then Al-Minya University with 78 percent. Testing the hypothesis found no significant differences among the related variables of age, major subject, or gender, and the viewing of the music satellite channels. Also, there were no statistically significant differences between the major subject studied and the gratifications gained, but there were significant differences related to the age variable.

In Palestine, Abu-Shanab (2004) studied the relation between Palestinian youth and music channels in order to find the extent of the impact of these songs on values, habits, and Palestinian identity. He found the number of those watching the musical channels reached 67 percent, against 33 percent for those watching the pictured musicals. He also found that viewing motives do not affect the patriotic Palestinian identity, since the viewers see that their motives are habit, time consumption, entertainment, escape from their problems, gratification, and curiosity. Statistically, the negative effects of place of residence, especially in camps, resulted in significant differences. There were no significant differences in the effect that video clips had on the type of university, living standard, or gender.

In Oman, Al-Rawas made a field study in 2004 using a random sample of four hundred university students in order to analyze the young students' usage of the music satellite channels and the gratifications gained. A high percentage of those watching the music satellite channels did so simply to spend time, to feel happier, or to imitate the singers. Other motives for watching were knowledge of other countries' songs, the development of romantic aspects, and the wish to increase links to people and the community. There were statistically significant effects of the music satellite channels on the traditional motives among the university youth, and between exposure and para-orientation, orientation and social gratifications; but no effect on parasocial gratifications. There were no significant effects of exposure to musical satellites on demographic variables like gender, age, or university (Al-Rawas 2004).

In Egypt, Galal (2004) studied the best methods to make Arabic song effective at showing Arab identity through song's thoughts, values, and inclusions. There were variations in the levels of Westernization of Arabic song according to the nationality of the singer. There was a positive relationship between the rate of broadcasting song and the nature of values present in it, as songs spreading negative values were broadcast more. There was a positive correlation between the broadcasting mode and type of song, whether it included high, medium, or low excitement.

A study by Al-Ali (2002) on television viewing habits of children in the United Arab Emirates indicated that children generally watch television programs during specific periods, as follows in the Emirates: the evening period (53.6 percent), the morning period (only 13.9 percent), noon time (24.5 percent), nighttime (7.82 percent), and free periods. The reasons are: (1) the evening is the prime viewing period because of the presence of children in the house at that time, and because schools are open in the morning in the Emirates; (2) most programs liked by children are broadcast in the afternoon—for instance, Arabic series, films, and plays; (3) the general results showed that 79.2 percent of the sample in the Emirates view children's programs on school days. The viewing period in the Emirates is three hours or more.

A study by Al-Abd and Al-Ali (1994) on media habits and children's viewing of children's television programs in Oman concluded that

- Males and females view in equal measure various television programs via satellite channels. These programs are: Arabic series, religious program types, Arabic films, Arabic plays, and acrobats and the circus.
- More males than females view five television program types with different probability levels, as follows: males more than females watch the news, and sport programs ($p < 0.95$), as all males watch the news, versus 93.7 percent of females, and all males watch tournaments and sports programs, versus 94.7 percent of females; more males (71.76 percent) than females (44.2 percent) watch foreign series; more males (97.9 percent) than females (70.5 percent) watch foreign films; more males (91.6 percent) than females (70.52 percent) watch newspaper statements.
- More females than males view these nine television program types; singing and dancing shows, miscellaneous programs, children's programs and cartoons, woman's programs, advertisements, cultural programs, documentaries, teletext services, and health programs.
- Single and married people view an equal amount of the following ten program types on satellite channels: Arabic series, children's programs and cartoons, cultural programs, newspaper statements, news shows, religious items, acrobats and the circus, musicals and dancing taboos, tournaments and sports programs, and Arabic plays.
- Singles watch the following five programs more than married people: foreign series, miscellaneous programs, advertisements, foreign films, and Arabic series.
- Married people watch the following four program types more than singles: woman's programs, teletext, services, documentaries, and health programs.
- Periods of extensive viewing of satellite channels are: the evening period (6–10 P.M.), which represents the most popular period of viewing, at 72.1 percent of studied groups; and the early night's period (10 P.M.–1 A.M.), which represents the second most extensive viewing period, at 65.8 percent of the studied groups.
- Males (95.7 percent) and females (93.6 percent) are almost equal in saying that their viewing of satellite channel programs affects their follow-up of television programs broadcast through nonsatellite channels in the Emirates.
- The most important disadvantages of viewing satellite channels are: vice can spread and be accessed easily; taboo subjects—for example, males and females together, courtship, and drug and alcohol consumption—can be presented as if they were normal and acceptable (100 percent); exciting methods for kissing can be shown and taught (98 percent); those committing crimes and violent acts can be presented as heroes (97 percent); the Islamic religion can be called into question and doubted (93 percent); morally depraved advertisements can

> use women and children in a bad way to increase consumption (77 percent); romance is made to seem exciting; women want to wear modern clothing, as seen in fashion videos, that does not fit in the Arabic community (69 percent); bad eyesight can result from constantly viewing and changing channels and staying up late (54 percent); time is wasted instead of being used purposefully to work, study, rest, or socializing—one researcher called this "time ghoul"—(49 percent); weakness and laziness can result as the viewer makes it a habit to continue watching different programs (36 percent); the time spent reading or listening to religious material is reduced (25 percent); and the young are taken away from studying (23 percent). Some respondents introduced psychiatric ideas, such as: if prison is a university for crime, then the satellite dish is the preparatory school for deviation, as it stops the creative abilities of children and their potential to become the men and women of tomorrow (1.7 percent; Al-Abd/Al-Ali 1994).

A study by Ali Al-Hail (2000) notes that most of the women portrayed in Arab media are shown performing domestic functions, and he suggests that both Arab and Islamic media should begin promoting the role of women as well-educated, professional members of society.

Sakr writes in her book *Satellite Realms: Transnational Television, Globalization and the Middle East* that the thirteen years between the first Intifada and the second Intifada that started in September 2000 were proof of the impact of media: "[It] provided a powerful indicator of the impact of transnational television among young people in the Middle East. When the first Intifada broke out in December 1987 there were no Middle Eastern satellite channels broadcasting far and wide to show scenes of Israeli troops shooting at Palestinian children throwing stones.... By the start of the second Intifada, the regional media landscape had changed dramatically" (Sakr 2001, 191). Sakr links the idea of television coverage to the impact this coverage has on people and whether or not it contributes to the creation of public opinion. She writes, "Television pictures of stone-throwing children challenging Israeli troops and wounded children had a galvanizing effect on young people throughout the Arab world" (Sakr 2001, 192). Images of children being shot by Israeli troops—particularly the devastating image of twelve-year-old Mohammad Al-Durrah being shot while huddling with his father behind a steel barrel, Firas Auda being driven over by an Israeli tank, or six-month-old Iman, who was shot in the chest—had a great impact on Arab viewers. Sakr goes on to explain that broadcasting these images to every Arabic-speaking home with satellite access caused an upsurge of anger far greater than what had occurred during the first Intifada. In Egypt, thousands of people participated in demonstrations at the universities of Cairo and Ain Shams despite heavy police presence, and school students stoned Cairo branches of the Sainsbury supermarket chain, suspecting it of having ties with Israel. Demonstrations by Saudi women took place for the sake of the Palestinian cause, and other demonstrations took place in most of the Arab capitals (Sakr 2001).

Conclusion

Conducting audience research in the region is full of barriers and constraints, from inconvenience to imprisonment. One of the many difficulties faced by researchers is the resistance presented by government bureaucrats and officials who maintain a proprietary, even paranoid, attitude toward information. Obtaining official permission to conduct research, particularly public opinion surveys for audience and market studies, is highly problematic. Researchers can only hope that someday there will be no need to have official permission. If the changing mass media help promote increased information flow, stronger civil society, and democratization in the Arab world, perhaps they will also promote a more open environment for mass media research.

Although a large number of scholarly works have been published on Arab media audience analysis in the past decade, the bulk of these works has both a low theoretical content and a lack of unbiased empirical data. This is partly a result of the barriers to obtaining primary data as well as a lack of accurate secondary data and trained communications researchers. But despite these problems, a number of interesting and informative studies have been generated. More research should be directed to documenting modern transitions in Arab social, cultural, economic, political, and media trends in order to generate solid scientific perspectives of Arab media. Thought should also be given to using research methods that surmount the barriers to survey and opinion research and capture the viewing habits and preferences of the lower-income segments that make up the vast majority of television viewers in the less-affluent Arab countries.

The media, both national and international, are profoundly affecting Arab governments and their relations with their citizens, their neighbors, and the world. Research is needed on the changing relationship between the state and the media, particularly as the media often has an impact on the direction of public policy and therefore impacts Arab audiences. Increased transnational/global media pressure and strengthening privatization trends are not only lessening the grip on information that state-owned media once enjoyed but are also increasing the pressure on independent audience and market research to guide business and advertising decisions and to spur progress toward increased democratization.

Finally, the cultural impact of the changing media environment needs to be assessed. Studies need to be done to measure and analyze the impact of the transnational/global media on Arab culture and society, to investigate the internal transformations that are changing the relationship between the media and the state, and to study how that change could further impact political evolution in the Arab world. The speed of technological and political change in the region calls for a renewed commitment to quality communication research, with a particular stress on understanding Arab audiences.

Notes

1. See Booz Allen Hamilton Inc., *Strategic Review of the Television Broadcasting Sector in the Middle East,* Dubai, 2005, http://www.boozallen.com/media/file/ME_TV_Landscape_Strategic_Review.pdf.
2. Ibid.
3. R. D. Rusch, Readers Pick Apple: 2004 Reader's Choice Awards, 2004, http://www.brandchannel.com/features_effect.asp?pf_id=248.
4. Media Research and Circulation Auditing, Newsletter 21, March 7, 2006, http://www.arabpressnetwork.org/articles.php?id=611; Lack of Credible Figures is the Biggest Challenge Facing Arab Media, Newsletter 10, December 13, 2005, http://www.arabpressnetwork.org/articles.php?id=368.
5. See Booz Allen Hamilton, *Strategic Review of the Television Broadcasting Sector.*
6. Ibid.
7. See Egyptian Radio and Television Union (ERTU), Evaluating the Public Opinion Regarding the Content of the Newscasts and the News Programs [in Arabic], 1995, Cairo: Central Department for Audience Research.

References

Abd, N. al- (2005), *Satellite Television and our Children.* Cairo: Dar al-Fikr al Arabi.

Abd, A. al-/F. al-Ali (1994), Satellite Television Viewing Habits [in Arabic]. *Journal of Communication Research* (Al-Azhar-University) 3, 326–407.

Abdel Rahman, H. (1998), Uses and Gratifications of Satellite TV in Egypt. *Transnational Broadcasting Studies* 1, http://www.tbsjournal.com/Archives/Fall98/Documents1/Uses/uses.html.

Abu-Shanab, H. (2004), Media Habits of Young Palestinians towards Video Clips and Their Relation to the Palestinian National Identity [in Arabic]. Paper Presented to the Scientific Conference of the Faculty of Mass Communication at Cairo University, May 4–6, 2004.

Ali, F. al-(2002), Television Viewing Habits and Exposure of the Children in the United States of America and the United Arab Emirates [in Arabic]. *Arab Journal for the Humanities* 78, 110–138.

Ali, S. (1984), Evaluating the Content of the Soap Operas Presented on Egyptian Television: A Content Analysis Study on Soap Operas Presented on Channel One [in Arabic]. Unpublished Master's thesis, Faculty of Mass Communication, Cairo University.

Alterman, J. B. (1998), *New Media, New Politics? From Satellite Television to the Internet in the Arab World.* Washington DC: Washington Institute for Near East Policy.

———. (1999), Transnational Media and Social Change in the Arab World. *Transnational Broadcasting Studies* 2, http://www.tbsjournal.com/Archives/Spring99/Articles/Alterman/alterman.html.

———. (2002), The Effects of Satellite Television on Arab Domestic Politics. *Transnational Broadcasting Studies* 9, http://www.tbsjournal.com/Archives/Fall02/Alterman.html.

Amin, H. (1996), The Arab World and North Africa. In A. Wells (ed.), *World Broadcasting: A Comparative View*, Norwood: Ablex, 121–144.

———. (1998), Media Studies in the Arab World: Issues and Concerns. Paper Submitted to the Broadcast Education Association's Annual International Conference, Las Vegas, April 3–7, 1998.

———. (1999), Satellite Broadcasting and the Building of Arab Information Society. Paper Presented at the Article 19 International Seminar, Cairo, February 20–21, 1999.

———. (2004), Nilesat: Current Challenges and Future Trends. *Transnational Broadcasting Studies* 12, http://www.tbsjournal.com/amin.htm.

Amin, H./H. Fikri (2002), Media, Sex, Violence, and Drugs: Egypt's Experience. In Y. Kamalipour (ed.), *Media, Sex, Violence, and Drugs in the Global Village*. Boulder: Rowman and Littlefield, 219–234.

Amin, H./J. Napoli (1997), The Politics of Accommodation: CNN in Egypt. *Journal of African Communications* 2, 18–36.

———. (2000), Media and Power in Egypt. In J. Curran/M.-J. Park (ed.), *De-Westernizing Media Studies*, London: Routledge.

Amr, N. (1981), Evaluating the Content of the Religious Programs on Changing the Family Values of Both People Living in Cities and in the Countryside [in Arabic]. Unpublished Master's thesis, Faculty of Mass Communication, Cairo University.

Auter, P./M. M. Arafa/K. al-Jaber (2004), Who is Al Jazeera's Audience? Deconstructing the Demographics and Psychographics of an Arab Satellite News Network. *Transnational Broadcasting Studies* 12, http://www.tbsjournal.com/Archives/Spring04/auter.htm.

Ayish, M. I. (1998), Communication Research in the Arab World: A New Perspective. *Javnost—The Public* 1, 33–57.

———. (2002a), The Impact of Arab Satellite Television on Culture and Value Systems in Arab Countries: Perspectives and Issues. *Transnational Broadcasting Studies* 9, http://www.tbsjournal.com/Archives/Fall02/Ayish.html.

———. (2002b), Political Communication on Arab World Television: Evolving Patterns. *Political Communication* 2, 137–155.

Boyd, D./H. Amin (1995), The Development of Direct Broadcast Television to and within the Middle East. *Journal of South Asian and Middle Eastern Studies* 2, 37–49.

Etefa, A. (2004), Transnational Television and the Arab Diaspora in the United States. *Transnational Broadcasting Studies* 12, http://www.tbsjournal.com/Archives/Spring04/etefa.htm.

Galal, A. (2004), Arab Identity as Reflected by Video Clips and their Impact on the Value System of Youth [in Arabic]. Paper presented to the Scientific Conference of the Faculty of Mass Communication at Cairo University, May 4–6, 2004.

Gher, L./H. Amin (eds.) (2000), *Civic Discourse in the Middle East and the Digital Age of Communications*. Stamford: Ablex.

Hafiz, S. (1993), *The Sorrow of Press Freedom* [in Arabic]. Cairo: Al-Ahram Center for Translation and Publication.

Hail, A. al-(2000), The Age of New Media: The Role of Al-Jazeera Satellite TV in Developing Aspects of Civil Society in Qatar. *Transnational Broadcasting Studies* 4, http://www.tbsjournal.com/Archives/Spring00/Articles4/Ali/Al-Hail/al-hail.html.

Hamada, B. (1996), *Media and Politics: Agenda Setting Case in Egypt*. Cairo: Nahdet Al-Shaq.

Kabha, M. (2004), Attitudes of Palestinian-Israelis to Arab Satellite TV. *Transnational Broadcasting Studies* 12, http://www.tbsjournal.com/Archives/Spring04/kabha.htm.

Labib, S. (1994), *Arab Policies in the Light of Current and Future Communication Trends* [in Arabic]. Tunis: Said Zidan.

Lynch, M. (2005), "Reality Is Not Enough": The Politics of Arab Reality TV. *Transnational Broadcasting Studies* 15, http://www.tbsjournal.com/Archives/Fall05/Lynch.html.

Marghalani, K./P. Palmgreen/D. A. Boyd (1998), The Utilization of Direct Satellite Broadcasting (DBS) in Saudi Arabia. *Journal of Broadcasting and Electronic Media* 3, 297–314.

Mohammad, H. A. (2004), Uses and Gratifications of University Students for Satellite Music Stations [in Arabic]. Paper presented at the Scientific Conference of the Faculty of Mass Communication at Cairo University, May 4–6, 2004.

Rawas, A. M. al-(2004), Uses and Gratifications of University Students for Arab Satellite Music Stations [in Arabic]. *Egyptian Journal of Public Opinion* 2, 1–78.

Sakr, N. (2001), *Satellite Realms: Transnational Television, Globalization and the Middle East.* London: I. B. Tauris.

Sayyid, L. (1999), The Egyptian Television Newscasts and their Impact on Increasing the Political Awareness among Youth [in Arabic]. Unpublished Master's thesis, Faculty of Mass Communication, Cairo University.

Shahin, H. (1996), The Uses and Gratifications of Cable Network Egypt (CNE) in Egypt [in Arabic]. Unpublished Master's thesis, Faculty of Mass Communication, Cairo University.

Al-Sharif, S. (1999), Communication and Culture and the Arab Reality [in Arabic]. Unpublished research paper, Cairo University.

Yussif, H. (1996), The Role of Television Newscasts in Promoting the Concept of Political Participation among Youth Living in the Capital City [in Arabic]. Unpublished Master's thesis, Faculty of Mass Communication, Cairo University.

Zayani, M. (2004), Arab Satellite Television and Politics in the Middle East. Abu Dhabi: Emirates Centre for Strategic Studies and Research.

CHAPTER FIVE

From Activity to Interactivity: The Arab Audience

Marwan M. Kraidy

Audiences, wrote the Australian cultural studies scholar John Hartley, are "invisible fictions (that) may be imagined empirically, theoretically or politically, but in all cases the product is a fiction that serves the imagining institutions. In no case is the audience 'real' or external to its discursive construction" (1992, 105). Though it may strike some readers as radically constructivist, Hartley's provocative statement is useful for a theoretical exploration of the notion of "audience" in the contemporary Arab world. In the context of major Arab media developments of the last two decades, Hartley's assertion compels us to ask a set of questions: Which institutions imagine the Arab audience? What are their agendas and how do these agendas inform the way they define their audience? Can the Arab audience be imagined as a unified multinational entity, or is it more accurately understood as a loose formation of transnational Arabic-speaking niches?

Clearly there is an ongoing battle over the Arab audience. Arab, Western and other governments; advertisers; and religious figures are competing for what practitioners of "public diplomacy" describe as the "hearts and minds" of Arabs. In the post-9/11 era, Arabs have been conceptualized variously as viewers, listeners, readers, citizens, consumers, subjects, and believers. The fabled "Arab street" has been the subject of often intense but seldom well-informed speculation. Institutions and individuals targeting the Arab audience today include odd pairs: the U.S. and Iranian governments, members of the Saudi royal family partnered with Lebanese entrepreneurs, and more recently, private Jordanian and Egyptian investors partnering clerics of various persuasions. Arab viewers are targeted through myriad genres: sensual music videos and ascetic religious sermons, reality television and newscasts. This eclecticism reflects various overlapping and competing agendas—political, religious, commercial—united in their search for that constructed category, the Arab audience, or, more accurately from an analytical perspective, Arab audiences.

The battle for Arab audiences is an auspicious opportunity to deepen our understanding and broaden the scope of the conceptual instruments that have so far been used to understand media audiences. Though scholarly research into media audiences has developed a strikingly broad and diverse body of theories and approaches, they share some common assumptions. First is the focus on television as the default medium. Although early research may have addressed film and radio, most scholarly audience research has focused on television, implicitly assumed to be the most influential medium in daily life, especially in those Western countries at the time when most audience theories were developed. Second is the national scope of audience studies. With a few exceptions (for example, Liebes/Katz 1990), scholarly, government, and corporate research has assumed the audience to be bound up in the nation-state. This chapter raises questions about both these assumptions. The existing focus exclusively on television is increasingly off the mark because of the advent of what I have called "hypermedia space," which is a seamless communication space bridging previously discrete media technologies like television, mobile phones, and the Internet (Kraidy 2006, 2007). The emphasis on the nation-state is also undermined by the flourishing of regional pan-Arab media. But before discussing these issues it is worth retracing the historical trajectory of audience research and revisiting some of its milestones.

Notions of activity and passivity have been central threads in research on media audiences. Concerns with whether audiences passively accept or actively decipher mediated messages betray various anxieties about political mobilization, social order, and cultural change, reflected in Hartley's ways of imagining the audience "empirically, theoretically, politically" (1992, 5). This chapter's first objective is to provide a brief summary of audience theories and establish links with Arab media. Rather than providing an exhaustive survey of audience theories, it focuses on theories relevant to contemporary Arab media. It provides a map of various theories of the audience developed in media and mass communication scholarship and then attempts to locate Arab audiences on that map. Also, rather than importing audience theories to the Arab context *mutatis mutandis*, it sets the former and the latter in dialectical tension. The chapter is therefore diagnostic, trying to evaluate various views of Arab audiences, and normative, proposing a research agenda on Arab audiences.

A Brief History of the Active Audience

Although audience activity permeates various schools of thought in media and communication studies, there is no monolithic conception of the active audience. Prompted by the rise of Nazism, scholars of the so-called Frankfurt school argued that the manipulation of audiences was instrumental in the rise of the fascist exploitation of masses leading up to World War II. From their perspective, urbanization weakened traditional social structures, alienating individuals and making them vulnerable to propaganda. Fleeing Nazi persecution in the late 1930s, leading figures like Adorno, Horkheimer, and Marcuse brought concerns about the audience to the United States, where scholars researching media impact disagreed with Frankfurt school perspectives. Lazarsfeld, et al.'s *The People's Choice* (1944), for example, refuted claims of powerful media influence on audiences, and Katz and Lazarsfeld's *Personal Influence* (1955) developed the "two-step" flow idea of mediated influence to undermine the notion of unmediated communication between social and political centers, on the one hand, and audiences on the other hand.

There were also theoretical and methodological differences between the humanistic critical approach of the Frankfurt school and the social scientific (and predominantly functionalist) methods of North American researchers. In what we can now see as a move to bridge some of those differences, Merton in *Mass Persuasion* (1946) advocated a shift from an emphasis on the *content* of media messages to a focus on the *process* of communication. However, his contemporaries "overshot" as they heeded Merton's call, switching from the study of content to the study of *effects* (see Morley 1993, for a detailed description of this shift). The same period saw the rise of Shannon and Weaver's mathematical communication model (1949), which understood communication in terms of cybernetics, focusing on information transmission. This model famously parceled the communication process into a "sender" transmitting a "message" to a "receiver" through a "channel" in spite of "noise," and in return, audience activity was understood as "feedback" bouncing back to the sender. Though simplistic for those committed to studying communication in its broader social and political contexts, this model reflected the rise of systematic theorizing of communicative processes and media audiences.

In an intellectual environment in which communication issues received increased attention, the first explicit and systematic discussions of audience "activity" arose when Katz (1959) stated that "less attention [should be paid] to what media do to people and more to what people do with the media" (1959, 2), encapsulating the rising "uses-and-gratifications" approach to media audiences (see McQuail 1984 for a detailed discussion of this school), which proclaimed, contrary to the Frankfurt school, that audience behavior is selective. The uses-and-gratifications approach (McQuail 1984, Rosengren et al. 1985) relies on a set of interrelated core assumptions focusing on gratification-seeking, individual motivation and the user's ability to consciously decide how to use different kinds of media. Although these assumptions continue to guide recent uses-and-gratifications research on mobile phones (Leung/Wei 2000) and the Internet (Papacharissi/Rubin 2000), criticism of the approach has been abundant. Scholars of political communication, political economy of media, and cultural studies (Morley 1980, 1993; Hall 1985, 1997; Ang 1991, 1996; Downing 1996; Nightingale 1996) have argued that the uses-and-gratifications approach is theoretically underdeveloped, ignores structural power, assumes social stability, and focuses excessively on the individual, critiques with which some uses-and-gratifications scholars (see, for example, Rosengren et al. 1985) agreed. This criticism notwithstanding, the uses-and-gratifications literature established audience activity as a major area of concern for social science inquiry.

Research on audience activity took another turn with the development at the University of Birmingham in Great Britain of the interdisciplinary intellectual formation known as cultural studies. An influential essay by leading cultural studies scholar Stuart Hall titled *Encoding/Decoding* (Hall 1980) proposed an approach to communication processes that focuses on the relationship that audiences have to both the media text and the social context of media use. Hall distinguished four stages of the process—production, circulation, distribution/consumption and reproduction—each of which, Hall argued, is necessary to the entire process but none of which would be the exclusive determinant of how people make use of mediated communication in their daily lives. Rather, media texts could be understood in terms of three hypothetical codes: (1) the "dominant-hegemonic," (2) the negotiated, or (3) the oppositional. Power exists throughout the process in the form of hegemonic, commonsensical practices. Hall essentially viewed the process of communication as the "reproduction of the meanings of the social formation" (Nightingale 1996, 29), but was later criticized for proposing an "assembly line" communication model. Nonetheless, implicit in the formulation was the assumption of audience activity, granting to audiences various levels of interpretive agency culminating in a hypothetically oppositional decoding of mediated communication.

Active audience research grounded in the cultural studies tradition grew in the 1980s, beginning in Great Britain and migrating to North America and later to Australia, Latin America, and Scandinavia. Several studies teased out the empirical implications of Hall's encoding/decoding, including some that preceded or coincided with the publication of his article: examples include Brunsdon and Morley's *Everyday Television: Nationwide* (1978) or Morley's *The "Nationwide" Audience* (1980). Other studies, mostly centered on single television programs, used the encoding/decoding model to focus variously on both media "production" and "reception" (Hobson 1982; Ang 1985; Buckingham 1987; Lull 1988; Liebes/Katz 1990). Most of these projects, and even the Scandinavian school of reception studies (Drotner 1994, Tufte 2000), which emphasized empirical, social scientific but qualitative research on media audiences, highlight the socially constructed nature of the television audience, echoing Hartley's statement that the audience "is a fiction that serves the imagining institutions" (1992, 105). To what extent do these seemingly disparate theories of the audience inform our understanding of Arab audiences?

Dreams and Nightmares about the Arab Audience

How the Arab audience has been imagined has changed over time. In the presatellite television era, roughly from the 1950s to 1991, Arab states launched television services with assumptions about audiences being subjects to be manipulated, citizens to be modernized, or potential sinners to be kept on the virtuous path. In some cases, as in Lebanon, advertising has been a part of television since its early days, imagining viewers as consumers. In others, like Saudi Arabia, it took several decades before advertising was allowed. There were a few cases, most notably that of Egypt under Nasser, in which broadcasting was explicitly harnessed to project political influence beyond national borders. With the advent of satellite television in the early 1990s, states attempted to maintain and expand their influence over Arab viewers, but commercial considerations became more important. Even for analytical purposes, therefore, it is nearly impossible to separate political and economic considerations of Arab audiences, as the two are tightly intertwined. Similarly, in the Arab context, the dichotomy between news and entertainment obscures more than it illuminates, since audiences of both kinds of programs are subject to overlapping combinations of political and economic calculation.

Since 2001 there has emerged a global struggle for Arab "hearts and minds" involving various Arab, U.S., and Iranian networks and forthcoming Arabic channels run by the BBC, France, and Russia. Most of these channels were, or will be, launched to counter Al-Jazeera, the subject of intense, even obsessive interest in Arab and Western capitals. The Qatari news and current affairs satellite channel greatly contributed to reversing decades of unidirectional news flows emanating from the West that were problematic on several fronts. As such, it provided an alternative voice in the global media sphere. However, the excessive focus on Al-Jazeera is revealing of assumptions made about its putative audience. After all, the audience itself is the linchpin of the entire media industry. In the case of Al-Jazeera, however, its geopolitical significance stems from its entanglements in the most contested events of the last decade, including the 9/11 attacks and the ensuing so-called war on terrorism launched by the Bush administration, the invasions of Afghanistan and Iraq, the Arab-Israeli conflict and related scandals and controversies such as Abu Ghraib, "extraordinary rendition," and the upheaval over the Danish cartoons of the prophet Muhammad, all of which Al-Jazeera covered extensively.

The shift in descriptions of Al-Jazeera pre- and post-9/11 in U.S. public discourse betrays a rising anxiety about Al-Jazeera's audience. This anxiety is premised on assumptions of audience passivity haunted by hypothetical audience activity. In other words, the shift of perception of Al-Jazeera exposes the inseparability of assumptions about audience activity and passivity while at the same time revealing various ways of imagining audience activity. Before 9/11, Al-Jazeera was hailed as a harbinger of democracy, stirring the Arab political soup, emboldening dissenters and exposing repressive and corrupt regimes. Post-9/11, perceptions of Al-Jazeera darkened, as expressed by Ajami when he writes that "Al-Jazeera deliberately fans the flames of Muslim outrage [its] virulent anti-American bias undercuts all of its virtues," concluding, that "It is in the final analysis, a dangerous force. And it should be treated as such by Washington" (Ajami 2001). Akin to Frankfurt school views of atomized individuals vulnerable to fascist propaganda, in the mind of the Bush administration and writers sympathetic to the administration's views, Al-Jazeera's audience was now reduced to a core subaudience of angry Muslim men, probably with long beards, angry smirks, fists in the air, and an inclination toward violence that they might act upon after watching the infamous bin Laden videos aired by the network. In the words of the *New York Times*, "[Al-Jazeera's] real importance stems from its Arab audience, where pictures of heavy casualties caused by American bombing could arouse anti-American feelings" (Perlez/Rutenberg 2003).

There are also corporate dreams about Arab audiences. Stretching from Morocco to Iraq there are a quarter billion potential Arabic-speaking viewers. Arabic speakers constitute one of the largest single-language audiences in the world—albeit with various Arabic accents and variations. Since the advent of satellite television in the early 1990s, the trade magazine *Arab Ad* has featured myriad articles about the advertising opportunities opened up by the regionalization of Arab media space. Corporate dreams about Arab audiences have been tempered by several factors, the first of which is the fact that those Arab viewers attractive to advertisers are concentrated in the Gulf Cooperation Council (GCC) states, especially Saudi Arabia, Kuwait, Qatar, and the UAE, with urban pockets of upper-middle-class affluence in other Arab countries. This means that large subsections would be able to watch free-to-air television signals without attracting advertising spending. Recently there has been renewed industry attention on North Africa, but there have been few concrete steps in that regard. Another obstacle is the state of corporate audience research.

Though some companies like the Pan-Arab Research Center and IPSOS-STAT have achieved a measure of respectability within the media industry, doubts remains about how fully "objective" their studies are, especially when it comes to their major clients. Focusing extensively on the countries of the GCC, audience researchers are confronted with various forms of resistance because of privacy or security issues. In this context there is a raging debate over "people meters" and other auditing and audience measurement techniques, which reflect both commercial anxieties over audiences and popular resistance to corporate surveillance. To be fully operational and sustainable, an advertising-supported media environment requires reliable audience research. A third obstacle facing corporate imaginings of the Arab audience is the fact that advertising spending in the Middle East and North Africa is the second lowest in the world after sub-Saharan Africa. In 2005, advertising spending was nearing five billion dollars, although this reflects rate-cards figures. The real figure, according to Arab advertising mogul Antoine Choueiri, was two billion dollars. Newspapers still get the lion's share, and television accounts for only 20 percent of the rate-card amount (Choueiri 2006). Because of these problems, commercially minded channels are trying to develop nonadvertising revenue sources. Hence the rise of game shows, music video channels, and reality TV, whose "interactive" features enable media companies to exploit alternative ways of profiting financially from Arab audiences.

Arab Audiences from Activity to Interactivity

If the obsession over Al-Jazeera stems from assumptions about the channel's impact on a putatively passive audience absorbing a relentless stream of anti-Americanism, it is the channel's reliance on "interactive" formats that have elicited much of the hype about its supposedly democratizing impact. Open microphone shows like *Minbar Al-Jazeera* (Al-Jazeera's Pulpit) and other shows that embed viewers' live telephone calls and e-mail messages have quickly become the channel's trademark, in sharp contrast with the scripted shows of its chief competitor Al-Arabiya. Through audience feedback, Al-Jazeera can thus claim to have its hand on the pulse of the Arab street. This is a harbinger of uses of "interactivity" as a basis for fundamental changes in the ways Arab media institutions view their audiences.

Like "activity," the notion of "interactivity" has elicited a lot of interest from media and communications researchers. Interactivity is generally defined as the "extent to which later messages recount the relatedness of earlier messages" and is defined as "a theoretical construct that grapples with the origins of captivation, fascination, and allure that can be inherent in computer-mediated groups" (Rafaeli/Sudweeks 1997, 159). Harking back to the Shannon and Weaver mathematical communication model, Rice defines "full" interactivity to "imply that the sender and receiver roles are interchangeable" (Rice 1984, 35), an emphasis echoed in Rogers's definition of interactivity as "the degree to which participants in a communication process can exchange roles in and have control over their mutual discourse" (Rogers 1994, 314).

The focus of these functionalist definitions of interactivity on a blurring of the boundaries between various participants in the communication process and their emphasis on user control, even if illusory, resonates with Arab media programmers and advertisers working within an unreliable advertising-supported media industry. Various media applications falling under the rubric of interactivity are seen by some Arab media corporations as a promising alternative to the partly and sporadically successful advertising-supported system. In addition to live telephone calls and e-mail messages, text messaging (known as the short messaging system, or SMS) and the multimedia messaging system (MMS) have been increasingly integrated into reality television, game, and music shows. In contrast to cybernetic understandings of communication in terms of senders and receivers, Arab media institutions have in recent years adopted what can perhaps be best described as a modified encoding-decoding model through which viewers are given a sense of agency and where various staged "oppositional" readings of the media text stand at the heart of the new trend in programming; an example of this would be in reality TV shows, where viewers have the "power" to compete with each other in order to influence the course of events.

For media institutions, reality TV is an attractive genre because it enables the integration of television with the Internet and mobile phones, creating "hypermedia space." Based on media convergence, hypermedia space is supplanting advertising as a source of profit. Nominations or votes for contestants via text-messaging or websites, requests and votes for favorite music videos, or calls to live music or game shows are now constant features of the Arab media industry. Although it is impossible to obtain completely reliable financial figures from Arab media corporations and market research companies, it is an open secret that very few satellite television channels are financially sustainable. The advertising-supported model does not quite work in the Arab world, for various reasons enumerated earlier. A combination of technological developments and commercial imperatives has turned the Arab media industry into an incubator of what is essentially a new economic model for media operations resting on a new conception of the audience. It is, therefore, no wonder that in one of several interviews I conducted with him, LBC general manager Pierre Daher said that "the future of Arab media is interactive television."

LBC has championed the new economic model in various programs, most notably *Star Academy*, its flagship reality TV show. As a result, a new economic model based on interactive uses of information technologies gives media corporations very precise demographic information that can, in turn, be used to target superconsumers much like political consultants in the United States target the so-called supervoters. In this context, reality TV "highlights the increasing importance not just of surveillance but of interactive technologies that rearrange the conventional distinctions between work and play and between consumption and production" (Andrejevic 2004, 17). Without viewers' participation, reality TV shows cannot proceed, literally, since their narrative and commercial logics are arguably more dependent on people nominating and voting via the Internet and mobile phones than on people watching via the television set. From a Marxist perspective, voting and nominating contestants in reality TV shows is a reversal of economic relations, since viewers have to pay for their labor instead of getting paid for it. Reality TV reflects the commercial attraction of television productions that integrate interactive elements.

Though it is clear that media interactivity has promising commercial applications, the broader societal implications of interactive media programs are not easily discerned. At face value, interactivity appears to have many positive connotations. By transforming communication into a two-way process, it vastly broadens the scope of participation in social communication. Insofar as interactivity brings in a larger number of participants to Arab television programs—whether as live callers on *Minbar Al-Jazeera*, voters in *Star Academy*, or players on any of the myriad Arab game shows—it contributes to the pluralism of Arab airwaves. But in a regional Arab context where there are few accountable social or political institutions whose responsiveness would make the bottom-up, citizen-to-leader, or citizen-to-institution communication—the first step in a chain of social or political processes of adjustment, redress or improvement—interactive communication is for the most part like talking in the wind. For this reason, commentary and debate about interactive media in the Arab world has occurred exclusively within the market research industry operating in the orbit of the advertising industry.

Indeed, the advent of interactive programs has triggered a debate about audience research in Arab countries. At a time when controversy continues over whether to introduce people meters to Gulf countries, some are beginning to question the necessity of such a move. Recently, a leading executive with Omnicom Media Group has commented, "'Everyone will tell you that people meters are crucial, and that's all good, but the issue in my opinion is that TV meters are passé, an old story.... We should go beyond TV meters and I think in this region we have the opportunity to go to the next stage. It's about doing engagement studies, how programmes are engaging with viewers—not just how long they're spending watching them."[1]

The shift from quantitatively measuring the time spent watching television to qualitatively assessing viewers' engagement with particular programs is theoretically significant but logistically arduous. Nonetheless, it springs out of the recognition that interactive programming genres are creating new dynamics in the industry and new kinds of audience engagement (see Ghosn 2005 and Badi 2006, for press commentary on these issues). The notion of "engagement" seems closer to Stuart Hall's encoding/decoding model than to market research. Significant in this regard to advertisers and propagandists is Hall's notion of meanings embedded in media texts that "win plausibility for and command as legitimate a *decoding* of the event within the limits of dominant definitions" (1980/1997, 99). These he called *dominant* meanings, which achieve their status through invoking commonsense (i.e. hegemonic) beliefs rather than trying to directly promote socially nonpalatable interpretations of media texts. This distinction hails from Hall's preference for Gramsci's notion of *hegemony*, where power is exercised by building broad consent around the interests of the elite through indirect co-optation, rather than Althusser's concept of *interpellation*, in which power works directly through powerful state and social institutions that "hail" people to adhere to certain ideologies. Whereas an Althusserian approach is compatible with the days of centralized, state-owned broadcasting, a Gramscian perspective on the Arab audiences is a better fit with the age of interactivity, narrow-casting and niche marketing, where audiences "reproduce" the social-economic system through their own participation in it.

Viewer participation can be seen by practitioners of various kinds of propaganda—public diplomacy or advertising—as amenable to the goals of creating better-informed citizens and, paradoxically, more compliant consumers. But the sense of viewer agency is contrived by Arab media institutions precisely because it is built on an economically successful use of interactive devices. Although the advent of fully interactive television programs is not yet a reality, it would be interesting to examine the ways in which interactivity articulates political and economic anxieties about Arab audiences. Voluminous theorizing and empirical research notwithstanding, how audiences decode mediated messages and how they act upon that decoding remains a black box—no wonder recent industry efforts to install people meters in the Gulf was officially named *Project Illumination*. Commercial and political anxieties will undoubtedly continue to fuel efforts to measure and understand (or perhaps illuminate?) Arab audiences.

This theoretical exploration of Arab audiences suggests that more empirical but theoretically grounded audience research in the Arab world is urgently needed. Such research should avoid the ultimately misleading focus on Al-Jazeera. This is not only because such a focus reflects, on the one hand, the diplomatic and propaganda needs of Western and Arab countries hostile to Al-Jazeera's editorial line, and, on the other hand, the tendency of many academics to view Al-Jazeera as a beacon of journalistic freedom and irreverence—both equally problematic—but because such a focus narrows down the range and scope of Arab audience research. Arab audience researchers should also avoid the sometimes untenable distinction between news and entertainment and should instead explore the overlap between politics and popular culture, evident in the controversies surrounding music videos and reality TV. Finally, future audience studies should go beyond the exclusive focus on television and build research frameworks that integrate the press, television, mobile devices, and the Internet. More concretely, there should be studies of national audiences during major political events, such as recent elections or referenda in Egypt and Syria; and comparative multinational studies of various national audiences in the context of a major global or regional event, such as the 2006 war in Lebanon or the Hamas takeover of Gaza. Other comparative studies would investigate the ongoing "culture wars" and moral panics over various programming genres. Other research could explore the intergenerational and intergender implications of hypermedia space in the Arab world. Research projects focused on one major program such as Al-Jazeera's *The Opposite Direction* or LBC's *Star Academy* would be worthwhile to the extent that they focus on the social, cultural, and political "embeddedness" of these programs. As they go about conducting these studies, faced with audiences that are increasingly transnational, mobile, and technologically savvy, researchers would do well to remember that "the field of audience studies goes on because its object is a fugitive" (Bratich 2005, 242).

Notes

1. We Must Go Past TV Meters, says OMG boss, *Campaign Middle East*, September 24, 2006.

References

Ajami, F. (2001), What the Muslim World Is Watching. *New York Times Magazine*, November 18.

Andrejevic, M. (2004), *Reality TV: The Work of Being Watched*. Lanham: Rowman and Littlefield.

Ang, I. (1985), *Watching Dallas.* London: Routledge.

_______. (1991), *Desperately Seeking the Audience.* London: Routledge.

_______. (1996), *Living Room Wars: Rethinking Media Audiences for a Postmodern World.* London: Routledge.

Badi, I. (2006), Where Is New Television Technology Taking us? Viewers are Now Able to Retrieve Broadcasts they Miss [in Arabic]. *Al-Hayat,* February 14.

Bratich, J. Z. (2005), Amassing the Multitude: Revisiting Early Audiences Studies. *Communication Theory* 3, 242–265.

Brunsdon, C./D. Morley (1978), *Everyday Television: Nationwide.* London: British Film Institute.

Buckingham, D. (1987), *Public Secrets: EastEnders and its Audience.* London: British Film Institute.

Choueiri, A. (2006), It's Time to Raise Ad Spending. *Campaign Middle East,* December 3.

Downing, J. D. H. (1996), *Internationalizing Media Theory.* London: Sage.

Drotner, K. (1994), Ethnographic Enigmas: The Everyday in Recent Media Studies. *Cultural Studies* 2, 341–357.

Ghosn, Z. (2005), Free-to-Air Channels Pull the Rug from under Encrypted Channels [in Arabic]. *Al-Safir,* March 18.

Hall, S. (1985), Signification, Representation, Ideology: Althusser and the Post-Structuralist Debates. *Critical Studies in Mass Communication* 3, 91–114.

_______. (1997), Encoding/Decoding, in: A. Gray/J. McGuigan (eds.), *Studying Culture: An Introductory Reader.* London: Arnold, 90–103.

Hartley, J. (1992), *Teleology: Studies in Television.* London: Routledge.

Hobson, D. (1982), *Crossroads: The Drama of a Soap Opera.* London: Methuen.

Katz, E. (1959), Mass Communication Research and the Study of Culture. *Studies in Public Communication* 2, 1–6.

Katz, E./P. Lazarsfeld (1955), *Personal Influence.* New York: Free Press.

Kraidy, Marwan M. (2006), Hypermedia and Governance in Saudi Arabia. *First Monday* 9, http://www.firstmonday.org/issues/special11_9/kraidy/index.html.

_______. (2007), Saudi Arabia, Lebanon and the Changing Arab Information Order. *International Journal of Communication* 1, http://ijoc.org/ojs/index.php/ijoc/article/view/18/22.

Lazarsfeld, P. F./B. Berelson/H. Gaudet (1944), *The People's Choice: How the Voter Makes Up his Mind in a Presidential Campaign.* New York: Duelle, Sloan and Pearce.

Leung, L./R. Wei (2000), More than Just Talk on the Move: Uses and Gratifications of the Cellular Phone. *Journalism and Mass Communication Quarterly* 2, 308–320.

Liebes, T./E. Katz (1990), *The Export of Meaning: Cross-Cultural Readings of "Dallas".* London/New York: Oxford University Press.

Lull, J. (ed.) (1988), *World Families Watch Television.* London: Sage.

Macmillan, S. (2007), Pitches Heard for Saudi TV Meters. *Communicate Middle East,* February 13.

McQuail, D. (1984), With the Benefit of Hindsight: Reflections on Uses and Gratifications Research. *Critical Studies in Mass Communication* 1, 77–93.

Merton, R. K. (1946), *Mass Persuasion: The Social Psychology of a War Bond Drive.* New York: Harper and Brothers.

Morley, D. (1980), *The "Nationwide" Audience: Structure and Decoding.* London: British Film Institute.

______. (1993), Active Audience Theory: Pendulums and Pitfalls. *Journal of Communication* 4, 13–19.

Nightingale, V. (1996), *Studying Audiences: The Shock of the Real.* London: Routledge.

Papacharissi, Z./A. M. Rubin (2000), Predictors of Internet Use. *Journal of Broadcasting and Electronic Media* 2, 175–196.

Perlez, J./J. Rutenberg (2003), Threats and Responses: Arabic Television; U.S. Courts Network It Once Described as "All Osama." New York Times, March 20.

Rafaeli, S./F. Sudweeks (1997), Net Interactivity. *Journal of Computer Mediated Communication* 4, http://jcmc.indiana.edu/vol2/issue4/rafaeli.sudweeks.html.

Rice, R. E. (1984), New Media Technology: Growth and Integration. In R. E. Rice (ed.), *The New Media: Communication, Research, and Technology.* Beverly Hills: Sage, 3–54.

Rogers, E. (1994), *A History of Communication Study.* New York: Free Press.

Rosengren, K. E./L. Wenner/P. Palmgreen (eds.) (1985), *Media Gratifications Research: Current Perspectives.* Beverly Hills: Sage.

Shannon, C./W. Weaver (1949), *The Mathematical Theory of Communication.* Urbana: University of Illinois Press.

Tufte, T. (2000), *Living with the Rubbish Queen: Telenovelas, Culture and Modernity in Brazil.* Luton: University of Luton Press.

Media Content

CHAPTER SIX

Arab World Media Content Studies: A Meta-Analysis of a Changing Research Agenda

Muhammad Ayish

Arab media have been around for the past century or so, yet systematic investigations of their contents have been carried out only in recent decades. The launch of academic and professional media training programs in the Arab world, coupled with the growing role of media institutions in the region, seems to have stimulated vigorous debates about how mass communications outlets handle community issues and events. Although research on Arab media contents has markedly been an academic concern, other contributors such as market research companies and national and international government organizations have been well noted.[1] In the 1960s and 1970s the role of media institutions in socioeconomic transition and cultural integration was questioned in the light of increasing foreign media share of the emerging Arab public sphere. A good number of content analysis studies were carried out primarily to prove or disprove arguments about foreign cultural and media imperialism theses. Other studies were produced in the context of international New World Information and Communication Order (NWICO) debates centering on media as both tools of national development and cultural dependency. Those studies sought primarily to identify how media mirrored national progress in economic, social, and cultural arenas and how that could possibly bear on achievements on the ground.

In the mid-1980s the advent of globalization generated new arguments about global political and cultural permeation of national media systems as reflected in increased advertising share for multinational corporations; Western dominance of foreign news sources; the proliferation of global media outlets through satellite television and the World Wide Web; and the expansion of foreign investments in national media operations. Yet, although these developments seemed to have induced significant shifts in content analysis research agendas, the overall scholarly approach to media contents in the Arab region remains captive to political, conceptual, and methodological constraints.[2]

From a historical perspective, communication studies in the Arab world have evolved in three distinctive post–World War II paradigm contexts: modernization, dependency, and globalization. In the three contexts, communication has developed largely in tune with Western-oriented perspectives about politics, culture and social change. Daniel Lerner's classic, *The Passing of Traditional Society* (Lerner 1958), seemed to have focused research on a presumed active media role in socioeconomic modernization. Almost fifty years later, communications research in the Arab world continues to be driven by deep convictions concerning the media's power and guided by Western-oriented conceptual models (Ayish 2003). It is within this region's research tradition that content analysis studies have evolved their distinctive agenda. In this respect, the writer argues that although the focus of media content analysis in the region has smoothly shifted from the traditional "development communication" to the "globalization" paradigm, this research tradition remains generally reactive, limited in scope, fragmented, descriptive, repetitive, and premised on an erroneous confusion of content characteristics with audience effects.

This study draws on a survey of over one hundred media content research works carried out in the Arab world over the past forty years. The study population is not meant to be exhaustive but to reflect major trends and issues associated with Arab researchers' endeavors to understand what the region's media have been delivering to their audiences. In a survey of communication research in the Arab world, Ayish (1998) notes that the research landscape is dominated by survey studies and descriptive/historical accounts of media institutions and events. Even when content analysis investigations were employed, they seemed to have drawn more on quantitative/descriptive rather than qualitative/critical methodologies. In addition, it is noted that Arab researchers, at least those in academia, seem to have failed to utilize content analysis research findings to generate new conceptual frameworks for better understanding the region's media systems.

Content Analysis Research Agenda

This section provides an analytical account of content research works carried out in the past four decades and centering on nine themes: national development, cultural globalization, politics, terrorism, women, children, military conflict, gatekeeping practices, and new media. In one way or another, these themes have been addressed by content researchers in reaction to global and local political, cultural and social concerns pertaining to potential media effects on the individual and the community at large. It should be noted here that researchers' handling of the nine study themes has been defined largely by ideological and cultural variables that seem to steer the research agenda in tune with dominant social and political orientations in Arabian societies. A significant implication of this societal "conditioning effect" is that the output of content research tends to be generally descriptive, seeking to throw light on how media institutions are supposed to echo rather than defy existing social and political arrangements in the region. In this sense, the role of content analysis research has been overwhelmingly administrative, seeking mainly to produce further media alignment with the establishment in its formal and informal manifestations.

Media and National Development

The history of research on media's relationship to nation building goes back to the early 1960s, when Arab countries were engaged in national development in the postcolonial era. Early modernization paradigm research argued that media could contribute to national development by informing, educating, entertaining, and creating empathy among audiences about the positive values of political participation, social integration, and cultural cohesion. The 1960s and 1970s were critical years for media research as they unraveled the tragic realities of media failures to induce desired socioeconomic transitions. Researchers and international development organizations interested in exploring media performance at the time sought to investigate a wide range of contents and how they promoted or frustrated nation-building endeavors. To the disappointment of many governments and international aid agencies aligned with the traditional modernization paradigm, media content appeared to have been far too mediocre to create needed public involvement in government-sponsored development. Around the world it was noted that television programming suffered from both low production quality and the dominance of imported foreign materials (Katz/Wedel 1977, Nordenstreng/Schiller 1979). In the Arab world, the dominance of foreign news film and press agencies was a common theme in content analysis research (Kandil 1985; Ayish 1989; El-Sarayrah 1994; Ziadat 1998). Reflecting growing international debates on the New International Information and Communication Order, content analysis research in the 1970s and 1980s primarily concluded that the information flow imbalance in the region was bound to undermine media contribution to sound social and economic transformation. Researchers seemed to have based their arguments mainly on the amount of airtime and print space allocated to different issues and topics in different state-sponsored media.

In the 1990s and beyond, significant aspects of the traditional "development communication" legacy were brought to bear on content analysis studies in the region. Media messages continue to be seen as a critical factor contributing to the promotion of state-initiated development in social, cultural, and economic fields. Hence, analysis has been very much concerned with identifying the quantitative volume of coverage given to government-sponsored projects and activities as an indicator of media contribution to national development. An example is a study by Abdul Ghani (1990) in which he analyzes coverage by three Egyptian national dailies of community development in the southern regions, concluding that *Al-Ahram* ranks first in terms of space allocated to this coverage. In another study, Shalabieh and Ayish (1991) point out that population programs were accorded generous time on Jordan's broadcast media despite the apparent absence of a national media policy concerning issues of birth control and family planning. The same conceptual and methodological approach to media content within the "development communication" tradition has been clear in studies conducted by the Institute for Arab Research and Studies (1991), Rostum (1994), Shalabieh (1996), Al-Mesallami (1998) and Abdul Fattah (2004). In one way or another, most of these studies seemed to have been initiated as part of broader regional or international development projects with exogenous policy agendas. A major problem with these studies seems to stem from their conclusions of specific media effects as derived from content patterns. Both Shalabieh (1996) and Al-Mesallami (1998) have noted in their studies that broadcast and print media in both Jordan and Egypt play central roles in health and environmental development by virtue of their extensive coverage. This approach seems inhibit genuine academic investigation of media-government relations, which need to be elevated to more critical levels of analysis that view the notion of development as a mere euphemism for state domination.

Media and Cultural Globalization

Since the early 1990s globalization has spread across the Arab world, spawning national and regional debates about the potential impact of communications carried by satellite television and the World Wide Web. It has been argued that globalization epitomizes a new wave of "cultural imperialism" that was bound to obliterate national identities and sow the seeds of moral decadence in society. The new media have been perceived as Trojan horses for communicating foreign values and lifestyles that adversely bear on indigenous cultures in the region. To add credibility to those claims, content analysis research has come to address a range of issues, the most outstanding of which pertain to identity. The central concept shaping those studies relates to the role of media, especially television, in promoting or inhibiting Arab identity. Yet, the challenge most content analysis researchers fail to meet has been about evolving clear and practical conceptions of Arab identity. Nasr (2004), for example, analyzes national identity in the Egyptian press as a construct of specific features that make Egyptians distinctive. He concludes that *Al-Ahram*'s mainly positive coverage of Egyptians abroad has been instrumental for safeguarding Egyptian identity against foreign encroachments. In another study of five leading newspapers in Egypt, Jordan, Saudi Arabia, the United Arab Emirates and Qatar, Ayyad (2004) notes that pan-Arab nationalism was accorded a minor position in these papers' coverage of the Iraq war when compared with political and security concerns. Ahmad (2004) notes Egyptian newspapers' advancement of pan-Arab unity as a means of safeguarding cultural identity in the region. Shams and Madhkour (2005) observe that Saudi Arabia enjoys positive representations in the Egyptian press without resorting to paid image-building efforts. In all these studies, the concept of cultural identity has been framed in normative terms with media content juxtaposed against traditional values and practices as components of cultural identity.

Television has been the most extensively investigated medium of communication as far as the issue of cultural identity is concerned. The proliferation of new satellite television channels with entertainment-oriented content in the age of globalization has encouraged more research into the potential impact of programming on Arab communities. For example, Abdul Aziz (2004) studies a sample of Arab-world video music channels and concludes that advancements in music video production techniques have brought about new hybrid concepts of video clips that could create social instability and cultural disorientation, especially among the younger generation. Armbrust (2005), on the other hand, notes that video clips would not undermine the foundations of society but would stay as part of long-standing tensions over the status of youth in a patriarchal culture. He concludes that video clips would not liberate the individual and usher in a blossoming of democracy, although there is no question that they are a useful tool for sketching out ideas about sexuality and the body. In other studies, researchers seem to take a rather reconciliatory position that recognizes television's adverse effects while accepting it as part of globalized world realities. In her study of video clips on Egyptian TV, Khairy (2005) notes that Arabic video clips are part and parcel of life in Egypt and the Arab world. They are hated and condemned, yet sought after and watched. People view them as a "foreign element" that they can enjoy and criticize. While religious authorities call for them to be ignored completely, parents fear the effect they might have on their sons and daughters, while coffee shops consider them a major business attraction. Similar studies on television and cultural identity also sought to investigate the role of new television shows like *Big Brother*, *Star Academy*, and *Super Star*, as well as commercials, in discouraging indigenous cultural expression (Tayea 1998; Abdul Aziz 2000; Fakhreddin 2003; El-Gazzar, 2004a, 2004b, Jalal 2004; Qulaini 2004; Kraidy 2005). These studies are taken to task for viewing Arab and global cultures as two mutually exclusive entities that are impossible to reconcile. The notion of culture evolving in a state of continuous fluidity and transition seems to be wholly absent in these investigations.

Media and Military Conflicts

The spread of military conflicts in the Middle East since the mid-1980s as exemplified by the Iran-Iraq War (1980–1988), the Iraqi invasion of Kuwait (1990–1991), the Palestinian Intifada (2000), the U.S. war on Afghanistan (2001–) and the U.S.-Anglo invasion of Iraq (2003–) have raised questions about the role of media in fomenting violence and unrest. Several conferences have been convened to address issues pertaining to media performance in war situations.[3] A principal concern of content analysis in this area has been the representation of different parties in the media sphere and how that could possibly reflect on the media's professional and political standing. Abdu (1995) analyzes coverage of the Iraqi invasion of Kuwait in two Egyptian papers, *Al-Ahram* and *Al-Shaab*, noting that the former explicitly condemned the invasion while the latter kept what seemed to be a neutral position on the issue. Al-Kindi (2004) analyzes coverage of the Afghan conflict in one government and one private Omani paper, also noting that despite their common approaches to the war issue, both papers failed to present identical treatment of military developments. In another study, Al-Kindi (2005) also analyzes Iraq war coverage in six Arabian Gulf newspapers in 2003 and concludes that five of them describe the U.S.-Anglo invasion of Iraq as illegal and contravening international law. Only Kuwaiti newspapers seemed to have supported the invasion. Other studies following this pattern include Ghareeb (2003), Junaid (2003), Abdul Ghani (2004), Abdul Maqsood (2004), Haiba (2004), and Sadiq (2004). Again, as in the "development communication" research tradition, studies of military coverage seem to stop short of addressing the political constraints that shape their coverage of conflicts in the region. It would be interesting to learn how newspapers with varying political and institutional backgrounds portray military conflicts. Even so, it is more important to utilize content analysis findings to explore how different variables yield different coverage patterns.

Television coverage of the war in Iraq has also attracted considerable attention among researchers. In a study of television's handling of the 2003 fall of Baghdad, Zayani and Ayish (2006) note that three leading Arab-world television channels presented divergent coverage of the events, depending on their political affiliations. While Al-Arabiya reflected a more favourable treatment of U.S. and new Iraqi government positions, the Abu Dhabi Channel showed more balanced attitudes. On the other hand, Al-Jazeera took a more antiwar stand, featuring a wide range of anti-American views on the war. Likewise, in other studies, Mustafa (1996) has found that Egyptian television focuses more on reporting war events and developments without deep analysis and commentary, whereas Abdul Azim (2002) notes that the conflict in Afghanistan received more time allocation than the conflict in Palestine on the three channels, with both Al-Arabiya and Al-Jazeera giving more coverage to Palestinian developments. Harb (2004) finds that news of the Palestinian-Israeli conflict figured highly on newscasts carried by both Palestinian and Israeli channels. The news shown on both these channels was dominated by conventional news items. Shahin (2004) notes that the Palestinian-Israeli conflict figured prominently in newscasts carried by the Israeli Arabic satellite channel. The Iraqi problem was the second most-covered issue. Ayish (2002b) also investigated coverage by three television channels of the 2000 Palestinian Intifada, noting that Al-Jazeera provided the most extensive and live reporting of events in Palestine while the Abu Dhabi Channel confined its coverage to pre-scheduled newscasts. In addition, both Juma (2003) and Mustafa (2004) provided a descriptive account of Egyptian television channels' portrayal of warring parties in Iraq with no solid explanations of the variables giving rise to their coverage.

Media and Terrorism

The global "war on terror" waged by the Bush administration in the post-9/11 era has unleashed heated debates about the potential role of Arab news media in fomenting anti-American sentiments and terrorism. El-Nawawy (2004) has found that the Arab media outlets, especially the new satellite channels, have proven to be strong rivals to the Western networks such as CNN and BBC, in their coverage of what the United States calls the war on terror. In a study of several Ramadan television series shown on Arab television channels and dealing with themes relating to terrorism, Lindsey (2005) notes that those shows are part of a well-established tradition in which Arab governments use the medium of the Ramadan soap opera to educate the public about issues they deem important. The popular "terrorist" theme of the 2005 TV series reflected an eagerness on the part of governments facing problems with Islamists to spread an antiterrorism message. Dick (2005) has analyzed some Ramadan TV series dealing with terrorism and noted that some of them have irritated the United States, Israel, and Islamists alike— namely, Egyptian and Syrian soap operas like *Faris bi Al-Jawad* (Knight without a Horse, 2002) and *Al-Shatat* (The Diaspora, 2003), and Abu Dhabi's 2001 sketch show *Irhabiyat* (Terrorism Tales). With little systematic knowledge available to substantiate growing claims of suspicious media contribution to anti-Western bigotry in the region, more research as part of broader discourse analysis seems to be needed to adequately address the Arab media's handling of terrorism.

Media and Politics

Researchers' interest in media relations with political events and issues goes back to the postcolonial era when media institutions were used as mouthpieces by emerging states. Although media reflected dominant state orientation on national and international issues, they were also central players in interstate propaganda wars in the 1960s and 1970s. There was little propaganda analysis done; yet when political conditions began to open up in the Arab world in the 1990s, the role of media in democratization began to receive remarkable scholarly attention. For example, El-Sarayrah and Ayish (1994) have investigated content patterns in three Jordanian newspapers in the democratic transition era and found greater diversity in views carried by the press. In Egypt, Abdul Maqsood (2000) has found notable correlations between partisan press affiliations and their attitudes toward candidates in parliamentary elections. In a similar study, Sherif (1995) has found that political issues were featured in news commentaries (86.67 percent) while economic topics received 10 percent, and military topics 13.33 percent, of allocated space. He also noted that radio news commentaries sought to highlight the role of Egyptian political leadership at regional, national, and international levels. Similar conclusions were reached by both Nassar's (1994) and Hamada's (1996) studies of media representation of political actors and events.

In addition to the analysis of general political communications, researchers have also investigated media coverage of democratic elections. Levinson (2005) notes that during the 2005 Egyptian presidential elections, the state news channels dutifully covered and aired equal-length clips from each event, about thirty minutes for each candidate. Nightly news viewers saw Mubarak speaking to a crowd of thousands, promising to create new jobs, battle corruption, and continue the process of democratization. Ayish (2001) observes that while television journalism in the Arab world shares significant features with American broadcast journalism, it also exhibits some of its own specific characteristics, noting that most television channels played up political news to the exclusion of information about cultural and human-interest activities. Television's handling of political events and developments has also been addressed by Bekhit (1996), Ayish (2002b), Hassan (2002), El-Nawawy/Iskander (2002), and El-Tounsy (2002). In recent years, the proliferation of global satellite television broadcasters affiliated with foreign governments has also renewed interest among researchers in investigating their programming as a form of public diplomacy. Mobarak (2004) has analyzed the news contents of the U.S.-sponsored Al-Hurra satellite channel and noted a discrepancy between Al-Hurra's actual agenda and what viewers perceived it to be. Conversely, the content analysis showed that Al-Hurra was found to be objective, informational, and nonopinionated in its coverage of Arab issues. In general, research on media and politics in the Arab world remains fragmented and lacking in conceptual sophistication. Beyond the political manipulation model, which defines media relations with Arab-world politics, these studies have failed to generate new ideas to account for the media's role in political transitions in the region. Many Arab satellite television channels like Al-Jazeera and Al-Arabiya are often hailed as the new institutions of the emerging Arab public sphere, yet our systematic knowledge of their political content remains highly scanty.

Media and Women

A growing body of content analysis research has accumulated over the past decade on the issue of how women are represented on Arab media channels. This research trend has surfaced as a result of rising interest in the role of women in modern Arab societies and how that is presumably undermined by negative media stereotyping. Hassan (2004) concludes that Egyptian drama presents women in a very negative way as playing marginal or secondary roles that are not consistent with traditional perceptions of women and society. Juma (2001) has found that women appeared in two-thirds of TV commercials analyzed in association with the sale of goods and services, generally playing secondary social roles as subordinates to men. In her study of women on Al-Jazeera, Dwaik (2004) has found a strategy vacuum in the channel's handling of women's issues. In dramatic works, Jamil (2003) has found that scenes featuring violence directed at women totaled four per hour on average on Egyptian TV while the total was five per hour in films. Verbal violence was dominant in 59.88 percent of violent scenes, while physical violence totalled 21.4 percent and a combination of both was 18.98 percent. Sulieman (1988) has found that only one television station catered specifically to women amounting to only 1.28 percent of programming. Most program components focus more on high-class women in urban areas. Similar studies giving credence to women media victimization include those by Al-Ali (1995b), Al-Dhaheri (2002), Abu El-Naga (2004), Jaweesh (2004), and the Center for Arab Women's Training and Research (2006). The problem with those studies is that they seek to investigate media representations of women fully detached from existing social and cultural settings, ending up with critical conclusions about media manipulation of women. In addition, most of those studies addressed the media's handling of women's issues on an empirical basis when qualitative approaches might have proved more useful in rendering a more accurate understanding of this issue.

Media and Children

By the early 1990s, it was clear that demographic transitions in the Arab world were changing the face of the region's communities, with over 65 percent of the population being classified as young. Many national and international programs were initiated to support this age group long perceived as being vulnerable to the cultural fallout of globalization. Again media, especially television, were placed at the center of Arab-world debates pertaining to their presumed effects on children's attitudes and lifestyles through mostly entertainment-oriented contents. Most content analysis studies saw media in the region as tools of cultural domination that contributed to the spread of social disintegration and moral decadence in Arabian communities. Examples include a study by Nasr (1995), who found serious flaws in imported children's cartoons as represented by graphic references to crimes that could adversely affect children by encouraging them to emulate what they view on the screen; and Al-Ali (1995a), who found that television channels in Milwaukee, Wisconsin (USA) and the United Arab Emirates promoted divergent values relating to community standards of youth socialization. For the Tunisian press, Qantara (1998) points out that most news catering to young people was dominated by short service-oriented items originating mostly from urban coastal centers to the exclusion of rural areas. In an edited volume on children's programs on local and international television channels Ayish (2002a) has found that while satellite television channels seek to cater to children with different contents, realities demonstrate that more program development needs to be demonstrated. It was concluded that children's programs continue to draw on imported materials; locally produced programs are monotonous and dull; and foreign competition continues to stifle solid production efforts. Other studies investigating children-oriented content were conducted by Abdul Khaleq (1996),

Hassan (1996), Yaqub (2003), and Mezyed (2004). Based on empirical analysis, these studies were primarily concerned with exploring features of children's shows to draw out conclusions about potential effects. At least three of these studies argue that children are likely to develop aggressive behavior as a result of their exposure to television. Such shortsighted conclusions seem to fail to grasp the findings of worldwide social and psychological research that view children's behavior as an outcome of multiple variables, one of which might be television.

Gatekeeping Practices

An enduring research question around the world has centered on investigating gatekeepers' decisions as a key to understanding media behavior. In the Arab world, this research tradition has received wide acclaim among communication scholars and students seeking to explain media relations with the state and society at large. Sherif (1996) studied Arab news coverage in six Persian Gulf daily newspapers from January 1 to April 30, 1994, noting that the UAE's *Al-Ittihad* newspaper showed the most interest in Arab world news, followed by the Kuwaiti *Al-Qabas* and the Bahraini *Al-Khaleej*. The study showed the newspapers' dependence on Western agencies and sources of information for their Arab news coverage. Abdul Hadi (1996) studied news coverage in Egyptian evening newspaper *Al-Messa* from 1956 to 1985 and found a dominance of political content over cultural and human-interest content. Al-Rami (1997) studied investigative journalism in Morocco and noted that while the serious press presents solid political news with intellectual substance, sensational newspapers tend to present news materials about crimes and rumors that require minimum intellectual propensity on the part of readers.

Gatekeeping studies were not confined to print media news selection practices, but embraced broadcast media as well. Ayish (1997) compared news content carried by the then London-based Middle East Broadcasting Centre (MBC) and Egyptian Satellite Channel (ESC) and found that commercial broadcasters were drawing on less formal and protocol-oriented news selection criteria. Sharif (2003) noted that Saudi Channel One had the largest portion of religious programs drawing on emotional appeals. In another study, Hassan (1997) found that MBC had the largest number of news items, at (38.2 percent), compared with 32.4 percent and 29.4 percent for Egyptian and BBC channels, respectively. Newscasts carried by the three networks were dominated by political news to the exclusion of cultural and human-interest news. Bayoumi (2001) analyzed the contents of several live news and public affairs shows carried by Al-Jazeera and Egyptian satellite channels in early 2000 and concluded that such programs had the potential to enhance popular participation in public discussions on political and social issues in the Arab world. Nasr (1994) found that the largest time slot is given to news on MBC (31 percent) followed by the Kuwaiti Channel (29 percent), Egyptian Channel

(28.5 percent), and Dubai Channel (27.5 percent). MBC was the only channel that dealt with a wider range of political, cultural, economic, and sports issues and events. In another analysis of program content carried by Kuwaiti television channels in the mid-1990s, Muawwad and Al-Yassin (1995) noted that topics ranged from news to economic, cultural, religious, sports, and drama programs. It was concluded that Kuwaiti television programs were designed more to meet local development requirements rather than regional concerns. The problem with these studies is that they are largely descriptive and seem to draw on empirical analysis that stops short of investigating the nature of newsroom and programming decision-making practices.

Online Media

The emergence of online media in the Arab world over the past decade has induced growing interest among researchers in studying Web-based content. In a collection of studies on cybermedia coverage of the war in Iraq, Ayish (2006a) notes that the www.aljazeera.net portal provided comprehensive coverage of the events from a perspective that viewed the U.S.-Anglo invasion of Iraq in negative terms. The qualitative analysis showed that the Al-Jazeera website presented the conflict in Iraq as involving protagonists (anti-American Iraqis) and antagonists (who supported the U.S. invasion of Iraq). In the same volume, Al-Marashi (2006) notes that the Internet provided an outlet for a wide range of political attitudes to the conflict in Iraq, especially among those affiliated with Iraqi resistance groups. The investigation of online media has also drawn on issues already tackled by conventional media content studies. In an analysis of online media coverage of women, Ayish (2006b) notes that women continue to receive systematic negative representation in three Arabic news portals (www.aljazeera.net, www.elaph.com, and www.alarabiya.net) although the Internet had been heralded as a major tool for women's empowerment. The potential role of the World Wide Web in shaping Arab youth attitudes has also been tackled by a volume edited by Ayish and Kirat (2005) as part of a conference on this subject. It was noted that Web-based content relating to the young ranged from education to entertainment to general e-commerce materials. In a study of bloggers in three Arab countries, Taki (2005) notes that materials posted on the Web in those countries touched on taboo issues pertaining to pan-Arab and domestic politics, thus concluding that blogs play a central alternative media role in the region. Another study looked at e-mail based communications involving readers and editors of online newspapers in the Arab world.

The technical characteristics of online media have also been examined by researchers. Shoman (2003) has found that elaph.com lacks many technical features available in online newspapers in the West; it offers few interactive links and no direct chatting and editor-audience forums, and its layout is closer to that of conventional print papers. Yet, it offers impressive immediacy and boldness. Fahmi

(2001) notes that while many Arab news organizations have raced to establish footholds on the World Wide Web, many features of the Internet continue to be underused, the most notable of which is interactivity. Al-Shihri (2005) draws on Google-based Web information to analyze how Saudi Arabia is represented in cyberspace. The study found that U.S.-based sources provide the majority of information on Saudi Arabia, as the country itself seems to fail to address Web users with its views and perspectives, especially in the post-9/11 era. Metwalli (2004) carried out a content analysis of a wide range of websites and found that the multiplicity of online outlets has not led to news independence, as websites have sought to cope with the round-the-clock work cycle by reproducing content from conventional media outlets. But despite these research endeavors, online media remains highly underinvestigated, perhaps because of the current state of transition to the new media landscape. It is clear that Arab researchers seem to be losing focus in handling Web-based communications. The expansion of online media within the evolving information revolution has had a disorienting effect on researchers who need to develop more appropriate methodological and conceptual tools to handle the virtual sphere better.

Summary and Conclusions

The Arab world has seen increasing debates on the potential contributions of media to social, economic, and political change. Yet, these debates seem to be poorly matched by systematic content analysis research that could substantiate arguments raised by different parties on this issue. As this meta-analysis shows, content analysis works have been carried out largely by academics in response to emerging concerns in different phases of postcolonial Arab history. In some way, interest in media content seems to have underscored growing conviction about the potential role of mass communication institutions in national development in its broadest sense. It has been widely believed that media have enduring effects on individuals and communities and therefore should be subjected to systematic scrutiny to check their disruptive role. It has also been believed that once the negative patterns within media content have been identified, relevant policies and plans of action would be initiated to counter their potentially subversive orientation. This formula has applied to a variety of situations ranging from building collective empathy, to cultural domination, to the misrepresentation of women, to political manipulation, to brainwashing, to the promotion of consumerism, and to delinquency reinforcement. Yet, if content analysis research is meant to alleviate existing media-induced social, political and cultural woes, its findings are rarely harnessed to achieve this end. The fact that an overwhelming majority of content analysis studies were carried out as part of purely academic projects seems to have inhibited their findings from trickling down into policy-making circles. The existing gap between academia and living realities has aggravated this sad situation.

Although content analysis will likely continue to attract interest among researchers, especially those in academia, this meta-analytical study reveals that the experience of the past four decades has been disturbing. In this respect, the writer believes that since research is intrinsically an information-gathering and analysis tool used to assist our understanding of different phenomena or to support specific actions for the benefit of community, it is unfortunate that accumulating content studies in the Arab world have failed to achieve this objective. In its basic configuration, content analysis research has been reactive to emerging social and cultural concerns at global and national levels. From the development thinking of the 1960s to the globalization paradigm of the 1990s and beyond, content analysis research in the Arab world has been merely responding to local and global political, social, and cultural debates on the perceived media roles in contemporary Arab societies. Mainstream research has centered on media content relating to the definition of national development as a sweeping process of social, political, cultural, and economic transformation. The genesis of this "overobsession" with development derives from the historical experiences of post-colonial Arab societies and their transition into modernity. In the 1990s the dominant development paradigm in content analysis research began to experience new cracks as Arab societies found themselves in the middle of a globalized world. The emerging content analysis agenda has come to embrace new issues like domestic politics, child-oriented content, women's representation, military conflicts, and virtual media. In one way or another, this agenda has been a product of new developments in Arab societies, as is evident in political and social reforms, military conflicts, and technological developments relating to online communications.

Content analysis research has been excessively descriptive, seeking to achieve administrative functions. Arab researchers' preoccupation with descriptive or exploratory studies has been a defining feature of content studies surveyed in this article. A major implication of this trend is the preclusion of critical/qualitative analysis studies that seek to generate new insights into how media institutions work in an Arab world traditionally associated with political authoritarianism and social and cultural taboos. Although the evolving content analysis agenda seems to reflect researchers' perceptions of the issues that need to be investigated, equally significant issues remain largely unattended. Corruption, globalization, the erosion of national identity, deteriorating economic conditions, and the decreasing sense of pan-Arab unity have been rarely addressed in content analysis research. This could perhaps induce us to think about how restrictive political and social conditions militate against researchers' venturing into nonconventional agendas. Another implication relates to the failure of this descriptive research to produce solid conceptual frameworks regarding media performance and relations with established institutions. Very few researchers have employed qualitative methodologies of semantics or semiotics to understand the use of the Arabic language as a tool of communication and how that could be related to political and cultural variables. In his study of Arab media discourse in the age of satellite television

Al-Qarni (1995) identifies four pillars: authoritarianism, unilateralism, formalism, and sacredness. Al-Jaberi (1994) notes that the concepts of modern Arab discourse do not reflect the current Arab reality as they are derived either from European thought or from medieval Arab-Islamic thought.

An important but sad facet of content analysis research is that it is fragmented, with no comprehensive efforts on the part of researchers to harness their findings in the construction of macroanalytical frameworks drawing on common Arab media features. Very few reasonable works on Arab media systems have been based on media content analysis. One of the reasons for this gap is, perhaps, the absence of networking mechanisms among Arab scholars who seem to operate in isolation. Content analysis research has not adequately covered communications developments pertaining to the institutions of the new Arab public sphere such as the Al-Jazeera Satellite Channel; new digital and Web-based media such as blogs and online journalism; and media relations to the changing social and political transitions in the region. There is a lot of discussion about the media's role in the emerging Arab public sphere, but little evidence to prove or disprove relevant claims. Finally, content analysis research has been premised on the erroneous notion of equating messages with effects. This writer has come across many conclusions made by content study authors that bad media content automatically means negative media effect. The obfuscation of the manner in which receivers handle media messages seems to have led to this misinformed conclusion. The implication of this orientation is that media are often blamed for social and cultural problems simply because they happen to carry unconventional content not in tune with existing community standards. This conclusion would also provide a scapegoat solution to community problems that result from nonmedia variables.

Notes

1. Examples include research works carried out by UNESCO, government media organizations, the U.S. State Department, and the Pan-Arab Research Center (PARC) in Dubai, UAE.
2. This trend has been evident in the nature and scope of topics selected for analysis in media content.
3. Among them are the Arab Media Summit in Dubai, October 7–8, 2003, and the conference on Arab and Western TV coverage of the Iraq War organized by the University of Cambridge, March 19–21, 2004.

References

Abdu, M. (1995), Propaganda Techniques in Press Coverage of the Second Gulf Crisis [in Arabic]. *Media Studies* (Al-Azhar University), July, 71–119.

Abdul Azim, A. (2002), Television Coverage of Events in Palestine and Afghanistan: A Comparative Study of the First, Nile and Al-Jazeera Channels [in Arabic]. *Media Research Journal*, 119–172.

Abdul Aziz, M. (2004), Arabic Music Video and Its Implications in the Realm of Arab Media. *Global Media Journal* 5, http://lass.calumet.purdue.edu/cca/gmj/fa04/graduatefa04/gmj-fa04grad-aziz.htm.

Abdul Aziz, S. (2000), Television Advertising Trends on Arab Satellite Channels: An Analytical Study [in Arabic]. *Journal of Arab Studies and Research*, 235–273.

Abdul Fattah, A. (2004), Media and Omani Community Issues: A Sociological Perspective [in Arabic]. In O. Shaqsi (ed.), *The Communication Revolution and GCC Societies: Realities and Ambitions*. Muscat: Sultan Qaboos University, 200–226.

Abdul Ghani, A. (2004), Iraqi War Coverage in International News Portals [in Arabic]. Paper presented at the Tenth Annual Convention of the College of Communication, Cairo University, May 2–3.

Abdul Ghani, M. (1990), The Role of Egyptian Press in Community Development [in Arabic]. Unpublished PhD dissertation, Sohaj University.

Abdul Hadi, I. (1996), *News Coverage in Evening Newspapers* [in Arabic]. Cairo: Telestar for Media.

Abdul Khaleq, S. (1996), Cartoons in Egyptian Television: An Analytical Study [in Arabic]. Unpublished Master's thesis, Cairo University.

Abdul Maqsood, H. (2000), The Egyptian Press and Elections: A Case Study of National and Partisan Press Treatment of the 1995 Parliamentary Elections [in Arabic]. *Egyptian Journal of Public Opinion Research* 2, 45–67.

Abdul Maqsood, J. (2004), Images of the Self in the Arab Press: A Case Study of News Discourse in *Al-Hayat* Newspaper [in Arabic]. In *Proceedings of the Tenth Annual Conference of the Cairo University College of Communication*. Cairo: 1101–1156.

Abu el-Naga, S. (2004), Arab Women and the New Media: Empowerment or Disempowerment? Paper presented at the Cambridge Arab Media Project, conference "Media and Political Change in the Arab World," September 29–30, 2004, Cambridge.

Abu Zaid, F. (1986), *Press Systems in the Arab World* [in Arabic]. Cairo: Alam Al-Kutub.

Ahmad, J. (2004), Attitudes of *Sawt Al-Arab* Newspaper toward Arab Unity [in Arabic]. In *Proceedings of the Tenth Annual Conference of Cairo University College of Communication*. Cairo, 849–896.

Ahmad, M. (2003), Values and Behavioral Patterns in Egyptian-Produced Children's Cartoons [in Arabic]. In *Proceedings of the Ninth Annual Conference of the Cairo University College of Communication*. Cairo: 1513–1553.

Ali, F. al-(1995), Children's TV Programs in the United Arab Emirates and Milwaukee: A Comparative Analytical Study [in Arabic]. In: F. al-Ali (ed.), *Emirati Children and the Media: An Analytical and Field Study*. Cairo: Dar Al-Fikr Al-Arabi, 161–231.

______. (1995b), Women in Radio Programs in the UAE [in Arabic]. *Media Research Journal*, July, 161–201.

Armbrust, W. (2005), What Would Sayyid Qutb Say? Some Reflections on Video Clips. *Transnational Broadcasting Studies* 14, http://www.tbsjournal.com/Archives/Spring05/armbrust.html.

Ayish, M. (1989), Newsfilm in Jordan Television's Arabic Nightly Newscasts. *Journal of Broadcasting and Electronic Media* 4, 453–460.

———. (1991), Risk Communication: A Cross-Cultural Study. *European Journal of Communication* 2, 213–222.

———. (1997), Arab Television Goes Commercial: A Case Study of the Middle East Broadcasting Center. *Gazette* 6, 473–494.

———. (1998), Communication Research in the Arab World: A New Perspective. *Javnost/The Public—Journal of the European Institute of Communication* 1, 33–57.

———. (2001) American-Style Journalism and Arab World Television: An Exploratory Study of News Selection at Six Arab World Satellite Television Channels. *TBS, Journal* 6, http://www.tbsjournal.com/Archives/Spring01/Ayish.html.

———. (2002b). Political Communication on Arab World Television: Evolving Patterns. *Political Communication*, 2, 25–136.

———. (ed.) (2002a), Children's Programs in Local and Pan-Arab Television Channels. In *Proceedings of the Conference on Children's Programs in Local and Pan-Arab Television* Channels. Sharjah: Supreme Family Council Sharjah.

———. (2003), Beyond Western Media Theories: A Normative Arab Islamic Perspective. *Javnost/The Public—Journal of the European Institute of Communication* 2, 79–92.

———. (2006a), Heroes and Villains in the Land of the Two Rivers. In: R. Berenger (ed.), *Cyber-Media Go to War: The Role of Converging Media During and After the War in Iraq*. New York: Marquette Books, 126–149.

———. (2006b), Women and Online Journalism in the Arab World: A Case Study of Women's Images in Three Arabic News Portals [in Arabic]. Paper presented at the Launching Meeting of the Arab Women Media Report, Cairo, June 17–19, 2006.

Ayish, M./M. Kirat (eds.) (2005), *The Internet and the Youth in the Arab World: Proceedings of the Conference on the Effects of the World Wide Web on Youth in the Arab World, University of Sharjah, Department of Culture and Information and the Sharjah Islamic Forum, Feb. 18–19, 2005.* Sharjah.

Ayyad, K. (2004), Arab Identity as a Variable in Arab Media Handling of the Anglo-American Invasion of Iraq [in Arabic]. In *Proceedings of the Tenth Annual Conference of the Cairo University College of Communication.* Cairo, 689–730.

Bayoumi, A. (2001) The Role of Arab Satellite Channels in Enhancing Audience Participation [in Arabic]. *Media Research Journal*, October, 233–270.

Bekhit, S. (1996), News Values in the Egyptian Press within Development Policies: A Case Study of National and Partisan Papers 1987–1990 [in Arabic]. Unpublished PhD dissertation, University of Cairo.

Center for Arab Women's Training and Research (2006), *Arab Women and Media Report: An Analytical Study of Research Works: 1995–2005* [in Arabic]. Tunis: CAWTAR.

Dhaheri, A. al-(2002), Women in Video Clips [in Arabic]. Paper presented at the Arab Women and Media Forum, Abu Dhabi, UAE, February 2–3, 2002.

Dick, M. (2005), The State of the Musalsal: Arab Television Drama and Comedy and the Politics of the Satellite Era. *TBS Journal* 15, http://www.tbsjournal.com/Archives/Fall05/Dick.html.

Dwaik, S. (2004), Media Discourse and Women's Issues on Arab Satellite Television Channels [in Arabic]. In *Proceedings of the First Conference of the International Communication Academy.* Cairo, 647–675.

Fahmi, N. (2001), Interactivity in Arab World News Portals [in Arabic]. *Egyptian Journal of Public Opinion Research* 4, 211–231.

Gazzar, N. el-(2004a), Arab Identity as Reflected in English-Language Youth Magazines [in Arabic]. In *Proceedings of the Tenth Annual Conference of the Cairo University College of Communication.* Cairo, 1361–1398.

______. (2004b), Reading Culture in Arab Television Advertising: A Content Analysis of Egyptian Advertising. *Global Media Journal* 5, http://lass.calumet.purdue.edu/cca/gmj/fa04/gmj-fa04-elgazzar.htm.

Ghareeb, S. (2003), Portrayal of the Anglo-American Invasion of Iraq by *Al-Ahram* and *Akhbar Al-Khaleej* Newspapers: A Comparative Study [in Arabic]. *Egyptian Journal of Mass Communication Research* 4, 265–321.

Haiba, M. A. (2004), The Role of Egyptian Columnists in Supporting Arab Identity during the War on Iraq [in Arabic]. Paper presented at the Tenth Annual Convention of the College of Communication, Cairo University, May 2–3, 2004.

Hamada, B. (1996), *Media and Politics: A Study in Agenda Setting* [in Arabic]. Cairo: Nahdat Al-Sharq.

Harb, G. (2004), Treatment of the Palestinian Issue in the Israeli and Palestinian Satellite Channels: A Comparative Study [in Arabic]. Unpublished Master's thesis, Arab Studies and Research Institute, Arab League, Cairo.

Hassan, A. (2002), Arab and Islamic Issues in Arab Media: A Comparative Analytical Study [in Arabic]. In *Proceedings of the Eighth Conference of the Cairo University College of Communication.*

______. (2004), Women's Images as Reflected in Satellite Television Drama and their Impact on Audience Perception of Social Realities [in Arabic]. In *Proceedings of the first Conference of the International Communication Academy.* Cairo, 457–712.

Hassan, H. (1997), News Mix and Technical Structures of Newscasts on ESC, BBC, and MBC [in Arabic]. *Media Research Journal,* January, 7–64.

Hassan, S. (1996), Educational Values Embedded in Children's Television Programs [in Arabic]. Unpublished PhD dissertation, Cairo University.

Jaberi, M. al-(1994), *Contemporary Arab Discourse: A Critical Analytical Study* [in Arabic]. Beirut: Arab Unity Studies Center.

Jalal, A. (2004), Arab Identity as Reflected in Video Clips [in Arabic]. In *Proceedings of the Tenth Annual Conference of the Cairo University College of Communication.* Cairo, 1027–1054.

Jamil, M. (2003), Violence Representation in the Man-Women Relations on Egyptian Television Drama. Unpublished Master's thesis, Cairo University.

Jaweesh, K. (2004), International Advertising between Cultural Compatibility and Alienation: A Study of International Ads in UAE Magazines [in Arabic]. In *Proceedings of the Tenth Annual Conference of the Cairo University College of Communication.* Cairo, 1157–1194.

Juma, I. (2001), Women's Images in Television Advertising: A Comparative Study of Arab and Foreign TV Channels [in Arabic]. *Journal of Arab Studies and Research,* December, 169–219.

______. (2003), Al-Jazeera Channel's Treatment of the Issue of the Iraqi Weapons of Mass Destruction [in Arabic], In *Proceedings of the ninth Conference of the Cairo University College of Communication,* Cairo.

Junaid, H. (2003), Press Treatment of the Anglo-American War on Iraq: An Analytical Study of Al-Ahram and New York Times [in Arabic]. *Egyptian Journal of Communication Research,* April–June, 34–53.

Kandil, H. (1985), *Satellite Communications* [in Arabic]. Cairo: Egyptian Book Establishment.

Katz, E./G. Wedel (1977), *Broadcasting in the Third World: Promise and Performance.* Cambridge: Harvard University Press.

Khairy, A. (2005), Arabic Video Clips Flirt with Desires of Egyptian Youth. *Transnational Broadcasting Studies* 14, http://www.tbsjournal.com/Archives/Spring05/khairy.html.

Kindi, A. al-(2004), Omani Daily Press Attitudes toward the American Campaign on Afghanistan: A Study of Editorials [in Arabic]. In O. Shaqsi (ed.), *The Communication Revolution and GCC Societies: Realities and Ambitions.* Muscat: Sultan Qaboos University, 315–336.

———. (2005), The Third Gulf War in Arab Gulf News Editorials: Questions on Professional Ethics [in Arabic]. *Tunisian Journal of Communication Sciences*, June, 17–47.

Kraidy, M. (2005), Reality Television and Politics in the Arab World: Preliminary Observations. *TBS Journal* 15, http://www.tbsjournal.com/Archives/Fall05/Kraidy.html.

Lerner, D. (1958), *The Passing of Traditional Society: Modernizing the Middle East.* New York: Free Press.

Levinson, C. (2005), The Role of the Media in Egypt's First Contested Presidential Elections. *Transnational Broadcasting Studies* 15, http://www.tbsjournal.com/Archives/Fall05/Levinson.html.

Lindsey, U. (2005), TV versus Terrorism: Why this Year's Ramadan Shows Tackled One "Controversial" Subject, but Were Barred from Broaching Others. *Transnational Broadcasting Studies* 15, http://www.tbsjournal.com/Archives/Fall05/Lindsey.html.

Marashi, I. al-(2006), Iraq's Cyber-Insurgency: The Internet and the Iraqi Resistance. In: R. Berenger (ed.), *Cyber-Media Go to War: The Role of Converging Media during and after the War in Iraq.* New York: Marquette Books, 234–251.

Mesallami, I. al-(1998), Environmental Issues in Weekly Magazines: An Analytical Comparative Study of *Al-Mussawwer, Rose El-Yousof, Akher Saaa,* and *October* [in Arabic]. *Media Studies*, January–March, 37–68.

Metwalli, A. (2004), Websites for Satellite Channels, Newspapers, and News Portals [in Arabic]. In *Proceedings of the First Conference of the International Communication Academy.* Cairo, 439–473.

Mezyed, M. (2004), Egyptian Television Cartoons and their Effects on Children's Sense of Identity [in Arabic]. In *Proceedings of the Tenth Annual Conference of the Cairo University College of Communication.* Cairo, 1287–1360.

Mobarak, R. (2004), International Broadcasting to the Middle East: A Case Study of the Al Hurra Network. *Global Media Journal* 5, http://lass.calumet.purdue.edu/cca/gmj/fa04/graduatefa04/gmj-fa04grad-mobarak.htm.

Muawwad, M./Y. Al Yassin (1995), Kuwaiti Television and Comprehensive Development: A Critical View [in Arabic]. In M. Muawwad et al. (eds.), *Media Studies.* Kuwait: Salasel Press, 262–296.

Mustafa, H. (1996), News Treatment of Arab Issues on Egyptian Television: A Case Study of the Gulf Crisis [in Arabic]. Unpublished PhD dissertation, Cairo University.

———. (2004), News Treatment of the War on Iraq in Arab Satellite Channels [in Arabic]. In *Proceedings of the First Conference of the International Communication Academy.* Cairo, 279–309.

Nasr, H. (2004), National Identity in International News: A Study of How Al-Ahram Handled Egyptians abroad in Light of Social Identity Theory [in Arabic]. In *Proceedings of the Tenth Annual Conference of the Cairo University College of Communication.* Cairo, 1247–1286.

Nasr, I. (1994), Arab News on Satellite Channels: A Study of News on Four Channels [in Arabic]. *Media Research Journal,* October, 7–48.

______. (1995), Delinquent Behavior of Television Cartoons Characters [in Arabic]. *Media Research Journal,* July, 5–68.

Nassar, S. (1994), The Column in the Egyptian Press: 1985–1989 [in Arabic]. Unpublished PhD dissertation, Sohaj University.

Nawawy, M. el-(2004), Terrorist or Freedom Fighter? The Arab Media Coverage of "Terrorism" or "So-Called Terrorism". *Global Media Journal* 5, http://lass.calumet.purdue.edu/cca/gmj/fa04/gmj-fa04-elnawawy.htm.

Nawawy, M. el-/A. Iskandar (2002), *Al Jazeera: How the Free Arab News Network Scooped the World and Changed the Middle East.* Cambridge: Westview Press.

Nordenstreng, K./H. Schiller (1979), *National Sovereignty and International Communication.* Norwood: Ablex.

Qantara, M. (1998), Youth-Oriented News: The Case of Shoroqu Youth Supplement [in Arabic]. *Tunisian Journal of Communication Sciences,* December, 39–54.

Qarni al-(1995), Media Discourse in the Age of Satellite Television: Toward a Restructuring of Communication Institutions [in Arabic]. *Journal of Humanities and Social Sciences* 1, 260–292.

Qulaini, F. (2004), The Role of Television Advertising in Fostering Global Culture among the Youth [in Arabic]. In O. Shaqsi (ed.), *The Communication Revolution and GCC Societies: Realities and Ambitions.* Muscat: Sultan Qaboos University, 227–266.

Rami, A. al-(1997), Yellow Journalism and the Issue of Press Freedom in Morocco. *Media Studies,* October–December, 147–155.

Rostum, A. (1994), The Role of Regional Media in Community Development [in Arabic]. Unpublished Master's thesis, Sohaj University.

Sadiq, S. (2004), The Role of News Photographs in Highlighting Arab Identity in Non-Arabic Newspapers during the Anglo-American Invasion of Iraq [in Arabic]. Paper presented at the Tenth Annual Convention of the College of Communication, Cairo University, May 2–3, 2004.

Sarayrah, M. el-(1994), Foreign News in two Jordanian Newspapers [in Arabic]. *Journalism Quarterly* 63, 363–365.

Sarayrah, M. el-/M. Ayish (1994), The Jordanian Press in the Democratic Transition: 1986–1992. *Moroccan Journal of Communication Research* 2, 107–152.

Shahin, H. (2004), News Treatment of Pan-Arab Issues on Israeli Satellite Channel in Arabic [in Arabic]. Paper presented at the Tenth Annual Convention of the College of Communication, Cairo University, June 6–8, 2004.

Shalabieh, M. (1996), Types of Broadcast Programs and their Utilization in Health Communication: Theory and Practice [in Arabic], *Journal of Humanities and Social Sciences* 1, 155–198.

Shalabieh, M./M. Ayish (1991), Population Communication on Jordan Radio and Television Programs: An Analytical Study [in Arabic]. *Abhath Al-Yarmouk* 1, 129–151.

Shams, S./M. Madhkour (2005), The Image of Saudi Arabia in the Egyptian Press [in Arabic]. *Arab Journal of Communication and Media* 1, 51–134.

Sherif, S. (1995), News Commentary on Egyptian Radio: Content and Format [in Arabic]. *Media Research Journal* (Al-Azhar University), July, 349–413.

______. (1996), Arab News in Gulf Newspapers: A Comparative Study [in Arabic]. *Journal of Humanities and Social Sciences* 1, 107–153.

Shihri, F. al-(2005), Images of Saudi Arabia on the World Wide Web [in Arabic]. *Arab Journal of Media and Communication* 1, 11–50.

Shoman, M. (2003), Arab Online Newspapers: A Case Study of Eilaph [in Arabic]. *Egyptian Journal of Public Opinion Research*, October–December, 227–263.

Sulieman, A. (1988), The Role of Women's Television Programs in Raising Rural Women's Awareness [in Arabic]. Unpublished Master's thesis, Sohaj University.

Taki, M. (2005), Weblogs, Bloggers and the Blogsphere in Lebanon, Syria and Jordan. In *Proceedings of the Conference on Online Journalism in the Arab World*, University of Sharjah, Nov. 4–5, 2005.

Taye'a, S. (1998), Advertising Trends on Arab Satellite Channels: An Analytical Study of Sample Commercials [in Arabic]. *Media Research Journal*, January, 137–171.

Tounsy, A. el-(2002), Reflections on the Arab Satellites, the Palestinian Intifada, and the Israeli War. *Transnational Broadcasting Studies* 8, http://www.tbsjournal.com/Archives/Spring02/arab_satellites.html.

Yaqub, T. (2003), Contents of Television Programs in the Gulf Region [in Arabic]. *Tunisian Journal of Communication Sciences*, December, 15–38.

Zayani, M./M. Ayish (2006), Arab Satellite Television and Crisis Reporting: Covering the Fall of Baghdad. *Gazette* 6, 473–497.

Ziadat, A. (1998), Arab Media Flows via Arabsat [in Arabic]. *Tunisian Journal of Communication Sciences*, December, 103–183.

CHAPTER SEVEN

The Political Elites' Dominance over the Visual Space: A Qualitative and Quantitative Content Study of Lebanese Television

Katharina Nötzold

Many Lebanese maintain that Lebanese TV stations are the mouthpieces of their political owners in regard to news and political programs. A first glance at the distribution of ownership of Lebanese audiovisual media and a zap through the evening newscasts may result in the ad-hoc conclusion that there is indeed some correlation to be found between ownership and content, and that each station's newscast reflects mainly the ambitions of the sectarian and political group of its majority owners. The existence of politically affiliated stations is not negative per se, especially when additional stations exist that serve the public beyond the interests of politically motivated owners. Yet, the state-owned television channel Télé Liban (TL) is unable to fulfill its role as a corrective mechanism because it is merely (mis)used as a mouthpiece by every government.[1]

To build up functioning social systems, it is important to underline the commonality of norms and values that are shared by people of a polity. Mass media have an important function in the interaction of powers in modern societies because they permit a large number of people to be reached. They package common social experiences and events in stories that used to be shared in daily rituals, festivities, and customs. Mass media can exercise an integrative function and may contribute to the "corporate identity" of a group or even a nation because they transmit messages—through repetitions and by using modern standard language—that lead to shared experiences among the audience members (Neuber 1993, 11). However, the technical abilities of mass media should not be equated with direct effects of transmitted content. This closer look at the content of Lebanese newscasts therefore will not concentrate on the possible effects of these messages.

Objective

This chapter's objective, instead, is to find out whether common social experiences and events exist at all in Lebanese news that could serve as a basis for the "corporate identity" of the Lebanese nation that has emerged from civil war. The political ownership of the audiovisual media sector and the audience's perception of the political bias of each station make it necessary to scrutinize more closely the claim of partisan reporting. To pursue this goal, a content analysis of Lebanese news will be utilized to look for similarities and differences among the contents of the different stations. The assumption here is that the political owners are able to create their own "public spheres" (Habermas 1962) with the help of their audiovisual media.[2] At the same time, it is assumed that the views of societal groups who have no access to the media because they are not represented in media production are ignored, especially when their views collide with those of the stations' political shareholders. To explore how events in Lebanon are presented on TV, national newscasts on the terrestrial Lebanese channels were selected because such a newscast format exists on every station and presents itself therefore as suitable format for comparative purposes.

The Lebanese Audiovisual Media within the Postwar Political System until 2005

During and immediately after the Lebanese Civil War (1975–1990), many small TV stations sprang up outside any legal framework. With the introduction of the Audiovisual Media Law of 1994 and its implementation in 1996, the Lebanese government licensed no more than six private TV stations alongside the state-run Télé Liban. Only stations whose major shareholders were politicians (e.g., former prime minister Rafiq Hariri, speaker of parliament Nabih Berri, former minister Suleiman Frangieh, former deputy prime minister Issam Fares) or parties (Hezbollah) that did not reject the postwar political system dominated by Syrian tutelage over Lebanon's political life received the necessary licenses (Dabbous-Sensenig 2003). At the same time, most of these politicians were representatives of Lebanon's major sectarian groups (e.g. Hariri for the Sunnis, Berri and Hizbullah for the Shiites, Frangieh for the Maronites, Fares for the Greek Orthodox). Thus, the political and sectarian affiliations of the different TV stations reflected the fragmented Lebanese society, with its eighteen recognized sects. Most stations, with the exception of NBN, are today general interest stations featuring entertainment programs, films, sports, drama series, sociopolitical talk shows, and the news. All licensed stations are private enterprises and have to attract the widest audience possible to generate enough income to be viable operations.

Lebanon's postwar years until 2005 were characterized by the dominance of Lebanese politicians who accepted Syrian interference in Lebanon's affairs, the co-optation of most warlords into the political system,[3] the suppression of the mainly Christian opposition to the postwar political system, the silence about the missing of the civil war and the lack of serious effort to establish a reconciliation process, the constant emigration of young educated Lebanese because of the shortage of economic and political prospects, and the continued Israeli occupation of southern Lebanon until May 2000.

At the same time, various actors tried to pursue different visions for Lebanon's future, among them: the massive reconstruction efforts of Hariri in downtown Beirut, the establishment of a "security regime" associated with President Emile Lahoud, the liberation of Lebanon and the continued resistance against Israel by Hezbollah, and small grassroots activities for reconciliation by some civil society organizations.[4] The relevant political and societal issues that were discussed in private and sometimes in the opinion pieces in the daily *Al-Nahar* were largely absent as topics on sociopolitical talk shows; nor were they to be found on the agenda of news programs. It is within these parameters that the private Lebanese TV stations LBCI (Maronite), Murr TV (Greek Orthodox), Future TV and New TV (both Sunni), and NBN and Al-Manar (both Shiite) operated in the postwar years prior to the withdrawal of Syrian troops in April 2005.[5]

Methods

Content analysis is the method used here to measure a number of the variables of the messages, such as the dominance of some topics, certain people, and religious groups in the news bulletins of Lebanese stations. It will be used here to compare the results of the analysis of all stations to draw conclusions as to whether each Lebanese TV station really gives preference to the news of the political owner and the sectarian group with which it is associated. The classic definition of Berelson (1952, 18), who described a quantitative content analysis as "a research technique for the objective, systematic, and quantitative description of the manifest content of communication," is limited in its approach when it is only used to count quantities, because without any further qualitative analysis the results of quantitative content analysis often lack meaningfulness. Therefore Holsti (1969, 11) recommends using both quantitative and qualitative methods "to supplement each other." Moreover, Früh (2004, 35, 67) considers a dichotomy of quantitative and qualitative methods for content analyses not very useful because even qualitative content analysis draws conclusions from quantities and every observation or identification of text characteristics regarding content is first a qualitative act of analysis. Consequently, I have decided to use a mixed approach combining quantitative and qualitative methods to measure the quantities of selected variables supplemented by a smaller textual analysis of selected news items that were comparable on the topic level.

Quantitative and Qualitative Content Analysis of Lebanese Newscasts

Selection of Newscast Populations and the Sample of Newscasts

The present analysis includes all Lebanese terrestrial television stations broadcasting in the years 2002–2003 with a valid license and included LBCI, Future TV, Al-Manar, NBN, New TV (NTV), and Télé Liban, all of which can be received throughout the country and transmit evening news bulletins containing Lebanese news items. LBCI has the highest audience ratings for its evening news bulletin, whereas TL and NBN only have a small audience share.[6] More important, the selected television stations represent different political figures in Lebanon who dominate the postwar political system.[7]

The analysis takes as its starting point national news items that would reflect topics relevant to all Lebanese and allow comparison. Taking into consideration that news is the ideal place for the political owners of television stations to highlight their visions for the country, news bulletins are the easiest way to detect similarities or differences in content. Hence, the main evening newscasts of all six terrestrial channels between 7 and 8 P.M. were selected.

The Sample of Newscasts

Initially, I wanted to analyze the newscasts of an artificial week over a period of two weeks (sample size) covering each weekday once (see Cohen et al. 1990, 56–57) to study continuing news stories. Due to technical problems, I had to readjust the sample size and compared the complete set of news from Friday, October 25, 2002; Sunday, October 27, 2002; Tuesday, October 29, 2002; Saturday, November 2, 2002; Monday, November 4, 2002; Wednesday, December 25, 2002, and two Thursdays, March 13, 2002 (Ashura[8]) and April 17, 2003. The reason for covering Thursday twice is that the Lebanese cabinet usually meets on Thursday (except holidays), and political decisions receive different appraisals afterward in the evening news bulletins. I considered the inclusion of religious holidays because religion and affiliation to one of the eighteen religious communities of Lebanon play a major role in the daily life of every Lebanese citizen and because religious leaders exert much influence.[9]

The Unit of Analysis and the Coding Process

The unit of analysis was the complete news item. The sample for the content analysis was drawn from the six existing TV stations on the above-mentioned dates. The sample size of eight days was forty-eight newscasts, which made up 742 news items that had to be coded. Using a broad definition, all items pertaining to

Lebanon were included. Not included were items concerning sports events and the weather forecast.

Coding was done in Beirut by a Lebanese student of communication studies.[10] She was given the newscasts on videotapes, a codebook, and coding forms. The videotapes already contained time indications. During several meetings, I explained the codebook, and the relevance and accuracy of the coding categories were sampled in a pretest and the codebook adapted. The relevant categories of the codebook included the code for the particular TV station, the date of the news bulletin, the run order of the items, the time length of each news item, how the news was presented, thematic coding categories (see table 1), the political attitudes transmitted in the news items, the location where the event of the news item was taking place, the major protagonist of the item, and his or her sectarian affiliation.

Reliability means and requires that different coders apply the same classification rules to the same content, which necessitates clarity in defining the coding categories and proper training of the coders. The coder repeated her coding of the sample after half a year. This intracoder reliability value was 0.9 (Früh 2004, 177–183), which is considered good.

Presentation of the Quantitative Content Analysis

The newscasts of the six stations have different lengths ranging from around thirty minutes (TL, Future TV) to forty-five minutes (Al-Manar, NTV, LBCI) to one hour (NBN). It is valid to say that more than three-quarters of the news were reserved for domestic items in the research period.

Coding Category: Content of Local News

Although news bulletins are often filled with reports about decisions taken in parliament, about the work of the government, party politics, or power struggles between politicians, other topics such as relations with foreign countries, the economic situation, the workings of the social services, relations among citizens on the local and the national levels, and their daily concerns ranging from health services to education are also part of news bulletins. Because the focus was on Lebanese news, a detailed list of Lebanese content was established after tests to see which topics were on the media agenda during the research period.[11]

A first look at table 1 shows the overwhelming dominance of political issues: an average of 64.2 percent of all news items, which is followed by an average of 5.5 percent each for news items that fall under the religious and economic categories. The coding category "political" news item included the coverage of meetings among politicians, elections, the introduction of new legislation, party politics, political appointments or dismissals, national administration, and internal security when not related to crimes. The category "religion" was only used for purely religious events. When in the numerous meetings between clerics and politicians the news item had political connotations, the coder was instructed to code

Table 1: Subjects of Local News

	FTV	LBCI	Manar	NBN	NTV	TL	Total
Political	60 65.2%	89 72.9%	80 64%	89 66.4%	78 61.9%	80 55.9%	**476** **64.2%**
Diplomatic	1 1.1%	1 0.8%	-	-	3 2.4%	10 7%	**15** **2%**
Military/Defense	2 2.2%	1 0.8%	3 2.4%	2 1.5%	2 1.6%	4 2.8%	**14** **1.9%**
Political Crimes	1 1.1%	-	-	-	1 0.8%	1 0.7%	**3** **0.4%**
Civil Crimes	1 1.1%	3 2.5%	3 2.4%	2 1.5%	5 4%	3 2.1%	**17** **2.3%**
Sectarian Crimes	1 1.1%	-	1 0.8%	-	1 0.8%	-	**3** **0.4%**
Religion	5 5.4%	9 7.4%	4 3.2%	4 3%	7 5.5%	12 8.4%	**41** **5.5%**
Economic	4 4.3%	8 6.6%	11 8.8%	9 6.7%	4 3.2%	5 3.5%	**41** **5.5%**
Labor	-	2 1.6%	-	1 0.7%	-	-	**3** **0.4%**
Infrastructure	3 3.3%	1 0.8%	3 2.4%	6 4.5%	7 5.5%	4 2.8%	**24** **3.2%**
Education	3 3.3%	-	4 3.2%	9 6.7%	3 2.4%	5 3.5%	**24** **3.2%**
Arts & Science	4 4.3%	4 3.3%	5 4%	4 3%	1 0.8%	6 4.2%	**24** **3.2%**
Communication	-	-	-	2 1.5%	3 2.4%	-	**5** **0.7%**
Social (Relations)	4 4.3%	3 2.5%	1 0.8%	2 1.5%	-	1 0.7%	**11** **1.5%**
Social Services	2 2.2%	1 0.8%	7 5.6%	2 1.5%	10 7.9%	6 4.2%	**28** **3.8%**
Environment	-	-	2 1.6%	2 1.5%	-	1 0.7%	**5** **0.7%**
Other	1 1.1%	-	1 0.8%	-	1 0.8%	5 3.5%	**8** **1.1%**
Total*	**92**	**122**	**125**	**134**	**126**	**143**	**742**

*number of units

it as a "political" entry. Many items showed endless meetings among politicians with the intention of providing evidence of the latest achievements of the political leaders; this kind of item was also termed "protocol news."[12] The audience usually does not hear what the politicians are saying to each other and very often the news reader sums up the meetings.[13] A comparison of stations shows that all have "political" items as their dominant feature.

The relatively high percentage of diplomacy reports on TL results from its function as a state-run station, meticulously reporting about all the official activities of ministers, including meetings with foreign diplomats. This again seems to be more a protocol obligation than a desire to explain sufficiently to the audience any important policy decisions.

The next ranking subject in all stations but Al-Manar and NBN is the coverage of religious events. TL has the highest number of religious items due to the fact that it covers fragments of the Friday and Sunday sermons of the main clerics. As a state-run television station, TL is obliged to give balanced coverage to all Lebanese sects. LBCI also devotes several news items to religious events—mainly, to excerpts from sermons of Maronite clergy. In October–November 2002, the reliquary of Ste. Thérèse was moved around Lebanon and LBCI covered in its newscasts the arrival of the reliquary in the different Lebanese regions. Since several LBCI news department staff members view themselves as catering mainly to a Christian audience, they deliberately included news items to specifically serve their Christian viewers.[14] (The relatively low score for coverage of religious events at Al-Manar and NBN is explained in the section "Clergy on Lebanese News.")

In comparison, Al-Manar, NBN, and LBCI transmit more news dealing with economic issues than does Future TV.[15] Lebanese Shiites feel as a group economically more underprivileged than any other sectarian group.[16] The need for the economic development of "Shiite areas" is therefore a recurrent theme in Shiite political discourse and may serve as an explanation for Al-Manar and NBN's coverage. Mainly, Shiites and adherents of leftist organizations have repeatedly demanded more welfare services, and trade unions have protested against the sinking income levels of people with small incomes. This is reflected by the fact that "social services" issues were most often covered on NTV and Al-Manar. Both stations don the image of fighting for "the man in the street" who suffered under Hariri's harsh economic policies. NTV has an affinity to Najah Wakim and leftist organizations whereas Al-Manar usually shows Hezbollah adherents.[17] In the period of research, LBCI gave considerable space to economic critics of Hariri and the correlation with "political attitudes" shows that not a single economic item matched a "pro-Hariri" stance but three alone were "pro-Lahoud" and two supportive of the "opposition."

The relatively high number of "education" items on NBN can only be understood by correlating the categories "sectarian affiliation" and "political attitude." The search result is that the majority of items that are coded "education" cover officials who are Shiite members of the Amal movement as they voiced "pro-Berri" attitudes. Since these officials are foremost seen as members of Amal and

Figure 1: Comparison of Political Attitudes in Lebanese News

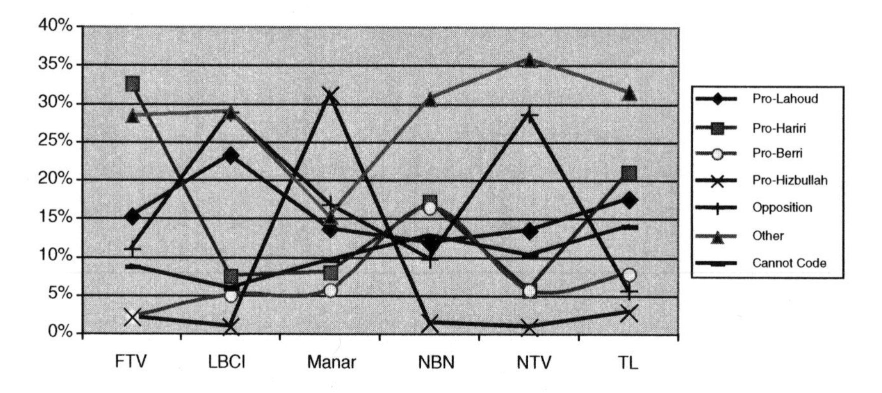

not as representatives of educational matters on a nationwide basis, they receive coverage only on NBN.

Coding Category: Political Attitude Transmitted in a News Item

The category "political attitude" is difficult to code and leaves room for subjective coding decisions. The coder was instructed to evaluate the general overtone in the news item and whether the content of the item embraced a particular political vision of one of the major Lebanese political leaders or blocs.[18] This point was discussed extensively before coding, and pretests showed that the coder understood to leave out personal political preferences. The categories of "political attitude" were defined as "pro" viewpoints.[19] It was decided to keep everything in "pro" categories and not to introduce "anti" categories to keep the data material manageable. Therefore, when the political attitudes could be better defined as "anti" categories and did not exhibit any specific "pro" tendencies, the coder was asked to use the "other" category. Only in those cases when the coder was completely unsure was she to use the "cannot code" category.

A first look at figure 1 proves that certain assumptions that are cultivated in Lebanon find their equivalent in the results determined during the research period. Future TV, indeed, has the highest rate of "pro-Hariri" reporting in its newscasts. Al-Manar is the station that has the highest percentage of "pro-Hezbollah" coverage, whereas NBN has the highest visibility of "pro-Berri" points of view. LBCI and NTV gave most space to opposition groups, compared to the rest of the other stations. Whereas LBCI mostly broadcast the activities of Christian politicians and groups who voiced their opposition to the pro-Syrian dominated *political* system, NTV's opposition was mainly made up of criticisms of the *economic* policies of Prime Minister Hariri.[20]

The most obvious difference exists among the results in the "pro-Hezbollah" category. Whereas LBCI and NTV each had only 0.8 percent "pro-Hezbollah" items, NBN had a mere 1.5 percent, Future TV 2.2 percent, and TL 2.8 percent. Al-Manar's newscasts, however, contained 31.2 percent "pro-Hezbollah" items. This big difference of 28.4 points between Al-Manar and the next station, TL, and the even bigger 30.8-point difference between Al-Manar and LBCI/NTV, is a first indication that Al-Manar is the most partisan of stations and that it carries the most support of its own provenance. It also shows that other stations did not give much space to supporters of Hezbollah and their political views in the news, partly because Hezbollah did not have any ministers in the government. Moreover, topics that were commonly associated with Hezbollah's agenda, such as activities against Israel, did not fare high on the agenda during the time of research.

Although Future TV has the highest percentage of "pro-Hariri" attitudes in its newscasts (32.6 percent), other channels such as TL (21 percent) and NBN (17.2 percent) still transmit a considerable number of "pro-Hariri" political views in their newscasts. The gap between Future TV and NTV (5.6 percent), which has the fewest "pro-Hariri" views, amounts to twenty-seven points. The latter number also highlights the fact that NTV indeed leaves little space to views that are closely associated with Hariri. This finding could correlate to the well-known antipathy of NTV owner Tahseen Khayyat for former prime minister Hariri.

Although President Lahoud does not own shares in LBCI, this station has the most favorable Lahoud coverage of all stations—at least in terms of the political views of the news items—with 23.1 percent, followed by TL with 17.5 percent. Surprisingly, even Future TV gives much room (15.2 percent) to news items with a "pro-Lahoud" attitude because the period of research was characterized by a power struggle between Lahoud and Hariri about the future economic direction of Lebanon. A more thorough look at the situation at LBCI may explain this high "pro-Lahoud" result. In October 2002 LBCI was the only "Christian" station left in Lebanon. Most staff members and many shareholders are Maronites—the sect to which the Lebanese president also belongs. Although many members of LBCI's political department disagreed with Lahoud's pro-Syrian stance, a favorable approach toward Hezbollah and his unwillingness to function as the political patron of the Maronites, they still supported the presidency as the highest political institution belonging to Maronites in the delicate sectarian power-sharing formula of Lebanon.[21] Shareholder Issam Fares and former shareholder Sleiman Frangieh were strong supporters of President Lahoud and were an integral part of the pro-Syrian faction in the Christian political camp. They exerted considerable pressure on the editorial policies of LBCI and fought with LBC-CEO Pierre Daher in court to install a censor in the station. Although Daher won the court battle, he did not risk losing his license but instead gave some space to political allies of Lahoud so as to enable LBCI to cover political affairs.[22]

Even though the coding was defined by "pro" policies, it is also enlightening to look at the figures from the opposite perspective. Low figures in the "pro" categories may either mean that a station tries to report neutrally about political attitudes or it has much "anti" reporting in its repertoire or that it does not report at all about certain events. Yet, since quantitative content analysis only provides information about manifest content and cannot make claims beyond that (Riffe et. al. 1998, 30), answers to low "pro" categories could be only found in a qualitative textual analysis of these news items.

Coding Category: Clergy on Lebanese News

Religious authorities play a dominant role not only regarding religious issues but also voice their opinions on political, social, and even economic issues.[23] This is reflected in the high level of coverage for clerics as the main protagonists of news items. Al-Manar's 20 percent coverage for clerics is the highest of all stations, followed by LBCI (16.4 percent), FTV (15.2 percent), TL (12.6 percent), NTV (11.9 percent) and a mere 10.4 percent on NBN news. Much more revealing about Lebanese society is, however, the sectarian distribution of the clerics on each station.

Figure 2 underlines some of the prejudices that are shared among the Lebanese people: the Shiite clergy is to be found mainly on Al-Manar, followed by NBN—both stations are associated with Shiism. The extraordinarily high number of Shiite clergy on Al-Manar (80 percent) can be explained by the fact that Shiite clergymen close to Hezbollah very often raise their voices on political issues and that their statements are extensively transmitted on Al-Manar. These figures alone do not say whether the clergy make only religious statements. Since many of Hezbollah's party members are clerics, it can be safely assumed that this double function finds its expression in political statements. A further analysis of this data reveals that indeed all Shiite clergy on Al-Manar (twenty items) have the coding category "political." Combined with the code "pro-Hezbollah" stance, fifteen out of the twenty Shiite clerics are featured in the "political" context and express "pro-Hezbollah" messages. This is a clear sign of Al-Manar's preference for giving voice to its "own" group. The very high number of Shiite clerics on NBN is expressed in the repeated appearance of Sheikh Abdel Amir Qabbalan, who is close to the Amal movement.

Christian clerics, especially Maronite ones, receive—in comparison to all other stations—the highest percentage of coverage at LBCI (45 percent), followed by NTV (40 percent) and NBN (35.7 percent). This again can be explained by the fact that LBCI is the only remaining station that is associated with a major Christian owner, and has almost exclusive Christian staff and a large Christian audience. Besides, clerics close to the patriarch acted as spiritual mentors for the Christian anti-Syrian opposition group Qornet Shehwan. Additionally, Maronite bishops issued during the sampling period several political statements about the tense political atmosphere after the politically motivated closure of (Christian) Murr TV.

Figure 2: Sectarian Distribution of Lebanese Clergy

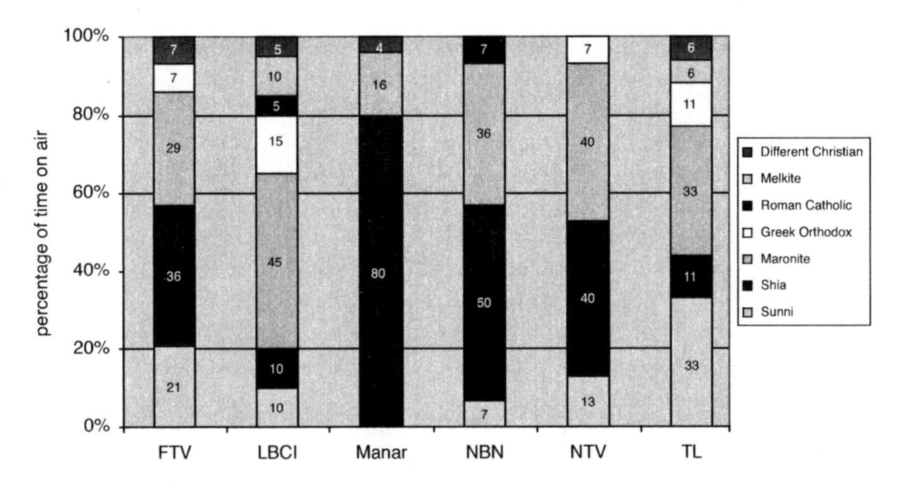

The overall higher coverage of Shiite and Maronite clerics on all stations is a result of the Lebanese postwar political system. Sunnis were mainly represented by Hariri and the current Sunni mufti of the republic is considered a politically weak figure. With the absence of a representative Christian political leadership after the civil war, Maronite Patriarch Sfeir has not only served his community as spiritual leader but has taken the role of highly valued mediator and political representative not only for Maronites but for all Christians. Shiites are represented by Berri and Hezbollah in the political realm but in Lebanese Shiism, starting with Imam Musa Sadr, the clergy also have outstanding political functions and give advice, guidance, and comment on political issues. Whereas Nabih Berri is a secular leader, Sayyed Hassan Nasrallah, Hezbollah's secretary general, is a cleric like some other Hezbollah leaders. A different reason for the overall high coverage of Shiite and Christian clergy is the inclusion of Ashura and Christmas in the sample.

More surprising is the high coverage of Sunni clerics on the state-run TL (36.3 percent). Less surprising is that it is followed by the "Sunni" stations Future TV (20 percent) and New TV (13.3 percent). Sunni clerics were rather silent about the politically charged atmosphere after MTV's closure, but during the sampling period a long-standing dispute between the Sunni Dar al-Fatwa/Hariri and a Sunni splinter group about the building of a mosque in downtown Beirut was settled. Hariri provided the money to build the Hussein Amin Mosque under the roof of Dar al-Fatwa, which was mentioned positively in Future TV but had slightly negative coverage on rival station NTV.[24] Al-Manar does not even mention a single Sunni cleric during the sampling period, which can be interpreted as meaning that Sunni clerics have no particular relevance in the current political system.

Figure 3: Distribution of Lebanese Regions in News Events on Lebanese TV

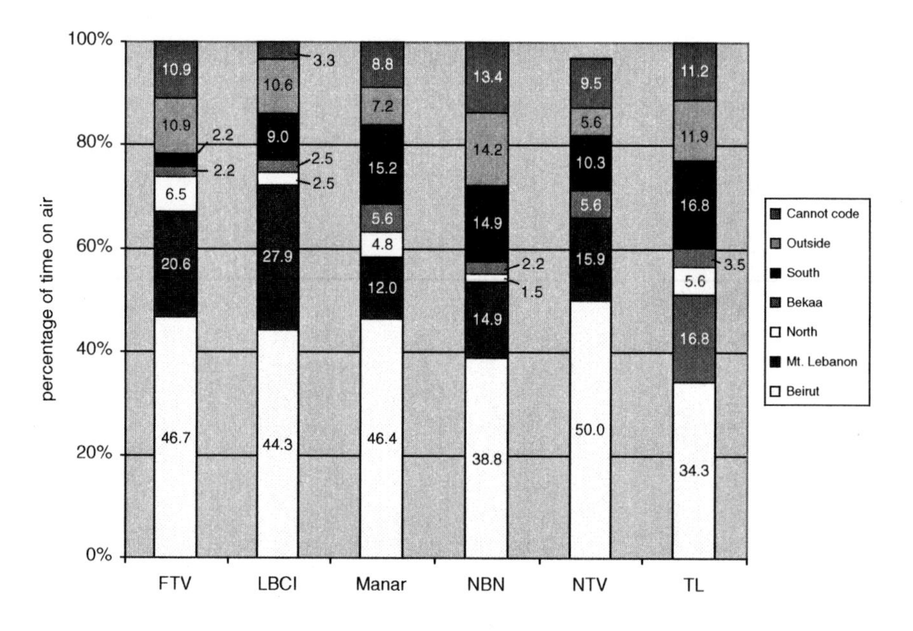

Coding Category: Location of Events in News Items

Beirut is the seat for the government and parliamentarians, for foreign embassies, high courts, all administrative directorates, and many educational institutions. Because political decisions are taken in Beirut in parliament or in long negotiations between the political and religious representatives outside parliament, it is unsurprising that the majority of news items originates from Beirut. It is also the place where all TV stations except LBCI are located. Figure 3 highlights Beirut as the center of coverage of news items. A look at Lebanese sectarian political geography is necessary to understand the relevance of this coding category. Lebanese regions are linked to specific sectarian groups.

Beirut is surrounded by the administrative and historical area of Mount Lebanon, which is densely populated and has the highest income levels in the country. It is the area that the traditional Lebanese power brokers, the Maronites and the Druze, hail from. LBCI, which is located in Mount Lebanon, reports most extensively from Mount Lebanon compared to the other stations. This figure can be explained by the fact that most Christian politicians live in this area and LBCI covers largely the activities of Christian politicians. Additionally, the seat of the Maronite patriarch is in Bkirki, Mount Lebanon. Since Patriarch Sfeir is not only a spiritual leader of the Maronite community but also acts in the absence of trusted and accepted Christian leaders as a political figure, his advice has been sought over the past fifteen years not only by Christian politicians but also by all other sectarian groups (Husseini 2004, 254–255). Therefore, many people visit Bkirki daily, and these meetings are widely covered by all stations, and this explains the relatively high degree of coverage of Mount Lebanon on Future TV, NBN, NTV and TL.

On the other hand, Al-Manar, NBN, and TL have a high level of coverage of events taking place in southern Lebanon, a predominantly Shiite area. This could be because Al-Manar and NBN are Shiite stations catering mostly to a Shiite audience. Shiite politicians have their electoral districts in southern Lebanon, and their activities there, such as attending graduations, receive wide coverage mostly at NBN (for Amal officials), Al-Manar (Hezbollah members) and TL (ministers with an Amal background). Since these activities are usually directed exclusively to their own sectarian community and do not have nationwide importance, it becomes clear that Shiite politicians feature prominently in items from Shiite regions in Shiite-affiliated stations. This is also mainly true of the Christian community and its relationship to LBCI.

All quantitative figures can only be understood if one possesses the necessary background knowledge about the political system, familial traditions, the sectarian distribution across Lebanon, the political activities taking place at the sampling time, and politicosectarian allegiances. Therefore it is necessary to include information gathered from other sources to come to a meaningful conclusion. Although I have already sprinkled in some results extracted using qualitative methods to embed the findings of the quantitative analysis in the necessary framework, one specific event should serve as an example for a qualitative analysis.

Qualitative Analysis: A Small Case Study

For the qualitative content analysis I have chosen news items of November 4, 2002, regarding the preparation for the Paris II Conference. This international donor conference, a recurrent topic in October–November 2002, intended to raise heavily needed funds and receive pledges of financial support for the reconstruction of Lebanon's economy. Since this conference was exclusively associated with Hariri and his economic policies, the plans for the conference also raised opposition from those who opposed Hariri's policies; they claimed that such a conference would merely lead Lebanon into more indebtedness. Such a controversial issue, which has found supporters and opponents within the Lebanese political elite and had an effect on all Lebanese, makes it possible to see how Lebanese TV stations with different political affiliations evaluate it.

The run order shows that only Future TV and TL ranked Hariri's preparations for the Paris II Conference as the second most important topic of news, whereas the other stations reported later on about it. Hariri's trip to Washington, D.C., was covered in reports of differing lengths as a separate news item by all stations except NTV (figure 4).

Moreover, LBCI and Al-Manar added to their short report about Hariri's tour another news item critical of Hariri's economic policies. New TV omitted Hariri's

Figure 4: Length of News Items for "Hariri in Washington" on November 4, 2002

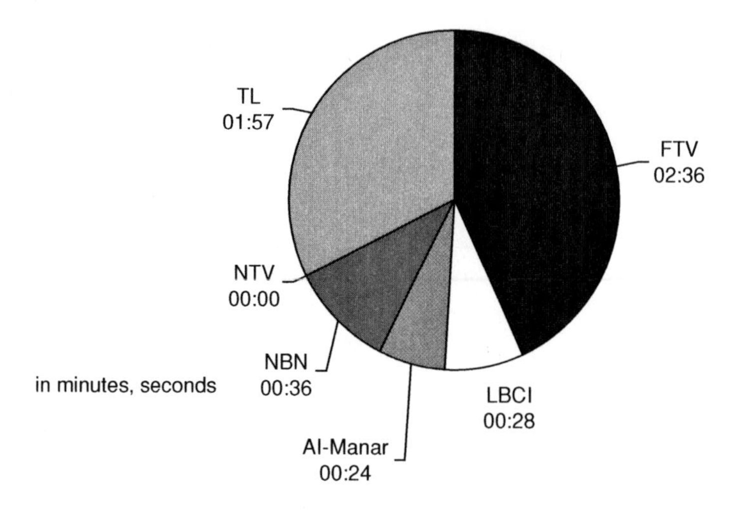

Washington trip altogether and had two news items in which the protagonists voiced their criticism of the economic policies of the government headed by Hariri. The most extensive report was aired on Future TV, which had sent its own reporter to report live from Washington about Hariri's various meetings.[25] The reference to Hariri's meetings, by showing that he was being received by two of the key players in the U.S. administration, was intended as a political signal to the audience. This political perspective of his visit was underlined by visits to the heads of the World Bank and the International Monetary Fund, clearly showing Hariri's economic agenda and political competence to his electorate.

LBCI neutrally stated that the prime minister was continuing his visits in Washington, where he would meet several personalities. Additionally, the viewer was informed that these visits were part of the preparations for the Paris II Conference.[26] Yet, the following news item reported that former prime minister Omar Karami had commented on the Paris II Conference. He was quoted as saying that "the conference may be successful. But at the same time we need some internal economic reconstruction. It is very important to stop the waste of money and it is very important to stop corruption."[27] Karami has repeatedly criticized Hariri and his economic policies. Hariri's dominance has been a thorn in the side of many Lebanese, especially to the traditionally notable Sunni families such as the Karamis, who had before almost exclusive rights to the premiership. Their displeasure with Hariri's continued presence at the head of most postwar governments was reflected in their accusing Hariri and his political allies of money squandering and corruption. Karami continued by saying, "The privatization file should be discussed thoroughly and slowly. It shouldn't be taken that easily and that quickly because it is one of the most important aspects of the country."[28] Hariri had to face continuous criticism about selling out the country to foreigners or his private interests, implying that he was amassing more wealth on the back of the "ordinary Lebanese" who were trying to earn their money honestly.

NTV also cited Karami. The news item is introduced by the news anchor thus: "Omar Karami has confirmed that the Paris II Conference is not a successful solution to get Lebanon out of indebtedness—the debt is becoming a burden to the citizens."[29] Al-Manar interviewed an economic expert who said that "Lebanon is going to the Paris II Conference not by its choice. However, we still can get out of this pressure by abiding to the schedules and know how to reshape our financial policies,"[30] which cryptically left room for speculation about who was forcing Lebanon to do it.

The different emphasis found in the reports of all TV stations about Hariri and his economic policies seem to confirm that each station is reporting with a specific agenda. Whereas Future TV positively stresses Hariri's mission for the good of Lebanon, especially economically, and does not give space to his critics, LBCI, Al-Manar, and especially NTV devote much space to his political foes or economic experts who disagree with Hariri's economic policies. This very brief case study may only serve as one example for the different assessments of events in Lebanon by various groups and how this is covered in the news.

Conclusion

A quantitative content study generates many values for the content variables of Lebanese news. Yet, these numbers alone serve only to describe the manifest content (Berelson 1952, 18). Therefore, here I have applied a mixed application of quantitative and qualitative methods to measure and interpret the content of Lebanese newscasts to arrive at more meaningful conclusions as to whether Lebanese TV stations indeed serve as the mouthpieces of their political owners and thus can be associated with certain sects.

The short answer to the Lebanese question would be that their observations are generally right—that on average each station's fare can be associated with the religious and political views of their majority shareholder.[31] A more differentiated look will highlight that many events that are of concern to all Lebanese or to the major sectarian groups receive a mention on all stations. More scrutiny through correlating variables and additional information taken from interviews and other sources will bring out the differences in coverage. These differences might be nuances in tone, the people invited to comment on events, the perceived value of a news item as reflected by the position in the running order of the news, or—decisively—the length of a news item because the longer the coverage, the more thorough the coverage.

The surprise of this content analysis is not so much that Future TV has the highest level of coverage of Hariri's activities but that Al-Manar does not have the highest percentage of coverage of religious events, even though many Lebanese and non-Lebanese consider Hezbollah a radical Islamic group. The key to understanding this figure and making it more meaningful is to correlate it with other coding categories.[32] TL, followed by LBCI, broadcasts the highest number of religious news items. Not only does Future TV *not* transmit the most items about economics—an assumption usually made because of Hariri's massive reconstruction drive for Lebanon—but Al-Manar, followed by NBN, has the largest coverage of economic topics. The numbers do not say anything about the quality of the news items. These might include positive evaluations, but also stories about ordinary people who suffer under the economic reconstruction plans pushed through by Hariri's government. A qualitative analysis of the texts can provide more detail, and the small sample of the coverage of Hariri's trip to Washington in the wake of the Paris II Conference hints that each station evaluated the events in a different manner depending on the political proximity of the major shareholder to Hariri.

To sum up, the newscasts in Lebanese stations reflect various realities, mostly dependent on the proximity of shareholders and sectarian groups to the issues—the persons or groups that are at the center of the reports. The divisions of Lebanese society are often reproduced in the different approaches taken by each station to cover the news. Even when the political owners do not interfere directly, news directors often enforce an editorial line close to the political attitudes of the majority shareholders.[33] An overall assessment comes to the conclusion that Lebanese news is elite-centered, often still presented in the form of protocol news, informing about the "good deeds" of the political or religious leaders, and containing mainly political news items; no station leaves much space to members of civil society groups, and there is only little room for the daily concerns of ordinary citizens. In fact, Lebanese news contributes little to the shared experiences of people living in Lebanese society, and the current state of Lebanese news cannot have any integrative functions. Instead, the different realities of the various political and religious groups are revealed through the newscasts, and differences are reinforced that do not contribute to a "corporate identity" but instead to a strengthening of factional identities.

Notes

1. Télé Liban is chronically underfinanced, and the political will is missing among those in charge to establish a framework for a sustainable public service broadcaster that serves all Lebanese groups and not only a few.
2. In Habermas's conceptualization, the "public sphere" is a modern institution and a set of values that bring private citizens together in public to engage in a context of reasoned debates (Habermas 1962).
3. Whereas Nabih Berri (now speaker of parliament), and Walid Jumblat and Elie Hobeiqa (both held the position of minister for the displaced for a short

while) as well as many others, have been co-opted into the political life, General Michel Aoun (who had fought the Syrians in the so-called War of Liberation in 1989 and 1990) went into exile to France, and Lebanese Forces commander Samir Geagea was indicted for the bombing of the Saydet Church in Zouq in 1994 and was incarcerated for several lifetime sentences, which he served in an underground prison in the Ministry of Defense in Yarzé. This left a bitter feeling among many Lebanese Christians, who perceived themselves as the only group punished for the civil war because their leaders could no longer represent them, whereas other militia leaders filled important public positions.

4. On the larger political scale, only Maronite patriarch Mar Nasrallah Boutros Sfeir and Walid Jumblat seriously pushed through reconciliation efforts in the Chouf area. The historic reconciliation visit of the patriarch in the Chouf Mountains on August 7, 2001, was watched suspiciously by the authorities and several Christian activists were imprisoned immediately afterward. This in turn only increased the growing anti-Syrian sentiment among many Christians and August 7 became a rallying day for them in subsequent years prior to Syria's withdrawal in 2005.
5. Lebanese Broadcasting Corporation International (LBCI) is the terrestrial channel of the LBC group. Murr TV is named after its majority shareholder Gabriel Murr but commonly known as MTV. Future TV is part of the Mustaqbal (Future) media group of the Hariri family. National Broadcasting Network (NBN) is jocularly named Nabih Berri Network. New TV (NTV) received its license only after a court decision. Al-Manar (the Beacon) started as "Channel of the Resistance" against Israel and has transformed itself in the "Station of Arabs and Muslims" and is closely associated with Hezbollah.
6. IPSOS: Lebanon—Top Ten in Prime Time. October–December 2002, http://www.agbgroup.com/public/countries/audiencedata/lebanon_402.htm.
7. With the closure of MTV only seven weeks before the sampling period started, an important voice of the anti-Syrian Christian opposition had been silenced and Lebanon's television landscape lacked an outspoken media outlet and excluded the representation of a large minority after September 2002. Although the politically motivated closing order of MTV has been revoked by Lebanese parliamentarians on August 16, 2005, the station is not on air despite Gabriel Murr's promise to resume broadcasting as soon as possible.
8. Ashura is the Shiite day of mourning commemorating the death of the Prophet Mohammed's grandson Hussein in the battle of Kerbala.
9. These holidays were Friday, Sunday, Christmas, and Ashura.
10. Despite speaking the Lebanese dialect, she understands and speaks the standard Arabic used in the newscasts. Additionally, she has an excellent command of English and knows the political situation of Lebanon well.
11. The coding categories for the content of Lebanese news items are found as headings in table 1.

12. This is a typical feature of traditional Arab newscasts; see, for example, Ayish 2001.
13. An example would be: "The President of the Republic, General Emile Lahoud, received today in the presidential palace in Baabda a delegation of parliamentarians representing Koura region and they talked about the necessity of economic development and they reiterated their support for the president's policies. Later, the president met with Metn MP Michel Murr to discuss the situation in the Metn region and Michel Murr ensured the president of the continued support of the people of the Metn, they also talked about the regional situation. In the afternoon, the president received a delegation of the Arab League headed by its president, Egyptian Amr Moussa. They talked about the regional situation and the need to stand united in the face of the aggression facing the Middle East. Moussa praised President Lahoud's pro-Arab stance and his continuous efforts for Arab unity."
14. This was voiced in several interviews conducted by the author with LBCI staff members in November 2002 and March 2003.
15. All items that talked about the state of Lebanon's economy and economic policies were to be included in this category.
16. Hanf (2007, 20) points out that already in the 1980s, all communities were stratified by income. Shiites were only underrepresented in the highest income group, but the lowest income groups were made up almost evenly by Shiites, Armenians, Greek Catholics, and Maronites. Thus, he rejects the often quoted equation of "poor Muslims" and "rich Christians." Until now, however, Sunnis and Shiites were slightly underrepresented in holding university degrees in comparison to other sects.
17. In Lebanon people can very often detect from the way a woman ties her head scarf to which group she belongs. Male Hezbollah members who are not clerics can often be identified because they never wear ties with their suits.
18. In a preceding step the political standpoints of different politicians were defined. The category "opposition" covered mainly those groups who represented the Christian anti-Syrian opposition but also Najah Wakim and the Communist Party.
19. For example, when the coder decided to code an item "pro-Lahoud" it meant that the political standpoint and policies of President Lahoud and his allies were expressed in this news item.
20. Najah Wakim, labor unions, and consumer societies were among those who rejected Hariri's economic plans for Lebanon.
21. Interviews with LBCI staff members in November 2002, March 2003, and 2004 in Beirut.
22. Interviews with LBCI staff in Beirut 2002–2004.
23. This happens either directly or very often through politicians who function as envoys of the religious figurehead.

24. The latter observations cannot be read from the figures but are results from a larger qualitative content analysis and may only serve as background information here.
25. To quote Future TV news, "Rafiq Hariri has a series of meetings, one just ahead with Secretary of State, Colin Powell and tomorrow evening he is going to meet with the National Security Adviser Condoleeza Rice. Hariri is concentrating more on the economic side than the political one on his visit to Washington and he is going to meet Finance Minister Paul O'Neal tomorrow after he is going to met tonight the Director of the World Bank, James Wolfenson again, but this time at the HQ of the Bank. It is the second meeting after he had another one with him at the Four Seasons Hotel. Hariri had also met the Director of the IMF Horst Köhler. Hariri is accompanied by Minister of Finance, Fouad Siniora, Minister of Economy, Basil Fleihan, and the Director of the Bank of Lebanon, Riad Salameh. The Lebanese delegation introduced during its visit its economical plan for Lebanon and the monetary plan of the Lebanese government to fix the economic situation which concentrates on the budget for the year 2003 in decreasing the spending and increasing the income and the desire after the Paris II Conference for lower interest rates in order to get the wheel of production going and increase employment. (...) It is true that the tour to Washington is a preliminary step to Paris II but the talks with the IMF have their own special importance. Hariri demonstrated Lebanese monetary plans for repairing the economic situation. The understanding of the IMF for this Lebanese program has the function of emphasizing the suitability of these procedures and encouraged the donating nations for an effective help of Lebanon at the Paris II Conference." Future TV News, November 4, 2002 (20:07:00–20:09:35).
26. LBCI News, November 4, 2002 (20:11:41–20:12:09).
27. LBCI News, November 4, 2002 (20:12:10–20:14:05).
28. LBCI News, November 4, 2002 (20:12:10–20:14:05).
29. New TV News, November 4, 2002 (19:52:01).
30. Al-Manar News, November 4, 2002 (19:40:43–19:44:52).
31. State-owned Télé Liban acts as mouthpiece for the government.
32. Al-Manar does not cover many religious events, but it has the highest number of clerics functioning as main protagonists. Further correlation reveals that these clerics are commenting on political issues.
33. Interview with various staff members of all Lebanese TV stations during October 2002 and March 2004 in Beirut.

References

Ayish, M. I. (2001), American-Style Journalism and Arab World Television: An Exploratory Study of News Selection at Six Arab World Satellite Television Channels. *Transnational Broadcasting Studies* 6, http://www.tbsjournal.com/Archives/Spring01/Ayish.html.

Berelson, B. (1952), *Content Analysis in Communication Research.* New York: Free Press.
Cohen, A. A./H. Adoni/C. R. Bantz (1990), Social Conflict and Television News. Newbury Park: Sage.
Dabbous-Sensenig, D. (2003), Ending the War? The Lebanese Broadcasting Act of 1994. Unpublished PhD dissertation, Sheffield University.
Früh, W. (2004), *Inhaltsanalyse. Theorie und Praxis.* Konstanz: UVK.
Habermas, J. (1962), *Strukturwandel der Öffentlichkeit: Untersuchungen zu einer Kategorie der bürgerlichen Gesellschaft.* Neuwied: Luchterhand.
Hanf, T. (2007), *E pluribus unum? Lebanese Opinions and Attitudes on Coexistence.* Lettres de Byblos Occasional Papers. Byblos: UNESCO Centre International des Sciences de l'Homme.
Holsti, O. (1969), *Content Analysis for the Social Sciences and Humanities.* Reading: Addison-Wesley.
Husseini, R. (2004), Lebanon: Building Political Dynasties. In V. Perthes (ed.), *Arab Elites: Negotiating the Politics of Change.* Boulder: Lynne Rienner, 239–266.
Information International (1999), *Televisions in Lebanon: Audience, Attitude and Programming Survey—1999.* Beirut: Informational International.
Neuber, W. (1993), *Verbreitung von Meinungen durch die Massenmedien.* Opladen: Leske und Budrich.
Riffe, D./S. Lacy/F. G. Fico (1998), *Analyzing Media Messages: Using Quantitative Content Analysis in Research.* Mahway: Lawrence Erlbaum.

Media Ethics

CHAPTER EIGHT

The Unknown Desire for "Objectivity": Journalism Ethics in Arab (and Western) Journalism

Kai Hafez

Journalism ethics is a system of values that, broadly speaking, defines aspects of "good" and "bad" journalism. Such a system can evolve under various circumstances and in different communities. Journalists in a specific country do not necessarily hold common values that are distinct from other national systems of journalism. Ethics is, however, based on a practical discourse on moral behavior among, for example, professional journalists and media workers or wider circles of interested public opinion. Academic media ethics has the task to analyze, systematize and evaluate the various ethical debates in order to discern the differences and commonalities in ethical standards that exist in national or transnational contexts. Ethics is certainly not the sole factor determining media output, but it is an important normative element. The interaction of political, economic, and social environments with individual and collective professional ethics is the driving force behind journalism. While the topic seems evasive and hard to define, ethics is at the same time a very "modern" issue. Since open media systems like those in Western democracies are hardly controllable by legal means or other repressive devices that interfere with the freedom of speech and publication, media ethics increasingly becomes the sole steering device binding systems together.

No matter how important media ethics might be, academic studies on Arab journalism on the subject are still extremely rare (e.g., Nimri 1995; Raffelberg 1995; Amin 2002; Hafez 2002, 2003; Abu-Fadil 2004). Searching for relevant material one can easily find a number of codes of ethics, mostly written by more or less state-controlled journalism associations around the Arab world,[1] but hardly any scholarly works can be found that systematically reflect on ethical problems of Arab journalism. At the same time, it would be totally erroneous to assume that ethical questions are not of any interest to Arab journalists—quite the contrary is true. Since 9/11 and the growing popularity of the Al-Jazeera TV network, there has been a huge number of conferences about Arab journalism around the world, all of them involving often heated debates on the quality of modern Arab journalism. Many of these debates were ignited by problems arising from the relationship between media and terrorism. The debate went so far that Al-Jazeera finally published a code of ethics.

However, there is a tremendous discrepancy between the vivid debates lead by practitioners on questions related to journalism ethics and the almost complete silence of academia. Journalism ethics seems to represent the "unknown desire" of Arab media studies. There are certainly a number of reasons for that situation. In general, many media scholars working on the Arab world face the inherent problem that the very concepts of "ethics" and journalistic self-regulation do not seem to make sense in the mostly authoritarian political contexts that still exist in the Arab world. How can we define "ethical behavior" in media systems that do not allow for the dialectic opposite—unethical behavior—and that do not grant the degree of liberal public debate needed for a free discourse on ethics? In fact, many governments in the Arab world have tried to hijack the issue of media ethics and have used it as yet another controlling device, with the result that many Arab journalists, while they love to speak about the challenges of their profession, hate performing under the label of media ethics.

Another reason for the underrepresentation of Arab journalism ethics in academic debates lies with the subject itself. Media ethics and journalism ethics are established branches of Western media and communication studies, but they are marginal compared to other fields like media effects, media audiences, or political communication. Although central for many public debates about mass media, the issue of journalism ethics seems to escape scholarly categorization. It lies at the crossroads of various disciplines like media and communication studies, philosophy, religious studies, and sociology—a fact that seems to complicate theoretical work. The interdisciplinary nature of the subject may well be responsible for the elusive character of many ethical core concepts like "objectivity."

This chapter will argue that the present situation is unhealthy for a number of reasons. First and foremost, many of the disagreements on the role Arab media have played since the attacks of 9/11 or during the wars in Afghanistan and Iraq are based on misunderstandings of the underlying professional ethical premises. The extreme polarization of views about Al-Jazeera, considering the network either a dangerous mouthpiece of terrorism or a herald of civil society and of democracy, is not only the result of a politically instrumentalized discourse that is being led by ideologues and politicians in the West and in the Arab world but also reflects the fact that the antagonists in that debate hold very different concepts of quality journalism; or, what is often more obvious, they share the same journalistic values but are incapable of explaining why media output in the Arab world and in the West often differs fundamentally, especially when the above-mentioned international conflicts are concerned. Such discrepancies between theory and practice are in many cases related to ill-defined and inconsistent ethical categories that leave too much room for interpretation and pose an obstacle to any realistic comparison between journalistic ethics in the West and in the Arab world.

The present chapter seeks a concise theoretical conceptualization of one of the core problems of journalism ethics: the roles of "objectivity," "balance," and "bias" in modern journalism. The aim is to highlight some commonalities and differences in Western and Arab theoretical and practical standards of objective reporting. The analysis will reflect on the formal ethical codes and journalists' attitudes and their publications. An overview of some of the existing research will be accompanied by suggestions for future research.

Objectivity, Balance, and Bias: Theoretical Deliberations

Objectivity has probably been the most important issue in journalism ethics debates over the last century. The basic idea is that journalists must seek for a representation of the world around them—of events, people, and circumstances—that can be shared with others as an appropriate description and interpretation of reality. Important positions of objectivity in modern media were formulated by, for example, Michael Schudson (2001). But the search for objectivity is not limited to the West. In his work on comparative, cross-cultural media ethics, Thomas W. Cooper argues that the search for truth and objectivity is a universal feature of global media ethics, much more universal than other values like privacy or freedom that are also much debated issues (Cooper 1989, 20).

It is surely fair to say that there are as many proponents as there are critics of the concepts of truth, reality, and objectivity in journalism. The notion that an assessment of absolute truth(s) is impossible has a long history in Western philosophy. Most accounts start with Plato's *Allegory of the Cave*. More sophisticated is the English philosopher George Berkeley's *A Treatise concerning the Principles of Human Knowledge* (1710), in which he elaborates at length that all existence can only be "perceived" and never be grasped absolutely (*esse est percipi*; Berkeley 1998). In the twentieth century the British philosopher and Nobel Prize winner Bertrand Russell discussed the matter. In his book *The Problems of Philosophy* Russell argues that the "table" in front of you cannot possibly be real and existent (Russell 1978). The reason for this is, as the author argues, that human perception is imperfect and incapable of an objective understanding of the nature of things. Is the table flat? It depends on how you look at it, merely through your eyes or with the help of a microscope. And it depends on the sensitivity of your fingers when touching the object. Is the table blue, or red? Every human eye perceives colors differently. In a strict sense, an object without any precisely describable aspects cannot be said to be existent, Russell concludes. However, one may reply, it is rather strange that we all seem to agree that the table stands in front of us—not objectively, but intersubjectively. We seem to share many culturally construed schemes of perception.

These epistemological debates are relevant for journalism. Although we might disagree on *how* we perceive the table, we all agree that the table is there. In the same way, journalists may disagree on many aspects of the "reality" they describe and report about, but they should be able to agree on some intersubjective facts and truths. While journalists might disagree on whether it is legitimate to lead a certain war, journalists and other observers should be able to agree on the number of people being killed throughout the war, and they should be able to isolate and describe certain core argumentations of the major protagonists involved in the war.

International reporting, like all other news making, should be judged on the basis of such moderate views of objectivity as intersubjectivity. Modern social science is based on a logic that transcends the fundamentalist clash between realists and radical constructivists—for example, when science theoretician Karl Popper highlights intersubjectivity as a core concept of modern scientific knowledge (Popper 1972). The systematization, verification, and falsification of intersubjective truth is characterized as the essence of scientific methodology. Without such methodology academics world be mere "storytellers," far from any superior claim to empiricism.

The same can be said about journalism. If there is nothing out there that "exists" in the sense that its representation in the media can be justifiably debated, journalistic reporting becomes as fictitious as poetry writing (and, honestly, most of us would probably prefer to read poetry because it is better written). Of course, media anthropologists, in particular, have rightly claimed that "entertainment is political" in the sense that entertainment is a reflection of social realities that must be taken seriously because it has an impact on societal change. Over the last decades many mass media have increasingly merged "news," "facts," and "fiction" in various forms of "infotainment" and "politainment." But does all that mean that the borderline between reality and fiction becomes blurred and that objectivity in journalism can be replaced by the principles of storytelling? Entertainment is political—but is journalism therefore mere entertainment?

Most journalists around the world would surely not subscribe to such logic. They consider themselves to be agents of reality transfer from events and actors to people and audiences (Shoemaker/Reese 1991, 31). If they amalgamate news and entertainment—for example, in political talk shows—it is to enhance the reach of news formats to information-averse audiences (a concept that is debated in political communication science; Baum 2003, Prior 2003), but not to negate reality. Even staged events like the public relations activities of prominent people contain some degree of intersubjectively describable reality.

In communication science Günter Bentele replicates a moderate approach to objectivity in his concept of "re-constructivism" (Bentele 1992), and recent accounts of journalism theory echo the paradigm of intersubjectivity as a modern middle ground. Guy Starkey, in his book *Balance and Bias in Journalism*, describes the problem as follows: "Representation being only a partial…account of a place, an event or an issue, necessarily involves choices being made over what is included and what is not. A representation that is selective might still be widely considered 'fair' if competing perspectives have been 'balanced' in such a way that none of them gain any advantage from the act of mediation taking place. However, bias lies in the absence of balance, it exists when one aspect of the place, one take of the event or one side of the argument has been given undue prominence that promotes it unfair over others, either to its advantage or to its disadvantage" (Starkey 2007, XVII).

Based on a moderate epistemology of objectivity as intersubjectivity, we can continue to conceptualize the field. Chris Frost, in his introduction to media ethics, mentions variations of the theme of objectivity—for example, "balance" (as used by Starkey), "impartiality," or "neutrality" (Frost 2000). Do they all have the same meaning? "Balance" is usually defined as the state whereby arguments that exist in a public arena are represented in a journalistic text. "Unfair" reporting in this perspective is reporting that emphasizes certain important actors and positions at the cost of others. Whereas "impartiality" means quite the same thing as "balance," "neutrality" implies that the journalist should not let personal opinions and biases interfere with his or her work.

Balance and neutrality are fine role models, but they are limited and do not fully describe what "objectivity" stands for. The problem is that all actors and public positions in a given field can be wrong or manipulative, and in that case "balancing" such views and taking a neutral stand would produce a dubious kind of media output not in touch with reality. "Balanced" journalism can also lead to an overrepresentation of certain public relations interests or articulated minorities, that are in fact much less relevant than many silent majorities in a society. In this sense, a journalistic contribution can be balanced without being objective. In German, the terms "Ausgewogenheit" (balance) and "Objektivität" (objectivity) express the differences in approach. Topics usually have a hidden agenda: perspectives on an issue, power relations, actors that are not yet known but nevertheless important. Objectivity, therefore, is not only what some people with effective public relations and high informal status in a public arena think about, but it is, in the ultimate sense, the knowledge shared by humankind *as a whole* about an issue. What sounds illusionary at first really marks the gulf between simpler and more sophisticated forms of journalistic understanding: between PR-oriented journalism and investigative journalism. Objective journalists are not mere moderators of the public discourse—they dig deeper.

It is therefore not astounding that Chris Frost and other authors in the field of media ethics see no contradiction between the notion of objectivity and the ability of journalists to "comment" on issues. Comments allow for analytical views on issues to bring in something other than the already established perspectives. This positive element of journalistic commentary, however, contradicts the fact that journalists have no democratic mandate that raises their individual views above those of any other person. Freedom of expression is a right all members of a community share without any privileges. Journalists' comments, therefore, mainly serve as a vehicle for representing not-yet-established views. They are not a forum for personal value judgements of journalists. The task is to help the audiences understand a case, not manipulate it, and to get as close to intersubjective reconstruction of reality as one can get.

Of course, journalistic reality is much more complex. Print, TV, and radio mass media systems are often embedded in ideological spheres—just think of the Right-versus-Left cleavage of many press systems around the world. In addition, some modern journalism concepts literally demand certain biases and ask journalists to take a firm stand on matters related to human rights or peace. For Starkey, antiracism is a case that commands partiality (Starkey 2007, XVII). Some authors within the modern peace journalism movement criticize objectivity as an ideology privileging war contestants, since their propaganda has a chance to enter the media (Fröhlich 2006). Even though such claims are highly contested, they are a marked departure from the old-style partiality of Right versus Left, since concepts like Starkey's or the peace journalists demand privileges only for a limited number of human rights positions that are the basis for any kind of objective discourse: peace and antiracism are needed prerequisites to become part of the intersubjective dialogue.

Objectivity is closely linked to content features of journalistic texts. It is only when we count and evaluate these features that we can arrive at a judgment whether a text reflects important viewpoints or represents core actors and whether it is objective, balanced, and neutral. Academic literature on media ethics has debated at length how to define objectivity, but it hardly ever reflects *how it can be measured.* However, the transfer of ethical standards to content features is all but easy, as the following examples will demonstrate:

- *Facts.* Facts are the natural antidotes to "opinion" or comment in the sense that they represent the highest degree of intersubjective reality that hardly anybody can doubt (remember Bertrand Russell's table). The checking of facts is therefore the prime journalistic virtue that is acknowledged in all media systems. Problems with the factual substance of media texts can, however, arise from the nonavailability of factual information, from manipulation or unprofessional research methods.
- *Agenda.* The topical agenda is one of the most analyzed features in modern content analysis of mass media. Whole theoretical branches like news value theory (e.g., Tuchman 1978) or agenda setting theory (e.g., Iyengar/Kinder 1987) are based on the fact that there are some things out there called "topics" or "issues" that represent journalistic value judgements of what kinds of facts, events, and developments are worth being selected for the media. Although it seems clear that presenting real facts must be part of any definition of objectivity, it is much harder to define what kind of media agenda can be called "objective." Problems arise from the breadth and the depth of the agenda. Is it fairer and more objective to treat a limited set of topics and report on them

with more facts, views, and opinions; or to present more topics but with a faster beat, incorporating more but also more superficial and perhaps less-balanced news? Given the limited resources the media have at their disposal, one can easily see that objectivity that wants to reflect both aspects ends up in a dilemma. There is no such thing as *the* objective media agenda, but any selection of topics can be debated and criticized, and must be justified against (intersubjective) alternatives. In this context, for example, journalistic routines for defining news have been repeatedly contested.[2] It is debatable, for example, whether the widespread prioritization of news about conflict and violence, so-called negative or bad news, is an intersubjectively justifiable mode of perception (e.g., Starkey 2007, 10).

- *Frames.* Over the last decade, the concept of "framing" has gained widespread attention in various academic disciplines (Entman 1993). Frames are core arguments in a given text defining how a topic that is on the media agenda is interpreted and presented. The basic function of journalism striving for inter subjectivity is to balance major frames representing the subjective viewpoints of all people involved in a certain event. It also explores hidden frames that are not articulated by any of the protagonists but, nevertheless, shed light on a certain case and bring journalistic expertise into perspective.

It is the aim of this chapter to exemplify elements of a future research agenda in the field of media ethics for Arab media. Therefore, this very limited set of theoretical considerations, linking the debate over objectivity to content features, will be applied to both Arab and Western media texts. The major question is whether Arab and Western media construct reality in such a way that they share inter subjective constructions of reality. Do Arab and Western media resort to the same facts? Do they highlight the same media agenda? Do they exchange and balance viewpoints?

"Objectivity" as a Value in Arab Journalism

Before these questions are targeted, it seems worth considering the professional attitudes of Arab journalists. Studies about professional norms, however, hardly exist. Arab media and communication studies have developed enormously over the last decades in centers like the University of Sharjah in the UAE, the American University in Cairo, or the Lebanese American University in Beirut. However, studies like those by David Weaver (1996) and others on attitudes of Western journalists are still very rare. Those that exist often do not cover the exact dimensions of objectivity that were discussed here, such as factuality, balance, and independent assessment of agenda and framing, but they are of great interest.

Jyotika Ramaprasad's and Naila Nabil Hamdy's article "Functions of Egyptian Journalists: Perceived Importance and Actual Performance" is in fact, as the authors state, a benchmark for future researchers. The study, which is based on an extensive questionnaire (n = 107), reveals that Egyptian journalists' attitudes can be broadly ranked as follows: support for Arabism and other community values was prevalent over their support for democracy, which was, however, still a strong and vested value when compared to lower-ranking values such as support for existing governments or the provision of entertainment (Ramaprasad/Hamdy 2006). The dimension of "support for democracy" included many of the characteristics that we have defined as core elements of objective journalism, such as accuracy of reporting, incorporation of society's views, and a critical assessment of government policies.

Those results seem to imply that truth and objectivity have increasingly become norms of Arab—or here, Egyptian—journalism. The old-style so-called mobilizational approach that the standard handbook of Arab media by William Rugh found typical of Arab authoritarian press systems, and which supported national governments, is no longer undisputed (Rugh 2004). On the contrary, it receives very low esteem. A new trend toward objectivity and impartiality as a value in Arab journalism seems to be emerging, and the values of Arab and Western journalism in this field have started to converge—even though many more studies will be needed to consolidate that finding.

One has to take into consideration that many Arab journalists are trying to practice journalism within a framework of support for their countries or other Arab countries and communities—and especially their fellow Arabs like the Palestinians—in times of crisis (see also Bekhait 1998). Such coexistence of values is not a distinctive characteristic of Arab journalism. A support for political aims like human rights, democracy, or peace would find great support among Western journalists. It is debatable whether support for Arab values is a sign of an essentially different cultural concept or merely a sign that journalists consider the resolution of certain vital crises, like the Arab-Israeli conflict, a prerequisite to democracy and an orderly public debate. Moreover, certain variants of Western journalism, like the American "public journalism" concept (e.g. Rosen 1999, Merritt 1998), also highlight community functions of journalism and demand that journalists exert objective journalism within the community paradigm. But those trends do not represent the mainstream ethics of Western journalism and are highly contested, whereas in Arab journalism they could very well represent the mainstream.

What we do not know in the case of Arab journalism—and this is the decisive aspect—is how political and professional aims are related and to what extent they contradict each other. In which regard can the promotion of Arab culture interfere with a journalist's assessment of accurate facts? And how does it influence the media agenda and the framing of texts when Arab journalists try to be balanced and fair? Is "Arabism" an illegitimate bias that contradicts objectivity and impartiality?

Existing studies on professional attitudes are not sophisticated enough to answer those questions. But there is some more evidence that Arab journalism is increasingly embracing objectivity as a norm. Truth, accuracy, and objectivity are almost consensual cornerstones of journalism ethics in Western and Arab codes of ethics that have mostly been designed by journalism associations (Hafez 2002). A comparison of Arab codes in diverse countries like Egypt, Morocco, Tunisia, and Saudi Arabia has confirmed Thomas W. Cooper's observation that the search for truth and objectivity is a universal feature of global media ethics (Cooper 1989, 20). Factual, correct, and unbiased coverage therefore can be considered a consensual value of journalism, which in all codes comprises the core and the essence of the journalistic profession and that distinguishes fiction from nonfiction.

Of course, identical codification is no proof of the fact that objectivity, accuracy, and fairness are practiced alike in all countries and media systems because this assumption would overlook the fact that information control, censorship, or tabloid journalism are widespread and the possibilities for verifying vary from country to country, medium to medium, and journalist to journalist. However, no cultural cleavage can be observed. The codes reveal that the search for truth is a common intercultural norm that is violated by all those forces within or outside the media systems that try to obstruct it. The possible hypothesis that Islamic countries might not be interested in "truth" and would rather propagate "Islam" as the single truth cannot be verified completely because even a code that limits journalists' freedom of expression to Islamic objectives and values, the Saudi Arabian code, demands that journalists present real facts (Hafez 2002).

The real categorical difference between Western and Arab journalistic codes of ethics lies not with the acceptance of truth and objectivity as a norm but with many communitarian regulations restricting freedom of expression. In general, the comparison of freedom regulations in different ethics charters shows that Thomas W. Cooper was right in his observation that the search for truth is much more clearly a universal value than adherence to freedom of expression (Cooper 1989, 20–39, 343–345). In many Arab codes of ethics, severe limits to freedom of expression are motivated by national, religious or other traditional values.

It is hard to say whether Arab journalists are generally less freedom-loving than their Western colleagues (Amin 2002). Many of the restrictive codes have been released by authoritarian governments rather than by journalists or other important segments of civil society. Those codes that were adopted by independent associations of journalists—for example, the Syndicat National de Journalistes in Algeria (Hafez 2002)—that express the democratic will of their constituents are clearly more freedom-oriented than those that have been dictated by the state.

In recent years, Arab media like Al-Jazeera have released individual codes of ethics. With respect to objectivity Al-Jazeera's code includes all the relevant reference terms, expressing the will to abide to "fairness," "balance," "independence," "truth," and "accuracy" while distancing itself from "bias" and "partiality."[3] Ethical codes like that of Al-Jazeera no longer incorporate cultural, national, or religious limitations to objectivity. However, in the case of Al-Jazeera, community orientations make themselves felt in the modern disguise of audience orientations when the code states that the network gives special attention to the "feelings of victims of crime, war, persecution and disaster, their relatives and our viewers." Such reference to a particular group, "our viewers," might be considered to conflict with the aim of objective reporting, because what about victims that are not related to Al-Jazeera? Will they be treated differently and be less represented?

In any case, the study by Ramaprasad and Hamdy suggests that community orientations are not *merely* dictated by governments but stem from the professional role models of Arab journalism that are, to a certain degree, still contained in modern codes of ethics. The crux, however, is that with the visible descent of governments' reputations, also observed by Ramaprasad and Hamdy, the decision whether any kind of objective reporting could be detrimental to the community tends to shift from governments to the journalists themselves (except maybe in times when a country is involved in war and societies rally around governments). If there is a contradiction between objective reporting and the well-being of a community, it seems increasingly clear that the individual Arab journalist has started to take over the professional and autonomous responsibility for defining that conflict.

Applied Objectivity: (Corporate) Media Performance in Arab and Western Journalism

Questions of objectivity in journalism can be considered on various levels. Although it is meaningful, as a first step, to analyze formal and informal attitudes that exist within the profession, as we have done in the previous section, such an approach has clear limitations. Formal ethical codification tends to declare professional aims or even official professional ideologies that are not necessarily identical with the real existing values of journalists. This is the reason why research on factual attitudes is needed—but even such research has clear methodological constraints for a number of reasons.

Attitudes to the profession, as formulated by journalists, are not necessarily identical with the journalist's or their media's actual performance. Integrating research on attitudes with content analysis would be a solution, but how do we pursue this? Ramaprasad and Hamdy chose to ask the journalists themselves how often they felt they were able to perform various journalistic functions (Ramaprasad/Hamdy 2006). This approach is legitimate, but, of course, involves the problem that journalists have to evaluate themselves. An assessment of performed objectivity is not pursued intersubjectively but subjectively. The authors do not pose the question whether journalists who want to be fair are really fair, but they ask whether they are fair within their own definitions of fairness.

An alternative to such research would be to contrast postulated norms with real news values or content features by comparing how different journalists achieve their ethical standards when covering the same events. The idea here is to measure the journalistic performance by confronting it with alternative reality constructs on the same issue and thereby getting closer to the concept of intersubjectivity. In the Arab-Western comparative context, such approach can reveal whether commonalities or differences that exist on the formal and informal ethical levels are only differences in professional ideologies or if they are effective in practical journalism. In other words, we could find answers to the question about whether objectivity, which is the undisputed core of Western journalism ethics and a strong and upcoming element of Arab journalism ethics, is practiced on the basis of an intersubjectively shared Arab-Western understanding of objectivity, of the reporting of facts and the balancing of viewpoints.

Of course, even such an approach has its limitations. First, to contrast media performance with journalistic attitudes does not take into account that objective reality could lie beyond the constructs of either Arab or Western media. Second, it does not take into account that media texts are conglomerates of various influences. Attitudinal research has rightly been criticized for being actor-centered, concentrating on the role of journalists while a considerable degree of the influence on texts stems from newsrooms, news organizations, and all kinds of organizational and societal influences (Weischenberg/Scholl 1998, 161).

Countering the latter criticism, however, we can argue that comparing ethical attitudes with journalistic performance is legitimate as long as it focuses on the ethics and the performance of *corporate rather than individual journalistic actors.* Since it is ultimately the media organizations that decide whether a journalistic product is published or not, any publication in the Arab or Western mass media can be expected to be in tune with the respective corporate ethics.

Given the heterogeneous body of content analysis of Arab and Western media that exists, we are still in a very early stage of research. Generalizations on whole national or regional media systems are impossible. But using the objectivity matrix of "facts," "agenda," and "frames" that has been outlined in the theoretical introduction, some preliminary observations can be made as a stimulus for future research.

As we stated earlier on, despite the fact that an assessment of absolute truth seems impossible, each event involves aspects of *a factual reality* that no observer would doubt. However, a close analysis of media output in the Arab-Western context shows that even "facts" easily become liable to manipulations since they are not always presented in the intersubjective context that is available. One example for this is the treatment of the death tolls of the Iraq War that began in 2003. While official figures cannot be trusted, a number of NGOs are nowadays determining the parameters of intersubjectivity—mainly, the Iraq Body Count (IBC), with an estimated number below 100,000 dead, and the American medical journal *Lancet,* which estimates more than 600,000 dead. A comparative study has revealed that over the years the biggest Egyptian newspaper, *Al-Ahram,* has much more often quoted the *Lancet* study, the conservative British newspaper the *Times* mostly referred to the IBC, and the British *Guardian* has balanced the two (Riehm 2006). Although there are no other studies in the field, an ad-hoc analysis in July 2007 of the English website of Al-Jazeera shows that the IBC has, indeed, been mentioned twenty-four times and the *Lancet* thirty-seven times.

Although all the media mentioned adhere to some code of ethics highlighting the accuracy of coverage as cornerstones of their professional ethics, the interpretation of what accuracy really is differs enormously. Instead of a sober presentation of the various and disputed figures of Iraqi death tolls as the sole legitimate expression of intersubjective truth, media coverage seems to reflect the underlying political ideologies, with the Arab media being *against* and the conservative *Times* being *for* the war. Only a liberal or even neutral position (as in the case of the British *Guardian*) seems to supply some accuracy of reporting. Although it is fair to say that over short periods of time governments and military censors can influence all media, the results of the study show that in the course of low intensity wars, media ideology can have a tremendous influence on accuracy and poses a challenge to intersubjectivity in reporting.

The Egyptian code of ethics demands communal restrictions on freedom of opinion only in cases when Egypt's values or security is concerned. Al-Jazeera's code of ethics demands respect of the audience giving "full consideration to the feelings of victims of crime, war, persecution and disaster, their relatives and our viewers." Both formulations, however, cannot be understood as a legitimizing of tendentious imbalance, and the same is true for the British press code, which asks for accuracy and nothing else. A tendency to manipulate facts even against ethical devices can be observed within some of the media in the West and in the Arab world.

If we consider the next element of objectivity, the media agenda, we have to remember that there is no such thing as an objective agenda. However, a comparison of Western and Arab media agendas makes one aware how the media in both spheres construct the basic orders of reality. Western media usually cover the Arab and Islamic world through the prism of a limited set of negative topics like wars, terrorism, fanaticism, and all sorts of religious, political, and gender repression (Hafez 2000b)—an agenda that is in contrast to the Arab media's own agendas, which usually highlight much more regular events and developments in politics, society, and culture. As a rule of thumb, the diversity of the Western media coverage on Arabs is low and often limited to topics that are of importance to the West. While content analyses of Arab foreign reporting of the West are rare, they would likely produce similar results. Even though foreign reporting cannot possibly be as diverse as domestic reporting, one cannot but state that reality constructions in the Arab-Western context are often extremely contradictory and void of any intersubjective thematic sensitivities.

This is not to say that the usually shared agenda that exists in the narrow field of international conflicts is in itself abnormal. The idea of a global public sphere is indeed based on the fact that different media systems are co-oriented toward the same issues, without which there could be no global exchange of facts, positions, and viewpoints. Despite this, however, there are very many topics that are prominent only in one or the other world sphere. There are still "white spots" and missing news that reflect a limited degree of intersubjectivity and topical awareness. For example, the issue of globalization and cultural development is high on the Arab media agenda while it seems rather low on the agenda in the West. Improved comparative agenda research could help to reveal the underlying differences in reality constructions in various media systems.

The major challenge for objectivity in the Arab-Western context, however, arises from the fact that "events" are not the same as "topics." Identical events can be treated under very different topical headings. One's "war against terrorism" in Iraq can be the other one's "imperialist crusade." Although generalizations are not appropriate, there is evidence for the fact that Arab and Western media quite often resort to contrasting frames when describing what they perceive as realities. The journalist and director of the Adham School of Journalism at the American University in Cairo, Lawrence Pintak, argues that Westerners and Arabs or Muslims inhabit "separate Information Ghettos, each seeing a view if the world largely at odds that of the other" (Pintak 2006b, 72). Such a view is supported by a number of works evaluating the conflict reporting of Arab mass media (Hafez 2006, 284–287). The French Panos study, for example, undertaken after the 9/11 attacks, argued that Al-Jazeera is more critical of the United States than are many other Arab news media(Panos Institute 2002, 17).[5] Political scientist Mamoun Fandy maintained as early as 2000 that, with the exception of regular news programs, Al-Jazeera represented a new kind of alliance between nationalists and Islamists (Fandy 2000, 388)—a view that until today is shared by some critical Arab journalists (Chimelli 2004). Muhammad Ayish argues that in the field of Arab regional conflicts Al-Jazeera lacks professional standards of objectivity (Ayish 2002, 150). Abdel Karim Samara observed that Arab television was generally not able to report the variety of political views on the war in Iraq in 2003, and oppositional perspectives against Saddam Hussein were not given sufficient attention (Samara 2003).

An interesting study by Antje Glück comparing representations of terrorism in Arab and German elite newspapers revealed that although terrorism as such is condemned in both media systems, the diagnosis of the phenomenon is completely different. While German papers concentrate on Islam and other internal Arab factors as a source of terrorism, Arab papers tend to pay much more attention to external causes like U.S. and British Middle East policies (Glück 2007).

Framing biases are therefore by no means a privilege of Arab media, and the resistance to understand the global discourse as an integrative balance of the viewpoints of all actors is paramount in both media spheres. The list of offenses against the principle of objectivity by American media before and during the Iraq War in 2003 is almost endless. This is confirmed in a study carried out by the American media watchdog FAIR during the war in March and April 2003.[4] According to this study, from the start of the invasion, government actors were in the majority on the major networks ABC, CBS, NBC, CNN, Fox, and PBS, while opponents of the war were underrepresented. Another recently published study by Samera Zagala on German TV news about the Arab world revealed that in reports on the Islamic world only around one-third of the actors represented were from the Islamic world (Zagala 2007).

As in all other cases, of course, the reality of the Iraq War allowed no exact reproduction. But one has to acknowledge that media reality in the Arab-Western context is often highly contested and that intersubjectivity can only be achieved by integrating the very divergent frames, arguments, and actors' perspectives in order to avoid biases and achieve a more balanced form of journalism on both sides. This is not to say that commentaries might not come to very different conclusions highlighting various interests. Communication and speech acts are much more than a "sterile" integration of meaning into texts. They involve interests, reflect the socialization of the authors, and express emotions. However, texts that deserve to be called "objective" need to be based on a balanced composition and exchange of reality constructions.

If they do not, as is often the case in Arab-Western media communication on international conflicts, they resemble what the Iranian media scientist Majid Tehranian has called "the dialogue of the deaf" (Tehranian 1999) in international communication. The existence of this kind of blocked "dialogue" is all the more astounding since many media around the world resort to the "dialogue between cultures" as a cornerstone of their news policies. Al-Arabiya, one of the most prominent Arab TV news networks, promotes the establishment of a "genuine dialogue across cultural, linguistic, ethnic, and national boundaries,"[5] and Al-Jazeera's famous slogan is "the other opinion."

Arabs and Westerners at the "Dead End" of Global Journalism Ethics?

Pintak believes that in the face of the reality of contemporary Arab and Western media reporting it is hard to see how something like a "global ethics" of journalism has emerged (Pintak 2006a). Although from his perspective such perception is a product of Western academic "ivory towers," Pintak argues that Arab journalists are first and foremost reporting from an "Arab perspective." In this sense, community values and orientations that have been proven to exist among Arab journalists (Ramaprasad/Hamdy 2006) are still stumbling blocks to the establishment of intersubjective ("objective") perspectives balancing facts and viewpoints.

However, Pintak's vision is not the only one. Although community orientations are still strong among Arab journalists, neutrality and objectivity have an improved standing in new Arab journalism. At the same time, the results of content analysis on international reporting in Western media point to the fact that community orientations seem also to exist in Western journalism, at least in times of conflict and crisis (Borden 2005). Such attitudes have hardly ever been under research in Western ethical studies, but they seem to be deeply entrenched at least on the level of media organizations, which are responsible for content that is often biased and unbalanced when it comes to reports about the non-Western world. Valerie Alia points to the "double standards" in Western journalism: an ethics of objectivity for the one group—the West—coexists with another standard of benign neglect and opinionated journalism for other parts of the world (Alia 2004, 57). If this assessment is correct, journalism ethics in the West and in the Arab world have much more in common than a look at codes and official ethical devices suggests.

The deep structure of journalism ethics on both sides, between Arab and Western journalists, seems to be a mix of professional attitudes that oscillate between values of objectivity and community orientation in international relations. It might not be *difference* but *identity* in journalism ethics that poses the real problem of world journalism today. Western journalism values, heralded throughout the world and increasingly embraced by Arab journalists, are not sophisticated enough to solve the crisis within global journalism. Western journalism ethics, although seen by many as a role model for professionalism, hardly ever reflect on problems of international and intercultural communication, although these are manifold: how to verify facts across borders; how to judge the importance of viewpoints that need to be represented and balanced if the domestic situation of many countries is a far away reality. Western journalism ethics is not yet *global* in nature, and Arab journalism modeling itself on that system of values will inevitably end up at a journalisitic dead end that tends to construct and reproduce the "clash of cultures" through a clash of journalistic perspectives (Hafez 2000a).

For journalism ethics to develop and to be effective, the biggest challenge might be that the very essence of ethical thinking, research, and practice might have to be shifted from the individual perspective of journalists and their attitudes to much wider horizons. "Professional ethics" transcends the individual by way of integrating media organizations, media entrepreneurs, and even whole journalistic cultures that exist as interrelated systems and deserve more academic attention as systems of ethical discourse. Moreover, the trend within new Arab media to point to the audience as a reference point for ethical behavior implies that professional media ethics is to a certain degree "audience ethics" (Zapf 2006). The journalist, the media owner, and the audience are interdependent, and it seems quite natural that they are also commonly responsible for the formulation of ethical standards. However, global markets are much less integrated than domestic national and regional ones (Hafez 2007). Global ethical standards will, if at all, only develop as regulatory systems of future global media markets and policies.

Notes

1. See the list in Hafez 2002, 247 ff. or the website The Ethics of Journalism Comparison and Transformations in the Islamic-Western Context, http://www.journalism-islam.de/con_codes.htm.
2. See, for example, the famous "McBride Report" that analyzed international communication: *Many Voices—One World: Communication and Society Today and Tomorrow* (1980), London: UNESCO.
3. See the Al-Jazeera Code of Ethics, http://english.aljazeera.net/news/aspx/print.htm.
4. Steve Rendall/Tara Broughel, Amplifying Officials, Squelching Dissent, http://www.fair.org/extra/0305/warstudy.html.
5. Al Arabiya News Channel, Overcoming Stereotypes, PowerPoint presentation by Mazen Hayek, director, marketing and business development, Bonn, October 12, 2006, http://www.agendasetting.com/2006/speakers/2006_10_12/08-Al-Arabiya-Mazen_Hayek_On_Stereotypes.pdf.

References

Abu-Fadil, M. (ed.) (2004), *Media Ethics and Journalism in the Arab World: Theory, Practice and Challenges Ahead. Proceedings of a Conference, Lebanese American University, Beirut, June 9–11, 2004.* Beirut: Institute for Professional Journalists/Heinrich Böll Foundation.

Alia, V. (2004), *Media Ethics and Social Change.* Edinburgh: Edinburgh University Press.

Amin, H. (2002), Freedom as a Value in Arab Media: Perceptions and Attitudes among Journalists. *Political Communication* 2, 125–135.

Ayish, M. I. (2002), Political Communication on Arab World Television: Evolving Patterns. *Political Communication* 2, 137–155.

Baum, M. A. (2003), Soft News and Political Knowledge: Evidence of Absence or Absence of Evidence? *Political Communication* 2, 173–190.

Bekhait, A. (1998), *The Egyptian Press—News Values and False Consciousness* [in Arabic]. Cairo: Arabi.

Bentele, G. (1992), Fernsehen und Realität. Antsätze zu einer rekonstruktiven Medientheorie. In K. Hickethier/I. Schneider (eds.), *Fernsehtheorien. Dokumentation der GFF-Tagung 1990.* Berlin: Bohn, 45–67.

Berkeley, G. (1998), *A Treatise on the Principles of Human Knowledge* (Orig. 1710). Oxford: Oxford University Press.

Borden, S. (2005), Communitarian Journalism and Flag Displays after September 11: An Ethical Critique. *Journal of Communication Inquiry* 1, 30–46.

Chimelli, R. (2004), Im Garten des Meinungsmonopols, in: Süddeutsche Zeitung, May 10.

Cooper, T. W. (1989), Global Universals: In Search of Common Ground. In T. W. Cooper/C. G. Christians/F. F. Plude/R. A. White (eds.), *Communication Ethics and Global Change.* White Plains: Longman.

Entman, R. M. (1993), Framing: Toward Clarification of a Fractured Paradigm. *Journal of Communication* 4, 51–58.

Fandy, M. (2000), Information Technology, Trust, and Social Change in the Arab World. *Middle East Journal* 3, 378–394.

Fröhlich, G. (2006), Emotional Intelligence in Peace Journalism: A Four-Part Paper. Section Two: The Evolution of Peace Journalism. *Global Media Journal* 8, http://lass.calumet.purdue.edu/cca/gmj/sp06/gmj-sp06-frohlich.htm.

Frost, C. (2000), *Media Ethics and Self-Regulation.* Harlow: Longman.

Glück, A. (2007), *Terror im Kopf. Terrorismusberichterstattung in der deutschen und arabischen Presse.* Berlin: Frank und Timme.

Hafez, K. (2000a), Islam and the West—the Clash of Politicized Perceptions. In K. Hafez (ed.), *The Islamic World and the West: An Introduction to Political Cultures and International Relations.* Leiden: Brill Academic, 3–18.

———. (2000b), *Islam and the West in the Mass Media: Fragmented Images in a Globalizing World.* Cresskill: Hampton Press.

———. (2002), Journalism Ethics Revisited: A Comparison of Ethics Codes in Europe, North Africa, the Middle East and Muslim Asia. *Political Communication* 2, 225–250.

———. (ed.) (2003), *Media Ethics in the Dialogue of Cultures: Journalistic Self-Regulation in Europe, the Arab World, and Muslim Asia.* Hamburg: Deutsches Orient-Institut.

———. (2006), Arab Satellite Broadcasting: Democracy without Political Parties. *Transnational Broadcasting Studies* 2, 275–297.

———. (2007), *The Myth of Media Globalization.* Cambridge: Polity.

Iyengar, S./D. R. Kinder (1987), *News that Matters: Television and American Opinion.* Chicago: University of Chicago Press.

Merritt, D. B. (1998), *Public Journalism and Public Life: Why Telling the News Is Not Enough.* Mahwah: Lawrence Erlbaum.

Nimri, J. (1995), Media Ethics and Freedom of the Press. In G. Hawatmeh (ed.), *The Role of the Media in a Democracy: The Case of Jordan. Proceedings of a Seminar Organised by the University of Jordan in Cooperation with the Konrad Adenauer Foundation, 27–28 September, 1995.* Amman: Center for Strategic Studies, University of Jordan, 112–121.

Panos Institute (2002), *One Year After: Media Comments on the First Anniversary of September 11.* Paris: Panos Institute.

———. (2006b), *Reflections in a Bloodshot Lens: America, Islam and the War of Ideas.* London/Ann Arbor: Pluto.

Pintak, L. (2006a), Arab Media: Not Quite Utopia. *Transnational Broadcasting Studies* 16, http://tbsjournal.com/letter.html.

Popper, K. R. (1972), *Objective Knowledge: An Evolutionary Approach.* Oxford: Oxford University Press.

Prior, M. (2003), Any Good News in Soft News? The Impact of Soft News Preference on Political Knowledge. *Political Communication* 2, 149–172.

Raffelberg, J. (1995), Ethics in the Media and Freedom of the Press. In G. Hawatmeh (ed.), *The Role of the Media in a Democracy: The Case of Jordan. Proceedings of a Seminar Organised by the University of Jordan in Cooperation with the Konrad Adenauer Foundation, 27–28 September, 1995.* Amman: Center for Strategic Studies, University of Jordan, 99–111.

Ramaprasad, J./N. N. Hamdy (2006), Functions of Egyptian Journalists: Perceived Importance and Actual Performance. *International Communication Gazette* 2, 167–185.

Riehm, J. (2006), *Die öffentliche Debatte über Kriegsopfer im Irak 2003. Akteure, Strukturen, Themen.* Unpublished Master's thesis, University of Erfurt.

Rosen, J. (1999), *What Are Journalists For?* New Haven/London: Yale University Press.

Rugh, W. A. (2004), *Arab Mass Media: Newspapers, Radio, and Television in Arab Politics.* Westport/London: Praeger.

Russel, B. (1978), *Probleme der Philosophie.* Frankfurt: Suhrkamp.

Samara, A. K. (2003), The Arab Media and the Iraq War. *Palestine-Israel Journal* 3, http://www.pij.org/current.php?id=10.

Schudson, M. (2001), The Objectivity Norm in American Journalism. *Journalism* 2, 149–170.

Shoemaker, P. J./S. D. Reese (1991), *Gatekeeping.* Newbury Park: Sage.

Starkey, G. (2007), *Balance and Bias in Journalism: Representation, Regulation, and Democracy,* New York: Palgrave/Macmillan.

Tehranian, M. (1999), *Global Communication and World Politics.* Boulder: Lynne Rienner.

Tuchman, G. (1978), *Making News: A Study in the Construction of Reality.* New York: Free Press.

Weaver, D. (1996), *The American Journalist in the 1990s: U.S. News People at the End of an Era.* Mahwah: Lawrence Erlbaum.

Weischenberg, S./A. Scholl (1998), *Journalismus in der Gesellschaft. Theorie, Methodologie und Empirie.* Opladen: Westdeutscher Verlag.

Zagala, S. (2007), *Kulturkampf in den Medien. Wie Fernsehnachrichten die arabische Welt abbilden.* Saarbrücken: Verlag Dr. Müller.

Zapf, I. (2006), *Medien-Selbstkontrolle. Ethik und Institutionalisierung.* Konstanz: UVK.

CHAPTER NINE

Agents of Change? Journalism Ethics in Lebanese and Jordanian Journalism Education

Judith Pies

Journalism ethics in democratic systems function mainly as an instrument of regulation and orientation for the profession. As a regulative tool, journalistic ethics may be understood as an integrating, legitimizing, and motive-building moment on two interacting levels, the individual and the institutional. A person working in the media may find orientation by reflecting his or her own profession, its structural conditions, and outcomes, as well as by justifying professional principles (Debatin 1997). But the weight and awareness of each functional aspect may vary in different societies at different times.

Particularly, in times of growing economic pressure and internationalization in the media sector, the functions of journalistic ethics become vital (Thomaß 1998, 15). In (semi)authoritarian systems media ethics must also be considered an instrument of governmental supervision often under the guise of professional self-regulation. Kunczik has concluded that in these countries ethical debates are often completely missing and codes of ethics are used by the government to control and manipulate the media (1999, 246ff.). On the other hand, the transformation processes in Eastern Europe have shown that awareness of professional ethics or guiding principles within the profession can be an effective means of defending journalism against external political and/or economic influences in times of extensive social, political, economic, and media internal changes (Thomaß/Tzankoff 2001, 247). Lebanon and Jordan have been undergoing changes for several years now, especially in the media sector. Therefore, a need for orientation and regulation within journalism can be presumed. But does a debate about ethics as a tool for strengthening the former or the latter function exist?

Although "to talk about ethics in Lebanon is still very new,"[1] a first glance already indicates the existence of such a debate within the two countries. For example, during the last few years, several conferences, roundtable debates, and public discussions on media ethics have taken place with the aim of creating a self-defined code of ethics in Lebanon. Another case is the Jordanian Journalists' Press Association, which announced a code of ethics under the supervision of the government to prevent new restrictions on the freedom of the press following 9/11. But does a continuously ongoing debate exist? And if it does, what is the content of this debate? The analysis of the role that ethics plays in journalism education can help to answer these questions. Journalism education can be the place to "form" future journalists with regard to ethics (regulative function), on the one hand, and provide a platform for discussion (orientation), on the other (Thomaß 1998, 51).

Thus, the aim of this chapter is to focus on the role of ethics within journalism education in Lebanon and Jordan. As journalism education in the Arab world has been changing and expanding only recently, it can be presumed that things are in a state of flux. Therefore, the way of dealing with ethics in the institutions of journalism education can be an indicator of how relevant journalism ethics is considered in the two countries within the profession in general. Besides the analysis of curricula and training programs, the concepts and attitudes toward journalism ethics among journalists' instructors can be employed as a methodological approach in any attempt to draw a picture of the actual situation in the field. Journalism instructors in their roles as experts can become active participants by stimulating the debates on ethics within the profession. At the same time, they function as mediators of ethics due to their positions as lecturers or course leaders and thus are important actors for raising awareness of specific journalism ethics and for teaching the ability to reflect on journalistic workings from a moral point of view. Consequently, their opinions about and conceptions of journalism ethics are vital for the concepts and discourses within the national journalistic field as a whole.

This essay focuses on university education—in particular, media or journalism departments, and external training courses for journalists organized by Lebanese or Jordanian organizations. Within fourteen institutions, eighteen interviews were conducted with experts who teach journalism courses at the aforementioned institutes or are responsible for the organization of the curriculum or the training programs. All interviews took place in Lebanon and Jordan in June 2006 and form the core of the analysis. In addition, curricula and seminar scripts of fifteen different departments in fourteen universities were taken into account.[2] After a short description of the training opportunities for journalists in the two countries the analysis follows three leading questions: First, which ethical problems do the instructors perceive in practical journalism in their countries, Lebanon and Jordan, and whom do they consider to be responsible for them? Second, do they believe that they may help to solve problems by teaching ethics courses, and do their opinions coincide with the content of these courses and the way they are taught? Third, what is the relevance of ethics for the society and/or the profession in the instructors' opinions?

Journalism Education in Jordan and Lebanon

Access to the Profession

Access to the profession in Jordan and Lebanon is defined by educational standards only to a minor degree. The decisive criterion is obligatory membership in the journalists' associations. In Jordan, a journalist is "any member of the [Jordanian Press] Association who has been registered in its records, and practices journalism in accordance to the law."[3] In Lebanon, a similar requirement exists,[4] but its application is very confusing and does not actually play a role for practicing journalists (Braune 2005, 93–96). But according to these definitions, people who want to become members and thus officially become journalists must have proof that they have been practicing journalism for a certain period of time. In Jordan there is no minimum qualification; in Lebanon one has to have at least a Lebanese high school education.[5]

Formalization of Journalism Education

Journalism education is hardly formalized in Lebanon and Jordan. There is a mixture of direct entry to the profession and journalism education at the university level. Stand-alone journalism schools, as commonly found in the United States, or Europe exist neither in Lebanon nor in Jordan. The principal qualification for the job is a university degree (BA or MA) in either journalism, TV and broadcasting, or mass communication. But this is still not the most common way to become a journalist.[6] The majority of journalists in both countries have no specific education in journalism.[7] In Lebanon, journalists obtain a BA in any subject and then start writing or producing. One Balamand university professor has noticed that the Lebanese journalism programs are diminishing in popularity. Instead, PR and advertising are more popular because they offer a more prosperous career.[8] In Jordan, Yarmouk University is still educating most of the journalists who have university degrees.[9] But a university degree is not always a precondition to becoming a journalist.[10]

Journalism studies and communication or media sciences are still in their early stages in Jordan. For a long time, the state-run Yarmouk University in Irbid had the only department for journalism and media. Since 1991 two private universities in Amman—Petra University and Philadelphia University—have been making attempts to improve and widen their range of journalism and/or mass communication courses.[11] Whereas Philadelphia University offers only a specialization for mass communication within the program for human and social sciences, Petra University already awards degrees in journalism. In summer 2006 they both mentioned plans to expand by adding further degrees in PR and advertising, journalism, and radio and television.[12] All three universities lecture in Arabic. The Jordanian choice seems to be very limited in comparison to the Lebanese, which has at least twelve universities offering degrees in journalism (for print and/or audiovisual media), mass communication, or both, in Arabic, English and French.[13] Lebanese University is the only state-run university in Lebanon. The others are private, mostly with special relations to a specific confessional group (Bashshur 2003).

In both countries, systematic on-the-job training is not common, and the lack of advanced training for experienced journalists is often criticized.[14] Nevertheless, the scene is developing further. Only recently, *Al-Nahar*—the leading Lebanese daily newspaper—has founded a training facility for journalists, the Al-Nahar Training Center. Jordan Radio and Television (JRTV), the state-owned broadcasting company, offers training sessions for its staff at its Media Training Center. Both *Al-Nahar* and JRTV mainly work on irregular training courses or workshops with external institutions. In addition to the training in media companies, a growing number of organizations outside the media companies offer technical and practical, and sometimes also theoretical and legal, training for journalists who are already working. Some of them are nongovernmental organizations (NGOs), and others are affiliated with universities. National journalist or press associations have training for journalists on their agenda, but whether these plans materialize, and in what form, is open to question (Braune 2005). As a reaction to a growing anti-Americanism or anti-Occidentalism among the Arabic public, Western governments and NGOs saw the necessity to train Arabic journalists in order to foster mutual understanding. One result is a huge number of American or European organizations offering journalism courses, sometimes also dealing with ethics (Robinson 2005). Many of them work together with national or pan-Arab organizations, which concentrate not only on national journalists but are open to journalists from all Arab countries. Two of the distinctive features of these organizations are as follows: their origin (Arabic vs. Western/international organizations) and the places were they hold their seminars (inside vs. outside the Middle East). Lately, pan-Arab institutions have also sprung up—for example, Al-Arabiya's Middle East Broadcasting Center in 2003 or the Al-Jazeera Media Training and Development Center in 2004.

Since this article concentrates on organizations that offer more or less regular courses and seminars with a focus on journalism in either Lebanon or Jordan, attention shall be addressed to the following: the Institute for Professional Journalism in Lebanon, Center for Defending the Freedom of Journalists in Jordan, and Arab Reporters for Investigative Journalists acting in both countries and Syria. The Center for Defending the Freedom of Journalists and Arab Reporters for Investigative Journalism can be described as NGOs, whereas the Institute for Professional Journalism is affiliated with the Lebanese American University as an academic institute. All three employ Arab trainers who have been working either in journalism and/or journalism education.

Ethics in the Journalism Training Field

Looking at the diversity of journalism education in Lebanon, one could presume that the debate on ethics is similarly diverse. But as we will see in the following paragraphs, the debate is surprisingly homogeneous. This is different in Jordan. Here, the discussions in the university departments differ from those within the training centers in many respects. But the heterogeneity is reflected also within university education. A closer look could reveal cleavages between state-owned university staff and private university staff, or among the Anglophone, French, Arabic, or Soviet academic backgrounds of the lecturers, for example.

What one should bear in mind is that the debate on ethics in both countries lacks empirical data and background information on journalism and the only recently growing interest in the scientific study of mass media and journalism in the Arab world in general. Without reliable data on the profession and theoretical approaches to the structures, functions, and effects of mass media in their societies, it is hard to reflect on the systems from an ethical perspective.

For the debate within the NGOs the cooperation with Western organizations—with regard to finance and content—should not be neglected. On the one hand, it enlarges their capacity to contribute to the debate on ethics. On the other hand, they have to fear the loss of credibility if their concepts are perceived as "Western ideological imperialism" and their financial support as another form of corruption.[15]

Which Ethical Problems Are Perceived, and Who Is Held Responsible for Them?

Asked about the most important ethical concerns in their home countries, academics prioritize different topics in Lebanon and Jordan. Whereas sensational journalism was ranked first in Jordan, the Lebanese were more concerned about the lack of objectivity and the overall bias in Lebanese journalism. This truly is a reaction to the media landscape in the two countries: Jordan has a "yellow" press, which has been challenging the regime, and there are some who have been active in journalism for several years because of its tabloid style and taboo breaking (Jones 2002). Ziadat considers the sensational journalism as a main cause of "dumping good laws."[16] But there are also voices, like that of Jordan's Center for Defending the Freedom of Journalists' director Nijal Mansour, that question these taboos and refuse to call them ethics.[17]

Lebanon has hardly any tabloids but faces a problem coinciding with the lecturers' and course leaders' concerns. More often, they demand topics that can be subsumed under "professional standards," like the use of sources, newsgathering, or double-checking of information.[18] This is because Lebanese newspapers, radio, and TV stations are often associated with a specific sectarian group or former militia and very generally speaking can be called partisan media (Dajani/Najjar 2003, 307ff.). As all media in Lebanon are political in one way or another, journalists cannot be independent. Professional training therefore is regarded as very important.[19]

Conflict of interest between a specific editorial policy and personal attitude is another problem mentioned in this context. This goes hand in hand with another relevant topic for both Lebanese and Jordanians: widespread bribery and blackmail. The reasons for this problem are multifaceted, and the interviewees mentioned several of them. One is the constant underpayment of journalists (average income per month in Jordan is about US$250 and in Lebanon US$500).[20] To make their living, journalists have to receive money from somewhere else. Whether bribery is justified by the bad economic situation of many media enterprises, which rely on such "extra payments," or by the advertising industry blackmailing journalists and editors, the responsibility is not apportioned to an "immoral" individual journalist but to the economic situation. A second justification is the influence of the government and secret services, especially with regard to blackmailing for political rather than economic interests. Financial support by "external forces" is mentioned in this context, too.[21]

All in all, apart from economic pressure, the interviewees held different groups or situations to be responsible for ethical problems: the editors and owners who provide bad working conditions and set bad examples; the regime and the political system that restricts free opinion and media; a lack of professionalism resulting from a lack of standards and journalistic self-perceptions, a state of war (with Israel) in Lebanon and (against terrorism) in Jordan that justifies taboos, stereotyping, and defamation.[22] The only woman among the academic staff in Jordan also mentioned general societal or cultural structures as a reason for ethical problems in journalism. She criticized teaching methods and the lack of critical thinking in the Jordanian education system in general and the lack of fundamental research in communication science.[23] Whereas none of the Jordanian teachers pointed to these problems, several Lebanese mentioned a lack of professional culture, the inability to think critically, and hierarchical and authoritative structures in society.[24] When ranking these accountabilities it becomes obvious that structural grievances are considered to be largely responsible in both countries. In Jordan, the interference of the government or secret service seems to be one big problem, whereas economic and editorial structures are the main culprit for the Lebanese. This result is not surprising, since there is more governmental interference in Jordan than in Lebanon. Yet it is only in Lebanon that there is a strong focus on the individual responsibilities of journalists and/or editors. Of course, the perceived responsibilities affect the valuation of the role of ethics in journalism education, as we will see in the following section.

Can Teaching Ethics Solve the Problems?

If you do not believe that you can change something on the individual level, why should you make efforts to "form" a moral journalist? Given this doubt, lecturers in Jordan often regret that the discrepancy between theoretical considerations at the university level and practical work in the newsrooms is too large to resolve.[25] As a lecturer from Yarmouk University argues, "The market demand is different from the educational or university demands."[26] This picture is reflected in the curricular representation of ethics, too. None of the three universities offers a special course in ethics. One department teaches law but not ethics; another has a course called "Journalistic Principles and Law" and a third—due to its specialization in (mass) communication—teaches neither law nor ethics. This result is in keeping with the concepts of Jordanian academics, who regard ethics mainly as a legal issue: "The journalists must know what the laws are and why they are there."[27] Hence, approaching the subject of ethics in special courses or within ethically nonspecific courses on journalism is considered to be necessary in order to caution students about possible social and legal consequences.[28] The legal aspect is emphasized because some Jordanian journalists have been sued and are thus perceived as being at risk of legal action, while moral self-regulation is considered a luxury.[29] Nonetheless, university lecturers in Jordan hypothetically back the teaching of what they themselves call "mores and tradition." But their own endeavor rests at a very abstract level. They call for objectivity, truth, balance, accuracy, fairness, honesty, or justice,[30] all claims that appear in almost every journalistic code around the globe (see Hafez 2003 for the Middle East and Muslim Asia). Their appeals, like "Don't write against religion," "Don't show violence," "Don't show a woman's body," or "Don't produce hatred among the people" can be found as similarly worded guidelines in the Jordanian journalistic code of ethics and even in the laws.[31]

In contrast to the academics, the nonacademic interviewees focused much more on the individual responsibility of journalists and media staff: "It has to come from the journalist and...from the chief editors."[32] Coinciding with that view, Rana Sabbagh of Arab Reporters for Investigative Journalism in Amman is convinced that role models can change the predominantly unethical journalistic culture in Jordan: "When you can look at a few role models and you see you can make it in this shit culture, then you just spend some effort on yourself to promote yourself and act with your values."[33] As a practicing journalist and chief editor, she has been trying to be such a role model, and as a trainer she is aiming to sensitize the workshop participants to ethical questions.[34] Mansour and the Centre for Defending the Freedom of Journalists combine the two approaches by offering tangible legal aid for journalists and courses to inform them about existing laws, on the one hand, and by making them aware in workshops and seminars of moral questions in journalism, on the other.[35]

Generally speaking, the importance of dealing with ethics in journalism education in Lebanon is not questioned by the interviewees. Although they do not deny the conflict between theory and practice, they are convinced that a specific way of teaching could reduce the shock of being, so to speak, thrown in the deep end.[36]

Thus, high priority is given to interactive forms of teaching, like role-playing, case studies, and discussions. Many universities also invite practicing journalists to share their experiences with the students and discuss conflicts within decision making. Balamand University lecturer J. Nader mentions former students who came to her and praised her ethics courses because "they remembered the class as a helpful forum to discuss moral issues for which their daily job did not leave enough space."[37] So, besides the mere knowledge transfer of laws and codes of ethics, increased awareness of moral problems in journalism, assistance in decision making, and provision of a platform for discussion are important learning targets for the university teachers. They identify with more general goals of education, which in their opinion are widely lacking in the Lebanese education and journalism system. One of these goals, for example, is confrontation with other opinions and the promotion of tolerance toward them.[38] Furthermore, critical thinking and an awareness of the need to become more credible by explaining controversial decisions are a major concern in Lebanon.[39] As in Jordan, the opinions are accompanied by the curricular representation of ethics in academic media institutes. In Lebanon seven out of twelve university departments offer courses in law and ethics, either separatly or in tandem. These courses are obligatory. Still, at two universities in Lebanon ethics is only an elective subject for the BA program. In all these courses a long list of topics touching on ethics can be generated: information on existing laws, regulations, and national, international, and institutional codes of ethics and their historical developments is an obligatory part of almost all courses in ethics and law.[40] Furthermore, prevailing problems in Lebanon are the starting point for discussions on case studies or role-playing—for example, on bribery and blackmail, the limits of privacy, depictions of violence, and conflicts of interest.[41] It is ambivalent that, on the one hand, the justification of moral decisions is mentioned as a learning target while the philosophical or religious basis used to justify ethical or unethical decisions is only taught in two universities. At the Greek Orthodox Balamand University they deal with the philosophical background of journalistic ethics,[42] whereas at Notre Dame University the ethics course includes "the Catholic Church's stand on legal and ethical functions of the mass media."[43]

Another widespread subject is the coverage of war, with an emphasis on historical cases that occurred during the Lebanese Civil War and current examples, especially those dealing with Iraq. Audiovisual and written illustrations are used to demonstrate the problems of showing violence, the attribution of different groups and persons, the reporter's or journalist's reaction toward violence and victims, and the handling of propaganda of conflicting adversaries.

In contrast to Jordan, representatives of the nonacademic institutes mainly agree with the aforementioned academics' opinions. In particular, the Institute for Professional Journalism in Lebanon has had a big share in stimulating discussions about ethics in recent years by organizing conferences, roundtables, workshops, and discussions with journalists, media managers, and experts, by elaborating professional codes of ethics, and by publishing materials on the issue.[44]

Why Is Journalistic Ethics Considered to Be Relevant at All?

The awareness of the functions and relevance of ethics among university instructors may have an impact on whether they deal with ethical topics during the journalistic education process or not. But it may also have an influence on their contribution to a wider debate within the journalistic field. As we have already seen, journalistic ethics in journalism education is ranked more highly in Lebanon than in Jordan.

Yet although the majority of Jordanian instructors do not believe that teaching ethics to journalists is useful, they consider ethics to be relevant to the society and the development of the profession. Their perspectives do not involve the individual journalist as the most important agent of change. It is not that the journalist may transform an unethical setting through his individual behavior but that a more ethical and freer setting creates more ethical journalists. In this view, institutional bodies have to promote change. The interviewees see ethics as an instrument for reaching an autonomy not beholden to the government, on the one hand; on the other hand, they see ethics as a step toward professionalisation. The way to reach this goal, in their opinion, is to support the journalistic institutions to cooperate with the state authorities to prevent the creation of a new law constraining freedom, for example. If they personally participate in such an endeavor they do not act in their roles as "instructors" but as "journalism experts" for these institutions. For example, two interviewees work as consultants for Jordan's Higher Media Council, which replaced the minister of information in 2002. The council was established by the recently appointed King Abdallah II as "an independent body comprised of both public and private sector organizations specialized in media. The council's responsibilities encompass formulating media policy, overseeing the regulation of the media sector and assisting in the creation of a responsible and accountable media environment."[45] Opinions among those working in journalism concerning this council are divided. Abu Ousbah, for example, who gave his expertise to the council when it was preparing a code of ethics, is well aware of the ambivalence of his work: "If you speak about any code [of ethics] you speak about more constraints against freedom of the press, [but] in the Arab world codes of ethics also protect journalists from the government."[46] Mansour is highly critical of it because he doubts its independence and reliability.[47]

Mansour is just one example of somebody who combines two roles; in his case, he is both instructor and expert. He tries to evoke ethical awareness among the journalists trained by the Center for Defending the Freedom of Journalists in his role as a trainer. As the head of a Journalists' NGO he is involved in working on new institutionalized regulations in journalism. He is convinced that "regulations grown within the journalistic field can push the borders and clean the mine fields."[48] One recent attempt was the handing over of a proposal for a new press and publication law by the Center for Defending the Freedom of Journalists with the aim of reminding King Abdallah of his aspiration for "a freedom of expression as high as the sky."[49] In January 2007 the center published a critical review of the draft law and expressed its reservations about the abandoning of former proposals (CDFJ 2007).

In their activities Jordanian instructors follow an approach that concentrates mainly on the regulative functions of journalism ethics. Only the two NGO trainers Mansour and Sabbagh combine this approach with an orientation-related access: they focus on individual journalists and accept that discussions about critical issues within the whole journalistic field are a useful way of coming to decisions that are more or less binding.[50]

The situation looks totally different in Lebanon. Governmental interference is not as significant as in Jordan. Instead, the situation for journalists in Lebanon in recent years has become dangerous because of political tension and the war with Israel in 2006 (IPI 2007). Consequently, ethics is seldom seen as a tool against governmental interference but as an instrument for resolving societal problems. This coincides with the perceived ethical problems in journalism in Lebanon. All interviewees are worried about the unbalanced journalistic culture, which they see as interrelated to their fragmented society. Political tension between different sectarian groups is mostly mirrored in the media. The lack of responsible journalism regarding societal unity is felt to be a threat to the whole society.[51]

One incident in June 2006 is a vivid example of this. LBC, a Christian-dominated TV station, airs a satirical show every week in which the presenter of the show makes fun of politicians. On June 5, 2006, he mocked Hassan Nasrallah, the chief of Hezbollah. After broadcasting the show, riots took place in Shiite South Beirut as expression of what the rioters—mainly followers of Nasrallah—felt was an insult. In addition to harshly criticizing the extreme reaction to this show, the interviewees were unanimous in criticizing the irresponsible behavior of LBC and its show's host and producer. Nabil Dajani of Arab Reporters for Investigative Journalism sees a clear violation of the law: "LBC has violated the law. This is very clear. Because there is a very clear item in the law that you cannot insult a sectarian. And here, see, you have to be professional; he [the LBC show's host] has to follow the law."[52] Nader points out that it is not only a legal matter but one of indifference to different social groups, which is reflected in editorial departments as well: "In this country you have a certain indifference towards certain structures. One hasn't got the same culture." This criticism highlights the opinion that an ethical journalism can only be practiced in an ethical media culture as a whole and thus includes journalists, editors, and media owners alike.[53]

In the interviewees' view, the development of a code of ethics that is at the same time a guideline for good journalistic practice is one way of achieving more ethical journalism. The training center of the Institute for Professional Journalism was the initiator of a first draft for such a code.[54] In a conference, "Professional Ethics, Media Legislation and Freedom of Expression in Lebanon," this guideline was proposed and discussed with journalists and others active within journalism. It was followed by several other activities such as discussions, roundtable debates, and article publication. On the one hand, this suggests that trainers perceive themselves as active members of a discourse within journalism. On the other hand, it underlines the widespread view that a code of ethics can be used as an instrument of orientation because it allows for discussion of content within the field and reflection on structures and participants' behavior. Interference by the government or the official bodies such as the press association or the journalists' association in this initial phase is unwanted except as participants in the discussion.

Conclusion

To summarize the value of ethics in journalism education in the two countries, it can be concluded that the focus of the aims of education in Lebanon is on the interaction of different fields of competence[55]: technical competence—for example, research or selection of news; communication skills, such as knowledge of different genres; and social orientation, which includes the ability to reflect professional behavior and the awareness of the role of the profession within the society. Within the last of these fields, ethics plays an important role and is accepted as such in Lebanon. In comparison, Jordan's journalism education focuses more on special expertise, especially in development topics.

Although ethics plays a minor role in Jordanian journalism education, the instructors are aware of their own potential for resolving current ethical problems in journalism by contributing to the debate within journalism. Both Jordanian and Lebanese lecturers see themselves as potential agents of change, but in different roles: whereas the university staffs in Lebanon regard their role as lecturers as the most influential, the Jordanian staffs see more potential for growth in their roles as experts. Both follow a higher objective, which in Jordan is the autonomy of the profession and in Lebanon—in addition to the search for credibility—the unity of the country. Thus, journalistic ethics is understood as a tool for regulating the profession in Jordan and as a tool for making the profession more ethical—thus, giving it the potential to change the society—in Lebanon. Coinciding with these aims, a code of ethics is seen as an instrument of regulation in Jordan and a base for discussion in Lebanon.

Notes

1. Interview with M. Tarabay, assistant professor, Lebanese American University, and trainer, Institute for Professional Journalism, Beirut, June 2, 2006.
2. The following institutions were taken into account: American University Beirut, American University for Science and Technology Beirut, Arab International University Beirut, Balamand University, Beirut Arab University, Jinan University, Lebanese American University, Lebanese University Sections I and II, Notre Dame University, Université Saint Esprit de Kasslik, Université Saint Joseph,

the Institute for Professional Journalists, Arab Reporters for Investigative Journalism, the Beirut Institute for Media Arts in Lebanon, Yarmouk University, Petra University, Philadelphia University, the Center for Defending the Freedom of Journalists, and Arab Reporters for Investigative Journalism in Jordan.

3. Press and Publication Law 1998, Art. 2, http://jpa.easycgi.com/english/JPALaw.aspx.
4. Loi sur les publications 1962, Art. 23–26, in: Derradji (1995), 257–269.
5. For Jordan Press Association Law 1998, Art. 5, see http://jpa.easycgi.com/english/JPASystem.aspx; for Lebanon cf. Loi sur les publications 1962, Art. 22, see Derradji (1995), 257–269.
6. Since reliable data on the educational background of working journalists is still hard to find, I refer to statements given by the experts.
7. Interviews with R. Sabbagh, executive director, Arab Reporters for Investigative Journalism, Amman, June 19, 2006; and E. Augé, professor, Balamand University, Balamand, June 5, 2006.
8. Interview with E. Augé, professor, Balamand University, Balamand, June 5, 2006.
9. Interview with A. Masannat, professor, Petra University, Amman, June 21, 2006.
10. Interview with R. Sabbagh, executive director, Arab Reporters for Investigative Journalism, Amman, June 19, 2006.
11. In the mid-1980s another BA journalism program started at the University of Jordan, but it was closed down only two years later (Rifai 1994, 89).
12. Interviews with S. Abu Ousbah, professor, Philadelphia University, Amman, June 20, 2006, and T. Abu Arjah, professor, Petra University, Amman, June 21, 2006.
13. The most popular degree at Lebanese universities is the BA in journalism and/or television and radio. Some universities call it a BA in mass communication with specialization in journalism or TV and radio, like the School of Arts and Science at Lebanese University. There are two departments that focus on practical training in television and film production, L'Institut d'études scéniques, audiovisuelles et cinématographiques at the Université Saint Joseph, and Département des Arts Visuels et Scéniques at Université Saint Esprit de Kasslik. An exceptional case is the program at the American University Beirut, in which the students obtain a BA in sociology/anthropology with specialization in mass communication.
14. Kirsten Maas of the Germany-based Heinrich Böll Foundation in Beirut mentioned also the difficulty finding journalists who get permission from their editors to leave their jobs for several days to participate in these programs. Interview with K. Maas, head, Heinrich Böll Foundation, Beirut, June 9, 2006.
15. A study on journalistic training by the Center for Defending the Freedom of Journalists found out that for most Jordanian (56 percent) and Lebanese (67 percent) journalists the nationality of the trainer does not play a role for

deciding in a specific training (CDFJ 2006, 424, 454), but 70 percent of the Jordanian and 33 percent of the Lebanese journalists consider the financiers of the training or the training institutions for their decision (434, 464).

16. "We used to have an excellent law in 1993, 'press freedom law' we call it, that has been amended against journalism in 1997." Interview with A. Ziadat, professor, Yarmouk University, Irbid, June 25, 2006.
17. "There are many taboos: don't criticize the Arab countries, don't write about sexual life, don't write about the Prophet, don't criticize the government. What kind of ethics is that?" Interview with N. Mansour, director, Center for Defending the Freedom of Journalists, Amman, June 21, 2006.
18. Interview with M. Tarabay, assistant professor, Lebanese American University, and trainer, Institute for Professional Journalism, Beirut, June 2, 2006.
19. Interview with M. al-Abdallah, professor, Lebanese University Section I and Beirut Arab University, Beirut, June 7, 2006.
20. Estimations for Jordan by R. Sabbagh, executive director of Arab Reporters for Investigative Journalism, Amman, June 19, 2006; for Lebanon by M. Abu Fadil, director, Institute for Professional Journalism, Beirut, June 2, 2006.
21. Besides, a variety of announced problems do exist in Lebanon, but they are not as striking as the aforementioned. Among them are the large number of pictures showing victims and brutal violence (interview with K. el-Fakih, professor, Notre Dame University, June 7, 2006), close relations between journalism and public relations, and the defamation and stereotyping of the "other" (interview with J. Nader, lecturer, Balamand University and Lebanese University Section II, Beirut, June 5, 2006). But the entanglement of journalism and public relations is regarded as an additional ethical problem in Jordan, too.
22. Interviews with Abu Ousbah, professor, Philadelphia University, Amman, June 20, 2006; R. Sabbagh, executive director, Arab Reporters for Investigative Journalism, Amman, June 19, 2006; A. Masannat, professor, Petra University, Amman, June 21, 2006; N. Mansour, director, Center for Defending the Freedom of Journalists, Amman, June 21, 2006; N. Dajani, professor, American University Beirut, and chairman of the board, Arab Reporters for Investigative Journalism, Beirut, June 8, 2006; R. Maalouf, professor, Lebanese American University, and director, Beirut Institute for Media Arts, Beirut, June 6, 2006; E. Augé, professor, Balamand University, Balamand, June 5, 2006.
23. Interview with R. Jadaan, lecturer, Philadelphia University, Amman, June 20, 2006.
24. Interviews with M. Abu Fadil, director, Institute for Professional Journalism, Beirut, June 2, 2006; and E. Augé, professor, Balamand University, Balamand, June 5, 2006.
25. Interviews with A. Masannat, professor, Petra University, Amman, June 21, 2006; and A. Nejadat, assistant professor, Yarmouk University, Irbid, June 25, 2006.
26. Interview with M. al-Muhtaseb, lecturer, Yarmouk University, Irbid, June 25, 2006.

27. Interview with T. Abu Arjah, professor, Petra University, Amman, June 21, 2006.
28. Interviews with T. Abu Arjah, professor, Petra University, Amman, June 21, 2006; and A. Masannat, professor, Petra University, Amman, June 21, 2006.
29. The number of arrested journalists in 2005 decreased in Jordan according to a poll among journalists conducted by the Center for Defending the Freedom of Journalists. 15.3 percent of the journalists said that they were apprehended in connection with cases related to the media before 2005. In 2005, only 1.3 percent of the polled journalists said they were arrested during this year (CDFJ 2005). According to the international press freedom monitoring institutes (Reporters sans Frontieres, International Press Institute, Arab Media Watch etc.) no journalists have been imprisoned for a longer period during the last four years in Jordan. One case caused international attention in 2006. Two editors were sentenced to prison for two months because of republishing the Mohammad cartoons (*Jordan Times*, May 31, 2006). Despite this improvement, the perceived danger is still vital (interview with N. Mansour, director, Center for Defending the Freedom of Journalists, Amman, June 21, 2006).
30. Interviews with T. Abu Arjah, professor, Petra University, Amman, June 21, 2006; A. Nejadat, assistant professor, Yarmouk University, Irbid, June 25, 2006; and A. Ziadat, professor, Yarmouk University, Irbid, June 25, 2006.
31. These "taboos" have undergone a heavy discussion and several legal changes in Jordan during the last years. The Press and Publication Law in 1998 listed fourteen content areas as off-limits for journalists. Among them were news disrupting national unity, disparaging religion, etc. (Najjar 2001, 102). The restrictions were removed from the Press and Publication Law in 1999 but were then introduced into the Penal Code, Article 150 again in 2001. Article 150 prohibited the publication of news articles posing a risk, such as harm the country's reputation or stirring up internal strife. Furthermore, Article 195 was introduced, setting a penalty of between one and three years' imprisonment for the crime of lese-majesté. Article 150 was largely reversed in 2003, but Article 195 is still in force (Memorandum on the Draft Press and Publication Law for the Year 2004 of the Kingdom of Jordan, Article 19, http://www.article19.org/pdfs/analysis/jordan.prs.2004.pdf). The discussion is still going on. In January 2007, the Center for Defending the Freedom of Journalists has handed over the parliament's National Guidance Committee its comments and reservations on the PPL draft underway (CDFJ 2007).
32. Interview with R. Sabbagh, executive director, Arab Reporters for Investigative Journalism, Amman, June 19, 2006.
33. Ibid.
34. Ibid.
35. For activities of the Center for Defending the Freedom of Journalists on ethics see www.cdfj.org, *Nashatat* (Activities)—(in Arabic).

36. Interview with M. al-Abdallah, professor, Lebanese University Section I and Beirut Arab University, Beirut, June 7, 2006.
37. Interview with J. Nader, lecturer, Balamand University and Lebanese University Section II, Balamand, June 5, 2006.
38. Interviews with J. Nader, lecturer, Balamand University and Lebanese University Section II, Balamand, June 5, 2006; and M. al-Abdallah, professor, Lebanese University Section I and Beirut Arab University, Beirut, June 7, 2006.
39. Interviews with E. Augé, professor, Balamand University, Balamand, June 5, 2006; and K. el-Fakih, professor, Notre Dame University, Kasslik, June 7, 2006.
40. For example, university programs at Balamand University, http://www.balamand.edu.lb/english/Arts.asp?id=1131&fid=117, or Lebanese University, http://www.ul.edu.lb/francais/faculte.htm.
41. Cf. the university programs at American University of Science and Technology (http://89.108.145.12/pages.asp?id=613&parentID=101&coParent=); Balamand University (http://www.balamand.edu.lb/english/Arts.asp?id=1131&fid=117); or Lebanese American University (http://www.lau.edu.lb/academics/AcadCat_2005-2006.pdf).
42. Interview with J. Nader, lecturer, Balamand University and Lebanese University Section II, Beirut, June 5, 2006.
43. Notre Dame University program 2005–2006, 329, http://www.ndu.edu.lb/.
44. For activities of the Institute for Professional Journalism on ethics, see www.ipj.lau.edu.lb, *Outreach* and *Events.*
45. Cited from the webpage of the Jordan embassy in the United States, "Information on the 'Jordan First' National Campaign," http://www.jordanembassyus.org/new/aboutjordan/er1.shtml.
46. Interview with S. Abu Ousbah, professor, Philadelphia University, Amman, June 20, 2006.
47. Interview with N. Mansour, at Arab Press Network, *Newsletter* no. 4, November 3, 2005, http://www.arabpressnetwork.org/articles.php?id=124&lang=fr.
48. Interview with N. Mansour, director, Center for Defending the Freedom of Journalists, Amman, June 21, 2006.
49. Interview with N. Mansour (see note 47).
50. Interviews with R. Sabbagh, executive director, Arab Reporters for Investigative Journalism, Amman, June 19, 2006; and N. Mansour, director, Center for Defending the Freedom of Journalists, Amman, June 21, 2006.
51. This concern has been continuously growing during the current tensions in the country. The National Audiovisual Media Council chief Abdel-Hadi Mahfouz's appeal is evidence of that. He addressed the media on January 30, 2007, requesting it to act responsibly: "The role of the audiovisual institutions should be constructive; they should not be a place to provoke confessional conflicts" (*Daily Star* online, January 30, 2007, "Media Council Chief Cites Perils of 'Tense Rhetoric'").

52. Interview with N. Dajani, professor, American University Beirut and Chairman of the Board of Arab Reporters for Investigative Journalism, Beirut, June 8, 2006.
53. Interview with J. Nader, lecturer, Balamand University and Lebanese University Section II, Balamand, June 5, 2006.
54. There had been an earlier code of ethics approved by the General Assembly of the Press Syndicate in 1974, which was one of many sources for the development of the new one (IPJ 2002, 63).
55. In reference to Weischenberg's fields of competence in journalism, I subdivide the education targets into technical competence, communication skills, special expertise, and social orientation, which is closely related to ethical awareness (Weischenberg 1990, 24).

References

Bashshur, M. (2003), The Deepening Cleavage in the Educational System. In T. Hanf (ed.), *Lebanon in Limbo: Postwar Society and State in an Uncertain Regional Environment.* Baden-Baden: Nomos, 159–179.

Braune, I. (2005), *Die Journalistenverbände in Jordanien und Libanon. Ein Teil der Zivilgesellschaft?* Hamburg: Deutsches Orient-Institut.

CDFJ (Center for Defending the Freedom of Journalists) (2005), Freedom of the Press...as High as the Sky. Media Freedom Status in Jordan 2005, http://cdfj.org/look/PDFs/Media%20Freedom%20Status%20in%20Jordan%202005%20EN.pdf.

———. (2006), *Investing in the Future: Strategy for Arab Journalists' Professional and Legal Capacity Building* [in Arabic]. Amman: CDFJ.

———. (2007), CDFJ Hands the Parliament's National Guidance Committee its Comments, Reservations on the Press and Publications Draft Law, http://cdfj.org/look/en-article.tpl?IdLanguage=1&IdPublication=1&NrArticle=3173&NrIssue=2&NrSection=2.

Dajani, N./O. A. Najjar (2003), Status of Media in Syria, Lebanon, and Jordan. In D. H. Johnston (ed.), *Encyclopaedia of International Media and Communication*, volume 4, R–Z. San Dieg Academic Press, 301–315.

Debatin, B. (1997), Ethische Grenzen oder Grenzen der Ethik? Überlegungen zur Steuerungs und Reflexionsfunktion der Medienethik. In G. Bentele/M. Haller (eds.), *Aktuelle Entstehung von Öffentlichkeit. Akteure—Strukturen—Veränderungen.* Konstanz: UVK, 281–290.

Derradji, A. (1995), *Le droit de la presse et la liberté d'information et d'opinion dans les pays Arabes.* Paris: Publi Sud.

Hafez, K. (2003), Journalism Ethics Revisited: A Comparison of Ethics Codes in Europe, North Africa, the Middle East and Muslim Asia. In K. Hafez (ed.), *Media Ethics in the Dialogue of Cultures: Journalistic Self-Regulation in Europe, the Arab World, and Muslim Asia.* Hamburg: Deutsches Orient-Institut, 39–68.

IPI (International Press Institute) (2007), Media in Lebanon: Reporting on a Nation Divided. Report on IPI's Finding Mission to Lebanon, 8–13 December 2006, http://

www.freemedia.at/cms/ipi/missions_detail.html?ctxid=CH0065&docid=CMS1166524 746992&category=missions.

IPJ (Institute for Professional Journalists) (2002), Professional Ethics, Media Legislation and Freedom of Expression in Lebanon. Proceedings of a Conference Held in Beirut, March 1–2, 2002 by the IPJ, http://ipj.lau.edu.lb/events/20020301/roundtable.php.

Jones, A. (2002), From Vanguard to Vanquished? The Tabloid Press in Jordan. *Political Communication* 2, 171–187.

Kunczik, M. (1999), Closing Remarks: Is There an International Ethics of Journalism? In M. Kunczik (ed.), *Ethics in Journalism: A Reader on Their Perception in the Third World.* Bonn: Friedrich-Ebert-Stiftung, 245–268.

Najjar, O. A. (2001), Freedom of the Press in Jordanian Press Laws 1927–1998. In K. Hafez (ed.), *Mass Media, Politics and Society in the Middle East.* Cresskill: Hampton Press, 77–108.

Rifai, Z. (1994), Status of Media Training in Jordan. In G. Hawatmeh (ed.), *The Role of the Media in a Democracy—The Case of Jordan.* Amman: Center for Strategic Studies, 85–93.

Robinson, G. R. (2005), *Tasting Western Journalism: Media Training in the Middle East.* Los Angeles: USC Center on Public Diplomacy.

Thomaß, B. (1998), *Journalistische Ethik. Ein Vergleich der Diskurse in Frankreich, Großbritannien und Deutschland.* Opladen: Westdeutscher Verlag.

Thomaß, B./M. Tzankoff (2001), Medien und Transformation in den postkommunistischen Staaten Osteuropas. In B. Thomaß M. Tzankoff (eds.), *Medien und Transformation in Osteuropa.* Wiesbaden: Westdeutscher Verlag, 235–252.

Weischenberg, S. (1990), Das "Prinzip Echternach." Zur Einführung in das Thema "Journalismus und Kompetenz." In S. Weischenberg (ed.), *Journalismus und Kompetenz. Qualifizierung und Rekrutierung für Medienberufe.* Opladen: Westdeutscher Verlag, 11–41.

Media Economy

CHAPTER TEN

Gaps in the Market: Insights from Scholarly Work on Arab Media Economics

Naomi Sakr

If, as the consensus would have it, the point of economics is to study choices people make about using scarce resources (Doyle 2002, 2), economics may not have presented itself as the most obvious discipline through which to grasp major features of Arab media in the early twenty-first century. With investment in an ever-growing profusion of media outlets, spurred after 2000 by several years of soaring oil revenues, scarcity of resources was understandably not the first issue to preoccupy scholars of the field. Of course, when economists use the term "scarcity," they simply refer to the fact that resources are not unlimited and can be put to alternative uses. Nevertheless, given the sums of money spent on Arab media output and a widespread lack of transparency about this spending, it is not surprising that the literature on Arab media economics remained rather sparse for more than fifteen years after the market upheaval that followed the emergence of satellite television channels in Arabic in the early 1990s.

The lack of literature is a problem not only for academic researchers but also for policy analysts and advisers. Buoyant oil rents have long been seen as providing authoritarian Arab governments with the means to avoid political and economic restructuring of a kind that would widen political participation (Luciani 1994, 131). Where the workings of Arab media markets remain obscure, questions of fundamental importance for future media law and policy are left unanswered. Markets are "not made in heaven" (Hills 1998, 459); they are made on earth by the decisions of politicians and regulators and the impact these decisions have on supply and demand. Because media products have special economic features that distinguish them from other goods, and because information is both a media product and a key ingredient of economic advancement (Garnham 2005, 289), regulation of media markets has structural ramifications that run deeper than the issues around taste, decency, cultural heritage, or political bias that are most commonly associated with media regulation.

A sparseness of published research dealing directly with the economics of Arab media, in Arabic, English or French, makes it unfulfilling to survey the literature from the point of view of industry subsectors (film, television, radio, newspapers, magazines, Internet) or individual countries. Equally, many insights will be lost if diverse media markets across the Arab world are treated as one. What seems more interesting is to try to understand how the microeconomics of particular subsectors connect with other subsectors in the same country and how they fit with the macroeconomic profiles of countries and the region as a whole. Movie making in Egypt and Saudi Arabia illustrates how striking contrasts between countries can coexist with industrial overlap. The first screening of a film in Egypt took place less than a year after Europe's first-ever film showing, in Paris in 1895. Through a combination of local and foreign investment and talent, Egypt became the only Arab country to develop a national film industry during the colonial period (Shafik 1998, 11). In doing so, it is said to have been on a par, in terms of confronting Hollywood exports, with "the British [film] industry, the rest of Europe, and the emerging film industries of Latin America and colonial Asia" (Vitalis 2000, 271). Egyptian experience in movies consequently gave the country a head start when it came to developing television (Boyd 1999, 38). In Saudi Arabia, in contrast, with a ban on cinemas long outlasting religious resistance to television, experiments in making or showing films remained highly localized and discreet until 2006. Yet, when the first Saudi feature film *Keif Al-Hal* (How Are Things?) appeared at the Cannes Film Festival that year, it represented a further milestone in the expansion of Prince Alwaleed bin Talal's Saudi-based media empire. That empire was partly built through television, via Alwaleed's involvement in the company ART (Arab Radio and Television), the Rotana record label, and Rotana network of television channels. ART has studios in Egypt, while both ART and Rotana have acquired libraries of Egyptian music and film (Sakr 2007).

It is proposed in this chapter to show some economic rationales for such relationships and developments by disentangling the economics of media production from the economics of distribution on one hand and the economics of consumption on the other. To the extent that they deal with the first of these categories, studies of Arab media should illuminate the costs incurred in media production, including labor costs. They should show how these are paid for, and what impact the various payment methods have on the type of content produced. Distribution raises questions that also relate to covering production costs, including protection of intellectual property and the market pressures on media producers to ensure outlets for their products by keeping control over distribution channels. To explore the economics of consumption means examining the allocation of resources involved in media use, including education, money, and time. It is possible to piece together primary data on all these issues from trade publications serving the advertising industry or from articles in listings magazines. That is not the purpose of this chapter. Instead it refers to studies by political economists, historians, and others, whose work has illuminated aspects of Arab media economics, sometimes intentionally and sometimes not. After a preliminary consideration of what makes media economics special in any context, the subsequent sections deal successively with production, distribution, and consumption, in each case looking at film, broadcasting, and the press in turn. The Internet, as primarily a means of distribution, is dealt with as such.

Special Economic Features of Symbolic Goods

Goods exchanged on media markets need a material carrier—whether sheets of paper, plastic discs, radio waves and receivers, or telephone lines. But media content itself is not material; it consists of meaning, and meaning is a commodity that cannot be physically destroyed. People watching a film or television program are not rivals with each other for that product, because one person's consumption does not reduce the supply to another in the way that it would with a kilo of oranges or a loaf of bread. Moreover, almost all the costs of creating a film, broadcast program, or single edition of a newspaper go into the original copy; once that has been made the costs of reproduction are, relatively speaking, extremely low. These special economic features of symbolic goods have been explored by Nicholas Garnham (e.g. 2000, 54–58) and others, whose work is cited and summarized by Gillian Doyle (2002, 10–13) and David Hesmondhalgh (2002, 17–22). For media producers the peculiarities are significant because they pose challenges for recouping production costs.

Raising the price to consumers of sought-after media content is not generally practicable because symbolic goods are not only nonrival but also nonexcludable: users cannot be stopped from watching unencrypted audiovisual products or sharing their newspapers, magazines, and compact discs. On the contrary, for financiers who have already sunk their money into a script, director, cast, set, editorial staff, camera crew, or singer, there is everything to gain and virtually nothing to pay for increasing the audience to the utmost. In the case of a car, washing machine, or other material good, each extra unit produced requires extra physical input that adds costs. By contrast, making extra copies of a publication, CD or DVD costs next to nothing and for broadcasters the cost of adding viewers or listeners for a program is zero. Since advertising shares many characteristics of mediated communication, media companies and advertisers' common interests create a situation in which the former can cover the costs of content creation by selling advertising space or airtime. By doing so, however, they introduce an influential third party into the relationship between producer and consumer. In the case of Arab media, competition among outlets that are at least partly funded through commercials has been good for consumers insofar as it helped to enliven and increase program choices. But it has also strengthened commercial influences, in the sense that advertisers favor certain types of content and certain types of audiences over others (Sakr 2006, 63–65).

Where the value of over-the-counter sales of media products cannot replace advertising revenue or offset the influence of advertisers, subsidies are another alternative. Here again, there is potential for beneficial or detrimental effects both within the media industry itself and in terms of externalities, or side effects. Producing information is an expensive business that may not be immediately profitable to the producer precisely because of the difficulty of excluding non-paying consumers (Stiglitz 1999, 8, 26). Since society as a whole benefits from the availability of information, including information that may annoy advertisers, the argument for subsidising it publicly is strong enough to have produced nonprofit public service broadcasters in Britain, Canada, and Australia in the form of the BBC, CBC, and ABC (Hoskins et al. 2004, 293–298). Some countries around the world have a publicly mandated system of subsidizing newspapers so as to promote the expression of a diversity of views. Some subsidize their domestic film industry through a national film council as the only guaranteed means to keep it alive.

Economics of Production in Arab Film, Broadcasting, and the Press

Since box office receipts are crucial to a film's financial viability, the lower a country's cinema admissions the harder it is to turn a profit on locally made films. Arab countries at opposite ends of the population spectrum demonstrate this economic rule, and studies about them expose the risks as well as the benefits of state support. Garay Menicucci points out that no Arab country apart from Egypt has a large enough internal market to sustain an independent national film industry (2005, 46), while Lizbeth Malkmus and Roy Armes draw on earlier studies to recount how low production costs and population size helped Egypt's film industry to enjoy a boom between the end of World War II and the 1952 revolution. With average output running at fifty films a year, Egyptian cinema not only attracted large Egyptian audiences but also brought in valuable export revenues up to that point (1991, 31). In small countries like Lebanon and Tunisia, however, box office receipts are also proportionate to population size, so that a feature film in Tunisia, for example, "can never actually pay for itself" (Shafik 1998, 33). Despite this disadvantage, Viola Shafik considers Tunisia lucky to have escaped the ideologically committed state interventions in film production and distribution that occurred under nationalizing governments in Egypt, Syria, and Algeria at various times (1998, 33). Dima Dabbous-Sensenig is not so sure that a lack of state support has been good for Lebanese cinema. But she is doubtful about the amount of difference that a planned Ministry of Culture subsidy could make, given that the sum promised in 2001 amounted to just US$200,000, to be divided among ten films (2006, 66–67). It might have been thought, as Shafik (1998, 40) notes, that pan-Arab coproduction of films could have helped to overcome disparities in the size of Arab markets. Instead it turns out that coproduction with Europeans has been much more common, even though it has been deeply problematic in orienting film content toward European rather than Arab audiences (Dwyer 2004; Menicucci 2005, 46–47).

Filmmaking is a risky business financially because a large number of profitable films are needed to keep the sector afloat. Low budgets can rarely secure proven talent, which makes low-budget movies generally less profitable in the long run. Hence, it makes economic sense to finance films from within media conglomerates that can ensure wide and effective distribution through being vertically integrated up and down the supply chain. Conglomerates can also cross-subsidize between profitable and less profitable output, because their horizontal integration enables them to generate and distribute a diverse range of cultural goods. Rotana's horizontal expansion from music and television into local film production was noted earlier. Egypt's biggest budget film, *Imaret Yaaqoubian* (The Yaaqoubian Building), released the same year as Rotana's *Keif Al-Hal?* (How Are Things?), was a project of GN4ME, part of the Good News Group, another conglomerate expanding both vertically and horizontally. Privately owned by Egyptian media magnate Imadeddin Adeeb, a television talk show host and owner of two daily newspapers as well as other publications, the Good News Group started two music radio stations in Egypt in 2003. Given Adeeb's close personal relations with Egypt's president, Hosni Mubarak, his business was widely expected in 2005 to benefit from eventual partial privatisation of the country's state-owned and government-run terrestrial broadcasting monopoly, the Egyptian Radio and Television Union (El-Amrani 2005, 331).

Expansion in the number of broadcasters under private Arab ownership has attracted ample scholarly attention, although the focus on satellite television has been greater than that on changes in terrestrial channels or radio. The key question for the present section is how the emergence of new broadcasters, and their subsequent expansion into multichannel digital networks, affected the economics of program production. One early effect was seen in rising demand by broadcasters for a still-limited supply of content, which prompted some broadcasters to call for collective action to try to curb rising content prices by averting head-on competition for top performers and sports rights (Sakr 2001, 117). If broadcasters failed to heed the call, it has to be assumed that their reasons for doing so were not wholly economic. Indeed, Oliver Boyd-Barrett, observing preparations for a Dubai-based channel, concluded that one of its principal goals was to promote Dubai; although this motive was linked to the emirate's macroeconomic future, Boyd-Barrett deemed it neither "exclusively" nor "directly" economic (2000, 325). Similarly, Saudi Arabia's satellite broadcasters, whose status as "private" has to be understood in the context of intertwined political and business interests between the Saudi ruling family and bourgeoisie (Luciani 2005, 145–148, 180–181), proved ready to allocate large sums to establish a dominant position in the market from which to control the scope and nature of television content rather than its price (Boyd 2001, 53–54, Ayish 1997, 490).

At least part of the large sums allocated to television in this manner has to be seen as a form of subsidy, since all the evidence points to a shortfall in the amount of advertising revenue actually reaching any of the new broadcasters, big or small. As Muhammad Ayish remarked in his study of Arab television, in a chapter titled "Economic Context," "private broadcasters seemed set to go beyond advertising-generated dollars to sustain their operations" (2003, 53). This is ironic, given that state broadcasters were seemingly forced into making way for private involvement because they could no longer sustain their own bloated budgets and mounting deficits. Neither Ayish nor Jihad Fakhreddine, writing in the early years of this century, were optimistic that advertising's contribution to programming costs could be boosted substantially in the short term. Ayish noted that, in theory, the pan-Arab television market should be attractive to advertisers. But he cautioned about the outcome of stiff competition for the "advertising pie." Fakhreddine warned explicitly that competition would increase downward pressure on the price of advertising slots. Having previously accused the pan-Arab satellite channels of trying to run before they could walk (2000), in the sense of making overoptimistic assumptions about advertising revenue, Fakhreddine reported five years later that his worries were well founded. By then market forces had indeed brought advertising rates down, while the "relaxed attitude" of the "big market players" had left advertisers in the dark about the size of audiences that television channels could deliver for them (2005, 158–159). To supplement advertising, channel executives were maximizing new revenue streams afforded by reality game shows whereby viewers vote for contestants by telephone calls or SMS text messages and television companies share the proceeds with their telecom counterparts. Joe Khalil, a specialist in program formats, has shown how Arab television companies were ready to pay steep fees for the license to make local versions of global reality formats (2004, 2006), while Gordon Robison (2005) has researched the reasoning that led some companies to screen imported versions of reality formats without taking the risk of making a local version.

If television executives made a relatively late start in using their ingenuity to diversify sources of revenue, owners and managers in sections of the Arab press have been playing the diversification game for a long time. Some papers enjoy direct subsidies, as detailed in William Rugh's updated typology of press systems in the Arab world (2004). For a more exhaustive catalog of subsidy mechanisms, however, Nabil Dajani's 1992 study of the Lebanese press seems relevant not only to Lebanon but other countries as well. Besides outright monthly or yearly payments by political patrons, money may be paid to put certain ideas or images into circulation, including by means of gifts to journalists. Advertising budgets may be directed to certain publications on the basis of content rather than readership and, in some cases, payments may be used to buy a newspaper's silence on certain issues or events (Dajani 1992: 49–53). Decisions about advertising are key to Egypt's newspapermarket, where a few dominant public sector agencies have enjoyed advantages over the private sector in being able to offer attractive discounts to advertisers, along with easy access to major outlets (Napoli et al. 1995, 52–53). Private operators are meanwhile liable to pay tax at 36 percent of the value of advertisements and, although newspapers and magazines produced in the free zone can escape the tax, the dominant position of government-funded newspapers and public sector agencies makes it hard for free-zone papers to compete (Berenger 2005). One way for nongovernment newspapers to scrape along is to payless than a living wage to their reporters. Data compiled by Yorck von Korff in his study of Egyptian journalists (2003, 116–13) implies that some journalists effectively subsidize their own jobs.

Distribution: A Key to Sustainability of Production

It follows from the nonrival and nonexcludable nature of media goods that owners of media content will seek to create some measure of rivalry and excludability by whatever means they can. Thus it is important in media economics to distinguish between content and carrier, since it is the latter that can create artificial scarcity by erecting barriers to access. Encryption technologies enabled the introduction of direct payment for television programming. Copyright enforcement campaigns were stepped up to protect Western film studios' and music producers' intellectual property at a time when the circuits through which they could be pirated increased in number. In this respect, the Internet presented itself as just one more channel for distribution of media content alongside other new distribution channels that expanded during the 1990s, such as satellite television and cable. Where the Internet differed was in the opportunities it offered for file sharing, or exchange of content on a many-to-many model, in place of the one-way, one-to-many flow that had prevailed for mass media distribution hitherto.

By analyzing Arab film production and distribution separately, it becomes possible to amplify the explanation already given for challenges faced by film industries across the region. A film producer will only benefit directly from the success of a film if he or she enjoys the proceeds from distribution, which is why there is a strong economic motivation for film studios to own chains of cinemas. Walter Armbrust (2000, 31) notes that, even in the heyday of Egyptian film, profits did not find their way back to the studios that made them. Robert Vitalis (2000, 275–76) recounts how Hollywood's MGM and Twentieth Century Fox built cinemas in Cairo and Alexandria in the 1940s and 1950s, thereby guaranteeing an outlet for American as well as Egyptian films. Antitrust legislation in the United States in 1948 had disrupted the vertical integration that linked studios and cinema chains in the United States, but it did nothing to interfere with efforts by the U.S. State Department and Motion Picture Association of America to build vertical integration abroad. This helps to explain the dominant global position of Hollywood films (Thussu 2006, 17–19). In more recent times, the number, location, and ownership of cinemas in Egypt has continued to play a part in the accessibility of Egyptian-made films, to the extent that the well-known director Yousef Chahine resorted to investing in his own cinema chain in Cairo to get his films screened to Egyptian audiences (Menicucci 2005, 46). Construction of new multiplex cinemas in Egypt has mostly been centered on what Menicucci describes as "upscale shopping malls and luxury hotels." Overall, according to the Arab Human Development Report (UNDP 2003, 80), the number of cinema seats per one thousand people in Egypt was around 1.5 in 2003, compared with an international average of 2.5. In some Arab countries the total number of cinemas is only in double figures. Roy Armes reports a steady decline in Tunisia, from 156 when the countries won independence in 1956 to 36 in the early years of this century, and a slump in Algeria from 300 at independence to "barely a dozen today" (2005, 181). Peter Lagerquist and Jim Quilty (2006) have shown how wealthy sponsors pour money selectively into an event like the Dubai International Film Festival, which has the potential to promote distribution of Arab films. Yet, where cinema attendance is restricted to a tiny elite, the prospects for local films enjoying big box-office receipts are limited.

Armes (2005, 181) points out that the "diminution of film theatres has been accompanied by a huge development of alternative distribution structures" using video, cable, and satellite television, which now reach large numbers of homes. Television has also become a significant distribution circuit for music in recent years, as is evident in the rise of Arab-owned music channels since 2002 and the expansion of single channels into a network of three or more. FM radio stations playing music have proliferated over the same period. But with the multiplication of alternative means of delivery come difficulties in extracting payment. Joe Foote (1998) followed the project to send CNN as an encrypted signal to tourists and diplomats in Egypt, showing how it underperformed after the 1991 Gulf War spurred the sale of satellite dishes, which made CNN available without subscription. The Arab world's three pay-TV operators have had to work hard to combat piracy of the programs they show, especially among communities where a single subscription can be shared among scores of households through unregulated cabling (Sakr 2001, 95, Madani 2003). ART, having monopolized rights to show 2006 World Cup football matches on its pay-TV network, ended up showing the semifinals and finals unencrypted (Sakr 2007). Low-income populations were not alone in regarding piracy as a natural response to the self-interested profit-oriented barrier ART had imposed on viewing.

Understanding how barriers to access can come about through distribution techniques is also important in relation to the economics of newspapers and magazines. Rugh (2004), despite looking closely at the press, fails to elaborate on the stranglehold placed by government-owned distribution houses on circulation of newspapers published by opposition parties or independent companies. In Egypt, for example, nongovernment papers lack their own printing presses and distribution networks, which puts them at a potential disadvantage in terms of reaching major book stalls and newsstands and makes them less attractive to advertisers who want circulation to be guaranteed (Bernard-Maugiron/Ibrahim 2001, 127). But such obstructions are not always insuperable. Historically, according to Ami Ayalon (1995, 155), oral circulation of texts through reading aloud was able to overcome, to some degree, barriers to access imposed by illiteracy and poverty. Thus, measuring the number of copies sold "may not be the best yardstick for measuring the size of the public exposed to the press" (154). Similarly, statistics for Internet connections in Arab households are not the best guide to determining exact statistics concerning Internet use because of the extent to which users rely on Internet cafés (Wheeler 2006, 34–35). Today, distribution of newspapers via the Internet overcomes some of the physical obstacles and facilitates access to newspapers across borders. Statistics show that visits to online versions of Beirut-based newspapers regularly surge in the aftermath of major political events (Gonzalez-Quijano 2003, 70–71). The challenge for newspaper publishers is to transform the public's interest into cash.

Audiences and the Economics of Media Use

Just as producers and distributors decide between alternative uses when considering the allocation of resources, media users do likewise when they devote resources to media use. The act of paying for a ticket to the cinema or buying a magazine obviously involves mobilization of financial resources, but another resource that is also required in these and all other cases is time. The significance of choosing to spend time on one media output rather than another becomes more apparent when it is realized that viewers, listeners, and readers do not know if they will benefit from watching, listening, or reading a particular item until after they have done so—at which point the time has already gone and cannot be regained. Different groups in society have different resources of leisure time and rules of supply and demand apply here, too, in the sense that the scarcer the free time available to an individual the more valuable that time becomes and the higher the stakes in deciding how to spend it. Where time is scarce there is increased demand for information about the options available, be it reviews, recommendations from friends, or previous satisfaction with particular media figures, whether actor, presenter, or writer.

That studies of Arab media audiences are notoriously rare is a contentious matter for advertisers, who repeatedly insist that they need to know more about audiences' preferences and choices if they are to increase their spending on advertising with Arab media above the levels still prevailing in the early years of this century, which remained low by global standards (Sakr 2001, 2007). A lack of audience data produced within the media industry itself (Fakhreddine 2005, 157–158) is mirrored by the rarity of scholarly studies relating media use to trends in media users' incomes and other spending, to demographic profiles, or changes in transport and the built environment that affect the accessibility of cinemas or outlets for print media. In a fascinating account of how and where Michael Moore's documentary *Fahrenheit 9/11* was screened in Cairo in the summer of 2004, Menicucci (2004) shows how considerations such as venue and timing are crucial to media use. Opening in Maadi, "nowhere near affordable public transportation," the film played to expatriates and owners of "sport utility vehicles and Mercedes sedans." When it finally reached a more central location "within walking distance of two subway stops," the film appeared on fewer screens and "at less convenient times."

Television viewing may take place in the home, but the question of which programs are watched in the era of satellite receivers and pay TV depends on disposable income and free time. Measurement of time spent watching television is tricky, because of the difference between leaving the television switched on and actually watching it attentively. But surveys suggest there may be a correlation between lower incomes and longer viewing times in some countries (Al-Abd/Al-Ali 1995, 113–114). They also indicate that viewing times had already increased so substantially in the five years before 2001, reaching levels of over four hours per individual per day in some countries, that massive increases in the quantity of television output would be unlikely to stimulate a proportionate increase in viewing times (Sakr 2002) and would instead force the ever growing number of channels to accept smaller shares of total audience hours. As to the growth prospects for pay-TV providers, these depend on changes in incomes, which vary among and within countries. Information on poverty and income distribution in the region is extremely weak (UNDP 2003, 139). But Lotfi Madani's research (2002, 184–186), drawing on data from Algeria's Institut Abassa, uncovers some reasons why communities in low-cost housing in Algiers moved from shared access to subscription channels via informal cabling arrangements to a much greater degree of individual ownership of satellite dishes during the course of the 1990s. He discusses the shift in light of push and pull factors such as the minimum wage, levels of education, state of emergency and extended curfews, and dissatisfaction with random channel selection and nonexistent after-sales service experienced by subscribers to a shared antenna. Even so, as Madani comments elsewhere (2003, 114), neither this nor any other data tell us who watches which programs.

Levels of education are as crucial to the economic survival of newspapers and magazines as they are to book publishing. Ayalon (1995, 143) considers widespread illiteracy to have been of "pivotal importance" in the history of the Arab press, because the small reservoir of readers placed a big constraint on the profitability of journals. The *Arab Human Development Report 2003* blames low demand for newspapers in the present era on low literacy rates and the high cost of newspapers relative to incomes (UNDP 2003, 59). However, the relationship between literacy and written content works both ways. Literacy is certainly a prerequisite for print media consumption, but it has to be remembered that it takes interesting publications to make people want to be able read. Equally, literacy gives no clues to reading habits. Where writers and editors lose their daily struggle with censors, markets for reading matter are distorted because supply is not available to meet potential demand.

Conclusion

As demonstrated by some of the research cited in this chapter, economic analysis of Arab media can go a long way to explaining why the region's pool of creative talent has largely failed to make headway in meeting demand for prized and vibrant media content that is made locally in the service of local populations. Filmmakers in Arab countries with large enough populations to support a viable national film industry suffered setbacks in the early postcolonial years through ill-advised government interventions, while those that could have benefited from strategic government support were often left to fend for themselves. A paucity of cinema seats drags down the box office receipts that are vital to a film's profitability, since the general public's access to affordable, nearby, welcoming cineplexes is a prerequisite for box office success. The situation whereby Arab broadcasters put political goals ahead of profits was shown to have continued into the satellite era. In this environment—characterized by broadcasters' reluctance to measure ratings, advertisers' reluctance to advertise without ratings, and widespread piracy of pay TV—radio and television output was pushed toward certain types of programming, including reality TV formats that could bring revenue from telephone voting, or imported shows that were deemed cheaper and less risky than equivalents made at home. The Arab press, meanwhile, has always faced market limitations caused by low literacy levels and low incomes, along with distortions caused by government controls on printing and distribution. It has survived through politically motivated subsidies. But these subsidies push content in predetermined ideological directions and thereby aggravate disparities between supply and demand.

These findings have clear implications for Arab media policy. There are strong arguments for subsidies in certain situations to counter factors that can undermine the profitability of locally generated media content. But subsidies linked to political agendas undermine profitability as well. Distribution networks need attention, bearing in mind that the profitability or otherwise of producing media content depends on the scale of access to it, and that concentration of controls over this stage in the supply chain further reduces diversity of supply. Meanwhile, the scale of piracy in lower-income Arab countries demonstrates that Arab consumers are hungry for the type of content that is currently reserved for an affluent elite. This much can be concluded from the existing patchy literature on Arab media economics. Implications of these conclusions point up the urgency of further research.

References

Abd, A.al-/F. al-Ali (1995), *Studies in Space Media* [in Arabic]. Cairo: Dar Al-Fikr Al-Arabi.

Armbrust, W. (2000), Introduction: Anxieties of Scale. In W. Armbrust (ed.), *Mass Mediations: New Approaches to Popular Culture in the Middle East and Beyond.* Berkeley: University of California Press, 1–31.

Armes, R. (2005), *Postcolonial Images: Studies in North African Film.* Bloomington: Indiana University Press.

Ayalon, A. (1995), *The Press in the Arab Middle East.* New York: Oxford University Press.

Ayish, M. (1997), Arab Television Goes Commercial: A Case Study of the Middle East Broadcasting Centre. *Gazette* 6, 473–493.

———. (2003), Arab World Television in the Age of Globalisation. Hamburg: Deutsches Orient-Institut.

Berenger, R. (2005), Tax Economics and Censorship of Foreign-Licensed Publications Distributed in Egypt: The Case of the "Cyprus Press." *Journal of Middle East Media* 1, 71–89.

Bernard-Maurgiron, N./G. Ibrahim (2001), Pouvoir de la censure ou censure du pouvoir? L'affaire Yusuf Wali c. al-Shaab. *Egypt/Monde Arabe*, 125–148.

Boyd, D. A. (1999), *Broadcasting in the Arab World: A Survey of the Electronic Media in the Middle East.* Ames: Iowa State University Press.

______. (2001), Saudi Arabia's International Media Strategy: Influence through Multinational Ownership. In K. Hafez (ed.), *Mass Media, Politics and Society in the Middle East.* Cresskill: Hampton Press, 43–60.

Boyd-Barrett, O. (2000), Pan-Arab Satellite Television: The Dialectics of Identity. In H. Tumber (ed.), *Media Power, Professionals and Policies.* London: Routledge, 314–331.

Dabbous-Sensenig, D. (2006), Ahead of the Bandwagon: Lebanon's Free Media Market. In S. Harvey (ed.), *Trading Culture: Global Traffic and Local Cultures in Film and Television.* Eastleigh: John Libbey, 61–75.

Dajani, N. (1992), *Disoriented Media in a Fragmented Society: The Lebanese Experience.* Beirut: American University of Beirut.

Doyle, G. (2002), *Understanding Media Economics.* London: Sage.

Dwyer, K. (2004), *Beyond Casablanca: M. A. Tazi and the Adventure of Moroccan Cinema.* Bloomington: Indiana University Press.

El-Amrani, I. (2005), The Long Wait: Reform in Egypt's State-Owned Broadcasting Service. *Transnational Broadcasting Studies* 2, 324–334.

Fakhreddine, J. (2000), Pan-Arab Satellite Television: Now the Survival Part. *Transnational Broadcasting Studies* 5, http://www.tbsjournal.com/Archives/Fall00/Fakhreddine.htm.

———. (2005), The Rise and Potential Fall of Pan-Arab Satellite TV. *Transnational Broadcasting Studies* 1, 156–160.

Foote, J. (1998), CNE in Egypt: Some Light at the End of an Arduous Tunnel. *Transnational Broadcasting Studies* 1, http://www.tbsjournal.com/Archives/Fall98/Articles1/CNE/cne.html.

Garnham, N. (2000), *Emancipation, the Media, and Modernity.* Oxford: Oxford University Press.

———. (2005), The Information Society Debate Revisited. In J. Curran /M. Gurevitch (ed.), *Mass Media and Society.* London: Arnold, 287–302.

Gonzalez-Quijano, Y. (2003), The Birth of a Media Ecosystem: Lebanon in the Internet Age. In D. Eickelman/J. Anderson (eds.), *New Media in the Muslim World: The Emerging Public Sphere*. Bloomington: Indiana University Press, 61–79.

Hesmondhalgh, D. (2002), *The Cultural Industries*. London: Sage.

Hills, J. (1998), Liberalization, Regulation and Development. *Gazette* 6, 459–476.

Hoskins, C./S. McFadyen/A. Finn (2004), *Media Economics: Applying Economics to New and Traditional Media*. London: Sage.

Khalil, J. (2004), Blending In: Arab Television and the Search for Programming Ideas. *Transnational Broadcasting Studies* 13, http://www.tbsjournal.com/Archives/Fall04/khalil.html.

———. (2006), Inside Arab Reality Television: Development, Definitions and Demystification. *Transnational Broadcasting Studies* 2, 51–68.

Korff, Y. von (2003), *Missing the Wave: Egyptian Journalists' Contribution to Democratization in the 1990s*. Hamburg: Deutsches Orient-Institut.

Lagerquist, P./J. Quilty (2006), Reel Casbah. *Middle East Report Online*, merip.org/mero/interventions/lagerquist_quilty_interv.html.

Luciani, G. (1994), The Oil Rent, the Fiscal Crisis of the State and Democratization. In G. Salamé (ed.), *Democracy without Democrats? The Renewal of Politics in the Muslim World*. London: I. B. Tauris, 130–155.

———. (2005), From Private Sector to National Bourgeoisie: Saudi Arabian Business. In P. Aarts/G. Nonneman (eds.), *Saudi Arabia in the Balance: Political Economy, Society, Foreign Affairs*. London: Hurst, 144–181.

Madani, L. (2002), L'antenne parabolique en Algérie, entre dominations et résistances. In T. Mattelart (ed.), *La mondialisation des médias contre la censure*. Brussels: Editions De Boeck/INA, 177–210.

_____. (2003), Une lofteuse à Alger. In G. Lochard/G. Soulez (eds.), *La télé-réalité, un débat mondial*. Paris: INA/MédiaMorphoses, 144–117.

Malkmus, L./R. Armes (1991), *Arab and African Film Making*. London: Zed Books.

Menicucci, G. (2004), *Fahrenheit 9/11* Plays Cairo. *Middle East Report Online*, merip.org/mero/mero091604.html.

———. (2005), Europe and the Political Economy of Arab Cinema. *Middle East Report* 235, 46–47.

Napoli, J./H. Amin/L. Napoli (1995), Privatization of the Egyptian Media. *Journal of South Asian and Middle Eastern Studies* 4, 39–57.

Robison, G. (2005), *The Rest of Arab Television*. Los Angeles: USC Center on Public Diplomacy.

Rugh, W. (2004), *Arab Mass Media*. Westport: Praeger.

Sakr, N. (2001), *Satellite Realms: Transnational Television, Globalization and the Middle East*. London: I. B. Tauris.

———. (2002), Satellite Channels between State and Private Ownership: Current and Future Implications. *Transnational Broadcasting Studies* 9, http://www.tbsjournal.com/Archives/Fall02/Sakr_paper.html.

———. (2006), The Impact of Commercial Interests on Arab Media Content. In Emirates Center for Strategic Studies and Research (ed.), *Arab Media in the Information Age*. Abu Dhabi: Emirates Center for Strategic Studies and Research, 61–85.

______. (2007), *Arab Television Today.* London: I. B. Tauris.

Shafik, V. (1998), *Arab Cinema: History and Cultural Identity.* Cairo: American University in Cairo Press.

Stiglitz, J. (1999), Public Policy for a Knowledge Economy. World Bank Paper Online, worldbank.org/html/extdr/extme/knowledge-economy.pdf.

Thussu, D. K. (2006), Mapping Global Media Flow and Contra-Flow. In D. K. Thussu (ed.), *Media on the Move.* London: Routledge.

UNDP (2003), *Arab Human Development Report 2003: Building a Knowledge Society.* New York: United Nations Development Programme.

Vitalis, R. (2000), American Ambassador in Technicolor and Cinemascope: Hollywood and Revolution on the Nile. In W. Armbrust (ed.), *Mass Mediations: New Approaches to Popular Culture in the Middle East and Beyond.* Berkeley: University of California Press, 269–291.

Wheeler, D. (2006), *The Internet in the Middle East: Global Expectations and Local Imaginations in Kuwait.* Albany: State University of New York Press.

CHAPTER ELEVEN

Orientalism and the Economics of Arab Broadcasting

Tourya Guaaybess

If the knowledge of Orientalism has any meaning, it is in being a reminder of the seductive degradation of knowledge, of any knowledge, anywhere, at any time. Now perhaps more than before.

(Said 1995, 328)

The idea people have about contemporary Arab media is often ambiguous. It is relatively common to see studies in international communication (by scholars or journalists) deal with Arab broadcasting not quite in the same way they deal with "Western" media. Indeed, rather than adopting a scientific (not prejudiced) methodology aimed at understanding the specific dynamics of the industry, the actors involved, their motives, and so on, they all too often link Arab media to themes that should normally remain outside their sphere. Indeed, Islam, the Israeli-Palestinian conflict, war, and the place of women all seem naturally attached to any study of Arab broadcasting. To take a short cut, "Arab media and Islamic fundamentalism" remains more probable as a title for an article than "American media and the Born Again"—even if, of course, all the perspectives are legitimate or some seem overused.

By trying to escape the geopolitical/religious/culturalist trap we may be able to gain a much better understanding of the changes occurring and get closer to their real motives. The complex geopolitical framework through which Arab media are seen, or in which they are entangled in some Western media or academic research, heavily weighs on our collective perceptions: if an Al-Jazeera journalist is linked to Al-Qaida it is never seen as absurd *a priori*; the proof must be made that it is not so (and even then, suspicion remains).[1] I am not stating that media and geopolitics is not a relevant topic: only that it is not relevant for Arab media alone and that, in this case, *geopolitics* is the real topic and media a by-product. I am also saying that very interesting things about Arab media probably lie outside the geopolitical sphere. However, in the first place, what is so outstanding about Al-Jazeera, that it overshadows the *system* from which it emerged? Why is it so common to fear its impact on the "Arab street"? These questions reflect confusions arising among the media, the message, and the context in which they emerge—be it political, national, or historical.

Thus, the economist's approach is crucial to gaining a global view and knowledge of Arab media; hence my stressing particularly the economical and financial environment of these media's development. I suggest that if the effects of the reforms can be of various natures—for example, social, sociological, political, anthropological, or geopolitical—very strong causes are clearly found in the economic arena, just as they are for media in the rest of the world.

This chapter is organized as follows. First, I will try to shed light on Orientalist attitudes. Then I will show that these media are in fact increasingly integrated into the international communications market. The argument will be more precisely delineated in the final part, where I deal more specifically with advertising, a major source of funding too often disregarded despite its being a very powerful reform trigger. Here too, the logics structuring the media industry in the Arab region—incidently, exactly those structuring other areas of the world—are strong.

Questioning the Arab Specificity

At all costs, the goal of Orientalizing the Orient again and again is to be avoided, with consequences that cannot help but refine knowledge and reduce the scholar's conceit. Without "the Orient," there would be scholars, critics, intellectuals, human beings, for whom the racial, ethnic, and national distinctions were less important than the common enterprise of promoting human community.

(Said 1995, 328).

It is a fact that when Arab media are analyzed in Europe or the United States, they are not always shown as they are. Neither are they analyzed with the same set of tools used to analyze media from elsewhere in the world. In France, for instance, if we speak of Arab media (be it in academia or in the media), it is often the "Al-Jazeera phenomenon" that will draw attention, or currently Al-Manar. If one wants to have a global or "wide" understanding of media, then the question of women and/or Islam will almost inevitably emerge. Much research has already been done about this question; we do not disqualify it here, only stress the importance of this prism when it comes to Arab media.

The TV channels that people focus on (Al-Jazeera and Al-Manar) are indeed quite peculiar; they are specific, and cannot be taken as a proxy for the entire Arab broadcasting system. The other channels, many of which resemble (too much?) the European channels, are rarely mentioned. This reflects an essentialist view of the Arab media production and, hence, of the expectations of the Arab viewers or "Arab public opinion." We will not elaborate here on the viewers; it is easy to see in the media the extent to which they are infantilized and considered as easily influenced or manipulated.

Concerning the TV channels, we will try to show through two examples the misrepresentations and misconceptions we can find in Europe regarding Arab media. This misrepresentation is not necessarily new (Said 1981; Turner 1994; Kamalipour 1995; Hafez 2000) but, strangely enough, it continues to exist in a field where it should not have: that of transnational and sometimes ultrasophisticated Arab channels.

The Question of Who Lies behind Al-Jazeera

The reaction of Arab states to Al-Jazeera has been, generally speaking, quite mixed and tainted with fear and skepticism. It was the first channel to reject the "traditional" rules applying to journalism—namely, the authoritarianism of Arab regimes and the prevailing "code of ethics" (which strongly recommended that any Arab media avoid criticizing the regimes of other Arab states). The channel was "free," at least much freer than the other Arab channels, and it is often regarded as an example to follow because it considers itself a challenger to transnational broadcasting (El-Nawawy/Iskandar 2002; Miles 2005; Zayani 2005).

Al-Jazeera is the most successful Arab transnational news channel. It has offices in the main capitals and correspondents all around the world, and news programs that maintain perfectly current "international standards" (i.e., those of the majors from the United States or the United Kingdom). The main specificity is that it is not a "Western" news channel, but one coming from a very small country that, in the news field, had not really existed until 1996: Qatar. It is also for many the "news channel of the South," for which it is increasingly becoming a model (for example, for President Hugo Chavez in Venezuela[2]). In addition, it is an Arabic channel and hence sometimes (mis)interpreted as being the mouthpiece of Islamists or as being directed exclusively at the "Muslim world" (Ajami 2001, Tatham 2006).

The quasi-immediate effect of Al-Jazeera's news has been a serious cause of concern for the United States and the United Kingdom, who set up a broadcasting arsenal to counter it. This concern and the resulting attacks on the channel were especially noteworthy after indirect and direct attempts to force the Emir of Qatar to rein it in proved unsuccessful. This failure saw the subsequent creation and launch of pro-American media like Radio Sawa, Radio Free Iraq, and Al-Hurra TV, launched in 2004. Other methods of a much more violent nature (bombing of the channel's offices in Kabul and in Iraq; Miles 2006) were also used. The latter bombing (April 8, 2003) led to the death of the correspondent Tarek Ayyoub.

For the past few years Al-Jazeera has been a discordant if not conflicting voice, especially in the Arab broadcasting sector, where we could see at least discomfort toward U.S. policy and many Arab countries. Al-Jazeera was hailed for bringing a sense of democracy or free speech. That, however, was before the wars in Afghanistan and Iraq; afterward, everything changed.

The idea of the "clash of civilizations," first mentioned by Huntington (Huntington 1996; Karim 2000) has resurfaced after the 9/11 terrorist attacks; it was used to legitimize this tendency to classify the channel as being part of the "other" civilization—that is, not the "Western" one. The reaction of the channel was to launch in December 2006 Al-Jazeera International, an English-speaking international news channel that would offer a multipolar alternative to the idea of the "clash of civilizations" in which one would show no sensitivity whatsoever to "the other side."

The other example we chose is a much smaller channel than Al-Jazeera. Nevertheless, at some point it was accorded all the attention that was directed at the Arab broadcasting sector.

Al-Manar and the Hypertrophy of the Subject in France

One channel enjoyed a significant level of publicity: the news channel Al-Manar. Nevertheless the station remains individual and by no means represents *the entire* Arab broadcasting sector. Al-Manar was created by the Lebanese Hezbollah in 1991, and is only one among many other Lebanese channels launched by the numerous communities living there (Dajani 1992). As is often the case in the region, it is considered a resistance organization by some and a terrorist organization by others (the United States and Canada). It was created in 1991 and initiated satellite broadcasting in 2000. It focuses its news coverage largely on the Palestine/Israel conflict, and enjoys wide popularity in the Middle East for obvious reasons.[3]

In October 2003 the U.S. State Department complained to the Syrian and Lebanese governments after Al-Manar announced it would broadcast the serial *Al-Shatat* (The Diaspora). This serial had an undeniably anti-Semitic content, leading all the other Arab channels to withdraw it from their grid, but not Al-Manar, which broadcast the serial during Ramadan. Finally, after the broadcasting of a clearly contentious episode, Al-Manar stopped broadcasting the serial.

An imbroglio between the channel and the French broadcasting authority, the Conseil Supérieur de l'Audiovisuel, led to the channel being banned on December 13, 2004, from broadcasting in France. What is interesting in this example is that the media campaign we saw in this matter often exposed Al-Manar to the "Western world." At the height of the "crisis," no less than twenty-two articles were devoted to Al-Manar in *Le Monde* newspaper for December 2004 alone. The government and media (press and broadcasting) finally dealt extensively with Arab media in a context of tension and opposition. The U.S. government now considers Al-Manar a terrorist organization and anyone dealing with it naturally faces the risk of sanction. The consequence of all this was to see the importance of Al-Manar swell excessively when compared to its actual role or place in Arab broadcasting. It remains a militant and partisan community channel, with very little effective influence, but its treatment has overshadowed the whole Arab broadcasting system—or worse, created a blurred representation of Arab television.

An interesting way out of the pitfall of Orientalism is to try sticking to the facts and avoid as much as possible any interpretation of those facts. Although political science is not always the most suitable prism for such an approach, economic science offers a priori safety in numbers. Naturally, we use the economic science prism because the research we have been doing in past years has convinced us that very powerful triggers to the current evolution and restructuring of the Arab media sector lie in the financial and economic sphere. Of course, this is not to underplay the other aspects (political, sociological etc.) of media development.

Media and the Economy

Politics: Mainly a Factor Preventing Change

It is useful to have in mind the recent history of the Arab media sector. Since its onset, the dynamics of broadcasting in Arab countries has had both a national and regional aspect, backed by a relatively homogenous linguistic community (Sinclair et al. 1996; see, for instance, the ambitions that Radio Baghdad had in as early as the 1950s, and above all the Egyptian Sawt-el-Arab; Nasser 1990). Another element of the regional dynamics is that, at the roots of one of their main industrial programs, Arab states shared the need to cooperate and set common tools in order to fight against the domination of "Western media."

Through the Arab League, the ASBU (Arab States Broadcasting Union) was set up in 1969 to implement the common view mentioned above, and it is within its framework that the first pan-Arab satellite was launched—namely, Arabsat. However, on the national level, the broadcasting authorities were centralized government bodies, controlled by authoritarian regimes. The reasons invoked to justify this domination were, invariably, the defense of national sovereignty and the necessity to educate the citizens. These arguments were also used by the managers of state broadcasting in Europe (France, for example) before the 1970s (Wolton/Missika 1983). At that time, the state's monopoly of Arab broadcasting was naturally accepted—hence the failure of the first generation of Arabsat satellites, which were largely underexploited (Kandil 1987). In the 1970s the use of television spread considerably, and the conditions for a broadcasting marketplace emerged in the Arab region, particularly through the export of Egyptian productions to the other Arab countries. Television was becoming a commercial business.

The political elements blocking the evolution and modernization of the sector will be only circumvented by the deregulation of Arab broadcasting. This will lead to the restart of a purely economic logic, like that existing in the 1990s (Ayish 2003). At that point, Arab countries had engaged, to a varying extent, in the liberalization of their economies, from which the broadcasting sector was excluded for obvious reasons. What has deeply affected the media in the Arab region and elsewhere is the globalization of broadcasting allowed by technological innovation.

This became apparent during the 1991 Gulf War as a result of the formidable attraction that CNN exerted on populations who were then given the chance to escape the news provided by the state television channels, which were somehow organically linked to regimes. Shortly after, the first Arab commercial television channels, aimed at a transnational audience, were launched on satellite. The Egyptian Satellite Channel (previously SpaceNet; Amin 1992), the Middle East Broadcasting Center, the two Saudi bouquets ART (Arab Radio and Television) and Orbit, the Lebanese Broadcasting Corporation, Future TV: they were all transnational, "deterritorialized," aiming and reaching with a wholly new content—fifty years after Sawt El-Arab—at a global Arab-speaking audience, and they were no longer the captive citizens/viewers of such a state.

Global Contents

Quite naturally, with a completely new commercial horizon, the newly born channels had to adapt their content, topics, and formats so as to attract and build a loyal audience among people widely spread geographically and comprising various identities. In these pan-Arab channels, there has been an organized loss of cultural identity in the sense that cultural specificities and local dialects have suddenly been reduced by the satellites through which they are seen to a mere set of local costumes and folklore. Cultural specificities cannot be the core of a medium's business. The rhythm of new formats is faster, as shows have to be shorter to catch the audience's attention without losing it and have to attract advertisers; set design has changed profoundly—now they convey a modern and dynamic image. The shows of the Lebanese Broadcasting Corporation are much closer to those of Rai Uno (colorful and joyful, with attractive young people) than to those of the dull channel of an autocratic regime. Be it out of lack of expertise or experience, or simply out of pragmatism (it is less risky to buy a program that has been commercially successful), many game or entertainment shows are bought from European or American producers. State television was forced to adapt in order to remain competitive. They changed their formats as well, and they bought new game shows and new entertainment shows. As pointed out by the CEO of the Algerian Entreprise Nationale de Télévision (ENTV), "this frantic race is not fortuitous, it obeys a purely commercial logic imposed by many transnational advertisers such as the mobile phone operators for whom our audience is an invaluable potential consumer that they want to capture at any rate...." State television stations have also begun to coproduce the shows with foreign partners in order to transfer know-how and offer higher-quality shows.[4]

The previous content of television broadcasts has undergone considerable rationalization. The shows that network the audience are the most likely to remain or be brought on board: games like *Who Wants to Win a Million*? (the Arabic version of *Who Wants to be a Millionaire?*), reality shows like *Star Academy* (on LBC), *Super Star* (the equivalent of *Pop Idol*, on Future TV), are all shows that have proved able to transcend national borders. They sometimes receive millions of SMSs from all around the world, generating substantial cash flow (Kraidy 2006). On the other hand, the productions that attract a too-limited audience are removed from the grid. On the music channel Rotana Clip, for instance, the clips showing attractive, young, often syrupy singers eclipse singers who are more original, more creative or more easily identifiable by their national origin. The latter shows now find it increasingly difficult to be broadcast on the transnational media; their situation is also getting harder on a national level, where they are underdistributed and face a sizable risk of being pirated.

News Program as Part of a Diversified Supply

News programs, wavering between sensationalism and information, can attract large audiences, and formats here also have to be short to succeed (Ayish 2001). The presenters, when they are not well-established figures or veterans known throughout the Arab world (like Hamdi Kandil), are young, dynamic, and often bilingual recruits. The way they dress, comb their hair, and do their makeup makes them very similar to the presenters we see on European or American transnational news channels—where they often had their first professional experience.

News bulletins are usually popular programs in the Arab world, too. MBC was one of the first channels to occupy the niche. When it was deposed by Al-Jazeera, its managers decided to change its concept (it became a global, diversified channel), which reveals the degree of "political commitment" of the channel. These channels are, in a way, a range of products being enriched, structured, and packaged for the audience in the region.

As in any commercial product, Arab transnational channels had to specialize and differentiate themselves—but not too much—to mark their territory and gain market share. The goal is not to broadcast or entertain for the sake of broadcasting or entertaining: the goal is to make a return on the investments made, to be profitable and beat the competition. Above all, promoters are entrepreneurs, many of whom often come from economic sectors having little to do with media—from finance to real estate development.[5] And to attain their ultimate aim—to make a return on their investments—they set out, just like the makers of any other product, to touch, seduce, and retain a creditworthy pool of clients, especially one that is potentially active (i.e., willing to consume). They use their specialist skills to reach as many segments of the population as possible. And within these segments, their prime target is young people. In 2005, 40 percent of the population in Arab countries was aged fifteen or under according to UNESCO figures.

Where Politics Are Back on Stage

Finally, the channels respond to a demand and stimulate it in return to keep it active; this process is very well known and effective in economically rich countries.

A few years ago, the supply side of the market was not so rich and was dominated by the British or French media. Now, and this is new, the "Western" supply has been pushed aside, even in the news field, in which its domination was the heaviest. The traditional players in this niche (the United States, the United Kingdom, France) understand this quite well, and have launched news channels to gain the lost market share among the Arab audience and reaffirm their views of the world—or at least, to get the public to understand them better. In particular, Al-Hurra was set up in 2004 by the U.S. Congress to amend America's negative image following the latest war in Iraq. We should also mention the BBC's Arabic Television (UK) and France 24. The political motives are quite obvious here: they have been clearly stated, just as they were by the Arab countries when they set up the ASBU some forty years ago. This is explained by the (geo)political effect of the change in market structure that we just mentioned; transational Arab news channels undeniably had a political agenda when they were launched. This is an agenda they have, to a certain extent, also implemented.

The other innovation in this field is that some Arab channels now have ambitions that reach well beyond the region's borders or the Arab-speaking audience. These channels want to be international media like Rupert Murdoch's News Corporation empire or the Bertelsmann Group: the ambitious newcomers are Arab Digital Distribution (managing the ART group) and more recently in 2006 the channel Al-Jazeera English (or Al-Jazeera International).

How to Finance This Buoyant Activity

Huge investments were made in the media sector: first, by states significantly upgrading the infrastructure, and then by the private sector (for motives that were largely economic, as the political arena was closed to them). The financing came from petrodollars or from the exports of TV productions. Now the further development of the sector cannot rely exclusively on these two funding sources. Advertising—private funds, in other words—emerge as the only credible alternative for both political and economic reasons.

From an economic point of view, advertising resources are much more flexible than state funding, as they do not depend on a restricted budget and its objectives. Advertising resources are also an attractive performance measurement within a liberal economy. Besides, they have growth potential and a recurring characteristic that state resources can hardly have. From a political point of view, the current international environment is clearly one in which states have to disengage from economic activity. Within this frame, advertising spending becomes an unavoidable funding source; all players are satisfied, advertisers and channel operators alike. In the Arab world as elsewhere, we see an increasing interdependence betwen media and advertising, as we will try to show in the next section.

Media and Advertising and Their Common Destiny

Overview: Sectors and Brands

The development of advertising in Arab countries is a relatively recent phenomenon, as it dates back only to the 1990s. Advertising spending has grown quite rapidly in the past two years, to reach $6.56 billion in 2006 (+21 percent after +17.6 percent in 2006[6]), though this amount remains small compared to the US (+4.1 percent to $149.5 billion). The amount of advertising spending is also quite small when considered per capita, although there are large disparities from country to country in the region: from $4 in Egypt and $38 in Jordan, $267 in Qatar and $372 in the Emirates. This compares to roughly $500 in the United States. The same observation applies to advertising spending as a percent of GDP (double in the United States, compared to the average of the Gulf Cooperation Council/GCC[7]). Finally, in terms of recipients we also note sharp differences: the main recipients are the GCC markets which account for 47 percent of total advertising spending ($3.3 billion). This can easily be explained by the high per-capita income of these countries. Then come pan-Arab media—those not affiliated with a predetermined national territory—which are responsible for 38 percent of total spending ($2.32 billion). Now if we look in detail at the media split, we see that television and newspapers get the largest share of the pie with $2.82 billion for television (42.9 percent of the total) and $2.75 billion for newspapers (42 percent of the total). In terms of growth rate, the two largest media we just mentioned had quite similar levels: advertising money spent on television in 2006 was 23.8 percent, and 21 percent was spent on newspapers.

Now, who are the main spenders? Since we are considering the broadcasting media, we focus our analysis on the pan-Arab sector, where television accounts for 90 percent of total advertising spending. The main spenders clearly belong to the consumer goods sector. We always find among the main spenders the most common house care, hygiene, car, food, and soft drinks brands that can be seen in European supermarkets or parking lots. From this point of view, a European consumer watching an Egyptian transnational channel will feel much less like a fish out of the water than would an Egyptian peasant from the Nile valley. The only distinction we can make between advertising spent on Arab media and that spent Western media is linked to growth rates, which can vary quite sharply with Arab media, and to the greater impact of the largest spenders in Arab media; but this is just a sign of an immature market that still has a long way to go.

The main point I have been trying to make is that, aside from the lack of maturity of the advertising sector on Arab transnational media, very little can distinguish it in terms of structure from its American counterpart—not in terms of brands, economic sector, or even the strategy of spenders, who target the most solvent consumers through the most efficient means. As in developed economies, advertising and media develop hand in hand.

Where Orientalism No Longer Holds

This detour via the advertising sector was necessary: media and advertising in the Arab region have indeed *already* converged with the Western model, as they are driven by the same stimuli. The data given confirm indeed that the consumer society is largely reflected on Arab transnational channels. The new logic instituted provides stable, measurable, and—to a large extent—foreseeable sources to fund their expansion; but this financial source constrains them in the content and formats they propose. The recipes and associations (format/content/advertising) that have been successfully elsewhere are being used here; transnational corporations are trying to sell in the Arab region, through Arab transnational media, the products that they have sold elsewhere in the developed economies, betting that tastes and customs are, if not universal, at least infinitely flexible. We are very far here from the viewer/citizen who is so often invoked when analyzing Arab media and speaking of *the* Arab audience; the political prism becomes outdated and obsolete. Arab viewers, like all the other viewers, are considered above all as potential consumers who will wash with Dove, quench their thirst with Coke or Pepsi, phone with Nokia, drink Knorr soup and Lipton tea, and drive a Nissan.

The operators, being entrepreneurs, would not miss such an opportunity, and this can certainly explain to a large extent the formidable burgeoning of satellite channels in the region; the number of Arab satellite channels grew to 263 in October 2006[8], catering to 130 million viewers. It seems obvious that we are witnessing overcapacity: there can hardly be 263 different concepts, and all these channels were certainly not established by "citizens" eager to make their voices heard in a political arena deprived of any freedom of speech—even though programs not exclusively commercial in nature do exist here and there.A majority of them have been established by entrepreneurs who simply want a share in the fast-growing advertising pie. This burgeoning has been made easy by the infrastructure put in place, which has significantly lowered the barriers to entry, as is the case in "media cities" with up-to-date infrastructure (A new generation of satellites, etc.) and no fiscal pressure—Cairo, Dubai, Tangiers, and Amman. Now we could say that the real barriers to entry heavily depend on the entrepreneur, and in particular on his or her agenda and ambitions. A tacit instruction might be similar to the one suggested to some oligarchs elsewhere: You can do as much business as you want, and this will make you rich if you succeed, but please, no politics. The state remains an active player in the field—with the specificity that it has the ability to amend the rules of the game—leading to what we would call a situation of "state capitalism." It is undeniable that some private players may have a hidden political agenda, but politics is very far from being the sole factor behind the development of the Arab media sector; and so, to adopt systematically a political science or religious prism to analyze them may lead to false conclusions. The roots of the dynamics we see are economic, and the Arab satellite media being created are by no means fundamentally different from the ones seen elsewhere in the world—they both grow out of a common compost.

One should generate analytical tools to examine the questions raised by the above developments. Some questions may require the researcher to use a diverse set of tools, especially if these tools have been efficiently used on media in other regions. We do not mean that political factors do not play a part, only that the current situation greatly limits the scope of their action, at least on an intraregional level. Thus, by contrast, the economic dynamics become overwhelming in their influence.

It Is about the Human Brain's Available Time, Even for Arab Media

We have seen in this section of the text that there are many channels through which advertising can influence the development of television. We have, above all, insisted on the great financial opportunity that the growth of the advertising market has offered to Arab operators and have suggested in this respect that advertising is indeed growing as a funding source. The results in terms of market size for the advertising sector show that spenders seem quite satisfied with the "environment" in which their ads are broadcast and that television seems to be evolving in the right direction. As we suggested earlier, both sectors seem to be growing together in harmony and cordially aware of the other's needs. The criticisms often made concerning the "quality" or "cultural content" of the shows broadcast are exactly the same as those expressed in France, for instance, about the two largest private commercial channels (TF1, M6): these criticisms are often about very poor cultural content, standardization, and the overwhelming presence of advertising, which imposes its norms and needs. These critiques culminate with a rather rough declaration by Patrick Lelay (CEO of TF1) in which he states that "*TF1's job is to help Coca-Cola, for example, sell its product.*...For an advertising message to be received, the brains of the viewer should be available. The shows we broadcast aim at making his brains available, or to entertain him, make him relax to get him ready between two advertising messages. What we sell to Coca-Cola, it is human brains' available time. Nothing is more difficult than to get this availability. There lies the permanent change. We have to search the programmes that work, move along with fashion, surf on trends, in a context where information moves faster, multiply and gets standardized."[9] We do not see anything fundamentally different on Arab commercial channels, as the strategy of many of those stations is very close to what Lelay describes.

Our goal here is not to discuss these growth strategies per se, which use to the maximum extent possible "market principles" in a sensitive sector like the media.[10] Our intention is to illustrate the fact that the development of transnational Arab channels is not an exotic phenomenon. Furthermore, a major group like the Saudi AMS (Ara Media Service) has perfectly integrated these principles, plus the necessity to be as economically and financially efficient and successful as possible. We can indeed read on their website that AMS "has been aware, since its establishment in 1994, that advertisers and advertising agencies do not buy channels; rather, they buy audiences." And that with respect to this, AMS has "learnt to be au fait with the viewer's feelings and wants, by reading into his reactions to various advertising environments, getting insights into his media consumption, and delving into advertising and brand exposures."[11] And AMS is probably only the first such player in the field. So there is ample room for other players to come.

What Next?

If the current trends continue, then we will very likely witness an increasing sophistication of the sector, coupled with rationalization: mergers, acquisitions, concentration, as in any economic sector in which the structure is not "cost-efficient" (see the evolution of the media sectors in Europe, for example). Concentration is a "natural" by-product of economic liberalism, as it permits synergies and reduction of costs. Furthermore, alliances may also develop, motivated by the will to enlarge and diversify the audience and hence increase advertising revenue (LBC and MBC, for example). This can occur without jeopardizing the states' political grip.

Conclusion: A Brief Look Back at the Attitude of States

We will conclude with a focus on the attitude of Arab states and the reform processes they have initiated. A step back to look at things more broadly will allow us to finish on a clear understanding of the elements mentioned above—especially their chronology. As Arab regimes can be classified as "authoritarian," the private sector has been and remains locked out of the political public sphere. This is very easily transposed into the media sector: no private channel has achieved absolute legitimacy as the political monopoly of the state cannot be challenged. However, the technological innovation in the broadcasting industry—namely the emergence of direct broadcasting satellites—has constituted a great challenge to the monopoly of states. The first materialization of this threat came through Al-Jazeera in the mid-1990s. The immediate reaction of the states was the "classical" banning and boycotting. But they soon realized that, given the nature of the technological evolution, this was an outdated and inefficient strategy that could prove dangerous for them: they perceived quite early the potential risks of a "tough" attitude, both from financial and political points of view. Besides, the potential market being the same for each channel (all countries in the region speak Arabic, so at least they have the possibility to understand the same language), the potential losses if one country moved first were sizable for all the others. For that reason, I call the Arab broadcasting landscape a system (the *Arab broadcasting system*) to underline the interdependence of all Arab channels (Guaaybess 2005). Then the classical "self-fulfilling prophecy" was observed, and so states adopted a more flexible and pragmatic approach, which allowed them to keep their grip on the political arena and gain resources (advertising, foreign direct investment) and influence from economic liberalization. As a result, reforms began to be implemented, media free zones established, partial privatization and demonopolization introduced—especially in Egypt, Jordan, or Morocco—and broadcasting licenses were given to (carefully selected) private actors. In other terms, a political opening "de-facade" for the sake of the economy and the image abroad was initiated. For instance, the private channels that were authorized in Tunisia were Hannibal TV, Nessma TV, and TT1 TV; all three are entertainment channels whose owners are businessmen close to the regime. Once the new rules were set, states were naturally the first movers; they became the first entrepreneurs in a system they had feared just a few years earlier, but that they had very quickly learned to tame and benefit from. But the new capitalism that was born remained state capitalism: states controlled quite drastically the gates to the satellite sector and kept their grip on the terrestrial grid. This is not specific to Arab states, but to authoritarian regimes where media is not organically independent from the state.

Notes

1. The ongoing detention without charge of the journalist Tayssir Allouni in Spain since 2005 and of Sami Al-Hajj, cameraman for Al-Jazeera, in Guantanamo Bay since 2001, and the absence of public reaction, are dramatic evidence of such attitudes.
2. The news channel Telesur launched in 2005 is also called Al-Bolivar in reference to Al-Jazeera.
3. During the latest Israeli-Lebanese conflict in July 2006, Al-Manar jumped from an 83rd to an 8th ranking in terms of popularity among Arab channels. IPSOS statistics, August 2006.
4. Taken from the website of the ENVT: http://www.entv.dz.
5. Examples are Saleh Kamel of the ART group; Rafik Hariri, who founded Future TV; Ahmad Bahgat, the owner of the private Egyptian channel Dream TV; or Walid Talal, the wealthy owner of Rotana Channel; and so on.
6. Source for the figures in this paragraph: Pan Arab Research Centre, except where otherwise stated.
7. The GCC, or Gulf Cooperation Council, created in 1981, comprises Saudi Arabia, Kuwait, the United Arab Emirates, Bahrain, Oman, and Qatar.
8. Arab Advisors Group Strategic Research Services, http://www.arabadvisors.com, December 2006.
9. AFP, November 2, 2004.

10. We use the word "sensitive" to highlight the political, social, and cultural ramifications or consequences (among others) that the current evolution of the media sector entails in the Arab countries.
11. http://www.amsarabia.com/sub_pages/begin.html. AMS is the representative for various media owned by the ARA group, including, for example, MBC, MBC FM, Channel 2, Showtime, Future TV and the newspaper *Al-Watan.*

References

Ajami, F. (2001), What the Muslim World Is Watching. *New York Times Magazine*, November 18, 2001.

Amin, H. (1992), The Development of Spacenet and Its Impact. In R. Weisenborn (ed.), *Media in the Midst of War: The Gulf War from Cairo to the Global Village.* Cairo: Adham Center Press, 15–20.

Ayish, M. (2001), American-Style Journalism and Arab World Television: An Exploratory Study of News Selection at Six Arab World Satellite Television Channels. *Transnational Broadcasting Studies* 6, http://www.tbsjournal.com/Archives/Spring01/Ayish.html.

———. (2003), *Arab World Television in the Age of Globalisation: An Analysis of Emerging Political, Economic, Cultural and Technological Patterns.* Hamburg: Deutsches Orient-Institut.

Dajani, N. (1992), *Disoriented Media Is a Fragmented Society: The Lebanese Experience.* Beirut: American University of Beirut Press.

Nawawy, M. el-/A. Iskandar (2003), *Al-Jazeera: The Story of the Network That Is Rattling Governments and Redefining Modern Journalism.* Cambridge: Westview Press.

Guaaybess, T. (2005), *Télévisions arabes sur orbite, un système médiatique en mutation.* Paris: CNRS éditions.

Hafez, K. (ed.) (2000), *Islam and the West in the Mass Media: Fragmented Images in a Globalizing World.* Cresskill: Hampton Press.

Huntington, S. P. (1996), *The Clash of Civilizations and the Remaking of World Order.* New York: Simon and Schuster.

Kamalipour, Y. (ed.) (1995), *The U.S. Media and the Middle East: Image and Perception.* Westport, CT: Greenwood.

Kandil, H. (1987), Le satellite d'Aladin. Le système de communication du satellite arabe. *Revue Tiers-Monde* 111, 659–670.

Karim, K. H. (2000), *Islamic Peril: Media and Global Violence.* Montreal: Black Rose.

Kraidy, M. M. (2006), Reality Television and Politics in the Arab World: Preliminary Observations. *Transnational Broadcasting Studies* 15, http://www.tbsjournal.com/Archives/Fall05/Kraidy.html.

Miles, H. (2005), *Al-Jazeera: How Arab TV News Challenged the World.* London: Abacus.

———. (2006), The Al-Jazeera Memo: To Publish or Not to Publish? *Transnational Broadcasting Studies* 16, http://www.tbsjournal.com/Miles.html.

Nasser, K. M. (1990), Egyptian Mass-Media under Nasser and Sadat. *Middle East Journal* 124, 1–26.

Said, E. W. (1981), *Covering Islam: How the Media and the Experts Determine How We See the Rest of the World.* London: Routledge and Kegan Paul.

______. (1995), *Orientalism: Western Conceptions of the Orient.* London: Penguin.

Sinclair, J. et al. (1996), *New Patterns in Global Television: Peripheral Vision.* Oxford: Oxford University Press.

Tatham, S. (2006), *Losing Arab Hearts and Minds: The Coalition, Al-Jazeera and Muslim Public Opinion.* London: Hurst.

Turner, B. S. (1994), *Orientalism, Postmodernism and Globalism.* London: Routledge.

Wolton, D./Missika, J. L. (eds.) (1983), *La folle du logis, la télévision dans les sociétés démocratiques.* Paris: Gallimard.

Zayani, Mohamed (ed.) (2005), *The Al Jazeera Phenomenon: Critical Perspectives on New Arab Media.* London: Pluto.

Media Law and Policy

CHAPTER TWELVE

Media Policy and Law in Egypt and Jordan: Continuities and Changes

Orayb Aref Najjar

In an address to the Foreign Press Association, in London, King Abdullah II of Jordan said, "Let me say a special word about terrorism and the tools of communication. Modern extremism depends heavily on its ability to deliver its message.... In the world they seek, there is no right to press freedom.... This is why a free and responsible press serves both humanity and its future when it refuses to be used as a tool—when it refuses to incite hatred and violence—and when it reaches for the truth of our common humanity."[1]

When the Egyptian government launched a campaign on Al-Misriyya government TV on March 26, 2007, to encourage Egyptians to vote in the referendum to ratify the thirty-four changes to their constitution, the program *The House Is Yours* scrolled down a timeline of terrorist incidents starting in the eighteenth century, lingering at 9/11 before arriving at scenes from bombing incidents in Egypt. Then, the announcer linked the need for new legislation to the need to protect against terrorism.

Without discounting the dangers Jordan and Egypt sometimes face, the attempt to link curbing press freedom to the need to curb extremism neglects both countries' history of controlling dissidents from the religious right to the secular left through press regulations (Abdul Rahman 1985, Najjar 2007). Michel Foucault asserts that law is "neither the truth of power nor its alibi. It is an instrument of power, which is at once complex and partial. The form of law with its effects of prohibition needs to be resituated among a number of other, non-juridical mechanisms.... The penal system makes possible a mode of political and economic management which exploits the difference between legality and illegalities" (Foucault 1977, 141).

Salah Eddin Hafez finds that one cannot separate the right to freedom of expression, speech, and belief and the right to gather and demonstrate from their economic, political, and social contexts. Nor can those rights be separated from the daily practices of ruling powers in any given country (Hafez 1993, 19).

Legal scholar Perry Keller observes that "[it] is only through an examination of the conditions that shape the media in different communities that a better understanding of the benefits and limitations of the global application of a liberal concept of freedom of the press will be obtained" (Keller 1992, 27, 372).

In this chapter, several approaches that include Pierre Bourdieu's field theory (2005), and Foucault's (1977) concept of resistance that resides at the site of power will be used to arrive at a more nuanced description of the spaces between "legality and illegalities." After summarizing problems that impede the development of a more liberal press legislation in the Arab world, I use the concept of *field* combined with a historical comparative overview of press legislation in Egypt and Jordan to explain how the social, political, religious, and leadership conditions under which the press operates have shaped the legal principles at stake in successive press legislation efforts.

I suggest that although the liberal legal framework for understanding press legislation is useful, it needs to be augmented with research on how different fields like journalism, politics, and religion interact with each other while press laws are being promulgated and how relations of resistance to unjust laws emerge in the "spaces between legality and illegalities" (Foucault 1977, 141). And finally, I take a look at how 9/11 has affected press legislation in Egypt and Jordan.

The Conceptual Framework

Bourdieu uses the concept of *field* to describe a social arena in which people maneuver and struggle in pursuit of desirable professional, material, artistic, or symbolic resources (for example, within the field of journalism, the field of law, and the fields of politics or religion). A field is relational in that it exists within a matrix of interfield relations as well as external relations with other fields of power with which it competes or cooperates (Bourdieu 2005).

The media field's power to determine what is important and what we should think about important things and people is based on legitimacy that journalists have collectively accumulated in the course of history (Champaign 2004). Those who deal professionally in producing discourses—sociologists, historians, politicians, journalists, and the like—struggle to have the way they categorize things recognized as legitimate categories of construction of the social world. Different political actors want to apply their categories of perception on others without duly noting that categories are socially constituted and socially acquired (Bourdieu 2005, 36, 37). Thus, the struggle among journalists, politicians, and the clergy on the definition of the social world and on speech and action boundaries is inevitable. Media law, then, is the instrument the state uses to rein in the definitional power of journalism. It is also contested space the religious and secular alike attempt to control. Rodney Benson (2005, 86) finds that field theory is "tailor-made for cross-national research" because it suggests "simultaneously examining historical geneses and trajectories, structural relations among fields, and the practices and worldviews of social actors within fields" (Benson 2005, 87).

In this Chapter, I illustrate how the changing relationship among different fields of power—the president/king, political parties, religious authority, external political actors, human rights organizations, and journalists' unions—has over time had a pronounced effect on the promulgation of media law. In short, this study examines media law in its social, political, religious, and foreign affairs contexts rather than studying it solely for its conformity with or deviation from the norms of the liberal tradition of lawmaking.

A number of constraints in various fields have had a profound effect on media law; some juridical, some nonjuridical. Below, I discuss each of these constraints, not as immutable impediments to free speech, but as *fluid fields* that have changed over time and may change in the future under different conditions.

Nonjuridical Constraints on the Press

The nonjuridical constraints on the press include weak political parties unable to challenge the executive branch, a judiciary weakened by successive restrictive press laws and emergency regulations, the presence of competing secular and religious authorities, and weak, co-opted or underfunded indigenous human rights organizations. As I discuss each of them, I note how each interacts with the press.

The Strength of the Executive Branch vis-à-vis Other Branches of Government

Both Jordan and Egypt have strong heads of state systems that prevent the proper separation of powers. Various political parties and other institutions have been forced to accept the principle of "acts of sovereignty" (Brown 1997, 124). In Jordan, the cabinet and the parliament are not as powerful as the royal court and the intelligence services. In Jordanian law, the king is "immune from any liability and responsibility." The king also appoints the prime minister and all forty members of the Senate, whose approval is needed for any proposed bill to become law (Hamed 2005). "Despite the clear and vocal demands for structural reform in Jordan," notes Julia Choucair, "fundamental issues have never really been on the table...there is little substance to show for the various initiatives and dialogues launched by the regime" (Choucair 2006, 10–11).

Two factors led to the strengthening of the centralization of decision making in Egypt; the first was the strengthening of the presidential system over the constitutional system in the constitution of 1956, which stipulated that the president of the republic is also the prime minister (unlike the constitution of 1923); the second, Article 192, gave the president the right to form the National Union (Al-Ittihad Al-Qawmi), later called the Arab Socialist Union (ASU), and made it the only legal party before giving the union responsibility for nominations to the National Assembly. In effect this structured the political field so that the head of the executive branch had more powers than the legislative branch because he controls the sieve through which those who are nominated have to pass. As head of the National Union, Gamal Abdel Nasser appointed editors of newspapers and chose a number of military men for that purpose—among them Anwar al-Sadat (Abdul Rahman 1985, 52–53, 55). By managing how dissent was structured and by changing the economic organization of the press from capitalist to socialist, President Nasser weakened his enemies, who were upper-class members who owned newspapers. This is what Foucault (1977) meant when he noted that the "penal system makes possible a mode of political and economic management which exploits the difference between legality and illegalities" (141).

Even when media were privatized under President Sadat, the control decision makers had over media only changed the way economic policies were decided, not the main actors within them. The president of Egypt remained the axis (*mihwar*) of the regime. The 1971 constitution gave the individual the right to establish newspapers, but stated that censorship may be exercised during emergencies, during war, or in relation to matters that deal with national security (Saleh 1995, 339). More recently an Egyptian blogger has written, "As all who know the 1971 Constitution are aware, the problem is not just the president's emergency powers but the codification of overwhelming presidential prerogatives in normal times. Trimming the edges will not dent the core."[2]

Egyptian columnist Mustapha Amin describes his "simple quarrel" with Sadat this way: "I call for freedom of the people, and he calls for freedom of the ruler! He thinks that the rule of one keeps him in office. I believe that the rule of the people safeguards him ... and preserves his eternal legacy as well!" (Amin 1989, 85). Some of the 2007 amendments introduced by President Hosni Mubarak's government appear to be designed to help him to stay in power or to enable his son to inherit it. Article 7 of the amendment to the constitution requires presidential candidates to be nominated by parties who have at least 3 percent of the elected members of parliament. This development was an insurmountable obstacle for the Muslim Brotherhood, which was banned but tolerated by the authorities, but which was declared unconstitutional in the 2007 amendments.[3]

"Taken together," write Brown, et al., "the amendments ... constitute an effort by the Egyptian regime to increase the appearance of greater balance among the branches of government and of greater opportunities for political parties, while in fact limiting real competition strictly and keeping power concentrated in the hands of the executive branch and ruling party" (Brown et al. 2006).

Weak Political Parties Unable to Challenge the Executive Branch

Despite the weakness of political parties in Jordan today, the parties have had an illustrious history since 1921, even before the state was founded. Parties at that time had a regional agenda that involved the liberation of Syria from French influence, and the establishment of an independent Arab state that includes Syria, Lebanon, Jordan, and Palestine (Al-Hournai et al. 1997, 11).

The most important period for political parties came after the displacement of Palestinian refugees from Palestine to Jordan after 1948, when the population of Jordan tripled and the West Bank was added to Jordan. A new Jordanian constitution was enacted in 1952, and the first Political Parties Law was enacted in 1955. The 1950s saw the development of fifteen political parties, as well as professional associations, labor unions, organizations for women and students, and charitable societies (Al-Hournai et al. 1997, 14). When the opposition won in parliamentary elections in 1956 and formed a government led by a socialist, King Hussein disbanded the government in April 1957 and jailed political activists (Al-Hournai et al. 1997, 14). After years of frozen parliamentary life (1967–1989), the government allowed elections, and in 1992 allowed the return of political parties. Despite the initial enthusiasm for political parties in which sixty-five were established, only thirty-five remained in 2007 (Al-Hournai et al. 1997, 38–39).[4] Only three parties are able to afford their own publications, and all suffer from low membership and poor financial clout, and there is a lack of public trust in their ability to affect change (Al-Hournai et al. 1997, 38–39).

Foucault suggests that we analyze punitive power—or in this case, the suppression of Jordanian Communist, Baathist, and Arab nationalist parties—"not simply as consequences of legislation or as indicators of social structure, but as techniques possessing their own specificity in the more general field of other ways of exercising power. Regard punishment as a political tactic" (1977, 170). The tactic succeeded in destroying the once-vibrant parties and inadvertently strengthened the Islamic movement, which continued operating in mosques. Reviving political parties in Jordan will not be easy even though the government is cautiously trying to do so.

The Political Parties Law approved by the Jordanian parliament on March 19, 2007, extends financial support to all political parties, but it supervises their sources of funding and requires them to appoint women to positions of responsibility.[5] The law raised from fifty to five hundred the number of members necessary for registering or maintaining party status and raised the minimum number of districts from which parties must draw their members. Existing parties that do not meet these requirements are to be disbanded. A coalition of parties is considering appealing the constitutionality of the law (DeBartolo 2007).

In Egypt, President Sadat kept the ban Nasser had imposed on private newspapers, but he distanced himself from some of the Nasserite positions by allowing political parties to operate in 1976 and abolished the one-party system of his predecessor. In his opening to the West, Sadat realized that economic liberalism, to be successful, has to be accompanied by political liberalism (Ahmad 1984, 18, 30). Several new political parties were founded under Mubarak's rule. The majority of political parties, however, were initially rejected by the government but were reinstated by the courts, which forced the government to register them after parties had sued. Furthermore, most of the new parties were small, insignificant, poor, and did not enjoy public support, while the rejected Islamic parties had a large popular base (Abdul Baqi 2005, 67). The Political Parties Law of 2007 gives President Mubarak and his ruling party broad authority to choose who may compete against them and under what terms. The regime has used the law to exclude Islamists as well as independents on those occasions when Islamists ran for office as independents (Whiston 2007).

Weak, Co-Opted or Underfunded Indigenous Human Rights Organizations

Egypt's Law 84/2002, pertaining to the governing of associations, gives the government control over the governance and operations of nongovernmental organizations. It provides criminal rather than civil sanctions for certain activities, including "engaging in political or union activities, reserved for political parties and syndicates."[6] The Egyptian Organization for Human Rights (EOHR) was legally recognized by the Ministry of Social Affairs on June 24, 2003, after eighteen years of work.[7]

Human rights organizations suffer from a lack of indigenous sources of funding. So, on the one hand, Western funding enables organizations to professionalize their operations, but on the other, it raises questions of ideological bias because religious groups are not recipients of this largesse (Carapico 2002, 395).

A Strong Religious Field as a Competing Source of Authority

Understanding the *changing relations* between the powerful political sector and the religious sector is crucial to understanding not just what type of legislation is enacted at any given time, but why. The tradition of the Egyptian constitution has been secular because the first constitution of 1923 was based largely on European constitutions. President Nasser, who was secular himself, did away with all of Egypt's religious courts (Muslim and Christian) when he enacted law number 462 in 1955. His government controlled private mosques, abolished private religious endowments and created new Islamic organizations to serve novel goals. Law 603 in 1961 reduced the independence of Al-Azhar and its power. The regime offered its own interpretation of Islam as the religion of freedom, equality and progress. Under Nasser, Islam was limited to a cultural role and was used to justify the "socialist" egalitarian policies of the regime (Abdul-Rahman 1985; Dalacoura 2003, 118–119). In contrast, Sadat, who was religious himself, appealed to an Islam that was a hybrid of modernism and traditionalism and used whichever element promoted his policies (Dalacoura 2003, 125), inadvertently strengthening the people who eventually assassinated him.

The growth of the power of Islamists in Egypt led to the enactment of legislation that gradually strengthened their position. Thus, in the 1971 constitution, the

Sharia, which is derived from the teachings of the Koran and from the practice of the prophet Mohammad, was described as "a principal source of legislation". In a 1980 amendment, the Sharia became *the* principal source of legislation (O'Kane 1972, 137–148).

In response to the rise of the power of observant Muslims in several Arab countries in 2000, the state accommodated them by posing as the guardian of religion. The state continues to allow itself be employed to suppress political and cultural products written or sung by liberals. Arab Press Freedom Watch finds that "fundamentalists are fighting cultural battles they wished they had fought in the 1980s when they were weak. In 2000, they objected to several works that had been published without protest in the 1980s."[8]

Al-Azhar got involved in censorship in 1985 when law 102 in 1985 gave it the authority to regulate publications of the Koran and the Hadith. In February 1994, however, its mandate was extended by a Fatwa making it the sole authority to which the Ministry of Culture must refer concerning Islamic matters. That authority gave itself the power to issue licenses for films, books, and tapes that discuss religion. Although the decision was merely an opinion, lawyers have pointed to it, arguing that books of a religious nature printed without Al-Azhar's permission are illegal (Engel 2004). Al-Azhar banned a book in which twenty-three "modern sheiks" discuss various contentious issues such as women leading prayers and challenging the Muslim Brotherhood members' claim that they represent the Egyptian people.[9]

Arab governments have stepped up censorship of Friday sermons to curb the rising power of Islamists. The Egyptian government decreed that the same official sermon would be delivered in 88,000 mosques across Egypt every Friday starting in July 2003. Some critics predict that narrowing the space for religious freedom could drive people into the arms of nonofficial religious groups.[10]

President Mubarak, a secular president, structured relations between the religion and politics fields through Article 5 of the 2007 constitutional amendments, which bans any political activity or the establishment of any political parties within any religious frame of reference (*marjaiyya*) or on any religious basis. It is a clear attempt to separate mosque from state that brings to mind the Turkish model, according to one Egyptian state official.[11] Legislation designed to remove the Muslim Brotherhood from political life is a naked bid to safeguard the power of the political field from power of the religious field by appropriating contested symbolic capital. The pattern of control is similar to that in Jordan, where the government closely supervises the content of sermons through its Ministry of Religious Affairs.

King Hussein of Jordan used a combination of modernity and traditionalism to challenge what he considered extremist interpretations of Islam: "I call upon you all to realize that the Arab Hashemite Hussein, who has been honored by the almighty Allah to be a descendant of the Prophet Mohammad Bin Abdullah, peace be upon him, is above all worldly titles and positions," as he put it in one of his speeches. After establishing his credentials as someone entitled to speak in the name of Islam, King Hussein then riled against "attempts to undermine and distort Islam from within the Islamic Ummah and from without."[12]

Juridical Constraints

Juridical constraints on the press include the long-term use of emergency laws, the use of multiple laws to limit the effectiveness of the press, and the use of restrictive regulations to constrain the press as well as press associations. Here I discuss each of these and describe their impact on the way the press functions.

A Judiciary Weakened by Long-Term Emergency Regulations

An Egyptian blogger writes that "Egypt's rulers have always understood that violent repression alone is never enough to control a complex society of guilds. So they have found in rule by law an utterly indispensable tool to certify and smooth the project of social control." President Sadat had a particularly apt expression whenever he embarked on one of his endless authoritarian maneuvers, "It's all by law!" (*kullu bi-l-qanun*;[13] Baheyya 2006).

Despite laws allowing freedom of speech, Egypt has been under a state of emergency continuously since 1967, except for the period from May 1980 to October 1981 when the emergency was lifted following the Camp David Accords between Israel and Egypt. The state of emergency was reimposed in the aftermath of President Sadat's assassination and since then has been regularly renewed; in 2003, for another three years, then renewed again until 2008.[14]

The Use of Multiple Laws to Control the Press

Since 1992 nearly all the provisions of Emergency Law 162/1958 in Egypt have been "quietly and methodically" transferred into the Penal Code and assorted other ordinary laws: "So Law 162/1958 is no longer needed, since its draconian provisions have been safely smuggled into the country's legal corpus" (Baheyya 2005). In fact, the laws that control the press include exceptional laws journalists call the "laws of bad reputation," such as the Law for Guarding and Ensuring the Safety of the People No. 33 in 1971; the Law Protecting National Unity No. 34 in 1971; the Law for the Safety of the Homeland and the Citizen No. 2 in 1977; Law No. 40, amended in 1977, dealing with Political Parties; Law No. 33 in 1978 for Protecting the National Front and Social Peace; Law No. 95 in 1980 for Protecting Values from Immorality; Law No. 105 in 1980 for the State Security Courts; and Law No. 148 in 1980 on the Authority of the Press, as well as Emergency Law (Hafez 1993, 246).

Similarly, Jordan's press is controlled through the Press and Publications Law; the Jordan Press Association (Law No. 15 for the year 1998; the Contempt of Court Law (1959); the Protection of State Secrets and Documents and the Defense Law (1992); and the Penal Code as amended in 2001,[15] Jordan's Protection of State Secrets and Documents Provisional Law No. 50.

Each tightening or loosening of press laws came as a result of events on the ground. The restrictive Jordanian Press and Publications Law of 1997, passed when parliament was not in session, appeared to be aimed at curbing objections to the peace agreement Jordan signed with Israel. The 1997 law's twentyfold increase of minimum capitalization requirements also put thirteen weekly newspapers out of business. Those regulations were struck down on January 26, 1998, by Jordan's High Court on technical grounds and replaced by the 1998 Press Law, which came into force on September 1, 1998.

After the ascension of Abdullah II to the throne in 1999, the 1999 Press Law nullified all content restrictions found in previous laws; but at the same time, the government amended the Penal Code on October 8, 2001, in an attempt to tighten antiterrorism laws and to prevent some of the country's fourteen weekly publications from publishing "lies and sensational stories" against the government. These amendments were introduced without prior public or parliamentary debate. Article 5, which replaces Article 150, states that anyone who prints "false or libelous information that can undermine national unity or the country's reputation" or "aggravate basic social norms" can be imprisoned. Other definitions in the article cover individuals who "sow the seeds of hatred" or "harm the honor or reputation of individuals." Individuals charged are subject to jail terms of up to six months and fines of up to US$7,100. Article 6, which replaces Article 195 of the Penal Code, criminalizes the publication of statements that insult or attribute false statements to King Abdullah II and other members of the royal family, whether they are published on the Internet, in print, or in cartoons.[16]

The Jordanian Lower House of Parliament voted on March 21, 2007, to scrap the provision in the Press Law for the imprisonment of journalists, after the Upper House (the King's Council) insisted that the relevant article 38 be canceled in response to demands by the Press Association. King Abdullah II had been petitioned by "some daring journalists" to reject the law. However, Parliament replaced the imprisonment provision with large fines of US$40,000 for defamation, libel, insult to religious beliefs, or publishing material that fuels sectarianism or racism or spreads rumors.

The Use of Restrictive Legislation in the Journalistic Field

In Egypt, censorship was imposed on the press for five months after the 1960 law and was imposed again after the 1967 war with Israel. The press was censored between 1960 and 1971. Even as he was censoring certain types of speech, President Nasser insisted that the press was free, provided it conformed to the socialist system he had created and provided it published news of interest to the working class instead of trivial news to sell papers (Saleh 1995, 334).

Despite repeated attempts by journalists to induce President Sadat to lift censorship, he did not lift it until February 8, 1974, when he felt that Egypt's performance in the 1973 October War with Israel legitimized his regime. Sadat chided journalists for stressing the negative, such as bribery and corruption, and for ruining Egypt's reputation in the world. He ordered the arrest of journalists, suspended them from their jobs, and prevented them from writing. Sadat criminalized criticizing the Camp David Accords between Egypt and Israel by making it punishable by fine or by imprisonment. When journalists resisted by writing in the Arab press, Sadat even imprisoned Egypt's most famous former editor of *Al-Ahram*, Mohammad Hasanein Haykal, for his criticism of Sadat's peace with Israel (Haykal 2003, 378). Sadat gave journalists working abroad an ultimatum to either return to Egypt and be pardoned, or lose their passports (Saleh 1995, 457–465).

The period of 1981–1985 under President Mubarak had some elements of liberalism in the sense that political parties were allowed to publish newspapers. But the resources the state press possessed in comparison to the opposition shrank the margin of that freedom (Saleh 1995, 618). In June 1995 the Egyptian People's Assembly passed a press law that increased punishment in libel cases from two to five years' imprisonment. The Press Syndicate's stiff yearlong opposition succeeded in forcing the law's repeal. The new law (1996) retained imprisonment for journalists but shortened it to one year maximum for libel and/or a fine of between 1,000 and 5,000 Egyptian pounds (Nafie 2003).

A new draft of the Press Law, prepared by the legislative committee in the Journalists Syndicate, was offered as a replacement for the much maligned 1996 Press Law. The draft annuls the article in the Penal Code that imposes imprisonment for publication crimes and replaces it with a fine; it guarantees the freedom to publish newspapers and guarantees journalists free access to information; it also imposes a penalty on any administrative body that refuses to comply with a journalist's request for information (Nafie 2003). These suggestions were not adopted by the government.

Despite Ibrahim Nafie's campaigning as head of the press syndicate for the deletion of imprisonment for journalists, he filed a direct misdemeanor case, No. 5155 in 2001, against journalist Ahmad Haredi Muhammad for libel for falsely accusing him of financial mismanagement as editor-in-chief of the *Al-Ahram* semiofficial daily. The offender, the editor in chief of *Al-Mithaq Al-Arabi*, an electronic newspaper, was sentenced to six months imprisonment and ordered to pay 1000 Egyptian pounds as a fine and 2001 pounds in temporary administrative compensation. Nafie sued, despite the fact that he had the right to publish a reply and a correction.[17]

Even though President Mubarak promised to remove the clause on imprisoning journalists in 2004, he did not introduce a special law amending articles on "publishing crimes" in the Penal Code until 2006. This he only did following even more pressure from the Press Syndicate. Nonetheless, the state retained laws forbidding the insult of state presidents. Journalists in Egypt could be imprisoned for up to five years for any one of the thirty-five "press offenses" listed under different laws.[18]

The weakness of the public sphere also extends to organizations that are supposed to protect journalists, such as professional associations. These organizations are often hampered in their work by legislation that affects every phase of their operations. In most Arab governments, notes Palestinian journalist Daoud Kuttab, membership in journalists' unions is open to publishers, editors in chief, and the "journalists" who work for wire services owned by the governments. Sometimes nonjournalistic staff and technicians are also allowed to join those same unions.[19] Even those who teach journalism may belong to the association in Jordan.

In response to the long ban on political parties, the fourteen professional associations in Jordan, which had over 120,000 members in total, took over the political functions of political parties and were in the forefront of resisting "normalization" with Israel. Jordan diligently supervises professional associations in an attempt to keep them from getting involved in politics. Three trade unionists of the Anti-Normalization Committee of the Jordanian Professional Associations were imprisoned because they advocated political changes to Jordan's diplomatic ties with Israel, but they were later released. The government has threatened to dissolve the Council of the Jordanian Professional Associations if it continues to be active in politics.

In Egypt, the independence of journalistic decision making declines when one of the government's men takes over the Press Syndicate but flourishes when an independent is elected. Under Kamel Zuhairi, who won elections in 1979, journalists supported by the Egyptian Bar Association rejected Sadat's efforts to turn the union into a press club. The government's interference in the 1981 elections, however, got its own candidate elected, decreasing the resistance to making peace with Israel that had been led by the former head of the union (Saleh 1995, 471). Then, in 2003, an independent from the opposition won the leadership of the Press Syndicate.[20]

Law No. 96 of 1996 indirectly imposed censorship by virtue of the presence of an appointed Higher Council of Journalism, giving the government a great deal of power over the press. Despite those measures, journalists went on strike in front of their syndicate to protest against the refusal of the government to annul imprisonment for journalists and to protest against the fact that a new penalty for insulting individuals was added to the penal code. Journalists argued that the article was reminiscent of Law 93 of 1995, described by the public as the "Corruption Protection Law."[21]

The Effect of the "War on Terrorism" on Journalism

Reporters without Borders noted that King Abdullah II of Jordan had pushed political liberalization since he came to the throne in 1999. Nevertheless, "the war on terrorism" since the 9/11 attacks on the United States still serves as an excuse for delaying reform. Jordan's government approved a new antiterrorism law on May 27, that includes provisions allowing security forces to place suspects under tight surveillance, seize their financial assets, and detain them for two-week periods (a detainment that may be renewed without a court order). Under the current Penal Code, suspects may be held for only twenty-four hours before a court order authorizing further detention is required. Leaders of opposition groups and professional associations decried the bill as turning Jordan into a police state and argued that the regular Penal Code already includes clauses pertaining to combating terrorism.[22] The history of the ebb and flow of freedom in Jordan, long before September 11, 2001, suggests that other perhaps more regional and domestic factors have more of an effect on press law than 9/11 did (Najjar 1998).

Similarly, although President Mubarak, during the September 2005 presidential reelection campaign, promised to let the Emergency Law (No. 162 of 1958) expire, his government renewed it in April 2006 until 2008. Mubarak later claimed the renewal was necessary because the government had not yet drafted "a firm and decisive law that eliminates terrorism and uproots its threats."[23] The Egyptian antiterrorism law is likely to be introduced before the state of emergency expires in 2008 (Brown/Dunne 2007). Amnesty International worries that the new 2007 amendments to the Egyptian Constitution would "simply entrench the long-standing system of abuse under Egypt's state of emergency powers and give the misuse of those powers a bogus legitimacy."[24]

The amendment of Article 179 would pave the way for the introduction of a new antiterrorism law that would undermine the principle of individual freedom (Article 41[1]); privacy of the home (Article 44); and privacy of correspondence, telephone calls, and other communication (Article 45[2]). The amendments would also grant the president the right to bypass ordinary courts, and refer people suspected of terrorism-related offenses to military courts.[25] Article 179 states that Articles 41, 44, and 45 (2) of the constitution must not "hamper" investigations into terrorist crimes (Asser 2007, 3).

Walid Kazziha, chairman of the political science department at the American University in Cairo, notes the emergency legislation has served two purposes: "It has been used—and continues to be used—against terrorism, but it has also been employed to suppress the opposition."[26]

Resistance Strategies: Speaking the Truth to Power

Foucault finds that "there are no relations of power without resistances" and the strength of resistance comes from the fact that it exists in the same place as power. "Hence, like power, resistance is multiple and can be integrated in global strategies" (Foucault 1977, 142).

Even though the judiciary branch in both Egypt and Jordan is weak compared to the executive, it is relatively strong compared to other institutions such as parliament, and has, in both countries, stopped some measures that were harmful to the press in regular times. As Brown (1997) notes, "The development of the Supreme Constitutional Court [in Egypt] from a check on the judiciary into the boldest judicial actor in the country demonstrates how institutional continuity does not preclude dramatic changes in the role of the judiciary" (102).

El-Gobashy describes the paradox of regimes that attempt to control procedures but end up giving people tools that decrease the reach of the regime: "Authoritarian regimes work by combining uncertain procedures with near-certain political results. However, some of these regimes develop elaborate judicial systems and legal procedures that may end up unwittingly providing opportunities for varieties of societal petitioning" (El-Ghobashy 2006, 21, 29).

The most effective form of resistance to the executive's power to shape political life came after political parties were banned in Jordan. Fourteen professional associations with a total of 120,000 members took over the role of political parties. The Jordanian Writers Association led the charge against "normalization" with Israel in 1993 when it protested against dealing with poets or writers who had participated in events attended by Israelis. Even though the association failed in a session held for that purpose to strip a poet of her membership, it still passed a set of by-laws governing normalization that became a model for the professional associations (Lynch 1999, 221). The Popular Committee to Resist Normalization and Protect the Nation's Name "conveys the public position carved out by the Resistance." The Jordanian government declared the committee as an illegal, unlicensed political organization and sued the papers for "publishing the name and statements of an illegal political organization" (Lynch 1999, 222). Even Jordanian prime minister Adnan Badran admitted that the associations were engaged in political life at a point in the kingdom's history when there was a gap in the political landscape caused by the absence of effective political parties.[27]

For years now, Arab journalists have been struggling to prevent the jailing of their kind. Ultimately, it was the sit-ins and agitation of journalists in both Egypt and Jordan—combined with international attention to their cause—that was responsible for the deletion of *some* of the articles allowing imprisonment of journalists for "press offenses."

Conclusion

A comparative analysis of different media laws over time suggests that the Jordanian and Egyptian governments, while genuinely fearing terrorism, did not depart from their usual way of making law over the years. In almost every case, the promulgation of laws was directed as much toward curbing the enemies and critics of both regimes as it was against physical terrorism. For example, neither government wanted the press to discuss the treaties they had signed with Israel, and criminalized such criticism. The continuity of practices is clear in the pattern of passing laws by stealth with little time for discussion or protest (Hamadah 1993). Change is evident in that information is now available from multiple sources, and so governments find it harder to prevent access to information.

As Foucault (1977) has observed, "The penal system makes possible a mode of political and economic management which exploits the difference between legality and illegalities" (141). Thus, the long struggle over the imprisonment of journalists for "press offenses" should be viewed in this light. The threat of imprisonment makes political and economic control and management possible.

The legal system, with its history of granting legitimacy to regimes, had power bestowed on it by history (Bourdieu 2005), and some judges used that power to push the limits of free speech. Thus, for both regimes, the legal system was a double-edged sword; they needed it to maintain their legitimacy, and yet, the power they had bestowed on the legal system was easily turned against rulers in Egypt and Jordan when the courts took their duty to protect free speech seriously.

When journalists were acting against the regimes' diktats, they were doing so not as individuals, as Bourdieu (2005) notes, but as members of a sector with a history of dealing with power; albeit, sometimes from a position of weakness. Thus, journalists had behind them various international human rights organizations that wrote insistent letters to the rulers of Jordan and Egypt, cajoling/chiding them for not keeping their promises. Partly because of that support, journalists were able to get enough concessions to advance the field of journalism slightly, but not enough to classify it as liberal by any stretch of the word.

As was illustrated above, the relations of the religious, political, and journalistic fields are not static and indeed changed under different presidents or kings. As Bourdieu (2005) has reminded us, those who produce discourses professionally struggle to have the their categories of construction of the social world recognized as legitimate. Different political actors want to apply their categories of perception on others without duly noting that categories are socially constituted and socially acquired (Bourdieu 2005, 36, 37). And finally, every one of those fields resisted encroachment on its definitional prerogatives by carefully threading them itself into the space between legality and illegalities.

Predictions for the future of journalism in Egypt and Jordan are not easy to make because *relations between the fields are fluid.* The future of journalism in both countries depends on whether the power of Islamists in both countries infiltrates the political field in sufficient numbers to matter. Additionally, much work remains to be done by press syndicates to remove antipress legislation from the numerous laws that contain articles that imprison journalists or harm freedom of speech.

Finally, the local legislation guaranteeing free speech is enhanced by the presence of an international climate for free speech. But the legislation enacted after 9/11 in Jordan and Egypt is modeled, in part, on the Patriot Act of the United

States. Thus, the real and imaginary fear of terrorism is expected to hamper the movement towards a free press in Egypt and Jordan for years to come. On the other hand, the constant agitation of journalists and their willingness to endure repressive measures will ensure that press laws in Egypt and Jordan will be liberalized, if only incrementally.

Notes

1. Abdullah II, Remarks by His Majesty King Abdullah II to the Foreign Press Association, London, November 23, 2004.
2. Baheyya, Egypt Analysis and Whimsy, July 29, 2005, http://baheyya.blogspot.com.
3. Asser, M., Egypt—A Permanent Emergency? BBC News, March 27, 2007, from http://news.bbc.co.uk/2/hi/middle_east/6481909.stm.
4. See also Latest House Parties in Jordan, March 24, 2007, http://www.black-iris.com/2007/03/24/the-latest-house-parties-in-jordan/.
5. UNDP Programme on Governance in the Arab Region; Jordan: United Nations Development Programme (UNDP), http://www.pogar.org/countries/civil.asp?cid=7.
6. Human Rights Watch, *Don't Enshrine Emergency Rule in Constitution*, March 26, 2007, http://hrw.org/english/docs/2007/03/26/egypt15566.htm; Events of 2006: *Human Rights Watch, World Report 2007*, http://hrw.org/englishwr2k7/docs/2007/01/11/egypt14701.htm.
7. *Country Reports of Human Rights Practices 2004*, U.S. Department of State, 2004, http://www.state.gov/g/drl/rls/hrrpt/2004/41720.htm.
8. *Arab Press Freedom Watch, 2001, The State of the Arab Media*, http://www.apfw.org/data/annualreports/2001/english/2001annualreport.pdf.
9. Egyptian Publisher removes the book *Modern Sheiks and the Manufacture* of *Religious Extremism* at the recommendation of al-Azhar, Al-Quds Al-Arabi, October 18, 2006.
10. Mekay, E. (2003), 88,000 Mosques, One Sermon. Interpress Service News Agency, July 24, 2003, http://ipsnews.net/interna.asp?idnews=19390.
11. Haggag, K. Part I: Point/Counterpoint on the Constitutional Amendments Rebalancing Powers and Rebuilding the Political Center, http://www.carnegieendowment.org/publications/index.cfm?fa=view&id=19113&prog=zgp&proj=zdrl,zme#point.
12. Hussein bin Talal, A Speech by His Majesty King Hussein to the People on August 17, 1993. Amman, Jordan: Ministry of Information.
13. Baheyya, Egypt Analysis and Whimsy, July 8, 2006, http://baheyya.blogspot.com.
14. Human Rights Watch World Report 2007 (see note 6).
15. Al-Zubaidi, L. (2004), Walking a Tightrope: News Media and Freedom of Expression in the Arab Middle East, Heinrich Böll Foundation, http://www.boell-meo.org/download_en/media_study.pdf.

16. International Freedom of Expression Exchange (IFEX), Changes to Penal Code a Threat to Press Freedom, October 16, 2001, http://www.ifex.org/en/content/view/full/29645/.
17. Press release by the International Freedom of the Press Exchange (IFEX) and the Egyptian Organization for Human Rights (EOHR), April 30, 2002.
18. Twenty-Two IFEX Members Urge President to Abolish Imprisonment of Journalists in Publication Cases, International Freedom of Expression Exchange (IFEX), January 10, 2007, http://ifex.org/en/content/view/full/80252/.
19. D. Kuttab, Good Governance and Arab Journalists Unions, Arab Media Internet Network, October 2002, http://www.amin.org.
20. H. Abdul Ghani, Jalal Aref: Egyptian Press Syndicate, Al-Jazeera.net, August 17, 2003, http://www.aljazeera.net/Channel/archive/archive?ArchiveId=92217.
21. EOHR's Report about Press Freedom in Egypt, Egyptian Organization for Human Rights (EOHR), 2006, http://www.eohr.org/report/2006/re0821.shtml.
22. Government Approves Anti-Terrorism Law. *Arab Reform Bulletin*, 2006/5, http://www.carnegieendowment.org/publications/index.cfm?fa=view&id=18413&prog=zgp&proj=z drl#jordanGovernment.
23. Human Rights Watch World Report 2007 (see note 6).
24. Amnesty International, Proposed Constitutional Amendments Greatest Erosion of Human Rights in 26 Years, March 18, 2007, http://64.233.167.104/search?q=cache:gsNaBoMBv1cJ:news.amnesty.org/index/ENGMDE120082007+write+into+permanent+law+emergency-style+powers+that+have+been+used+to+violate+human+rights&hl=en&ct=clnk&cd=3&gl=us&lr=lang_ar|lang_en|lang_fr.
25. Ibid.
26. Morrow, A. (2006), Opposition Fights Martial Law Extension, Interpress Service News Agency, May 5, 2006, http://ipsnews.net/news.asp?idnews=33141.
27. Badran Asks Association Presidents for Observations on Draft Law, *Jordan Times*, August 26, 2005, http://www.jordanembassyus.org/08262005001.htm.

References

Abdul Baqi, I. (2005), *The Press and the Corruption of the Elite: A Study of Reasons and Solutions.* Cairo: Al-Arabi.

Abdul Rahman, A. (1985), *Studies in the Contemporary Egyptian Press.* Cairo: Dar Al-Fikr Al-Arabi.

Ahmad, M. S. (1984), The Future of the Political Party System in Egypt. Cairo: Dar Al-Mustakbal Al-Arabi

Amin, M. (1989), *Forbidden Ideas.* Beirut: Al-Asr Al-Hadith.

Benson, R. (2005), Mapping Field Variation: Journalism in France and the United States. In R. Benson/E. Neveu (eds.), *Bourdieu and the Journalistic Field.* Cambridge: Polity, 85–112.

Bourdieu, P. (2005), The Political Field, the Social Science Field, and the Journalistic Field. In R. Benson/E. Neveu (eds.), *Bourdieu and the Journalistic Field.* Cambridge: Polity, 85–112.

Brown, N. (1997), *The Rule of Law in the Arab World.* Cambridge: Cambridge University Press.

Brown, N./M. Dunne/A. Hamzawy (2006), Egypt's Controversial Constitutional Amendments: A Textual Analysis. *Arab Reform Bulletin* 9, http://www.carnegieendowment.org/experts/index.cfm?fa=expert_view&expert_id=238.

Carapico, S. (2002), Foreign Aid for Promoting Democracy in the Middle East. *Middle East Journal* 3, 379–395.

Choucair, J. (2006), *Illusive Reform: Jordan's Stubborn Stability.* Carnegie Paper No. 76, http://www.carnegieendowment.org/publications/index.cfm?fa=view&id=18900&prog=zgp&proj=zdrl.

Dalacoura, K. (2003), *Islam, Liberalism and Human Rights.* London: I. B. Tauris.

DeBartolo, D. (2007), Attention Turns to Electoral Law. *Arab Reform Bulletin* 3, http://www.carnegieendowment.org/files/debartolo_april07.pdf.

Engel, R. (2004), Book Ban Exposes Azhar Censorship. *Middle East Times,* November 10.

Foucault, M./Gordon, C. (eds.) (1977), *Power/Knowledge: Selected Interviews and other Writings, 1972–1977.* New York: Pantheon.

Ghobashy, M. el-(2006), The Year of Elections in the Middle East. *Middle East Report 1, 20–31.*

Hafez, S. (1993), *The Sorrows of the Press.* Cairo: Al-Ahram Center for Translation and Publishing.

Hamed, S. (2005), Jordan: Democracy at a Dead End. *Arab Reform Bulletin* 4, http://www.carnegieendowment.org/files/May_Full_Issue5.pdf.

Hamadah, B. I. (1993), *The Role of Media in Decision-Making in the Arab World,* Dissertation Series 21. Beirut: Center for the Study of Arab Unity.

Haykal, M. (2003), *Between Journalism and Politics.* Cairo: Dar Al-Shuruq.

Hournai, H. al-/Urdun Al-Jadid Research Team (1997), *Jordanian Political Parties.* Amman: Al-Urdun Al-Jadid Research Center/Sindbad.

Keller, P. (1992), Freedom of the Press in Hong Kong: Liberal Values and Sovereign Interests. in *Texas International Law Journal* 279, 371–417.

Lynch, M. (1999), *State Interests and Public Spheres: The International Politics of Jordan's Identity.* New York: Columbia University Press.

Nafie, I. (2003), The Future of Journalistic Self-Regulation and Journalism Associations in Egypt and the Arab World. In K. Hafez (ed.), *Media Ethics in the Dialogue of Cultures.* Hamburg: Deutsches Orient-Institut, 162–168.

Najjar, O. (1998), The Ebb and Flow of Press Freedom in Jordan, 1985–1997. *Journalism and Mass Communication* Quarterly 1, 127–142.

———. (2007), After the Fall: Palestinian Communist Journalism in the Post–Cold War World. *Rethinking Marxism* 3, 337–360.

O'Kane, J. (1972), Islam in the New Egyptian Constitution: Some Discussions in Al-Ahram. *Middle East Journal* 2, 137–148.

Saleh, S. (1995), *The Crisis of the Freedom of the Press in Egypt.* 1985–1945, Cairo: Egyptian Universities Publishing House.

Media Cultures

CHAPTER THIRTEEN

Arab Media and Cultural Studies: Rehearsing New Questions

Tarik Sabry

Before we begin the process of recentering ourselves, we must first decenter ourselves.
(Abu-Rabi 2004, XIV)

[T]he media are changing the world in ways important enough for a study of these changes to become part of formal education.
(Hall/Whannel 1964, 21)

I started work on this chapter with a genuine intention that the final product would be an exposé or critique of key canonical texts on Arab media and culture so that it would possibly serve as reference point for the scholar and student working in this area. It took me a long while to realize that this was not only an unattainable task but also a kind of academic queue-jumping, if one can use such language to denote the order, logic, and understanding of things. It took me even longer, I must confess, to convince myself that my digression to dealing with rather more basic questions on Arab media and culture studies was not intellectual laziness on my part. Most discouraging was the prospect of text selection (there are literally hundreds of varied sources that one can classify under the "rubric" of Arab culture). There was also the worry that the outcome would merely serve as a bibliographic summary of texts. Without wanting to undermine such intellectual exercise, for I sincerely think it necessary, I simply think that this task must be preceded by another: that of establishing the nature of the epistemological framework within which we can engage in thinking and rationalising the relationship between media, culture and society in the contemporary Arab world. The problem I encountered was unavoidable: How does one write or rehearse a historiography of a field—in this case, the latent field of Arab media and cultural studies—when such a field only exists in a latent, incoherent, and unconscious form? So, rather than opting to compile bibliographic material on who wrote what,[1] using what methodology and to what effect, I am content, for now at least, to take a step back and rehearse what I believe to be basic yet fundamental questions about the development of the field, hoping that this will open up a sustained debate and discussion on the possibilities or impossibilities of its appropriation and "academization".

I see this chapter as the logical progression from work I published recently, titled "In Search of the Arab Present Cultural Tense" (Sabry 2007), in which I attempted to articulate the necessity for an epistemic space where the study of Arab cultures (media and other new forms of artistic expression) could become central objects of scientific enquiry. Without wanting to police the boundaries of such a field, I argued that the latter would be far more useful were it informed by, and reconnected with, sociological and philosophical problematics raised by contemporary Arab thought. Taking lessons from the vantage point of the well-established and mature fields of British media and cultural studies, I also argued for a flexible hermeneutics that would allow for less deterministic interpretations and theorizations of Arab media and cultures. I also argued that this epistemic space was necessary as an intellectual project for the reworking of the idea of Arab cultures in such a way that our reference points are informed not merely by the sacred and the timeless, or even by what Mathew Arnold calls "the *best* knowledge and thought of the time" (Arnold 1993, 79) but also by the grittiness and ordinariness of culture as it unfolds in its everyday, ontological, time-based world structure. In what follows, I hope to rehearse and problematize both old and new questions relating to the development of this new, latent, and still incoherent field: Arab media and cultural studies.

The Arab academe and its intellectuals have been very slow (almost stubborn) in realizing the centrality of media to experience in the modern Arab world, and they have not therefore been able (with the exception of some journalism courses scattered here and there) to see the benefits in fighting for the institutionalizing of media and cultural studies in Arab higher education.

The study of Arab cultures, it is important to add (since the study of culture is crucial to the development of the field), has been almost completely left to the Western anthropologist and social scientist who have, for the last century, at least, been *the* main observers and interpreters of Arabs and their cultures. This work, however important (and a lot of it is), has unfortunately failed to spark enough interest in the Arab academe for it to materialize into an active and coherent field of enquiry into Arab cultures. It is certainly odd that this has never happened, since the study of culture is not entirely alien to the Arab cultural repertoire. Ibn Khaldoun, now celebrated by some Western observers as the father of social science, impressively argued in the thirteenth century that a comprehension of any nation's history requires a study and exploration of the structure of its culture or *umran* (Ibn Khaldoun 1996).[2] Just as no Arab scholar, with the exception of Jabri, has, for nearly a millennia, cared to build on Ibn Rushd's rational project, no Arab scholar, it seems, cared to develop Ibn Khaldoun's ideas in any systematic way. I am not unaware of the myriad of theses and writings on Ibn Khaldoun in Arab libraries, but this compendium shows no linearity in thought, nor has it produced scientific paradigms into the study of culture. This absence of continuity in the Arab sciences is part of a wider and more problematic phenomenon inherent to Arab "reason" and its structure, which Jabri famously dealt with in his philosophical treatise *A Critique of Arab Reason*, where he blames digression in Arab thought and sciences on the inactivity of *la raison constituante*—that part of reason that produces knowledge, and on the dominance of *la raison constituée*, which limits its activity to the reproduction of *les idées reçues*.

Middle East Studies Revival: A Trojan Horse?

Exactly a year before the events of 9/11, it was commented that interest in the Middle East, as an area study in the U.S. academe, was undergoing a process of decline and that African and Asian studies were emerging as more favored subjects of study (Armbrust 2000).The events of 9/11 and their aftermath changed all this almost instantaneously. Very large sums of taxpayer money in the West, especially in the United States, have since been channelled to resuscitate academic interest in the subject. What is the nature and *telos* of the recent revival of the Middle East as an academic subject in Western academe? My main concern with this hasty renewed interest in the old Middle East relates to (1) its motives and (2) epistemological situatedness. In his 2003 preface to *Orientalism*, Edward Said took the opportunity to voice his concerns, yet again, about the state and somewhat dubious motives of Middle East Studies in the United States: "[T]here is of course a Middle East Studies establishment, a pool of interests, 'old boy' or 'expert' networks linking corporate business, the foundations, the oil companies, the missions, the military, the foreign service, the intelligence community together with the academic world. There are grants and other rewards, there are organizations, there are hierarchies, there are institutes, centres, faculties, departments, all devoted to legitimising and maintaining the authority of a handful of basic, basically unchanging ideas about Islam, the orient, and the Arabs" (Said 2003, 301–302).

Although it would be incongruous, if not misleading, to view all of the motives behind a resurging interest in the Middle East as a Trojan horse, it's still fair to say that this renewed interest was precipitated into being without allowing enough time for the thinking through of the methodological considerations and epistemological implications to be utilized in the study of the region. Both Arab and Western scholars researching the field in Western academe have a number of questions with which to deal, questions they ought to have been allowed to tackle prior to completing their grant and sabbatical applications. To what field of study does their work belong? What is its main reference point? Is it sociology, area studies, Orientalism, or mere intelligence for the consumption of Western foreign offices? Who will it serve and for what purposes? How will their approach to studying the region differ from that pursued by the classic Orientalist? And if their work deals with the contemporary Arab and Middle Eastern world, its media and societies, in what ways is it (their work) attempting to bridge or inform questions and problematics posed by Arab and Middle Eastern intellectuals vis-à-vis, let's say, the "cultural question" or reactions to modernity's pathologies? If linkages are not made, then who and what does this intellectual repertoire serve? In other words, what is the nature of the epistemological passageway into the subject of Arab media, culture, and society in Western academe today? The Orientalist dogma inherent to studying the Arab and his culture persists in different forms and is more than likely to continue to do so in the future. Said, who did much to unclothe Orientalist dogma and reveal its discourse, observed,"The principle dogmas of Orientalism exist in their purest form today in studies of the Arabs and Islam...one is the absolute and systematic difference between the West, which is rational, developed, humane, superior, and the Orient, which is aberrant, undeveloped, inferior. Another dogma is that abstractions about the Orient, particularly based on texts representing a 'classical' Oriental civilization, are always preferable to direct evidence drawn from modern oriental realities. A third dogma is that the orient is eternal, uniform, and incapable of defining itself; therefore it is assumed that a highly generalised and systematic vocabulary for describing the orient from a Western standpoint is inevitable and even scientifically 'objective'. The fourth dogma is that the orient is at the bottom something either to be feared...or to be controlled [by pacification, research and development, outright occupation whenever possible]" (Said 2003, 300–301).

However, rather than doing away with these recurrent reincarnations of Orientalist dogmas in researching Arabs and their cultures, I suggest that this kind of knowledge becomes an object of sustained and systematic enquiry for the field.

The Problem of Arbitrariness between Intellectual Formations and Historical "Moments"

The establishment of new academic fields does not take place in a haphazard fashion, nor does it develop outside history. Stuart Hall's early writings, in which he makes the case for the centrality of the media to experience, confirm this. The media, he argued with Whannel, "are not the end products of a simple technological revolution. They come at the end of a complex historical and social process; they are active agents in a new phase in the life-history of industrial society. Inside these forms and languages, the society is articulating new social experiences for the first time. In fact, the emergence of new art forms is closely linked with social change" (Hall/Whannel 1964, 45). The question that needs to be asked in the Arab context is: Are the historical and sociocultural conditions in the Arab region suited to the development of an academic field that takes culture and the media as the objects of its enquiry? If so, what are these historical events and what shape should this field take? What ought to be its main concerns? One of the important lessons we learn from the historiography of studies into media and communication, especially the development of mass communication in the United States in the 1930s and cultural studies in Britain in the 1960s and 1970s, is that their development was not accidental, but the product of historical moments. They are "a determinate effect of the historical process; responses to the pathologies [the disorders] of modernity" (Scannell 2006, 4).

Thus, a study of the development of these fields, or of any academic field, cannot take place outside the historical, political and socio-economic contexts that determined them nor the historical formations that shaped them. Scannell observed that academic fields "show up, in particular times and places, as one response to contemporary anxieties about the world. The form that such responses take is an effect of history in the first place, not of the founding institutions and their founding fathers. Thus, if the two key moments in the academic study of the media in the 20th century are Columbia in the 30s and 40s and Birmingham in the 60s and 70s then what must be accounted for, in the first place, is why each moment took the form that it did: why did it appear as a social question in 30s America and as a cultural question in 70s Britain and why in that order [i.e. why does the social question appear, historically, before the cultural]?...Thus there are two quite distinct and separate historiographies to the formation of intellectual fields: the endogenous histories of particular developments [sociology at Chicago, say] and the exogenous history to which they are a response. The former is a plurality, the latter a singularity: histories and History" (Scannell 2006, 4).

If we were to accept Scannell's reasoning here as a more sophisticated and useful way of *doing* media and communication historiography, how then do we appropriate it to make sense of the study and enquiry into media, culture and society in the Arab world? What do we know about the intellectual formations of the scholars now engaged in the study of the region's media and culture? Upon what hermeneutics do they rely to interpret the world? What paradigms, if any, have emerged from their enquiries? To what historical moment are they responding? Answering these questions is certainly beyond the scope of this chapter; what follows, however, is not entirely detached from the problems they pose. If I am contributing a paper, let's say, on Moroccan or Egyptian popular culture, or the political economy of Arab media, to what epistemic space will I be contributing? This question applies both to the Arab scholar who writes in Arabic and publishes his work mainly with an Arab audience in mind and the scholar dealing with similar issues in English, French, or German in different locales of Western academe with a mainly Western readership in mind. It is not so much the geographical situatedness of the "field" that is of concern but its "epistemological" situatedness.

One problem that emerges from the "situatedness" question is methodological. Since the development of academic fields is partly shaped, as we learn from Scannell, by intellectual formations that are in turn affected by certain historical "moments," then how is this going to affect the structural and methodological development of a field such as Arab media and cultural studies, to which both Western and Arab scholars have been contributing not only from different geographies but also from different historical moments? Here, the problem is one of confusion caused by arbitrariness between the cultural temporality and the historical "moment" within which knowledge is produced about Arab media, culture, and society. Arab and Western scholars contributing to the field may not share similar intellectual formation or motives. In fact, a lot of them are likely to be unaware of each other's work, since what has so far been produced on the region's media and culture is isolated work, exhibiting little linearity of thought and argument. This is not to say, of course, that established academic fields such as British cultural studies were clearly defined from the outset or were even "coherent." The field of British cultural studies was, and still is, the product of competing paradigms, different intellectual formations, and even endless turf wars.

Nevertheless, what brings this field together in a way that Arab media and cultural studies may not is inherent to the commonality of the historical moment and the cultural temporality within which it operates. To this we also need to add the existence of sustained debate, not only about media, culture, and society, but how these are thought and rethought from within the field. It is a debate about the field itself, which is also evidence of its maturity (Garnham 1986; Hall 1986; Morley/Chen 1996; Silverstone 1999; Curran/Morley 2006; Scannell 2006). If the cultural "turn" was, according to Scannell, the result of a shift in the nature of political discourse in the West (from politics of poverty to politics of abundance), and if this was also to play a part in shaping British cultural studies in the 1960s as an intellectual discipline, then to what "moment" or political shift do we attribute the rationale for an Arab media and cultural studies? In the same vein, since a shift in political discourse implicates change in meanings ascribed to "politics," should we not also be rethinking what is meant by *politics* in today's Arab context?

Scannell's analysis is rather plausible, but his justification for the shift in political discourse is clearly framed within a Western context and cannot therefore be generalized. In the case of the poor South, of which the Arab region is part, the politics of poverty is still dominant, and so is the emancipatory discourse with all its different struggles. South American and African cultural studies emerged in societies where the politics of poverty were predominant. They still are, and so I think it safe to say, in the case of these geographies at least, a shift from the politics of poverty to the politics of abundance was not a prerequisite for the establishment of African or South American cultural studies. The intellectual formations that shaped African cultural studies in the 1950s and 1960s (especially Frantz Fanon, Ngugi Thiong'o, and Kimani Gecau) shared a common experience: colonialism. Their work was a response to anxieties caused by colonialism and its aftermath. Here again, we can also say with some certainty that the postcolonial "moment" was the *exogenous* element that shaped African cultural studies. The Arab region, like sub-Saharan Africa, was spared neither the physical nor the mental brutality of the colonial system. As I write, the latter is still relevant in Iraq, Afghanistan, and the Palestinian territories. It is therefore required of Arab media and cultural studies to explore not only the dynamics of postcolonial consciousness but also imperialism and its consequences on regional peoples and cultures. What I have tried to show by giving examples from the two different intellectual traditions of African and British cultural studies is that although they were shaped during the same period (mainly the 1960s) both their reference point and the historical moments to which they responded were different.

Nevertheless, in today's globalized world, we really cannot afford to conceptualize or theorize an Arab media and cultural studies through the prism of the local alone. The Arab region has long been subject to the globalizing structures, temporalities, and institutions of modernity. So, just as critical theory was a response to what Adorno and Horkheimer called the "dialectics of the enlightenment" (Adorno/Horkheimer 1979), Arab media and cultural studies must also intervene to describe, make sense of, and theorize on the region's reaction to modernity and its disorders. It is through the prism of the *glocal* (the global and local) that Arab media and cultural studies must position itself. I am not unaware of the varied attempts from within the Arab and Islamic world at unpacking and making sense of modernity as a project. This has resulted in a myriad of discourses, some embraced, that ruthlessly worked to propagate modernity as an answer to Arab and Islamic ahistoricity; others rejected it outright as a mere imperialist project. Some today are calling for modernity from within, adapting cultural particularities that are inherently Arab and Islamic. What this compendium failed to do, however, is explore modernity as lived experience. Moreover, its narratives have seldom enquired into the role played by transnational media and other forms of artistic expression in conveying meanings of modernity and what it means to be modern. Arab media and cultural studies will need to build on this debate by exploring the different ways in which the Arab world encounters Western modernity today and how these encounters have affected its cultural temporality and its structures of feeling about the world.

Problematizing the Discourse of "Culture" in "Arab-Islamic" Culture: A Very Brief Sketch

The intellectual formations that shape academic fields usually dictate the kind of hermeneutics that are relied upon to interpret the world. When we say "Arab media" and "cultural studies," to what "culture" are we referring exactly? How are the meanings of culture articulated from within the Arab world? There are many competing and contested discourses about what Arab "culture" is or what its function should be. The same could be said about Arabness. The pan-Arab interpretation of culture's function is an interesting one. The term "Arab world" can be divided into two further unifying terminologies: *al-watan al-arabi* and *al-ummah al-arabiya.* The first denotes geographic unity; the second alludes to some sort of spiritual *din* (religion) common experience (Jabri 1994, 25). According to Jabri, the main historical characteristic of "culture" is inherent to its function as a unifier. Here, the awakening of Arab consciousness is predicated on culture's ability to unify. Culture's historical function, according to Jabri, a pan-Arabist par excellence, is to help transform the Arab world from a mere geographic space (*al-watan al-arabi*) to *al-ummah al-arabiya*, a space bound by common shared experience (Jabri 1994, 25–27).

This shift from the spatial to the symbolic has of late been skillfully managed by certain transnational Arab media in ways no print media could ever achieve. Al-Jazeera's highly perceptive understanding and communication of the "common frames of injustice" shared by Arab and Muslim audiences is inherent to its success. The communication of these "frames" is not unintentional or hazardous; rather, it is part of a coherent intentional "care structure" that is intentionally embedded in most of Al-Jazeera's programming. It is these "frames of common injustice" and how they are communicated that transform an otherwise stratified and heterogeneous audience into a homogenous one. These frames are the product of internal and external elements. The former can be summarized in the Arab and Muslim masses' dissatisfaction with their repressive and undemocratic regimes and lack of civil freedoms. The latter are the product of external historical events including, in order of importance: the occupation of Palestine and the plight of the Palestinian people, the occupations of Iraq and Afghanistan and the United States' continual bias toward the state of Israel.

The "Popular" in Arab Popular Culture

To speak of an Arab popular culture in a homogenous fashion is to mask the particularities of the very voices, heard or unheard, that make up Arab popular cultures and thus conceal dialectics of power relations inherent to Arab societies (Sabry 2007). Discourses of unity and reconciliation, often mediated through Arab mass media, mask difference and competing antagonistic forces inherent to Arab societies. To give just one example from the Arab world, Moroccan society is stratified into different popular tastes and cultures, so much so that we cannot really talk of *a* Moroccan culture. We have the popular culture of the *Aroubi* (derogatory, of Arab descent, also meaning "peasant", "irrational," and "mostly uneducated"); the *Fessi,* the elitist who appreciates Andalusian music and knowledge, and unlike the Aroubi only fills his glass of Moroccan tea halfway. We also have the *Amazigh* or *Shelh,* the native of Morocco and the modern—usually a Francophile who consumes mainly French culture. The Amazigh appreciates Amazigh music, the Aroubi likes the Shaabi (a type of Moroccan folk music), and the modern appreciates Western pop music and maybe some Egyptian classics.

These tastes can and do overlap, but the Shelh and the Aroubi's popular tastes are often mediated as subordinate to those of the modern and bourgeois Arab whose mannerisms, individuality, and culturedness are presented as the distinguishable traits of a superior and modern culture. How the stratification of tastes in Arab popular cultures is played out by Arab mass media, be it in Egyptian soap opera, Moroccan popular comedy, or other forms of cultural production, is often mediated through discourses of power. So what appears as "popular" in Arab popular culture is in many ways pseudo-popular, which speaks with and for the voices of the center. Manifestations of Arab "popular" cultures are more visible in noninstitutionalized popular cultural spaces, such as popular jokes, music, cafés, and mosques. In her study of Egyptian soaps Abu-Lughod has observed the following: "State television and those who produce for it can try to reflect certain social transformations, to gain popularity, just as they have made efforts for years, in line with ideologies of development, to shape or mould their audiences and bring them into a national modernity. Yet they cannot control the experiences people seek outside of television-watching or the everyday social worlds in which people live their lives" (Abu-Lughod 2002, 129).

These "everyday social worlds" are taken-for-granted popular cultural spaces that are largely understudied. The wisdom in calling the field "Arab media and cultural studies," rather than "Arab media studies," is that the latter confines the "cultural" to media, whereas the former is more encompassing and provides wider scope for analyzing what Abu-Lughod calls the "everyday social worlds." To this, we need to add what During (2005) terms the "global popular." Arab television and radio stations and cinema halls are saturated in global popular artifacts that range from Mexican soaps, to American sitcoms, to Chinese Kung-Fu, to hip-hop. This is the reason why culture in the Arab world should be analyzed through the prism of the *glocal* rather than that of the local.

It is difficult to raise the issue of culture in the Arab context without reference to religion. Religion—mainly, Islam—plays an important if not fundamental role in conceptualizations of Arab cultures. Religion is indeed ingrained in the everyday structures of Arab societies. It is visible, heard, and smelled, and it is part of what binds much of Arab identity together. Without wanting to make generalizations about Arabs, for fear of falling into the same trap previously dug by many an Orientalist—and many of them have done little but generalize on the Arab and Arab culture—I can say with certainty that no comprehensive study of Arab cultures can afford to ignore the role played by religion in determining such cultures. Walking down the "popular" streets of Morocco, Egypt, and Tunisia just before the time of the *Iftar* (breaking the fast),[3] one is intoxicated by the wonderful mix of food smells: *harrera* (soup), cakes, and other mouth-watering delicacies, not to mention the care structures with which certain rituals are observed, forming a common experience and structure of feeling. In short, religion permeates many spheres of Arab social and cultural life, and this varies from the voices of the Adan (call for prayers), to people's greetings and language, popular jokes, satellite religious programs, the Internet, and so on. We also need to add the momentary encounters with the "traditionalizer": the father, sister, friend, Imam, storyteller and the taxi driver, the quasi-prophets who see it as their duty to remind their people of God's sacred words and the prophets' good conduct. Religious discourse in the Arab world is part of the fabric of Arab structures of feeling and must therefore be studied as a cultural phenomenon. To grasp the totality of cultural experience, the hermeneutics upon which Arab media and cultural studies rely to interpret social and cultural reality in the region have to incorporate a category that precedes both the social and the cultural, if not life itself: the existential. This is a category much ignored in Western media and cultural studies because of the intellectual traditions that helped shape them.

However, a rearticulation of Arab cultures within the category of the "existential" must not necessarily lead to the latter's Islamization or Christianization. For at that very moment we would limit analysis of culture to the realm of the sacred, we would destroy not only its ontological structure but also the prerequisite for a creative and critical consciousness. By enveloping culture in the realm of the sacred, we risk losing sight of its gritty and profane nature. This line of argument, however, must not be misunderstood for a call to secularize or, even worse, to desacrilize the study of culture. Religion must be allowed to shape culture, to be part of its fabric; but culture, any culture, must not be defined or determined solely through religiosity. In their many attempts to recontextualize Western communication theory within an Islamic context, Arab scholars (see Glass 2001) have ignored a very important intellectual task: that of decentring or troubling meanings of "Islamic" culture from within. This intellectual task of recontextualization and "acclimatization," to use Jabri's term, must be preceded—if it is to adhere to any form of radical consciousness—by the act of decentering exactly the subject it seeks to center (in this case, "Islamic culture"). By failing to do so, we risk building a cultural repertoire that is erected on binary differentiations between "us," the Muslims *and* the West, as if we have no shared cultural or historical affinities, therefore reproducing dogmatic Orientalist discourse for which we have so vehemently criticized Orientalism (Said 2003). As Berque puts it, "Altercation and affinity with West has always characterised the Arabs" (Berque 1978, 3). The risk of adhering to this futile and obsolete discourse of "us" and "them" is that it often detracts from a far more important intellectual task: reworking the idea of culture and cultural heritage in contemporary Arab societies in ways through which the past is reconciled with the present.

Processes of theory recontextualization are not innocent. They often come in the form of discourse and rarely resist claims to authenticity. In the case of Iran, conforming to a particular interpretation or discourse of "Islamic culture" happens at the expense of keeping quiet about and allying with state ideology, no matter how unjust or wrong it is—which is, ironically, far from Islamic. In his sustained critique of Mowlana's work, Khiabany has observed, "Commentators such Mowlana adhere to the simplistic notion that Muslim societies [and Islamic states are monolithic] are homogeneous entities with ideally disciplined sacred structures and clear and irreversible visions. It is the state that imposes unity and coherence on culture and creates a forced unity out of a whole set of complex practices, diversities and inconsistencies ... contrary to Mowlana's assumptions, it is not Islam that gives meaning to the state but rather it is the coercive force of the state that makes the 'particular' Islam what it is in a particular national context" (Khiabany 2006, 19).

What is thus required of us is a dual process of recontextualization, one that deals with the task of reconceptualization and reappropriation of the Western episteme to fit local cultural contexts, the other reconfiguring and troubling these very processes themselves, by way of theoretical and reflexive revision.

Arab Higher Education and Lack of Critical Reason

This brings us to the issue of intellectuals and the role they can and should play in making the media and their role intelligible. An Arab media and cultural studies project led by uncritical reason is a failed project. "We study the media," argues Silverstone, "because we are concerned about their power ... in our everyday lives; in the structuring of experience, on the surface and in the depth and we want to harness that power for good rather than ill" (Silverstone 1999, 143). Facile empiricism now being imported from uncritical regions of Western academe and taught or, shall I say, force-fed en masse in Arab universities to obedient Arab students happy to regurgitate what they have been taught will simply not do. What's more, Arab universities, with very limited exceptions, are heavily policed and remain part of the state apparatus par excellence. The hierarchy of the Arab university is answerable to the authoritarian state and plays a major role in maintaining the status quo. Critical rationality is discouraged. The "lack of autonomy has resulted in a situation where universities are run according to the requirements of the governing political logic, and not a plan or wise educational policy" (AHDR 2003, 56). Another cause for concern that has hampered the development of media and cultural studies in Arab higher education must be attributed to the weakness of the social sciences in the region.

Sociology departments in Arab higher education would have been a preferred, if not the ideal, site for developing and engaging with the question of the media, but the weakness of research in this field, which I attribute to authoritarian states' sabotaging of any form of critical reason, has unfortunately stood in the way of such development. Describing the state of sociology studies in the Arab higher education of the early 1970s, Badawi remarks, "sociology sections in different faculties of Arab universities ... have not yet produced the fruits we expected of them. Investigations, theses and Monographs are meagre and have little substance ... the study of this discipline leaves a lot to be desired" (Badawi 1972, 784).[4] The Arab Human Development Report of 2003 provides an even bleaker picture of the state of education and the social sciences in the Arab world today: "Arab researchers in the humanities and the social sciences, frequently work in a vacuum. They are integrated with neither global nor Pan-Arab groups. This isolation adds the report, 'has led in several cases to observable frustration that has begun to turn into a general mood, reflected in a withdrawal into individual pursuits and a kind of indifference, not only to public affairs but also to questions of knowledge per se in addition to social and cultural limitations inherited and internalised, there is the intervention of politics and laws associated with politics, which directly or visibly draw red lines for research in the humanities and the social sciences" (AHDR 2003, 75–76).

However, it is fair to say that modern Arab universities are still relatively young, with three-quarters of them only established in the last twenty-five years of the twentieth century (AHDR. 2003, 56). Developments of educational curricula happen through a compromise between "inherited" and new interests: a process that, as Raymond Williams argues in his assessment of education in British society, "may be long delayed and will often be muddled" (Williams 1961, 172). And "the rate at which the curriculum adjusts to the changes in society," argue Hall and Whannel, "is slow and even the most established subjects have had to be fought for" (Hall/Whannel 1964, 387).

As it stands, Arab higher education is clearly out of sync with social change and employment demands. The rapid growth of the Arab media market over the last decade, and the occupational demands resulting from this development are certainly not catered for by the Arab higher education curriculum. Arab higher education has to expand to meet these social needs: otherwise it, and with it a whole cultural repertoire, is doomed to further digression and stagnation. If we are to act on Jabri's answer to challenges to modernity by modernizing the Arab cultural heritage so that it can deal with problems of the present (Jabri 1991, 1994, 2001), then this process must begin with the university and education.

Conclusion

What I have attempted to do in this chapter is to further rehearse some of the questions I originally posed in a previous work, articulating the possibility and importance of an epistemic space that examines media and culture in the Arab world. This attempt leaves many questions unanswered, perhaps intentionally so, to invite more debate and discussion on the topic. The question is not only one of subject; it is also one of methodology (Williams 1961). What should we teach in Arab media and cultural studies, and how do we teach it? How do we "distinguish serious intellectual work from mere shifts in taste and fashion?" (Hall/Whannel 1964, 22). These are questions that beg more discussion and debate on the topic. Suffice it to say, the field of media and cultural studies is inherently interdisciplinary, as it draws from many traditions and schools of thought, and this has to be reflected in the ways in which we teach Arab media and cultural studies through allowing for a plurality of hermeneutics in analysing cultural phenomena. The field should also avoid imported, ready-made facile empiricism and encourage the deployment of innovative methodologies. The success and credibility of a field such as Arab media and cultural studies, I argue, will depend on its ability to articulate and assess not only the dynamics of power as they emerge from the cultural text (both written and visual)—and how the latter is encoded and decoded—but also on its articulation of the economic and political structures that govern and influence cultural production in the Arab world. It is important to reiterate this well-known political economy fact: cultural products are dual commodities. Yes, the culture industries are there to entertain, inform/misinform and educate; but they are, above all, businesses and profit-seeking institutions. As Silverstone puts it, "Global economies and global finance cannot work without a global information infrastructure...global politics depends on the rapid communication between the relevant parties, in peace time and in war" (Silverstone 1999, 144).

Notes

1. A very useful bibliographic work by Dagmar Glass traces trends in Arab-Islamic Media and Communication Perspectives from the 1950s to the late 1990s and can be found in Kai Hafez's edited collection *Mass Media, Politics and Society in the Middle East* (Glass 2001). The article is titled: "The Global Flow of Information: A Critical Appraisal from the Perspective of Arab Islamic Information Sciences." Glass stratifies Arab media and communication scholars into five different intellectual traditions: group 1 (1950s–1996), whose work was concerned with public opinion and the social functions of communication and was largely influenced by American communication models; group 2: also established in the 1950s, this group worked hard to institutionalize the teaching of media practice; group 3, which was established in the 1960s and was mainly concerned with classical Islamic theories of communication; group 4, which was established in the 1970s and called for the re-Islamization of Arab information; and group 5, described as the product of the 1980s, an advocate of an "Arab conceptualization of information" (Glass 2001, 220–222).
2. Al-Umran, in the work of Ibn Khaldoun, denotes both culture and civilization.
3. There is a sociological distinction between the use of the term "popular" in Morocco and that in the West (see Sparks 1992). No academic work has so far examined meanings of the popular within Moroccan popular culture. Gassous (1988) and Belkbir (1991) came close to doing so, as their work deals with, among other things, the relationship between Moroccan popular culture and the discourses of power inherent to Moroccan society, but neither of them has directly dealt with meanings of the "popular" in Moroccan popular culture

per se. There is a linguistic and sociological distinction between the use of the word "popular" in the English language and that used in Moroccan Dareja "Moroccan dialect." In the latter, a popular or Shaabi person does not necessarily denote a successful or rich person, but someone who is accepted as being from, of, and for the people. In the Moroccan sense of the word, the linguistic sign "popular" connotes meanings of belonging, modesty, and humility. A "Shaabi" person can be rich or poor, educated or uneducated. To be "popular" in the Moroccan sense of the word is to be one of the people. A rich man wins Shaabeya "popularity" not through his material possessions, but through his modesty and acceptance of the poor and their way of life. If you are rich, what wins you popularity among the Moroccan working classes is not money or wealth but the capital of sociability: the ability to mingle with the poor, speak to them, joke with them and eat with them as equals and not subordinates (Sabry 2005, 5–6).

4. Author's translation from French.

References

Adorno, T. W./M. Horkheimer (1979), *Dialectic of Enlightenment.* London: Verso Editions.

Abu-Lughod, L. (2002), Egyptian Melodrama—Technology of the Modern Subject? In F. D Ginsburg/L. Abu-Lughod/B. Larkin (eds.), *Media Worlds: Anthropology on New Terrain.* Berkeley: University of California Press, 115–133.

Abu-Rabi, I. (2004), *Contemporary Arab Thought: Studies in Post-1967 Arab Intellectual History.* London: Pluto.

Arab Human Development Report (AHDR) (2003), *Building a Knowledge Society.* New York: United Nations Development Programme.

Armbrust, W. (ed.) (2000), *Mass Mediations: New Approaches to Popular Culture in the Middle East and Beyond.* Berkeley: University of California University Press.

Arnold, M. (1993), *Culture and Anarchy and Other Writings.* Cambridge: Cambridge University Press.

Badawi, A. R. (1972), The Human Sciences and Cultural Life in the Modern Arab World. *Journal of World History (Contemporary Arab Culture)* 4, 771–788.

Belkbir, A. (1991), On the Meaning of Popular Culture [in Arabic]. In *Popular Culture: One of the Principles of Maghribi Unification.* N.p.: Moroccan Cultural Centre, 15–27.

Berque, J. (1978), *Cultural Expression in Arab Society Today.* Austin: University of Texas Press.

Curran, J./D. Morley (eds.) (2006), *Media and Cultural Theory,* London: Routledge.

During, S. (2005), Popular Culture on a Global Scale: A Challenge for Cultural Studies. In A. Abbas/N. Erni (eds.), *Internationalising Cultural Studies: An Anthology.* London: Blackwell, 439–453.

Garnham, N. (1986), Contribution to a Political Economy of Mass-Communication. In R. Collins et al. (eds.), *Media, Culture and Society: A Critical Reader.* London: Sage, 9–32.

Gassous, M. (1988), Observations on Transformations in Contemporary Moroccan Popular Culture [in Arabic]. In *Popular Culture: One of the Principles of Maghribi Unification.* Kunitra: Manshurat Al-Majlis Al-Baladi, 33–56.

Glass, D. (2001), The Global Flow of Information: A Critical Appraisal from the Perspective of Arab Islamic Information Sciences. In K. Hafez (ed.), *Mass Media, Politics and Society in the Middle East.* Cresskill: Hampton Press, 217–240.
Hall, S. (1986), Cultural Studies: Two Paradigms. In R. Collins/J. Curran/N. Garnham/P. Scannell/P. Schlesinger/C. Sparks (eds.), *Media, Culture and Society: A Critical Reader.* London: Sage, 33–49.
Hall, S./P. Whannel (1964), *The Popular Arts.* London: Hutchinson Educational.
Ibn Khaldoun, A. (1996), *Al-Muqadima* [in Arabic]. Beirut: Institute of Cultural Books.
Jabri, M. (1991), *A Critique of Arab Reason: The Construction of Arab Reason* [in Arabic]. Beirut: Arab Cultural Centre.
______. (1994), *The Cultural Question* [in Arabic]. Beirut: The Studies of Arab Unity Centre.
______. (2001), *A Critique of Arab Ethical Reason* [in Arabic]. Casablanca: Moroccan Publishing House.
Khiabany, G. (2006), Religion and Media in Iran: The Imperative of the Market and the Straightjacket of Islamism. *Westminster Papers in Communication and Culture* 2, 3–21.
Morley, D./K. Chen (ed.) (1996), *Stuart Hall: Critical Dialogues in Cultural Studies.* London: Routledge.
Sabry, T. (2005), Emigration as Popular Culture: The Case of Morocco. *Journal of European Cultural Studies* 1, 5–22.
______. (2007), In Search of the Present Arab Cultural Tense. In N. Sakr (ed.), *Arab Media and Political Renewal: Community, Legitimacy and Public Life.* London: I. B. Tauris, 154–168.
Said, E. (2003), *Orientalism.* London: Penguin.
Scannell, P. (2006), Broadcasting and Time. Unpublished PhD dissertation, University of Westminster.
Silverstone, R. (1999), *Why Study the Media?* London: Sage.
Sparks, C. (1992), Popular Journalism: Theories and Practice. In P. Dahlgren/C. Sparks (eds.), *Journalism and Popular Culture*. London: Sage, 24–45.
Williams, R. (1961), *The Long Revolution.* London: Penguin.

CHAPTER FOURTEEN

Through the Back Door: Syrian Television Makers between Secularism and Islamization

Christa Salamandra

Over the past decade, Syria has developed a television drama industry rivaling that of Egypt, long the center of Arab media production. With the spread of satellite technologies and the proliferation of Arabic-language satellite stations, Syrian dramatic series reach audiences throughout the Arab world and in numerous diasporic communities beyond. In neoliberalizing Syria, TV makers must contend with a new set of dictates and constraints imposed by conservative Islamic markets. The thematic strategies they adopt relegate religion to a colorful but safely remote past. By invoking the golden ages of Islamic empire, cultural producers promote a back-door secularism, incorporating Islamic imagery while avoiding direct contemporary political or social reference. Islam is often folklorized as bygone custom and tradition or aestheticized as costume history.[1] This strategy seemingly allows a nod to contemporary proclivities without compromising TV makers secularist agendas. Yet within the contested field of Syrian cultural production, accusations of pandering to Islamic revivalism serve as modes of distinction and critique. My fieldwork among Syrian television makers reveals that these ambiguous historical motifs are often read by industry figures as acquiescence to an Islamification process many feel is antithetical to their understandings of art and progress.

The Musalsal

With the spread of satellite access, Arab television audiences can now choose between a range of locally produced genres—situation comedies, reality TV, talk shows, and the news-as-entertainment offerings of Al-Jazeera and its competitors. Yet one form stands out, both in volume of production and in numbers of viewers: the miniseries, *musalsal* (meaning, literally, "series").[2] This is particularly true during the holy month of Ramadan, which has given the musalsal its form and has in turn been shaped by it over the past thirty years. In Syria, it is referred to simply as *dramah*, having eclipsed the shorter dramatic form, the *sahrah* (meaning, literally, "evening") television film. It is also the television genre that has attracted the bulk of scholarly (particularly anthropological) interest.[3]

In Syria, the Ramadan series was born in with pioneer director Ghassan Jabri, Hani al-Rummani, and Faisal al-Yassiri's 1967 *The Misers* (Al-Bukhala), a thirty-episode dramatization of ninth-century author Al-Jahiz's *Kitab Al-Bukhala* (Book of Misers). Over the next thirty years, the holy month developed as the prime broadcast season for locally produced drama programs—a time of year when work hours shorten, expatriates return to visit, and families gather to break fast and tune into *musalsals* afterward. Television watching became as much a Ramadan tradition as praying the *tarawih.* An Egyptian, and later Syrian, industry developed, that produced a handful of Ramadan series each year, avidly watched and heatedly debated in both private and public culture. The representations of self and society, group and nation, tradition and modernity, men and women in these series created opportunities to discuss sensitive topics, and they became the stuff of social distinction (Abu-Lughod 1993, 1995, 1997, 1998, 2003, 2005; Armbrust 1996a, 1996b; Salamandra 1998, 2004).

The rise of pan-Arab television stations and the spread of satellite access dramatically transformed and expanded Arabic-language media. While Western attention has focused on news media—notably Al-Jazeera—the Ramadan musalsal was central to this burgeoning. Over one hundred Arab series were produced—and almost as many aired—for Ramadan 2006 (Dick 2007). Producers compete for a coveted Ramadan time slot for first airing, although many series are rebroadcast at other times of the year. Their fragmented audiences no longer provide the ethnographer with discrete instances of viewer engagement (Salamandra 2005). Yet some series resonate more than others, and thematic patterns emerge—among them an Islam-colored authenticity.

Islamification

In Syria, as in much of the Arab world, mass culture remains one of the few remaining bastions of secularism. Nevertheless, television makers operate in a cultural milieu where authenticity has become elided with Islam.[4] In contemporary Arab intellectual discourses, authenticity, *asalah,* is associated with religion, and with revivalist Islam in particular, where it refers to fundamentalism in the literal sense, to a return to a pure Islam of scripture, of Koran and *hadith,* and the era of the Prophet Muhammad (Kubba 1999, 132).

This elision of authenticity and religion is a hallmark of local modernities and marks a shift in twentieth-century Islamic thought from the jurisprudential to the cultural and symbolic. The era of the Prophet Muhammad and early Islamic history form an authentic golden age. Both subsequent Islamic historical experience and traditions, and non-Islamic cultures are rejected by some contemporary Islamists concerned less with whether acts or ideas are legal or illegal—as was the case for traditional Muslim jurists—but whether they are sacred or profane. Whereas Muslim scholars of preceding centuries employed concepts of *istihisan* (juridic discretion) and *maslahah* (the common good), revivalist Islam adopts a method of authentication, *tasil*, reflecting the notion that the Koran contains a comprehensive guide to the proper conduct of individuals, organizations, and governments (Al-Sayyid 1999, 109–110).

Amid the dramatic civilizational dichotomy emerging in last quarter of the twentieth century, Arab intellectuals find themselves under pressure to defend themselves against charges of inauthenticity (Safi 1994, 173). To thwart accusations of Westernization, former secularists have incorporated notions of cultural authenticity in attempts to cope with tensions between tradition and modernity. This trend marks a radical departure for leftist and liberal thinkers, many of whom once thought notions of heritage and tradition irrelevant or antithetical to future possibilities (Safi 1994, 193). For instance, Syrian philosopher Tayib Tizini, who sought to uncover the roots of Marxism in Islam, argues for a more broadly defined notion of Islamic authority, pointing to the cosmopolitan golden ages of Islamic civilization as models for authentic tolerance and social justice (Safi 1994, 177–182). Muhammad Abd Al-Jabiri, a liberal, believes that religious and cultural heritage must be understood and redesigned rather than rejected (Safi 1994, 188–192). Likewise, Egyptian historian Tariq al-Bishri, a former secularist, argues that his fellow leftist intellectuals erred in omitting culture, and especially religious heritage (*turath*), from their analyses (Meijer 1989, 3).

It is essential to note that the Islamification of public culture is far from complete; many of the most watched and talked-about series of recent years are contemporary social dramas with little mention of religion. Yet as prominent members of Syria's intelligentsia, some television makers feel pressure to portray an Islam-inflected cultural authenticity, one out of keeping with their progressive sensibilities. The themes of recent programs reflect efforts to reconcile locally conceived authenticity with secular politics.

A few directors have chosen to address the Islamification of society and polity head on, by entering the debate in religious terms. When approaching that most sensitive of red lines—religion—TV makers strive to be relevant and topical by advocating liberal, even progressive interpretations of Islam. Najdat Ismail Anzur, one director, has attracted attention from the Western media, broaching the timely topic of suicide bombings with *The Beautiful Maidens* (Al-Hur Al-Ayn) of 2005, and *Renegades* (Al-Mariqun) of 2006. Anzur cites the tarring of Islam as a prime motivation: "I see that we need are of clarification on this matter. Is it really rising from within the society, or is somebody inventing it? We see that there are many reasons for it, and without going into political details, we can say that the reasons are the struggle, the cold war between America and the former Soviet Union, and how they [the Americans] were able to attack [the Soviets] by supporting the groups in Afghanistan. One way or another, they invented the character called Bin Laden. Maybe they now have changed their way of thinking towards the region, and we are suddenly faced with a phenomenon called terrorism. And Islam is implicated, considered a religion of terrorism. We have tried, as far as we were able—we're not religious or committed, we're secularists. But at the same time, we see that this is affecting our society. Drama is very useful in this, because it clarifies things. Drama does not solve problems, but it can sheds light on matters like this phenomenon, and can begin to get into details—like where did this phenomenon come from, what are the reasons behind it, what is it's history—not in a didactic way, but in a dramatic way, one that is pleasing (muhabbab), close to the people."[5]

Terrorism occasionally forms a subplot of other series, notably Marwan Barakat's *Buried Resentments* (Ahqad Khafiya) of 2006. In many of these treatments, would-be bombers are thwarted or, more often, have a change of heart before carrying out their deed and adopt a more liberal, state-sanctioned interpretation of Islam in the end.

Uniquely, new-generation star director Hatim Ali's 2005 offering *Unable to Cry* (Asiy Al-Dama) treats the growing women's piety movement in urban Syria. In one subplot, protagonist Samir cites both classical Islam—the acts and deeds of the Prophet Muhammad—and the early-twentieth-century friendship between Christian writer May Ziadeh and Shaikh of Al-Azhar Mustafa Abd Al-Raziq, to argue for a religiosity more progressive than that of his mother, leader of a piety group. The shy, pious young judge, played by Ali himself, debates the Sharia's position on women with his mother as he fixes alarm clocks in his bedroom. A vocal advocate of women's emancipation, Samir agonizes when forced to render decisions on custody cases that contradict his own belief that Islamic law should evolve with changing circumstances. His sympathies lie with divorced mothers who lose their children upon remarriage. In the final episode, Samir has resigned from the bench, unable to reconcile his own understanding of Islam with the rigidity of Syria's personal status law. When a former colleague visits his newly opened clock repair shop and asks if he still enjoys fixing clocks, Samir ponders the metaphor: "Sometime I watch people passing by, and I'm filled with despair. It's like our clock has stopped at the beginning of the last century—the same questions, and the same problems. Look around you, listen to a news broadcast, and judge for yourself. The modernization and reform projects, the search for identity, and I don't know what else, they all failed. Look at where we were, and where we are now: the ignorance, illiteracy, fanaticism, closed mindedness [*inghilaq*], backwardness, and takfir."[6]

In an interview with the author, Ali echoes his character Samir: "We tried to answer the question surrounding the reality of Arab women, and where they have arrived at the rise of the twenty-first century. It is basically a question that intellectuals have been debating since the beginning of the last century, with what was called, in literary terms, the age of Arab Renaissance [Asr Al-Nahdah]... In this era, there was a famous woman, a writer, poet and journalist, May Ziadah.... This [Lebanese] woman went to Egypt, lived there, and was among the first women to go to university, and she was not muhajibah [did not cover her head]. She had a literary salon in which the leading artists and intellectuals of the day used to gather. One of these was Mustafa Abd Al-Raziq, who was Shaikh Al-Azhar, and the Azhar was the biggest religious institution, not only in Egypt, but probably in the entire Islamic World. This shaikh walked in her funeral procession and stood at her grave, where he recited a poem and wept bitterly. And she was a women firstly, and secondly, a Christian. Whereas less than a year ago, for example, the current shaikh Al-Azhar came out with a fatwa forbidding the decoration and display of statues in homes. So we see that our society, our intellectuals, have not only not been able to answer the questions raised in the Nahda; they are also sunk in the shadow of increasing extremism, and closed mindedness [*inghilaq*] of which women are often the primary victims."[7]

Unable to Cry is exceptional in its direct treatment of matters of faith. When Islam is alluded to in TV drama, it is most usually aestheticized, folklorized, and relegated to the past. Hatim Ali himself most often sets his clock very far back, to the golden age of Islamic Spain. His four-part treatment of Al-Andalus, *Hawk of the Quraysh* (Saqr Quraysh) of 2002; *Cordoba Spring* (Rubi Qurtuba) of 2003; *Petty Kingdoms* (Muluk Al-Tawaif) 2005; and *The Fall of Granada* (Suqut Gharnatah), planned for 2007, joins a host of other blockbusters set in the distant past of Islamic empire.[8] Historical works are seemingly designed to appeal to pan-Arab audiences and attract funding from conservative sponsors. These big-budget historical epics combine elaborate period sets, luxurious costumes and extra-filled battle scenes with themes of good and evil and the Muslim community pitted against foreign enemy. Al-Andalus offers an opportunity for social and political commentary. It reconfigures a cosmopolitan disposition within terms that are safely, Islamically authentic, as one interviewee argued: "I think we are on the brink of a true war of civilizations, one that is not limited to a battle of ideas, but is about to develop into a confrontation using traditional and probably not traditional weapons, in the future. In light of this, I began a project about the rise of the Andalusian state, which is probably a unique, exceptional experiment in the history of human kind, were you found, in one place on earth, Muslims of all ideologies, ideas, and aspirations, along with Christians—the original inhabitants of the land, and Jews. The presence of all of these in one place, in a democratic atmosphere, in a dialogue of civilizations, allowed for the establishment of one of the most important human civilizations, the Andalsuian civilization, which was, I think, the gate through which Greek civilization entered what is today called Europe."

In previous decades, TV makers rarely depicted the Islamic empire as a social and political nirvana of tolerance and democracy; secular political struggles in the recent past served this purpose. Audiences got the message, noting a level of participation missing from the Baath-dominated contemporary polity. Haytham Haqqi's 1996 *The Silk Market* (Khan Al-Harir) is a prime example.[9] Here we find the merchant class of 1950s Aleppo debating the merits of unification with Egypt and the loss of an elected parliament it would entail. Some characters advocate unity with Baghdad instead, a move that would have preserved Aleppo's position as Syria's main commercial center. Social and political struggles are framed in the secular terms of that era, with religious references largely limited to a blind shaikh, an unsympathetic bit character.

Production and Producers

To understand the shift toward Islamic authenticity, one must look to the transformations that began in the early 1990s, with the advent of Syria's de-Baathification process. Throughout most of its history, Syrian television was state owned as well as state controlled; its employees were uniformly low in status, socially marginal, and relatively impoverished. A move toward economic liberalization in 1991 opened the door to private production companies. These emerged in the most Syrian of ways: they tended to be owned by individuals with strong links to the regime, most notably the son of the former vice president.

With expansion of the industry, television drama has become the contemporary Syrian cultural form par excellence, to the detriment of all other cultural forms. Syrian television now encompasses much of the local intellectual and artistic community. Informants note that when political parties were banned in the early 1970s, activists became writers and journalists, but employment opportunities have now rendered them TV makers. The industry attracts—and to varying degrees employs—writers, directors, photographers, visual artists, designers, composers, musicians, and actors from various sectarian, regional, and class backgrounds. The rise of a star system has produced increasing social fragmentation, as some have become wealthy and famous, while many more struggle.

The Syrian state still produces a few low-budget productions each year, but most series are now privately produced. TV makers must compete for funding from—and please an exacting set of—censors in the conservative Gulf Cooperation Council (GCC) states. Gulf stations fund most series and receive exclusive right for Ramadan broadcasts in return. On occasion, private producers, often from the GCC, will fund series and then market them to stations. One significant development is the emergence of the star/executive producer, the actor with enough name recognition and industry clout to attract large-scale funding from sources in Saudi Arabia or Dubai, who then, informants argue, pockets, much of the budget. Tales of price undercutting and other cutthroat tactics abound.

An average of thirty-five Syrian series now air each Ramadan on various terrestrial and Arab satellite stations, both private and public, in what industry figures have dubbed *al-fawrah al-dramiyyah*, or "outpouring of drama" (Dick 2005). Increased production and expanded access have obliterated the annual media sensations that once united the Syrian nation in the act of viewing and responding and created space for subnational identity expression. The mediascape now encompasses the entire Arab world, but many television makers argue that as the industry has grown and its products have commodified, drama's progressive potential has been diffused. Syrian TV makers are aware of—indeed, perhaps exaggerate—the power of their medium to transform Syrian society, and they often see themselves at the vanguard of a secularizing process. They feel that GCC domination of the market has usurped this important role. Elitist assumptions about mass culture persist in the absence of ratings or formal channels for viewer feedback. Syrian TV makers see Arab audiences as unsophisticated and impressionable. Viewers, they believe, will absorb and conform to television's messages. Industry figures argue that the potential for promoting progressive political or social agendas has decreased with globalization. In the absence of reliable viewership research, it is Gulf station managers, who are often Arab expatriates, who decide what is aired. As one industry figure notes: "With satellite television, I now have twenty-two censors". Another notes: "In the old days, we were poor, but our art was our own. We produced work that we felt was good for Syria. Now we have become like merchandise, slaves to a bunch of Beduins who have no appreciation for our urban civilization."

Artists in many cultural contexts bemoan commercialism; laments over popular taste and ratings exigencies pervade media and publishing industries in America. Yet in Syria, the "enemies of art" are not a generalized national audience, or even amorphous "market forces." Rather, they are a specific group of wealthy foreigners perceived as overprivileged and parochial, out of touch with what Arab audiences need, if not what they want. Syrian cultural producers often elide the conservative Islam of the Gulf ruling elites and the political Islam of movements such as the Muslim Brotherhood as forces against art and progress. With regionalization, industry informants point to a worst-of-both-worlds situation, as economic liberalization without democratization leaves them vulnerable to both Syrian censors and Gulf buyers. "People like me feel betrayed by authority, be it capital or the gun," argues a well-known cinema director, "We have lost the historical moment."

Such dissatisfactions reveal nostalgia for the Baathist socialist project and the accompanying state support. They also point to an underlying faith in the benefits of a strong state, a belief that deregulation leads to disaster and a fear that the form this disaster will take is political Islam. Here Syrian TV industry figures employ a mode of expression akin to what Michael Herzfeld refers to as "structural nostalgia." In Herzfeld's formulation, both state and nonstate actors refer to an Edenic age of harmonious social relations, a time before social disintegration and moral decay mandated state intervention. This imagining legitimizes accommodation of the state as a necessary evil (1997, 109–138). Syrian television makers invoke what might be called a structural nostalgia in reverse, harkening back to a more recent era of state support for "art," cushioning cultural producers from the vicissitudes of market forces and what they see as an Islamization of the public sphere.

Treatments of Islamic Andalusia and biopics of heroic figures of the past such as Salah al-Din Al-Ayyubi and Omar Al-Khayyam compete with treatments of the more sensitive and more local present. The ambiguous messages encoded in these distant historical narratives can be ignored by censors and denied by producers. They avoid the social complexities of the contemporary world, gliding past conservative GCC censors and appealing to GCC buyers. A story of medieval heroism is often more marketable than a contemporary urban tale of poverty and oppression.

Many industry "have nots," those who either refuse to join or were left out of the most lucrative projects, argue that golden-age themes pander to two dreaded, seemingly opposed enemies: the Syrian regime and political Islam. They accuse big-budget epic creators of selling out to what screenwriters Mazen Bilal and Najib Nusair call "prevailing values in the societies of the oil states" (1999, 8). Claims of compromise become part of the competitive fray among cultural producers, reflecting a mode of sociability common among elite groups in Syria that I have referred to elsewhere as a "poetics of accusation" (Salamandra 2004). Themselves largely secular Muslims, Syrian cultural producers argue that imperial epics work to bolster these two seemingly opposed forces, both united by non-urban orientations. A director argues: "These works reviving the glories of the past amount to indirect support for the Islamists. The project is to make money, but the results play into the hands of the Islamists: look to the past, look to our own values, which should be revived. Their major crime is that they glorify the past, falsify the present, and ignore the future. This trend goes along with the Arab regimes. Tribal relations and values are promoted. Islam provides a framework for this: 'obey those who are leading you'. It promotes regressive social values. This is all very much blessed by the people in charge, who want everything to remain as it is. This is why we see that there is no effort to deal with the actual lives of people. This is society as expressed by the ruling system, not society as it really is."

In contrast, contemporary social dramas and comedies, often produced on modest budgets, are less desirable to the major GCC funders and buyers, but they are purportedly—and ironically—much loved by GCC audiences.[10]

Conclusion

In Syria, as in much of the Muslim world, essentialist notions of the West and its evils require cultural producers to create a local authenticity tinged with Islam. Dramatic depictions of Islamic empire suggest a back-door secularism—an attempt to reconcile the progressive politics of TV makers with the didactic demands of buyers and the perceived religiosity of audiences. Yet like the uninvited party crasher, such strategies do not proceed uncontested. Accusations of pandering to "prevailing values," be they those of Arab regimes or retrograde audiences, permeate the discourse of Syrian cultural producers. They reveal a nostalgia for the modernist and nationalist projects Arab cultural producers once participated in—some reluctantly, others enthusiastically. The demise of socialism and the promise of democracy produce a sense of ambivalence and uncertainty among media people, uniting them, paradoxically, with the very audiences they deem in need of secular enlightening.

Notes

1. The folklorization and aestheticization of religion was a cultural strategy common in socialist contexts (Vertovec 2001, Peyrouse 2004).
2. There are no reliable audience figures for the Arab world. Advertisers, television producers, and station managers rely on informal methods—e-mail, Internet sites, word of mouth—to get a sense of a program's popularity. For the musalsal, discrete length is part of the problem, as there is no point in tracing ratings on a thirty-episode series. Yet most media figures emphasize the enduring popularity of this genre (Rami Omran, Syrian advertising agent, interview with the author, January 13, 2007).
3. For anthropological approaches to the Arab miniseries, see Abu Lughod 1993, 1995, 1997, 1998, 2003, 2005; Armbrust 1996a, 1996b, Diase 1996; Lane 1997; Seymour 1999; Salamandra 1998, 2004, 2005; Shoup 2005.
4. For a discussion of this phenomenon in popular music, see Pond 2006.
5. Najdat Ismail Auzur, interview with the author, December 27, 2006.
6. *Takfir* refers to a practice of declaring fellow Muslims apostates. It has become associated with extremist Islamism, most notoriously in recent years, the Al-Qaida network.
7. Hatim Ali, interview with the author, January 7, 2007.
8. See Shoup 2005 for a detailed discussion of Andalusian series.
9. For a more detailed discussion of *The Silk Market*, see Kawakibi 1997.
10. Mandana Limbert notes that Omani audiences prefer contemporary social dramas set in urban Syria to Islamic golden age or fantasy epics (personal communication).

References

Abu-Lughod, L. (1993), Finding a Place for Islam: Egyptian Television Serials and the National Interest. *Public Culture* 5, 493–513.

———. (1995), The Objects of Soap Opera. D. Miller (ed.), *Worlds Apart: Anthropology through the Prism of the Local.* London: Routledge, 191–210.

———. (1997), The Interpretation of Cultures after Television. *Representations* 59, 25–50.

———. (1998), The Marriage of Feminism and Islamism in Egypt: Selective Repudiation as a Dynamic of Postcolonial Cultural Politics. In L. Abu-Lughod (ed.), *Remaking*

Women: Feminism and Modernity in the Middle East. Princeton: Princeton University Press, 243–269.

______. (2003), Asserting the Local as the National in the Face of the Global: The Ambivalence of Authenticity in Egyptian Soap Opera. In A. Mirsepassi/A. Bassu/F. Weaver, (eds.), *Localizing Knowledge in a Globalizing World: Recasting the Area Studies Debate.* Syracuse: Syracuse University Press, 101–127.

______. (2005), *Dramas of Nationhood: The Politics of Television in Egypt.* Chicago: University of Chicago Press.

Armbrust, W. (1996a), *Mass Culture and Modernism in Egypt.* Cambridge: Cambridge University Press.

______. (1996b), The White Flag. *Mediterraneans,* 8–9, 381–389.

Bilal, M./N. Nusair (1999), *Syrian Historical Drama: The Dream of the End of an Era.* Damascus: Dar al-Sham.

Diase, M. (1996), Egyptian Television Serials, Audiences, and the Family House, a Public Health Enter-educate serial. PhD dissertation, University of Texas–Austin.

Dick, M. (2005), The State of the Musalsal: Arab Television Drama and the Politics of the Satellite Era. *Transnational Broadcasting Studies* 15, http://www.tbsjournal.com/Archives/Fall05/Dick.html.

______. (2007), Going for Broke: The Musalsal Industry Revs up for Ramadan 06. *Middle East Broadcasters Journal* 1/2, http://www.mebjournal.com/component/option,com_magazine/func, show_article/id,207/.

Herzfeld, M. (1997), *Cultural Intimacy: Social Poetics in the Nation-State.* New York: Routledge.

Kawakibi, S. (1997), Le role de la television dans la relecture de l'histoire. *Maghreb/Machrek* 158, 47–55.

Kubba, L. (1999), Towards an Objective, Relative and Rational Islamic Discourse. In R. Meijer (ed.), *Cosmopolitanism, Identity and Authenticity in the Middle East.* London: Curzon, 129–144.

Lane, S. (1997), Television Miniseries: Social Marketing and Evaluation Egypt. *Medical Anthropology Quarterly* 2, 164–182.

Meijer, R. (ed.) (1999), *Cosmopolitanism, Identity and Authenticity in the Middle East.* London: Routledge.

Peyrouse, S. (2004), Christianity and Nationality in Soviet and Post-Soviet Central Asia: Mutual Intrusions and Instrumentalizations. *Nationalities Papers* 3, 651–674.

Pond, C. (2006), The Appeal of Sami Yusuf and the Search for Islamic Authenticity. *Transnational Broadcasting Studies* 16, http://www.tbsjournal.com/Pond.html.

Safi, L. M. (1994), The *Challenge of Modernity: The Quest for Authenticity in the Arab World.* Lanham: University Press of America.

Salamandra, C. (1998), Moustache Hairs Lost: Ramadan Television Serials and the Construction of Identity in Damascus, Syria. *Visual Anthropology* 2–4, 227–246.

______. (2004), A *New Old Damascus: Authenticity and Distinction in Urban Syria.* Bloomington: Indiana University Press.

______. (2005), Television and the Ethnographic Endeavor: The Case of Syrian Drama. *Transnational Broadcasting Studies* 1, 4–17

Sayyid, R. al- (1999), Islamic Movements and Authenticity: Barriers to Development. In R. Meijer (ed.), *Cosmopolitanism, Identity and Authenticity in the Middle East.* London: Curzon, 103–114.

Seymour, (1999), Imagining Modernity: Consuming Identities and Constructing the Ideal Nation on Egyptian Television. Unpublished PhD dissertation, State University of New York–Binghamton.

Shoup, J. (2005), As It Was and Should Be Now: Al-Andalus in Contemporary Arab Television Dramas. *Transnational Broadcasting Studies* 15, http://tbsjournal.com/Archives/Fall05/Shoup.html.

Vertovec, S. (2001), *Religion and Diaspora.* Transnational Communities Working Paper, http://www.transcomm.ox.ac.uk/working%20papers/Vertovec01.PDF.

The Authors

Dr. Hussein Amin is currently the chair of the Department of Journalism and Mass Communication at the American University in Cairo. Professor Amin holds several key positions in national, regional, and global media. He is chairman of the Egyptian Radio and Television Union's (ERTU) Research and Development Committee and a member of ERTU's Board of Trustees, the governing body of Egypt's radio and television broadcasting organization. Dr. Amin is the former president for the Arab-US Association for Communication Educators (AUSACE) and past chairman of the International Division of the Broadcast Education Association (BEA). He serves on the advisory board of the World Congress for Middle Eastern Studies (WOCMES), the *Journal of International Communication* (JIC), and the International Association for Mass Media Research (IAMCR), the *Journal of African Media Studies*, and the *Journal of the Middle East Media* (JMEM). Dr. Amin is the senior editor of *Transnational Broadcasting Studies* (TBS), Arabic editor of the *Global Media Journal* (GMJ), and Middle East editor of the *Journal of Global Media and Communication*. Dr. Amin's research interests include Egyptian and Arab media systems, media convergence, global and transnational broadcasting, Arab media laws and regulations, new information and communication technologies, and the impact of these new technologies on development. Dr. Amin has published extensively on a wide range of topics related to the media with a specific reference to the Middle East.

Professor Muhammad Ayish is a professor and Dean of the College of Communication at the University of Sharjah, United Arab Emirates. Prior to that he had worked at Yarmouk University, Jordan, and United Arab Emirates University (UAE). He has had over fifty articles published in Arabic and English in international journals, as well as having his book *Arab World Television in the Age of Globalization* published in 2003. He serves on the editorial boards of seven Arab and international journals. His research interests cover Arab media, political communication, media convergence, and cultural studies.

Dr. Tourya Guaaybess is a researcher in information and communication sciences and affiliated with the GREMMO (CNRS, University of Lyons) and the

Laboratoire Communication et Politique (CNRS) in Paris. She is currently teaching at the Catholic University of Lyons. She was a Marie Curie Fellow at the Robert Schuman Centre for Advanced Studies in the European University Institute of Florence (2001–2003), and has written several articles on Arab media as well as the book *Télévisions arabes sur orbite, 1960–2004*. She has coedited an issue of the journal *Hermès* on contemporary media in Arab countries.

Kai Hafez is a professor (chair) for international and comparative communication studies and currently the director of the Department of Media and Communication Studies at the University of Erfurt, Germany. He was a Senior Research Fellow of the German Institute for Middle East Studies in Hamburg, Germany (1995–2003), and is a guest professor at the Institute of Sociology, University of Bern, Switzerland. He was a Senior Associate Fellow of St. Antony's College, University of Oxford, and has been a frequent academic political advisor to German governments. Hafez is on the editorial boards of several academic magazines (*Political Communication, Arab Media and Society, Journal for International Communication, Global Media Journal*, and *Journalism: Theory, Practice and Criticism*). Among his English publications are: *Islam and the West in the Mass Media* (2000); *The Islamic World and the West* (2000); *Mass Media, Politics, and Society in the Middle East* (2001); *Media Ethics in the Dialogue of Cultures: Journalistic Self-Regulation in Europe, the Arab World, and Muslim Asia* (2003); and *The Myth of Media Globalization* (2007).

Marwan M. Kraidy, PhD, is associate professor of communication at the Annenberg School for Communication at the University of Pennsylvania, specializing in global communication and Arab media. He was a fellow at the Woodrow Wilson International Center for Scholars (2005–2006), and director of the Arab Media and Public Life (AMPLE) project, both in Washington, D.C. (2006–2007), and scholar-in-residence at the Annenberg School (2007). He has published two books, *Global Media Studies: Ethnographic Perspectives* (2003) and *Hybridity, or, The Cultural Logic of Globalization* (2005), and numerous articles and essays about Arab media, international communication theory, and global culture and communication.

Marc Lynch, PhD, is associate professor of political science and international affairs at George Washington University. He received his PhD from Cornell University, and has taught at the University of California–Berkeley, and Williams College. His most recent book, *Voices of the New Arab Public: Al-Jazeera, Iraq, and Middle East Politics Today*, was published by Columbia University Press. He writes frequently on Arab politics, Iraq, and Islamist movements in journals such as *Foreign Affairs, National Interest, Wilson Quarterly, Foreign Policy, European Journal of International Relations, Arab Media and Society*, and *Politics and Society*. He also runs the influential Middle East politics blog Abu Aardvark (www.abuaardvark.com).

Dr. Russell E. Lucas is an assistant professor of political science at Florida International University in Miami, Florida. He has previously taught at the University of Oklahoma and at Wake Forest University. His publications include *Institutions and the Politics of Survival in Jordan: Domestic Responses to External Challenges, 1988–2001* (2005) and articles in *International Studies Quarterly, International Journal of Middle East Studies, Middle East Journal, Middle Eastern Studies, Middle East Review of International Affairs,* and *Journal of Democracy.*

Dr. Orayb Aref Najjar is associate professor at the Department of Communication, Northern Illinois University, DeKalb, IL. Her publications center on media law in the Middle East and North Africa, and new technology, and include: "New Palestinian Media and Democratization from Below" (2007), in *New Media in the New Middle East,* ed. Philip Seib; "After the Fall: Palestinian Communist Journalism in the Post-Cold-War World," in Rethinking Marxism (2007); "Cartoons as a Site for the Construction of Palestinian Refugee Identity: An Exploratory Study of Cartoonist Naji al-Ali," *Journal of Communication Inquiry* (2007); and "New Trends in Global Broadcasting: Nuestro Norte es el Sur," *Global Media Journal* (2006).

Dr. Katharina Nötzold is a RCUK Research Fellow at the University of Westminster CAMRI's Arab Media Centre, UK. She completed her PhD about Lebanese television in the postwar years, *Defining a Nation? Lebanese TV Stations: The Political Elites' Dominance over the Visual Space* at the University of Erfurt in Germany. She worked as a research fellow at the Center for International Peace Operations (ZIF) in Berlin (2005–2007) and served as an international election observer. She has been a junior research fellow at the German Orient Institute in Beirut (2002–2003), and has written several articles about Lebanese and Arab media.

Judith Pies, MA, is a PhD candidate at the Department for Media and Communication Studies, University of Erfurt, Germany. She graduated in journalism and mass communication from the University of Mainz, Germany, with her master's thesis on media reception among young Arabs in Germany. She was a research assistant at the Centre of Excellency Orient-Occident Mainz (KOOM) at the University of Mainz (2003–2006). The focus of her PhD thesis is the changing field of journalistic norms in Jordan.

Carola Richter, MA, is a teaching and research assistant for international and comparative communication studies at the University of Erfurt, Germany. She is currently working on her PhD thesis on media strategies of moderate Islamists in Egypt. Among her English publications is: *Has Public Diplomacy Failed? The U.S. Media Strategy towards the Middle East and the Regional Perception of U.S. Foreign Policy,* in *Great Powers and Regional Orders: The United States and the Persian Gulf,* ed. Markus Kaim.

Dr. Tarik Sabry is a senior lecturer in media and communication at the University of Westminster, UK, where he is member of the Communication and Media Research Institute. He is cofounder of *Westminster Papers in Communication and Culture* and coeditor of the *Middle East Journal of Culture and Communication.* His publications have appeared in several academic journals, including: *European Journal of Cultural Studies, Global Media and Communication, Transnational Broadcasting Studies, Middle East Journal,* and *Westminster Papers in Communication and Culture.* His research interests include media and migration, Arab popular cultures, and Arab contemporary thought. He is currently working on a book *Cultural Encounters in the Arab World: On Media and What It Means to Be Modern.*

Dr. Naomi Sakr is a reader in communication at the Communication and Media Research Institute (CAMRI), University of Westminster, and Director of the CAMRI Arab Media Centre. She is the author of *Arab Television Today* (2007) and *Satellite Realms: Transnational Television, Globalization and the Middle East* (2001) and has edited two collections, *Women and Media in the Middle East: Power through Self-Expression* (2004/7) and *Arab Media and Political Renewal: Community, Legitimacy and Public Life* (2007). She has written background papers for UNDP, the European Parliament, and the UK House of Lords, as well as numerous journal articles and book chapters related to media flows, television policy, the making of journalists, international news, the regionalization of transnational television, media reform, and governance in the Persian Gulf countries. Her principal research interests are the political economy of transnational media; Arab media policy and development; and human rights and media law reform in the Arab Middle East.

Christa Salamandra, PhD, is assistant professor of anthropology at Lehman College, City University of New York. She received her PhD from the Institute of Social and Cultural Anthropology, University of Oxford, where she also served as postdoctoral research associate. She has been a visiting lecturer in the Department of Anthropology, School of Oriental and African Studies (SOAS), University of London; and a Fulbright Scholar and visiting professor at Lebanese American University in Beirut. She is the author of the book *A New Old Damascus: Authenticity and Distinction in Urban Syria* (2004) and numerous articles on Arab media and expressive culture.

Index

Abdel-Rahman, H., 75
Abdullah I, 39
Abdullah II, 173, 217, 225, 227
Abu Dhabi TV, 20, 69, 82
  Iraq war and, 110
accuracy, 154–55, 158
Adeeb, Imadeddin, 189
advertising, 72, 96, 99, 186–95 passim, 206–09 passim
  degree programs, 167
  television, 95, 109, 190, 207–08
Afaq Arabia, 50
Afghanistan, 109, 110, 148, 201, 244, 254
Africa, 242–43. *See also* North Africa
aggression in children
  television and, 114
Akif, Muhammad Mahdi, 50
Al-Ahram, 52–61 passim, 108, 110, 157, 226
Al-Ahrar, 50, 60
Al-Akhbar, 60
Al-Aqba Intifada, 42
Al-Arabiya, 20–25 passim, 110, 160
Al-Azhar, 222, 223, 256
Al-Daher, Pierre, 98, 133
Al-Dawa, 49
Al-Dustur, 59, 61
Al-Gumhuriya, 60
Al-Hajj, Sami, 211n1
Al-Hawary, Anwar, 60–61
Al-Hayat, 51
Al-Hroub, Khaled, 29
Al-Hurra, 3, 112, 201, 206
Al-Ittihad, 114
Al-Ikhwan Al-Muslimun, 49
Al-Jabri, Muhammad Abd, 238, 239, 244, 248, 254
Al-Jahiz, 253
Al-Jazeera, 1–4 passim, 9, 18, 23–30 passim, 95–100 passim, 199–202 passim
  audience research, 79–80
  critical of United States, 159
  global brand ranking, 70
  ideology and, 51
  Iraq war and, 110, 115
  journalistic ethics and, 147–48, 155–56, 158
  market share, 20
  polarized views of, 148
  staffer detained without charge, 211n1
  thematic channels, 70
  website, 115
  women's issues and, 112
  Zogby polls and, 81
Al-Jazeera International, 206
Al-Jazeera Media Training and Development Center, 168
Al-Jihad, 49
Al-Khalej, 114
Al-Majali, Hazza', 39
Al-Manar, 12, 20, 127–41 passim, 143n32, 200, 202
  popularity rise, 211n3
Al-Masry Al-Yawm, 52–61 passim
Al-Messa, 114
Al-Miriyya, 217
Al-Mithaq Al-Arabi, 226
Al-Nahar, 127, 168
Al-Nur, 50

Al-Qabas, 114
Al-Qaida, 26, 260n6
Al-Razik, Mustafa Abd, 256
Al-Sadat, Anwar, 48, 49, 220–27 passim
Al-Shaab, 50, 110
Al-Wadi, 82
Al-Wafd, 50, 52–61 passim
Algeria, 3, 4, 155
  film industry, 188, 192
  satellite television, 194
Ali, Hatim, 255, 256
Alia, Valerie, 161
Alluni, Tayssir, 211n1
Althusser, Louis, 99
Alwaleed bin-Talal, 186
Amal, 131, 127
Amazigh, 244
Amin, Mustapha, 220
Amnesty International, 228
Andalusia, 256
anti-Americanism, 18–22 passim, 25, 33, 96, 110, 111
  journalist training and, 168
antiterrorism laws, 225, 228
Anzur, Najdat Ismail, 254
Aoun, Michel, 141
Ara Media Service, 210
Arab Ad, 96
Arab cultural studies, 237–51
Arab Digital Distribution, 206
Arab immigrants, 83
Arab League, 142n13, 203
Arab League Educational, Scientific, and Cultural Organization, 82
Arab media and cultural studies, 237–51
Arab Press Freedom Watch, 223
Arab Radio and Television (ART), 76, 80, 186, 192, 204
Arab Reporters for Investigative Journalism, 168, 171
Arab Satellite Television and Politics in the Middle East (Zayani), 82
Arab Socialist Union, 219
Arab States Broadcasting Union, 82, 203, 206
Arabic language, 10, 210
Arabic song, 84
Arabism. *See* pan-Arabism
Arabsat, 80, 203
Armenians, 142n16
Aroubi, 244–45
arrests of journalists, 178n29, 226
Asharq Al-Awsat, 51
Ashura, 141n8
audience studies, 8–9, 19–21, 69–102
authenticity, 253–54
Ayish, Muhammad, 159, 190
Ayyoub, Tarek, 201

BBC, 206
  global brand ranking, 70
Baath Party, 258. *See also* de-Baathification
Badran, Adnan, 229
Baghat, Ahmad, 211
Baghdad Pact (1955), 38–42 passim
Balamand University, 172
balance, 149–61 passim
Balance and Bias in Journalism (Starkey), 150–51
Barakat, Marwan, 255
Bartels, L., 17, 21
Beautiful Maidens, The, 254
beheadings, 26
Beirut, 136
Bennett, Lance, 26–27
Benson, Rodney, 218–19
Berkeley, George, 149
Berque, J., 246
Berri, Nabih, 126, 131–35 passim, 140n3, 141n5
bias, 25, 126, 149–61 passim. *See also* partisanship
Big Brother, 109

Bilal, Mazen, 259
Bkirki, 136–37
blackmail, 170, 172
bloggers, 115, 220, 224
bombings, 201
  in television dramas, 254, 255
Booz Allen Hamilton, 73, 79
Bourdieu, Pierre, 218
boycotts, 41
Boyd-Barrett, Oliver, 189
"bread riots," 3
bribery, 170, 172, 226
Britain, 206. *See also* Baghdad Pact (1955)

CNN, 8, 25, 77, 160, 192
  Gulf War and, 3, 204
Camp David Accords, 224, 226
cartoons, 28, 95
cartoons (television), 113
cell phones, 97–98
censorship, 4, 48
  civic responsibility and, 74
  Egypt, 49, 223, 225, 227
  Lebanon, 133
  military, 158
  television, 257, 258
  violence and, 75
Center for Defending the Freedom of Journalists, 168–73 passim, 176n15
Chahine, Yousef, 192
children
  television and, 77, 84, 113–14
Choucair, Julia, 219
Choueiri, Antoine, 96
Christians
  Lebanon, 131–37 passim, 141, 142n16
cinemas, 191–95 passim
  banned in Saudi Arabia, 186
circulation auditing, 72
civil war
  Lebanon, 126–27
clergy
  television coverage, 134–35
codes of ethics, 155, 158, 165, 166, 171–74 passim, 180n54
  Al-Jazeera and, 148, 155, 201
  studies of, 147
college students
  television viewing, 83
colonialism, 242–43
Communist Party
  Jordan, 221
  Lebanon, 142n18
community, 154, 161
  limits to freedom of expression and, 155
conflict of interest, 172
constitutional amendments
  Egypt, 56–59, 217, 220, 228
constructivism, 34, 91, 150
consumerism, 207, 208
content studies, 52, 105–24
  Lebanese TV, 125–44
corruption, 138, 170, 226
  advertising industry, 170
  media coverage, 54–55, 117
  newspaper industry, 190
Council of the Jordanian Professional Associations, 227
courts
  Egypt, 229
critical thinking, 170
cultural globalization, 105–06, 108–09
cultural studies
  African, 242
  Arab, 237–51
  British, 242

Daher, Pierre al-, 98, 133
Dajani, Nabil, 174
Danish cartoon crisis, 28, 95
Dar al-Fatwa, 135
death tolls, 157–58

de-Baathifiction, 257
defamation, 177n21, 225
democracy, 4, 5, 29, 33, 154
  foreign policy and, 35
democratization, 22, 29, 111
  Egypt, 48, 57, 58
demographics, 72, 98, 113
demonstrations, protests, etc., 22, 24, 29, 38, 40, 86
  right to demonstrate, 217
digital broadcasting, 81
diplomats and diplomacy
  television coverage, 131
dissent, 29
  management of, 220
distribution, 191–93
diversity, 5, 21, 98
Dubai International Film Festival, 192
Dubai TV, 20, 76, 189

e-mail, 115
economics
  television coverage, 131
Egypt, 3, 4, 24, 46–65
  advertising, 207
  censorship, 49, 223, 225, 227
  constitution, 222–23
    proposed amendments, 56–59, 217, 220, 228
  elections, 112
  film industry, 186, 188, 191–92
  journalistic attitudes study, 153–54
  journalistic code of ethics, 158
  media law, 217–233
  newspapers, 49–63, 107, 108, 190–91
  radio broadcasts, 38, 111
  television, 69, 73, 76–77, 82, 83, 95, 203
    constitutional amendments and, 217
    soap operas, 245
    video clips, 109
Egyptian Bar Association, 227
Egyptian Organization for Human Rights, 222
Egyptian People's Assembly, 226
Egyptian Radio and Television Union, 82, 189
Egyptian Satellite Channel (ESC), 76, 204
elections, 32, 112. *See also* voting
emergency laws, 224
Encoding/Decoding (Hall), 94
encryption technology, 191, 192
entertainment, 79, 109, 113, 150, 205, 211. *See also* reality television shows
Enterprise Nationale de Télévision (Algeria), 204
epistemology, 149–50
ethics, 7, 147–81. *See also* codes of ethics
executions, 26
executive power, 219–20

facts, 152
  liability to manipulation, 157
Fahrenheit 9/11, 194
FAIR, 159–60
Fakhreddine, Jihad, 190
Fallujah, 26
Fandy, Mamoun, 159
Fares, Issam, 126, 133
fear of terrorism, 229, 231
Fessi, 244
film theaters. *See* cinemas
films, 9
  censorship, 70
  distribution, 191–92
  economic aspects, 186–98 passim
financing, 206
foods, 245
foreign policy
  public opinion and, 33–45
foreign relations
  television coverage, 131
Foucault, Michel, 217, 220, 228, 230
framing, 6, 23, 52, 153, 159, 244

France, 80, 200–06 passim, 220–21, 244
Frangieh, Suleiman, 126, 133
freedom of expression
restrictions, 155, 158, 166, 173, 177n16, 217–33
See also censorship
freedom of religion, 223
Frost, Chris, 151
Future TV, 20, 80, 127–40 passim, 143n25, 204

Gagea, Samir, 141
Gamaat Islamiya, 49
game shows, 204
gatekeeper role, 5, 7, 114–15
Germany, 160
Glass, Dagmar, 249n1
globalization
broadcasting, 203–04
cultural, 105–06, 108–09
Glubb, John Bagot, 38–42 passim
Glück, Antje, 159
Good News Group, 189
Graber, D., 17
Gramcsi, Antonio, 99
Great Britain, 206. *See also* Baghdad Pact (1955)
Greek Orthodox Church, 126, 127
Guardian, 158
Gulf Cooperation Council, 257–59 passim
Gulf War (1991), 3, 192

Habermas, J., 140n2
Hafez, Salah Eddin, 217
Hafiz, S., 76
Hall, Stuart, 9, 94, 99, 240
Hajj, Sami al-, 211n1
Hamada, B., 76
Haqqi, Haytham, 256
Hariri, Rafik, 21, 126, 127, 131–40 passim, 143n25
Hartley, John, 91, 94
Hashemite Kingdom of Jordan. *See* Jordan
Hawary, Anwar al-, 60–61
Haykal, Muhammad Hasanein, 226
health programming, 108
hegemony, 99
Herzfeld, Michael, 258
Hezbollah, 62, 126, 127, 131–40 passim, 142n17, 202
Higher Council of Journalism (Egypt), 227
higher education, 247–48
Higher Media Council (Jordan), 173
historical epics (television), 256, 258–59
Hobeiqa, Elie, 140n3
Hollywood, 191
Hroub, Khaled al-, 29
human rights organizations, 222, 230
Hussein I, 38–42 passim, 221, 223
Hussein Amin Mosque, 136
Hussein, Saddam, 159
"hypermedia space," 98

ideology, 152
immigrants, 83
immunity (law), 219
impartiality, 151. *See also* bias
imperialism, 105, 108, 159, 243
imprisonment of journalists, 48, 75, 178n29, 211n1, 221, 225–29 passim
Institute for Professional Journalism, 168, 172, 174
insult of kings and presidents
forbidden, 225–27 passim
intellectual property, 191
intellectuals, 247
interactivity, 97–100, 115–16, 190
International Association of Media and Communication Research, 9
International Communication Organization, 9
international relations, 33–35. *See also* foreign policy

Internet, 1, 3, 6, 9, 59, 71
content, 115–16
distribution, 191, 193
immigrants and, 83
reality TV and, 98
See also websites
Intifada, 42, 86, 110
Ipsos-Stat, 72, 96
Iraq, 3, 24, 108, 109, 159, 244
death tolls, 157–58
online media coverage, 115
television coverage, 26, 28, 55
Al-Jazeera coverage, 19
Islam, 245
Egypt, 222–23
Jordan, 223–24
in Syrian television dramas, 252–62 passim
journalistic ethics and, 155
Islamism and Islamists, 4, 6, 230
Arab states and, 63n3
defined, 62n1
Egypt, 222–23
Jordan, 223
Syrian television dramas and, 252–62 passim
Western pop culture and, 74
See also Muslim Brotherhood
Israel
Israeli-Palestinian conflict, 55, 71, 80, 81, 86, 110
Al-Manar and, 202
Jordan and, 38–42 passim
Lebanon and, 141n5
Issa, Ibrahim, 61

Jabri, Muhammad Abd al-, 238, 239, 244, 248, 254
Jordan, 3, 4, 38–42, 55, 108
advertising, 207
executive power, 219–20
journalism education, 165–81
media law, 217–33
newspapers, 111, 225
Jordan Radio and Television, 168
Jordanian Journalists' Press Association, 166
Jordanian Writers Association, 229
journalism education, 165–81
journalism ethics, 7, 147–81. *See also* codes of ethics
journalists
arrests, 178n29, 226
imprisonment, 48, 75, 178n29, 211n1, 221, 225–29 passim
underpayment, 170
judges
in television dramas, 255
Jumblat, Walid, 140n3, 141n4

Kamal, Abdallah, 60
Kamil, Issam, 60
Kandil, Hamdi, 205
Karami, Omar, 138–39
Kazziha, Walid, 228
Keller, Perry, 218
Khaldoun, Ibn, 238
Khalil, Joe, 190
Khayyat, Tahseen, 133
Khiabany, J., 246
Khouty, Rami, 29
kidnappings, 26
King Abdullah I, 39
King Abdullah II, 173, 217, 225, 227
King Hussein, 38–42 passim, 221, 223
Kitab Al-Bukhala (Jahiz), 253
Koran, 223, 253–54
Kuttab, Daoud, 227
Kuwait, 3, 110, 115

LBC, 20, 76, 79, 98, 141n5, 174, 204
alliance with MBC, 210
LBCI, 127–143 passim
labor unions, 131, 142n20
Lahoud, Emile, 127, 131, 133, 142n13

Lancet, 157–58
law, 171, 177n16, 178n31, 217–33
lawsuits, 226
League of Arab States, 142n13, 203
Lebanese Broadcasting Corporation. *See* LBC
Lebanese Broadcasting Corporation International. *See* LBCI
Lebanese University, 168
Lebanon
  journalism education, 165–81
  newspaper industry, 190
  television, 125–44, 202
leisure time, 193, 194
lese-majesté, 178
libel, 226
licensing, 48, 50, 126, 128, 133, 211
literacy, 194–95
Lynch, M., 28–29

MBC, 20, 76, 79, 114–15, 204, 205
  alliance with LBC, 210
  thematic channels, 70
magazines, 49, 71
  distribution, 192–93
Majali, Hazza' al-, 39
Mansour, Nijal, 169, 174
markets, 185
  fragmentation, 20, 28
  research, 72–73
Maronites, 126, 127, 131–35 passim, 141n4, 142n16
media agenda setting, 23, 152–53, 158
"media cities," 7, 208
"media democracy," 1
media interactivity, 97–100, 115–16, 190
media ownership, 125, 161
media regulation. *See* censorship; law
media research 6–10
Middle East Broadcasting Center. *See* MBC
military courts, 228
Minbar Al-Jazeera, 97, 98
Misers, The, 253
mobile phones, 97–98
Monde, Le, 202
Moore, Michael, 194
Morocco, 3, 4, 114
  popular culture, 244–45
movies. *See* films
Mubarak, Hosni, 48, 56, 61, 112, 189, 220–28 passim
Muhammad, Ahmad Haredi, 226
multimedia messaging (MMS), 97
Murr, Michel, 142n13
Murr TV, 127, 141
musalsals, 252–53
music television, 73, 83–84, 97–98, 109, 192
Muslim Brotherhood, 4–5, 46–65, 74, 223, 258

NBN, 127–138 passim, 141n5
Nader, Jo., 172
Nafie, Ibrahim, 226
Nasrallah, Sayyed Hassan, 28, 135, 174
Nasser, Gamal Abdel, 49, 220–25 passim
National Democratic Party (Egypt), 57
national development, 107–08, 117
national film industries, 186, 188
National Union (Egypt), 219–220
nationalism, pan-Arab. *See* Pan-Arabism
Nazism, 92
neutrality, 151, 160
New TV (NTV), 20, 127–139 passim, 141n5
New World Information and Communication Order, 105, 107
news, television, 79, 125–44
newspapers, 108, 110, 114
  advertising, 190–91, 207
  banning of, 221
  distribution, 192–93

Egypt, 49–63, 107, 108, 110, 221, 226
Jordan, 111, 225
literacy and, 194
put out of business by new law, 225
sensationalism in, 114
subsidies, 190–91
Nielsen ratings, 72
Nilesat, 82
9/11 terrorist bombings, 95, 202, 239
Nisbet, Erik, 18–19
nonprofit broadcasters, 188
North Africa, 96
Notre Dame University (Lebanon), 172
Nusair, Najib, 259

objectivity, 147–164 passim
Oman, 84–86, 110, 260n10
Omnicom Media Group, 99
online media. *See* websites
opinion surveys, 19, 21, 70, 72, 73
Al-Jazeera and, 81
Orbit (television station), 20, 80, 204
Orientalism, 199–203 passim, 239, 240, 246
Oslo accords, 40
Ousbah, Abu, 173
ownership, 125, 161

Palestine and Palestinians, 24, 26, 41, 221, 244
Israeli-Palestinian conflict, 55, 71, 80, 81, 86, 110
media coverage, 55
television viewing, 83–84
pan-Arab media, 23, 24, 26, 28, 49, 51, 81–83
Intifada and, 86
Ramadan television programs, 253, 257
satellite television, 203–05 passim
Pan Arab Research Center, 72, 96
pan-Arabism, 154, 243–44
media coverage, 108, 117
Paris II Conference, 2002, 137–140 passim, 143n25
partisanship,
Lebanon, 169
press, 52, 76, 111, 192, 226
television, 125, 126, 202
Passing of Traditional Society (Lerner), 106
passivity, 92, 97
Patriot Act, 230–31
pay-TV, 69, 73, 191, 192, 194
peace journalism movement, 152
"people meters," 96, 99–100
perception, 149
Petra University, 167
Philadelphia University, 167
phone surveys, 73
Pintak, Lawrence, 159
piracy, 192, 195
pluralism. *See* diversity
political participation, 77
political parties, 48, 220–22
banned in Jordan, 229
party presses, 52, 76, 111, 192, 226
polls, 19, 21, 70, 73
Al-Jazeera and, 81
government permission, 72
Pop Idol, 69
"popular" (word), 249n3
Popular Committee to Resist Normalization and Protect the Nation's Name, 229
popular culture
Arab, 244–45
Morocco, 244–45, 249n3
Western, 74, 75
presidency
Egypt, 219–220
press legislation. *See* law
press partisanship, 52, 76, 111, 192, 226
Price, Monroe, 26
privacy, 228

privatization of media, 220
professional associations, 227, 229
propaganda, 3, 4, 60, 70, 72, 111, 172
  peace journalists', 152
protests, demonstrations, etc., 22, 24, 29, 38, 40, 86
  right to demonstrate, 217
public opinion, 1–4 passim, 8, 71
  foreign policy and, 33–45
  of newscast content, 77
  surveys, 19, 21, 70, 72
    television, 73, 79
public relations, 72, 151
  degree programs, 167
  governmental, 4, 6
  Muslim Brotherhood and, 61

Qabalan, Abdel Amir, 134
Qatar, 3, 29, 95, 201
  advertising, 207
Qornet Shehwan, 134
Qur'an. *See* Koran

radio, 38, 111, 192
  degree programs, 167
Radio Baghdad, 203
Radio Free Iraq, 201
Radio Sawa, 201
Rai Uno, 204
Ramadan
  television and, 73, 111, 252–53, 257
Razik, Mustafa Abd al-, 256
reality television shows, 82–83, 97–98, 190, 204
regionalizing, 27
regulation. *See* law
religion
  coverage restrictions, 171, 177n17, 178n31
  in Arab culture, 245–46
  in Syrian television dramas, 252–62 passim
  television news coverage, 130–31, 134–35
religious courts, 222
religious freedom, 223
religious television programming, 73, 78, 114
Renegades, 254
Reporters without Borders, 227
repression, 28–30 passim, 217–31 passim
resistance, 218
right to free expression. *See* freedom of expression
riots, 3, 38, 174. *See also* "bread riots"
Rotana, 186, 189
Rotana Clip, 205
Rucht, Dieter, 48
Russell, Bertrand, 149
Ruz Al-Yussif, 59, 60

SMS. *See* text messaging
Sabbagh, Rana, 171, 174
Sadat, Anwar al-, 48, 49, 220–27 passim
Said, Edward, 199, 239, 240
Sakr, Naomi, 6
Samara, Abdel Karim, 159
Samir, Muhammad, 61
samizdat, 2
Sar, Musa, 135
Satellite Realms (Sakr), 86
Saudi Arabia
  film industry, 186
  in Egyptian press, 108
  online media coverage, 116
satellite television, 1–2, 111, 112
  Algeria, 194
  Arab states and, 6, 95, 190, 203–04, 208–09
  audience research, 71, 76–86 passim
  censorship and, 258
  Egypt, 76–79 passim
  entertainment orientation, 109
  financial unsustainability, 98

influence, 17, 29
news agenda of, 23
programming for children, 113
Saudi Arabia, 189
Saudi Arabia, 29
journalistic code of ethics, 155
satellite dish prohibition, 75
television, 69, 73, 189
Sawt-el-Arab, 203, 204
Scannell, P., 241, 242
scapegoating, 18, 118
scientific method, 150
self-censorship, 4
sensationalism, 27, 28, 29, 114, 169
September 11, 2001, terrorist bombings, 95, 202, 239
sex in films, 70
Sfeir, Mar Nasrallah Boutros, 135, 136, 141n4
Shaabi, 244, 250
Shanahan, Jim, 18–19
Sharabi, Hisham, 29
Sharia, 223
Shelh, 244–45
Showtime, 73
Sigal, Leon V., 7
Silverstone, R., 247, 249
small media, 6, 47
soap operas, 1, 78, 111, 245
socialism, 225, 258, 260
Somalia, 55
song, 84
spin doctoring, 6
sports news, 63n8
Star Academy, 69, 82, 98, 109, 204
Starkey, Guy, 150
state capitalism, 208, 211
storytelling, 150
subsidies, 188, 195
Sudan, 55
Sunni Muslims, 126, 135, 142n16
Superstar, 82, 109, 204
Supreme Constitutional Court (Egypt), 229
surveys (polls), 19, 21, 70, 72, 73
Al-Jazeera and, 81
Syria, 41, 220–21
film industry, 188
Lebanon and, 126, 132–34 passim, 141
television drama industry, 252–62

taboos, 177n17, 178n31
takfir, 260n6
Talal, Walid, 211n5
talk shows, 5, 28, 127
Tarrow, Charles, 23
Tehranian, Majid, 160
Télé Liban (TL), 125–40 passim, 143n31
Telesur, 211
television, 1–2, 6, 24–27, 260n10
advertising, 95, 109, 190, 207–08
audience research, 69–90, 92, 94–102
degree programs, 167
economic aspects, 189–90, 207
Egypt, 69, 73, 76–79, 109, 112–13, 253
Kuwait, 115
Lebanon, 125–44
political coverage, 129–31
Ramadan and, 73, 111, 252–53, 257
Syria, 252–62
viewer participation, 97–100
violence and, 26
women in, 112–13
See also game shows; music television; pay-TV; reality television shows; satellite television
Telhami, Shibley, 20
terrorism, 111, 148, 159, 170, 217
fear of, 229, 231
in television dramas, 255
press restrictions and, 217
See also antiterrorism laws
text messaging, 97, 205
theaters, film. *See* cinemas

Tilley, Charles, 23
Times, 157–58
Tizini, Tayib, 254
totalitarianism, 4
transformation theory, 2
transnational Arab media. *See* pan-Arab media
treaties, 38–42 passim
truth, 154–55
Tunisia, 113, 188, 192, 211

UK, 206. *See also* Baghdad Pact (1955)
Unable to Cry, 255, 256
underpayment of journalists, 170
unions, 131, 142n20
United Arab Emirates
  advertising, 207
  television, 69, 84
United States
  Al-Hurra and, 206
  Al-Manar and, 202
  film industry, 191
  Jordan and, 41
  mass media and Iraq war, 159–60
  Patriot Act, 230–31
uses-and-gratifications approach, 9, 76–79 passim, 93–94

Venezuela, 201
victims, 156
viewer participation. *See* interactivity
violence, 26, 29, 75–76, 153, 172, 177n21
  in films, 70
  in television, 112–13
voting, 22. *See also* elections

Wafd Party (Egypt), 52
Wakim, Najah, 131, 142
war, 109–110, 150–56 passim, 170, 172
  death tolls, 157–58
websites, 115
  Muslim Brotherhood, 46, 50–63
West Bank, 221
Who Wants to Be a Millionaire, 69, 204
Who Wants to Win a Million, 204
Wickham, C. R., 50
Wolfsfeld, Gadi, 5–6, 7, 47
women in media, 86, 112–13
  coverage restrictions, 171
  online media, 115
  television dramas, 255

Yarmouk University, 167, 171
Yemen, 24, 55
youth, 115

Zagala, Samera, 160
Ziadeh, May, 255–56
Zuhairi, Kamel, 227